PLANNING FOR AN URBAN WORLD

The MIT Press
Cambridge, Massachusetts, and London, England

PLANNING FOR AN URBAN WORLD:
The Design of Resource-Conserving Cities

Richard L. Meier

Library of Congress Cataloging in Publication Data

Meier, Richard L.
 Planning for an urban world.

 1. Cities and towns—Planning—1945- 2. Natural resources.
I. Title.
HT166.M424   309.2'62   74-9740
ISBN 0-262-13112-9

Scenarios

Tables

Figures

The ideas for this study of future urbanization had been growing for a long time, but they finally came together in 1965 while I was a member of a team of planners working with the Venezuelans. Five years earlier, the Venezuelan government had decided to build a new port city on the Orinoco River with the intent of maximizing the social product obtainable from the extraordinarily rich combination of resources in the region.

In many ways this was an ideal assignment for the American planners convened by the Joint Center for Urban Studies of Harvard and MIT, because the hypocrisy and autism normally associated with "foreign aid" was not present; the Venezuelans had committed a large part of their oil royalties to the implementation of the development plan and were willing to pay for the best advice available. This was not an exercise in utopianism but a practical effort to accomplish as much as possible for the nation within a short span of years.

Gradually the vision of a new city for more than a quarter of a million people was built up out of the crosscurrents of proposals, critiques, and experiments in the field. Meanwhile immigrants were arriving at a rate of a thousand a month to occupy the site of the new city; a smaller, variable number left disappointed. Over 75,000 were in residence before the consulting planners departed.

Most of us from the United States had gone into the project hoping to learn through experience how to plan and design humane cities that were capable of developing regions and possibly whole societies. The outline plan for Ciudad Guayana may not have been optimal, but it was close to the best that planners from developed and developing countries, when yoked together, knew how to do. Nevertheless, as I reviewed the prospects, I came to believe that this was a kind of plan that should never be done again on this scale or any larger one. Although designed to develop and export natural resources, the city was too wasteful of those resources to be repeated elsewhere. No combination of deposits of highly marketable minerals, waterpower potential, and forests is ever again likely to be found in such proximity on this earth. Reluctantly I came to the conclusion that although the approach taken was adequate for this instance, I could not as a responsible planner transfer what I had learned to other places in the world. That determination set me to speculating how a developmental metropolis should be planned when, as would be universally true in the future, the society has limited access to natural resources. What strategies were open that would conserve these resources?

Thereupon I found myself working many hours at night in a small Caracas hotel room spelling out policies for conserving water, energy, materials, capital, and human time, while during the day at the office my calculations for the Guayana region of the 1970s would allocate them almost profligately. I knew that my contemporaries working on urban development in India, Pakistan, Nigeria, Turkey, Thailand, and elsewhere were reaching approximately the same official recommendations about the resource mix as the teams with which I worked, because we were all using world prices and had available to us the same basic urban technologies. Our proposals could not be completed, however, because even if those plans were accepted for the development of these countries, severe scarcities would appear and frustrate them. My knowledge of geology and technology was sufficient to recognize that the anticipated urban population was so large its needs could exceed prospective supplies by two- to fivefold. I felt a bit uncomfortable in the role of a professional who presumed he was doing as much and as well as he knew how but who also recognized that, through the lessons he was teaching by example, he was reinforcing a trend likely to resurrect the Malthusian specter.

These arguments were sufficient to explain my concerns to others, but were still too superficial to suggest solutions. I also needed a conceptual framework that would indicate how an assembly of new facts and ideas might shift strategies for development. That framework did not exist in any single discipline, but would have to range over a number of established fields and encompass subjects that had still not emerged from the mother discipline—philosophy.

I would have been incapable of thinking of urbanism as an outgrowth of living systems had it not been for associations with James G. Miller, Ralph Gerard, Anatol Rapoport, Kenneth Boulding, John Platt, and the circle around them that started ten years earlier in Chicago and Ann Arbor. They patiently (and on some occasions impatiently) disentangled nested levels of organization and formulated a number of cross-level principles. As a consequence, it became possible for a few of us to jump to the realization that the city may be usefully considered to be a *self-created environment that determines the continuation of the evolution of the human species.*

The Ford Foundation, in providing a grant for sabbatical travel, enabled me to see firsthand the changes wrought within cities by economic development in Japan, and the means of coping with unprecedented residential densities in Hong Kong. I was able to observe how the Industrial Revolution, with its strong organizational implications, was being installed quite ingeniously by all kinds of Indians in the alleys of Howrah and other smoky extensions of Calcutta, but disastrously in the huge complex adjoining the new city of Durgapur. The threat of famine in India became very real at that time, and I moved on to other cities where I developed further a technique for identifying new developments in a metropolis when the native language was known only through a dictionary.

Since then I have been particularly indebted to students who came from all disciplines, and from many countries of the world. First in Ann Arbor, and then in Berkeley, they enrolled in classes on Regional Development and Futures of Urbanism and the City. There the implications of resource-conserving strategies were mapped out for several of the metropolises where conditions were due to become critical over the next several decades. Other trips to Asia were undertaken with the help of a small grant from a fund provided by the Ford Foundation for overseas training in professional schools.

I am indebted in a very different way to the National Institute of Mental Health, particularly its Metro-Studies Center, for a grant entitled "Gaming Simulations of Community and Social Organization." It provided an opportunity for experimentation with new techniques in modeling urban development and yielded a variety of new insights, particularly for testing political and administrative feasibility. The Institute of International Studies and the Center for South and Southeast Asia at Berkeley assisted me in making further checks in the field, and for library research as this stage of the study was being completed and a follow-through organized. The staff in the Institute of Urban and Regional Development helped produce the intermediate working papers and drafts. Kiki Skagen Munshi and her

South Asian experience became available at a critical time, as did Arthur Stamps and his design background. It always comes as a shock to an investigator to discover how many people spend so many hours on the preparation of a single book, and their efforts are gratefully acknowledged.

Richard L. Meier

Berkeley, California
May 1974

PLANNING FOR AN URBAN WORLD

Although I consider this study a contribution to economic development, I rarely use a strictly economic argument, and the results do not fit into the genre devoted to the maximization of the Gross National Product. The study is also devoted to the achievement of social justice, but it seldom uses the language of socialist ideology or of advocacy. It attempts also to introduce a major reformulation of city planning that will soon be needed. Since the conceptual framework encompassed all of these considerations, and more, the problem of choosing what language to use and how to order the ideas became serious; no line of progenitors has set a tradition for this kind of discourse.

I chose a living-systems idiom for two kinds of reasons. The first has to do with the structure, which is multileveled in abstraction and therefore powerful enough to encompass a wide variety of phenomena, yet open enough to admit bodies of independently conceived theory. Economic principles then become special cases of ecological principles, and technological forces can be made to serve instead of dominate. Politics and culture can be conveniently superimposed as developmental potentials. Ecology is obviously a more suitable frame than organismic biology because the urban world almost always lacks purposive control and a discussion of the future of cities requires a macro outlook.

The other reasons for adopting a living-systems mode of discourse, instead of sociological, politico-economic, or journalistic, lie with the audience. A new readership is emerging. The wave of environmentalist enthusiasm in the 1960s brought about a popularization of ecology—a word stretched to include an ideology, a body of legal opinion, a dogma, an ethic, and an aesthetic that shared very little meaning with the scientific subject of many decades standing. Nevertheless the movement generated a huge amount of curiosity; ecology was adopted almost everywhere in America, and increasingly in Western Europe, as a component in general education. Humanists were forced to admit its relevance to their concerns, and they, too, began to read widely in the subject. The principal transmitters of ecological concepts overseas are those young people who feel comfortable communicating in the English language in addition to their own. In Asian cultures, in particular, they found the holistic outlook of ecology very appealing, and the new kinds of political action it engendered were very exciting. Penetration of other parts of the world has been significant, although it has proceeded more slowly.

The mood transmitted by the environmentalist movement has been one of antipathy for the city and its technology. They are viewed as joint causes of an impending collapse of natural systems and populations. Therefore, the formulation of designs for resource-conserving urbanism must combat a series of preconceptions that have diffused worldwide. The objective can be carried out most persuasively by starting with basic principles affecting the survival of man and his communities.

Biologists long ago pointed out that the *fitness* to survive and reproduce in humans is now determined more by cultural factors than by the challenges presented to individuals by the natural environment. Fitness now depends neither upon quickness of wit nor upon alertness to threat. Brawn is equally obsolete. Fitness now represents the capacity of a population to survive and reproduce itself in a given matrix of environmental forces. Cities have encapsulated a variety of significant cultural forces, causing them to become loosely institutionalized so that most individual crises are succored now by some body of specialists, such as doctors, police, welfare workers, and the like. By differentiating peoples into social classes and occupational groups, cities are introducing new capabilities for the collective control of the total environment of man. Once these conditions are recognized, we can proceed to ask what selective pressures exist that are traceable to the kinds of competition maintained in the urban environment. What are the genetic and somatic characteristics of the generations that will succeed in getting along in urban environments while consuming much less in the way of familiar natural resources per head than city dwellers at present?

Some of the facts cause apprehensions of doom. Note, for example, the larger implications of the principle that once a species has established itself in a new environment its biomass increases to a level close to the limits set by the energy chain. This can be disastrous for a growing population that is rapidly depleting limited supplies of both its fossil and fissile fuels. The generalization drawn from living-systems theory causes us to measure the biomass of man, comparing it with what is known about other species, leading to the discovery that *Homo sapiens* appears to be second already among all species, while the first—a combination of some 231 breeds of cattle—is a species that is now fully domesticated by man, and whose fitness depends upon human protection and manipulation. Most of the other plentiful species, plant and animal, have also been domesticated. Moreover, present trends suggest that humans will shortly reach the top in the protoplasm contest, and that most of the human biomass will converge upon cities for life supports because systems involving the closely integrated organization promoted by urban life can be more efficient for utilizing scarce resources than those that are dispersed over a countryside.

As cities have grown and developed, they have streamlined the food web so that an increasing proportion of the original calories of energy fixed from sunlight is used in the metabolism of the city. Surprisingly, though hortatory argument abounds, *no scientific literature as yet takes up the synthesis of balanced urban ecosystems,* even though millions of dollars have been expended in researching closed systems for spaceships. Fortunately, one can find abundant bits and pieces, even some subassemblies, in the technological literature so that several quite different systems for the transfer of energy and recycling of protoplasmic building materials can be proposed that appear to be both technically and economically feasible.

Back in 1965 the idea of recycling certain key components, such as water, phosphate, fixed nitrogen, metals, and polymeric materials of construction was rather novel. Shortly thereafter the recycling concept was picked up as a popular fad and then incorporated into the ideology of Nature worship. It has by now accumulated many unneeded connotations so that public discussions can generate many misunderstandings. For all of this, an economically integrated program for recycling, a true urban metabolic system, cannot yet be found in the literature, and it is time that the attempt at formulating such a program be made for situations where scarcities are most keenly felt.

Constructive approaches to meeting a food and energy crisis do not follow directly from ecological analysis. The living system, as understood by biologists, has directions for development or evolution but not goals. It is influenced in the directions it takes by forces and structures in the environment, but it cannot make decisions that are subsequently implemented. The theorist of living systems plays the role of external observer-analyst, endeavoring to discover an economical means for presenting the range of possibilities that actually exists for the continuation and evolution of man, while estimating the likelihood of each distinctly different outcome. As long as he employs the discipline of biology, or of "black box" psychology, he remains an outsider to the system, similar in many respects to the traffic analyst interpreting the movements of impersonal automobiles and trucks through a maze of freeways, arterial roads, and parking places. Both are able to provide warnings based upon observed trends, but observational science by itself offers no strategy for avoiding catastrophe.

In fairness, however, it should be said that the observational methods occasionally identify points in the system where a small intervention can have amplified effects of a largely predictable kind. Nevertheless, for *decision,* or calculated avoidance of inferior alternatives, we must start from inside the living system, looking at the individual in the population and his means for affecting his immediate environment by interacting within a group or by his participation in institutions.

This other body of systems thinking applicable to cities starts from a belief that man can gain some control over his collective destiny. History shows that there have been ways of evading catastrophic losses of life and welfare of individuals arising from famines, epidemics, and breakdowns in social order which may be quite independent of the biological forces influencing the survival and maintenance of populations. Strategies for planned action can advance the middle-run welfare of individuals and their organizations.

My behavioral model of the typical autonomous urbanite presumes he bargains with organizations, offering a portion of his own time, effort, and attention in order to obtain goods and services. He walks around in a synthetic environment viewing the living system from the interior as a "participant observer" who is altruistic on only a few occasions, follows along in the rut of tradition most of the time, while calculating self-interest on a number of occasions. An individual living in a metropolis must make repeated decisions about what niche is best for him. In order to make satisfactory decisions for himself, however, he needs to have a relatively stable environment that holds a large share of the less important factors constant. It should not be dead or static, but should offer a limited variety of opportunities for self-improvement at low risk to the individual, and should provide a basis for ordering his decisions. A review of the ways in which urban dwellers spend their time suggests that they allocate 10% to 30% to restoring order in their immediate physical environment. This is time spent in personal grooming and the maintenance aspects of housekeeping. However, an even greater amount of attention is devoted to making choices affecting others— family, friends, peer groups, face-to-face associations, firms, offices, and others. In all of these a kind of micro-order must be created by cooperation. There the individual needs to appear altruistic or conforming in order to gain the needed cooperation of others.

The urban system, from the insider's vantage point, is no larger than the microcosm which includes the detectable effects of a choice. External effects tend to disappear the further one moves away from the locus of that choice. Normally the initiation of a branching chain of transactions is reviewed in prospect and the net consequences calculated. The problems of project appraisal are well known to economists because they have specialized in formulating techniques for optimization; the individual is assumed to use the same approach to choice but in an informal way. These methods fail frequently in the metropolis, however, because unprecedented chain reactions can occur very easily in a densely packed space. Experiences with unanticipated reinforcement or a damping out of secondary effects of a choice cause the decider to ask for much more information at very little cost to himself. Control over the essential features of the urban environment therefore depends upon a flow of relevant information to a population of decision makers acting relatively independently of each other.

Increasingly, therefore, the urban environment must be designed to produce reliable signals for the micro decision makers. It also needs to record data on its flow of transactions for the managers of the environment to assess.

They, too, must improve their strategies for conservation and utilization. Almost certainly there are ways of defeating the stringent effects of well-established biological principles, or at least ways for deferring or mitigating their impact. This hope seems most possible in the modern metropolis, because the dependence upon the chanciness of weather and disease has been greatly reduced by constructing an artifact surround.

A participant's view of urban control systems draws upon law and tradition for its source of order. Physical property and the spatial ordering of the environment provide another set of phenomena one expects to remain constant for a sizable part of a human lifetime. These factors provide the setting for the metabolic activity in the city, the features of system maintenance that call into play a multiplicity of feedback loops. The modern city has evolved many mechanisms for reporting deviations from the steady state, and urban institutions have set up alarm systems for detecting shifts that may become destructive. Action mechanisms for restoring the status quo, or making an adjustment upon it, have often been prepared in advance—contingency plans. Response times range from a matter of minutes in the marketplace to years in the case of some political and social reactions.

We need growth models for the metropolis that go beyond the shifts in structural proportions and spatial relationships as size increases. We need models for enhancing capabilities—learning by planning as well as learning by doing—of metropolitan decision systems. How can a Tokyo-scale rate of economic development be installed in other metropolitan areas? How has this record achievement sometimes been improved upon as it is transmitted to Taipei, Seoul, Singapore, and elsewhere? Tokyo comes as close as anything yet invented to the leviathan that reports continuously about itself to itself concerning how it is doing and what may happen in a few days or months. To its present regret, Tokyo has discovered that it has much less competence in techniques for coping with the middle to long run; it has, for example, waited for pioneering to be done in America or Western Europe before attending to the effects of insults to the natural environment.

The modes of metropolitan government are obviously relevant to the social and economic development process,

but so are the operations of headquarters offices of trans-
regional and multinational organizations in both the private
and public sectors, because the relative competitiveness
of urban regions shows up in the data assembled. Rapid
improvements in security and welfare are possible when
the mobile capital and skills can be attracted away from
the less effective urban environments. Competition of this
sort offers an indirect but higher order equivalent of
"predation at a distance." We need now the kinds of
metropolises that not only can provide opportunities for
life superior to those available in rural areas and the small
towns but are strong enough to compete with other large
cities as the supply of capital, material, and scarce skills is
expanded.

Therefore, the presentation of ideas must oscillate from
the philosophical, detached observer's view of living systems
to the internal, advice-oriented image of the way a city
should work on the basis of what is known. The first allows
for the assessment of what new challenges cities may have
to face in the future as a result of increasing size, age, resource depletion, and new knowledge available to all.
The second allows for the devising of strategies, the definition of policies, or the description of institutions that
should be able to cope with the prospective challenges.
The most powerful strategy appears to be that of expediting the self-organization of residents, sojourners, and inmigrants; the best policy seems to be that of substituting
information or communications channels for the most
scarce resources; and the key institutions are those that
find devices for operating across national boundaries. The
principal difficulty is that of communicating to other observers who are intellectually anchored in either the detached viewpoint or the advice-oriented one, but not in
both. To bridge this division, the rules of disciplined reporting must be violated. I shall commit this sin as long as
productive insights emerge.

REDEFINING URBAN ECOSYSTEMS   Chapter 1

Cities are destined to become the normal habitat for man.
When human populations are numbered in the multiple
billions, the metropolis must become home for all but a
minor fraction. Only in the highly organized, carefully
designed, and globally interconnected metropolis does any
hope exist for coping successfully with prospective resource
scarcities. Cities must diversify activities, acquire new com-
petencies, preserve knowledge, and accumulate structure
in dimensions and directions that are only now becoming
evident. In the long run they should be able to provide the
stable, natural environment within which the further evolution of living species, including man, will be accelerated.

The prospect is quite contrary to the widely circulated and
commonly believed reports that our modern metropolises
are about to die.[1] Actually our great cities appear to be
undergoing natural changes due to maturation, since after
a long period of growth starting from insignificant origins
the rates of increase of the first of them to be established
appear to be leveling off. Many associations and institutions in such cities are feeling the emotional storms and
uncertainties that accompany adolescence. The most
highly developed of the great cities of the world—London,
New York, Paris, Boston, Toronto, Chicago, Stockholm,
and others—must now anticipate a "middle-aged spread,"
with rates of increase in the range of 0-2% per year in
biomass and physical supports instead of the 3-10% rates
previously experienced. With maturity comes a willingness
to engage in the creation of enduring organizations so that
growth is transferred to a nonphysical realm. Preservation,
renewal, and conservation of scarce local resources then
become the central issues for such cities, though elsewhere
in the world the urgencies are more elemental. Newer
metropolises must still learn how to overcome the grave
threats to survival that arise from an increasing scarcity of
natural resources and the consequent rates of social change.

Critics of cities usually repress facts embarrassing to their
theses. They should be encouraged to explore in depth the
recent histories of a few representative metropolises and
compare their series of formal reports and statistics with
others. Selecting any of the commonly used definitions
of welfare they like, they should judge the shifts in such
welfare generated in these cities over time. Those who

have already done so cannot find a single city that is not a significantly better place to live for a majority of the population than it was a generation or so ago. The "bads" that have been recently recognized as potentially debilitating, such as the deterioration of atmospheric quality, traffic congestion, and crowding, are strongly outpointed by improvements in education, communications, most aspects of health, and in spatial mobility. More impressive yet is the performance in meeting emergencies, because an ability to detect threats in advance and to mobilize resources to counter them is evidence for the viability of a community in the environment with which it must interact. Reduced typical reaction times, which can be used as sensitive indicators of improved capability to overcome crises, prevail all over the world.

The great fault in the standard intellectual opinion about cities is that judgments are reached by comparing current urban conditions with concepts of what should be, and not at all with what has existed in the recent past.[2] Such specifications of ideal conditions are not invariant, but as information about best examples is acquired, and the technical possibilities that allow further improvement are explored, they are strengthened over time and made more demanding. It is not unexpected then that the gap that separates the present situation from the utopian ideal continues to grow larger, nor is it unanticipated that shortcomings will excite a litany of pessimistic predictions that cities will become unlivable. The objective data that point to improving conditions are ignored, because they are not relevant to programs for action that, one hopes, will bring about truly substantial amelioration. Past gains, it is commonly believed, have been far from good enough—because felt deficiencies have increased still more.

Having contested current "doomsday" doctrine by indications of the existence of strong contrary evidence, an alternative concept for visualizing future society is required. Simply stated, it is the following: *The fundamental problem for most people presently living and soon to be born is still that of survival, preferably at a state noticeably above bare subsistence.* The fundamental problem is *not* how to achieve affluence for everyone. Moreover, the emergence of levels above subsistence must be achieved with increasing equity. Since resources are limited, how might a secure existence be achieved, which also allows hope for improvement? What are the principles connecting scarce resources with the functioning of cities? It is possible to take them up in order: first the significance of resources for cities, and then the city as ecosystem in a synthetic (designed?) environment.

A living system is characterized by a set of inputs (or resources) and a set of outputs, with multiple, cybernetically stabilized pathways inside the system that effect the transformation. The metropolis therefore converts resources into something else; resources, together with the internal institutional environment, are used to grow *people*. The function of cities for generations to come will be to "create human capital" from inputs of unskilled immigrants and their newborn cohorts.[3] The metropolis must gather in commodities won from the earth's crust and convert them into civilized, whole people able to make their way in an increasingly interdependent world. Neither waste, nor rubble, nor pollution should be allowed to accumulate, nor should instabilities in the internal pathways be permitted to develop to the point where they affect the survival and competence of the next generations.

As yet metropolises have achieved very little coordinated control over their resource supply or their own organization. The national state still jealously retains formal responsibility for constructing modern environments and programming the development of human resources. Thus far national states have done little to increase the efficiency of the consumption process (although they have on occasion instituted effective procedures for equitable rationing), and they tend to intervene in production schemes that draw directly upon natural resources in the hinterlands, insisting upon a more orderly exploitation. Nationalism is losing its hold upon loyalties, however, and, with the spread of television, its control over character development. Multinational organizations are inventing ways of moving knowledge, cash, people, commodities, and organizational forms across national boundaries faster than new controls are being devised. Therefore the future opportunities for great cities are more diverse than at present.

What is a resource? Everyone has a generalized idea of what resources are and the ways in which they may be identified. Each of us puts minerals and forests and waterfalls into this category almost automatically. Any person

THE METROPOLIS AS A RESOURCE TRANSFORMER

living near the sea will add fisheries to the list. Those who are in food enterprises recognize the significance of the living soil—micro-organisms, worms, moisture, and humus— as a fundamental resource. More recently, highly unusual environments, the kinds that excite wonder in man, have been marked as a scenic resource. The common meaning of the word is based upon these agreements between people with quite different personal experiences.

It is important to examine further the implications of the *idea* of a resource. It starts with some unusual quality found in a locale that makes the area appear different from the typical physical environment. This difference is great enough to assign a functional name (e.g., clay banks, oil pools, pine woods, fishing reefs, fruit belts, waterfalls, and natural harbors, to name a few) to the type of locale. Each is a resource, however, only when the information about it can be passed along from one place to another and one generation to the next. Only then can the locale produce something of value to man and become a resource. The knowledge embodied in a technology is, by definition, general enough to be diffusible across cultural boundaries; it can also evolve or develop over time, accumulating small-scale improvements as it is applied. Normally a technology is made up of a sequence of operations or processes that can be spelled out as a series of directions or recipes for what should be done with one or more resources in order to accomplish the conversion to a desired commodity or service.

The knowledge component of resource use has been increasing in quantity and significance over time. It is recorded in images—diagrams, blueprints, laboratory analyses, mathematical equations, sets of specifications, technical terminology, and so on. The resource has real value only if the effort invested in its use is more than compensated for by the returns to people. Most of the so-called natural resources in the world are not worth the expense involved in extracting or making use of them, and are therefore relegated to the submarginal class. They become true resources only when the scarcity of the primary commodities or services produced from such resources has increased, and price rises have occurred, or when a significant improvement in technological efficiency has been established. Of the two, advances in applied science have been more effective recently in creating resources worthy of development than has a rise in prices brought on by the exhaustion of deposits of richer concentration.

Most of the common mistakes in future-oriented public policy can be easily avoided when thinking about resources as grounded in this information-based formulation, rather than upon depletion-obsessed doctrines. According to the teaching of a past generation, we could look forward to a day when resources essential to civilization would be universally depleted; this would be a time when our great-grandchildren would be doomed to a way of life sustained only by the renewable resources of soils, vegetation, and waterpower. Feature stories in magazines and newspapers and university lectures on conservation have dwelt upon the hard times in the future brought about by the accelerated exhaustion and waste of our richest resources. These early projections were inadequate because they did not consider the specific effects of the steady growth of knowledge about technology; nevertheless this mode of thinking has continued up to the present.

The acquisition, storage, and transmission of knowledge are all uniquely human activities. Some individuals have greater aptitude for this work than others, but almost everyone can improve his mastery of such knowledge by the expenditure of time and attention. As natural resources are depleted, the knowledge about substitutes and alternatives that specific people possess or can quickly obtain may be drawn upon to prevent deprivation in the population as a whole. As far as society is concerned, the possessors of knowledge are a resource—the human resource produced by cities—and as valuable and dependable as any options on a new discovery of oil or the mapping of a new fishery.

These recent insights are a revelation; they greatly broaden the development strategy for a modern society. The planning horizon was once limited by the expected depletion time of energy sources, but now it can be extended by building up knowledge of substitutes that are more plentiful, just as nuclear fuels can replace coal and fuel oil by advancing the technology of nuclear reactors. Having dispensed with the misconceptions of the extreme pessimists, however, we should not make the mistake of extreme optimism. Energy and most other basic nonrenewable natural resources will become relatively more scarce and expensive over time; their price is likely to rise as rapidly as that of skilled, organized attention by permanent employees.

THE INTERDEPENDENT CONSTITUENT POPULATIONS

Continuing this analysis of the urban ecosystem, we must consider the *interactions of populations*—the relations of men, machines, animals, and plants with each other and with the supporting environment. Knowledge about environment is acquired by men, but embedded and stored as information and pattern in the other populations. When existing together as a community, the location, appearance, and responses of each of these populations is chosen so that it becomes better adapted to the others. Interdependencies can become very strong as the community matures and approaches the climax stage. These interdependencies are not merely day-to-day relationships but of a kind that can heal wounds and redress insults as long as the injuries are normal for the community and have been sustained several times before. All the principles by which we have come to understand living systems apply, as well as others barely glimpsed as yet.

Human populations are significant forces in a wilderness and controlling agents in the countryside, but in the city they became clearly *dominant.* Note that the plural of population has been used; the biologists' assignment of a single species to *Homo sapiens* is based upon the same criterion that is applied to animals—the capacity to maintain a common gene pool—but the peculiar properties of men allow them to transmit much more information from one generation to the next through nurture of the young and through highly organized social institutions than through gene recombination, so subspeciation is exceedingly important. Cities have always had markedly plural human societies, and the tendency is toward increased pluralism rather than homogenization. When urban locales dominated by a single ethnic, religious, occupational, or avocational group (now often referred to as ghettos, quarters, or districts) are dissolved, several new subcommunities find a place in mosaic structure; in them a significant number of individuals study and discipline themselves voluntarily to a distinct set of traditions that maintain the community against forces of assimilation. Cosmopolitan groups do not demand the total commitment of their members, and a single individual may belong to several different subspecies, dividing his time according to the requirements of the separate roles to be filled. The boundaries of the territories maintained by respective populations are marked in ways knowable only to initiated members of the communities, because they are increasingly overlapping and interpenetrating each other in the multistoried metropolis. An observer of the cityscape sees nothing but a jumble of partially decipherable patterns, but because he is an acknowledged member of some of the groups he will see the phenomena of dominance in the urban system with a personal interest not available to the field biologist observing a community of plants and animals.

The populations that men most dominate and control in the urban communities are *machines.* They are slave populations, imported mostly from other cities, that come in all sizes, appearances, and many specializations. In the workshops of cities that still operate close to subsistence, the transition from tools to machines is still incomplete, and the supply of the actuating juice of electrical power is not drawn upon universally as yet. The growth and elaboration of these electrical machines require a huge expansion of the segment of the human population specializing in their maintenance. More potent self-propelled species of machines, which range in dimensions from diesel locomotives and jet aircraft to wristwatches and battery radios, consume refined or predigested energy sources instead of electricity, consuming up to 20% of all energy in the urban community. (Anticipated energy consumption in cities is summarized in figure 1.1.) An even greater proportion of humans addresses itself to their direction and maintenance as a full-time income-producing occupation, and the population of the self-propelled species expands even more rapidly than their masters.

Just as the first wave of machines in the nineteenth century relieved humans of most of the backbreaking labor required for civilized existence, the *automata,* a prolific new breed of machines possessing complex cybernetic capabilities, are now relieving humans, in turn, of mind-deadening routines and similar drudgery.[4] Automata entered the most advanced cities in the 1950s and penetrated the poorest before the end of the 1960s. The basic input for these new machines is *information,* which may come from the physical environment through a sensor type instrument from records of human transactions, or, to an increasing ex-

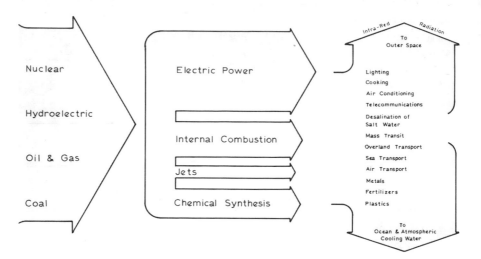

Figure 1.1 Possibilities for a New Metropolitan Energy Economy
This sequence of energy transformations for urban activity can be designed for temperate-to-tropical environs for about 800-1200 kg of coal equivalent per capita per year. That is about a tenth of the present consumption in the United States. Substitutes for the automobile and space-saving dwelling designs provide the principal opportunities for fuel savings.

tent, from the action of other machines. The automata of our era rarely locomote because they need minor but very steady sources of electrical power, but they are now going through a process of micro-miniaturization, reducing size for a given capability by a factor of a hundred, so that the 1980s will bring a huge variety of peripatetic automata. Normally, automata affect situations and conditions at a distance through the networks and switching gear of a telephone system which was originally designed to meet human communication needs. Computing centers, which provide the physical supports for most of the automata, are coming into continuous contact with each other and most of the information-based transactions among metropolises are carried out through them with the aid of microwave beams that reinforce the coaxial cables.

This new population of actors does not seem to have affected the numbers of animals living in cities. The urbanized wild animal species are primarily parasitic upon man, living off of the surplus and inadvertent waste from his household. Rats, mice, birds, and insects are the most common, although they stay out of sight most of the time. Almost as numerous are the domesticated species of animals, which have been bred into diverse strains and have extraordinarily little resemblance to the original wild type. Their associations with humans are very close and their presence is especially evident in the less densely populated portions of the metropolitan area, where individually they often serve as human companions. Carefully bred populations reappear as delicacies providing variety in the diet. Populations of the parasitic species are usually kept down to convenient levels through indirect controls over habitat and food supplies, while reproduction in the domesticated species is generally controlled directly by men. The biomass of these tamed species tends to range between 5% and 20% of the human, depending heavily upon the subcultural values attached to associations with them, since dog lovers, cat owners, equestrians, and bird keepers are usually quite different kinds of people. Some city dwellers are beef eaters, some consume pork, many like chicken, but quite a few are vegetarians. Some modern cities maintain, in addition, large populations of domesticated animals at a distance, on ranches and market farms, from which they import milk, carcasses, and packaged flesh. Other cities are hosts for communities of fishermen who engage in organized predation on marine life.

Very few of the plant species native to the territory occupied by the city can continue to live in an urban community. Even weeds, the wild species springing up untended in the less trafficked interstices, most often belong to the introduced category. In the parts of the city where activity is most incessant, domesticated trees, shrubs, flowers, and grasses predominate. Their function is purely ornamental since the fruits, if any at all, are rarely harvested. Edible plants begin to be numerous out toward the edges of the metropolis; the ornamentals still hold sway in the land facing the roads, but patches and rows of fruit and vegetable monoculture are found very often behind the houses.

A metropolis consumes huge quantities of vegetable materials, many of which are imported from great distances, but almost all of them have been preprocessed before arrival into commodities like flour, sugar, lumber, paper, cloth, and soap, and have been rendered sterile so that they can be safely stockpiled. Once introduced and digested, most of these plant substances also sustain life among the animal species and the micro-organisms.

Invisible plants in the soils and water bodies of the urban community are less modified from the natural state. Even the quantity of such life, considered as biomass, is not greatly changed, because the huge volume of imported organic substances needs to be decomposed. Thus ponds, streams, and tidal pools are likely to have more bacteria, and the soils have at least as much litter for them to decompose as elsewhere; the wild species of micro-organisms present are very much the same as those before urbanization. Civilization intervenes to the extent of introducing pure cultures for a few purposes—domesticated strains of yeast for breweries, distilleries, and breadmaking, molds for cheesemaking, and varieties of bacteria for commodities like vinegar or yogurt. Close inspection of the city also reveals that special cultures of aerobic and anaerobic micro-organisms are maintained in large stirred tanks in sanitary facilities that have been explicitly designed to expedite the decomposition of waste organic matter. The domestication of the various microbiological species has proceeded further in Japanese cities than in Occidental metropolises.

These populations, with all their relationships and transformations, are not as simple as suggested by the foregoing generalizations, but actually constitute the most complex ecosystem ever evolved. It must be further emphasized that they form total communities which are not in equilibrium. Many are invading new territory and expanding their dimensions by as much as 10% per year. Quite a few observers regard the growth as "cancerous"; Ian McHarg has called it a "brown fungus" attacking Earth. In North America the chief populations in the front lines of the invasion seem to be made up of a variety of piloted automotive vehicles, while in tropical Asia and Africa the frontiers of the metropolis are usually extended by human squatters, often accompanied by vehicles and domesticated animals.

Taken together, urban ecology is a fascinating subject. It is a pity that it is not studied as such, but only as a series of limited specializations. The term itself was appropriated by a subspecialty of sociology; bio-ecological investigators drew upon relatively undisturbed natural distributions to inspire their theories. Though ignored by the systems scientists, maintenance of the urban ecosystem has become a series of interrelated arts that are improved and transmitted from one generation of practitioners to the next. Thus, while we have not been conscious of it, the web of life in cities has become ever more intricate, and the overall system can more consistently restore conditions to the viable range than in earlier times. Neglect of this newly synthesized system cannot continue for long, however, because a huge pressure of human population is building up in the countryside, and it requires life supports regardless of where individual persons decide to live. The crucial life supports can be put together only with the semi-manufactures and machines produced within an urban framework.

Cities contain the most intensively constructed habitat. Nature offers no real parallel for building and controlling physical environment, so theoretical systems based upon natural observations can be stretched to encompass cities only with difficulty. The structures are so elaborate that they are seen, when approaching a city, much sooner than the populations—towers, office slabs, factory chimneys, water tanks, church steeples, and microwave relay stations come into view very often even before entering the first

THE DESIGNED URBAN HABITAT

suburb. The first living population to be seen—trees—stand out at a somewhat smaller scale—not only are they abundant, but most are carefully ordered and spaced, thus moderating the severity for the eye of the architectonic structures. Once inside the city, where the populations actually interact, one sees objects at the scale of the individuals—poles, fences, hedges, signs, mailboxes, waste receptacles, parking spaces—all of them subject to certain constraints because they are not randomly distributed, but are nevertheless in a kind of complex disarray that produces low-level generalizations. A practiced eye, able to detect aging processes in materials, would note that networked subsystems were introduced piecemeal into the built city, and the resulting local conflicts are either tolerated or treated cosmetically with paint or landscaping.

An efficient means for discovering order is to watch a modern urban precinct grow, from below the ground to the roof tops. Kings and emperors sometimes made it their lifetime ambition to will a new city into being, reserving many of the crucial decisions to themselves while delegating the major effort to architects, clerks, and builders. Today the launching of an urban shell is carried out by an entrepreneur backed by public or private corporations, the gestation period is about five years, and the period of high speed assembly is eight to fifteen years.

SCENARIO ONE

Creating a
Contemporary
City

The recipe for a modern new city, without technique, finance, and style, runs as follows: Take a few thousand hectares of land, well-drained, preferably with a rolling surface, used until then for orchards, pastures, and some row crops. Reshape the land form with bulldozers, scraping off brush, rubble, and sod from most hillsides. Fill the ravines and gullies, and guide the brooks into underground drains. Dig ditches in the flat areas to conduct away surplus runoff, and prepare special hollows for lakes, reservoirs, and ponds. Sculpt the hillsides into terraces 20-100 meters wide, but save a few middle-aged trees to break up the symmetry. Set out stakes at measured intervals with coded plastic ribbons which tie into the blueprints for the next wave of construction activity.

Install a series of distributive networks on the site. First the street and road pattern is cut more deeply into the soil. Then ditchdiggers come to lay water lines and sewer pipe. A smaller machine can follow to put down gas pipe

(soon to become an anachronism for new urban settlements, unless it becomes feasible to distribute hydrogen) and then the lines for the electric power and telephone grids. Nowadays an extra cable is laid alongside them to be ready to transmit cable television and computer signals. Then tidy up everything by compacting and paving the roads and leveling the mounds of spoil. Finally bring in new teams to dig up the interiors of the blocks, lay foundations, and erect the buildings. Import young new trees and shrubs for the more open and public spaces.

The various urban populations are expected to stream in at this stage—vigorous people come with still-growing families and bundles of artifacts, the vermin species originally displaced by the bulldozers reinvade the territory battling those brought in with the domesticates that live with humans, stationary machines are installed, and vehicular types stand by the doorways ready to move. New trees and shrubs are planted, seed beds for annuals are freshly prepared, patches of lawn are laid down, and the native weeds are pulled out wherever they appear. Within a few years of interaction, a totally new set of associations among humans, animals, plants, machines, and buildings has been instituted.

The automata are introduced more gradually into special niches, primarily the central business district, the industrial estates, the medical districts, and the school system. Arriving as metal boxes with dial or television-screen faces, semiconductor guts, and servomechanism limbs, they speedily take control of the routine backroom type of operations. They maintain flows through the networks and the transactions between individuals and groups within the new city, especially their contacts with the rest of the world (see figure 1.2). Automata are particularly needed for holding down the frequency of error in the goods and services (thus maintaining their quality) that are exported from the new city in exchange for commodities and assistance obtained from elsewhere.

The urban habitat is incomplete without its signs. The central business districts use neon and fluorescent-backed lighting for emphasis, as do most roadside installations, and for announcing the function of the site at night. Billboards go up along principal channels of movement, street signs are placed so as to direct vehicular traffic and to label roads and plazas in the residential areas, poles carry ephem-

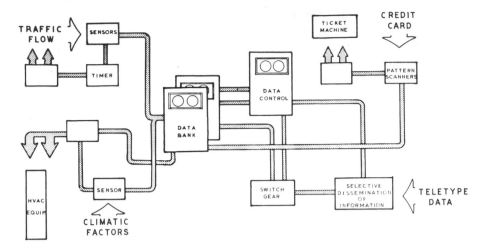

Figure 1.2 A Simple Automaton

Wherever transactions between the human population and the designed environment become repetitive and routine, the person who acts as a "gatekeeper" is made to feel like an extension of the machinery; his behavior becomes unfeeling and automatic. Routine exchanges at the gates of a mass transit station might be handled by a system with a flow diagram that looks like this (taken from the plans of the Bay Area Rapid Transit System). The design became more complicated when it was required to assume more human qualities, especially those of outwitting ticket forgers, preventing fraud, and minimizing the possibility of accidents under unusual conditions. These automata were less susceptible to start-up problems than those controlling the operations of rolling equipment. Introducing an automaton into a new role and getting it to work smoothly in a human organization often presents great difficulties.

eral notices of opportunity at eye level, and the vehicles often carry insignia identifying the corporate operator. Images, displayed as form or presented on the face of buildings, together with the kinds of order imposed upon landscaped plots, serve as unlettered signs that tell strangers (and remind residents) moving about in this complex habitat much of what they need to know concerning the standing of the respective households and organizations in the "pecking order" of the locale. As a result, the strangers in a locale are able to judge better what proprieties to use when approaching a citizen of the new city.

This version of metropolis is energy-intensive, water-wasting, and it uses land, scarce materials, and labor in a profligate fashion. Whatever displaces the present formulation of the "modern" urban environment must nevertheless be competitive with it from the point of view of the human population. A large fraction of humans must prefer the successor habitats to those provided by the metropolitan areas now in existence. Fitness of a subspecies now implies its ability to fit the environment to human capabilities more intimately than at present. This need for close fit means that the web of interdependencies that evolves in an urban ecosystem should be made more explicit so that networks installed in the habitat will permit easy adaptation to external stresses.

The concern thus far has been with requirements for a viable urban habitat. The respective ingredients can be combined with the populations who transform the habitat into a city. What does a city do that a noncity finds difficult or impossible? What is the output of a city? Objectively, how can one formula for a city be said to be better than another? The metropolis has been pictured here as a self-repairing, homeostatic social reactor that can, when necessary, obtain from its hinterland or from other cities whatever it needs in the way of natural and human resources.

THE PRODUCT OF CITY LIFE

The fate of the natural resources, once they have been removed from the original site, is quite readily traced. The first step refines the crude product; therefore we see grain dried and winnowed, trees trimmed and debarked, petroleum de-emulsified, gas desulfurized, and ores milled at sites not too far removed from the original mine. The graded and standardized products are then moved on to processors at crossroads, many of which have not become urban centers but have remained mill towns and factory settlements. There a wide variety of basic commodities are produced—grain reappears as flour and middlings, trees as paper and board, petroleum as a hundred different refinery products, each of them held to strict specifications, gas is transformed to electric power or petrochemicals, and ores are moved on as ingots and shapes of metal. The ultimate destination for 80% or more of the tonnage of these commodities is a metropolitan area where the complex, market-oriented manufacturing is carried out in as many as a dozen successive steps. Moreover the *inorganic* transformation of mineral resources has now reached a physical volume twenty to thirty times as great as that observed for formerly living materials, such as crops, animal products, and wood.

A few months or years later, the usefulness of the manufactured products runs out, and they become only so much scrap. A bit of salvage may be possible, so that some materials go through another cycle of refining, fabrication, and distribution, but even then the end is ultimately the same. Nothing remains but some polluted water, some solid waste, carbon dioxide, a small amount of the more noxious gases, and a quantity of heat that escapes built-up areas (mostly as low-grade infrared radiation because the metropolis itself is maintained as a "warm body" with a temperature several degrees higher than its immediate environment). The material balances and the energy accounts for the urban system are thereby settled. As much goes out of the ecosystem or is stored in it, as originally went into it.

It is important to consider these residues over the long run, because they change the immediate physical environment. The solid stuff transported to an urban settlement becomes an indigestible waste; the most convenient use is to fill low places in and about the city, especially to build up levels and dry up marshland. After a generation or two, however, the detritus and rubble accumulate on-site so that the city raises its average ground level above the surrounding plain a half meter or so each century. Long-lived ancient cities left *tells* raised as much as twenty meters above the desert, but much of that material—dressed stone, sun-dried brick, and ordinary clay-based stucco—was employed for defense purposes rather then ordinary living. Nowadays most major defense installations have been moved out to the empty, interstitial areas. The modern metropolis, if abandoned, would very likely be seen not as a mound of rubble but as a jungle of grass-grown girders, reinforced slabs, with interstitial shrubs and forest undermined by elaborate grids of wire and pipe, much of it connecting catacombs made up of subbasements and storm drains. The most time-resistant material below the surface would be the enamelware, particularly toilet equipment, much of it more lasting than potsherds of past millennia. The trend thus far, however, points directly away from any significant abandonment of cities and rather moves in the direction of an increasing scale of urban settlement. Momentous forces have been released by the processes conducted within the urban social reactor and they are enabling the metropolis to become still more influential and populous.

Social reactors produce the opportunities that stimulate the appearance of new autonomous units, called organizations, with larger-than-human capabilities. Human organizations are created much more readily in the city because density promotes frequent interaction among individuals and the facilities are designed to keep the conflict level low. These organizations remain in the city after the fuels have been expended and the imported commodities have been used and returned to the earth's crust as solid and liquid waste. Vital, active groups will achieve a higher degree of organization, since the transactions of city life produce both an accumulation of knowledge, and a diffusion of it, that can be readily drawn upon. In thermodynamic terms, at the same time that a city catalyzes reactions with high entropy gain, it conserves negentropy or order in small, carefully protected cells.[5] In the long run, such new organizational structures—for example, the IBMs, Comsats, Social Security Administrations, health maintenance organizations, and university institutes—comprise the surviving output from urban life.

In an urban milieu organizations are continually formed and others dissolve. They are more highly specialized in modern cities, and there are many more of them than for the same dimensions of human population in rural areas. The reasons are readily apparent—organizations imply transactions among members (otherwise their names may remain, but they no longer exist as living entities), and a city distributes its physical facilities so as to expedite high

Table 1
Net Consumption of Natural Resources in Metropolitan Areas, 1970 (Metric tons per million population per year)

Mineral	United States[a]	India[b]
Water[c]	1,800,000,000 (10% domestic; 35% industrial, 55% cooling)	180,000,000 (30% domestic)
Fuel[d]	8,000,000 (30% coal, 40% oil, 30% gas)	400,000 (80% coal, 20% gas)
Sand, gravel, and stone	8,000,000 (60% sand and gravel, 40% stone)	1,000,000[e]
Clay, lime, cement, gypsum, salt	1,600,000	300,000[f]
Iron ore, and ferroalloy ores	800,000	200,000
Nonferrous ores and metals	100,000	10,000
Renewable Organic		
Wood, paper, and natural fibers	400,000	30,000[g]
Foodstuffs, Staples[h]	150,000 (50% cereals, 30% sugar)	200,000
Foodstuffs, perishables[i]	600,000 (25% dairy, 25% poultry, 20% veg.)	100,000

Source: *Proceedings of the Second International Future Research Conference, Kyoto 1970: Challenges from the Future* (Tokyo: Kodansha, 1971), p. 389.

[a]The Standard Metropolitan Statistical Area (SMSA) based upon county lines is becoming steadily more obsolete, so it is assumed here that 70% of the U.S. population was living in metropolitan areas in 1970.

[b]The urban population of India was set at 120,000,000 persons for 1970.

[c]This assumes that water use in an industrial nation is somewhat greater than in nonurban areas. The total for nonirrigation uses in the United States is 2,300 tons metric per year per capita. Indian domestic use is set at 25 gallons per capita per day, since reports from various cities range 22-30 gallons per day. Perhaps 30% more than that is filtered and treated, the difference being lost in leakage. Industrial water appears to demand comparable volumes of water, on the basis of very scattered reports.

[d]Railroads are a heavy user of coal in India, so only 60% of the total fuel consumption was assigned to urban users, but 90% of all U.S. fuel was assigned to these consumers.

[e]No figures available; this level of consumption was deduced from the amount of cement used and the scale of flood control projects designed to protect urban areas.

[f]Figures not available; these numbers were deduced from the amount of pukka housing and facilities installed (cement and brick) while allowing one kilogram of salt per capita per year. Sulfur is known to be very scarce.

[g]Assumes that only half of the timber products get to the city, but about 70% of the paper and board are used there. Fibers have small volume.

[h]Adjusted upward from the estimated consumption so as to allow for spoilage.

[i]About 20% more is re-exported to surrounding nonurban areas.

rates of social transaction. Over time we see an enhancement of the number and variety of human organizations in
cities; there can be organizations of organizations as well,
which try to cap the pyramid with still further organization. If a minimum set of conditions for existence is used,
it is possible to count the organizations present in a city;
at the least, a viable organization has a name, an address at
which it can be reached (which at a minimum may be only
a telephone number or a post office box), a membership,
and a mechanism for transferring the responsibility for
communication in the organization's name to other individuals.

If the founding rate for organizations is higher than the
dissolution rate, the city is productive. Although no counts
have been published, a number of indirect indicators suggest
that virtually all cities are currently increasing their number
of organizations, although for periods up to several years at
a time a city under great stress may experience heavy mortality (via bankruptcy, dissolution, amalgamation, removal,
and the like) among its organizations.

The principle of "survival of the fittest" among organizations, together with the observation that cooperation in a
variety of groups serves as one of the traits most likely to
ensure an individual's own survival, suggests that human
evolution has been displaced upward to this level. The idea
by now is quite old, since geneticists, anthropoligists, and
philosophers such as Haldane, Julian Huxley, Linton, Waddington, and their successors agree that the selective pressures which led to the appearance of the remarkably plastic
Homo sapiens as the dominant predator species in nature
have ceased to be effective.[6] They recognize that the less
fit individuals, whether measured biologically or intellectually, now do survive and, even more significant, reproduce
strongly (although the least fit, the bottom decile, do not).

Thus the succeeding generations of man adapt to the
challenges set by nature no longer as individuals or bands
but as members of groups formed with other men, animals,
plants, machines, and automata. The other species multiply
man's adaptability by at least a thousand times—as judged
by the intensity and variety of forces he is able to withstand. A few modern organizations now promote ad hoc
groups in a way that yields still greater adaptability, while
most others find ways of incorporating some of these behavioral modes into their standard operating procedure.

The organization is preserved as long as it appears to be efficient for controlling the external environment or response to change in it. These organizations with their artifacts comprise a social system operating in an almost wholly synthesized environment.

Thus a special function for cities can be proposed. They are the places in which new controls over the interface with the environment are devised and the base of operations from which such controls are field-tested and implemented. The best indicators of control are extension in operating range—distance, bigness, smallness, grossness, fineness, invariance, speed, purity, evenness of distribution, heat, and cold. Each year, teams in one or another of the most highly cultured cities announce their capacity to move one of these frontiers a bit further out. A decade or so later an organization advertises its ability to do so routinely. First the knowledge is added to the presently existing stock and then, as long as it remains potent, it is distributed to an ever-widening circle of users.

In summary, then, a metropolis is a social reactor—an engine for sociocultural and economic growth that works by expediting interaction among humans. It also contains special facilities for the acquisition of new information about nature. The first product of urban life is flux of public transactions, each of them a voluntary internal adjustment intended to improve or maintain the welfare of an individual or group. Information is diffused through such transactions, leading to decentralized stocks of knowledge. A few of the transactions will be novel and therefore add items that have never before existed in anybody's stock of knowledge. Novel diagrams, images, later often new words are invented to convey the knowledge, making them part of the culture. Repeated voluntary transactions among individuals, animals, their machines, and automata, taken two or three at a time, create bonds of trust. The bonds often close to form groups, and the groups stick together in organizations. Therefore new organizations represent another special product of cities, a few of which may last for decades, even centuries after the initial expenditure of resources for their founding. Finally it becomes apparent that biological evolution can be propelled at a vastly accelerated rate, perhaps in a new direction, by the environments maintained in the great cities because human organization sets the criteria for reproduction and survival of individuals of the other species brought into the city.

The concept of efficiency for the design and operation of a social reactor follows directly from these observations. The idea of "resource-conserving" implies *obtaining greater flows of voluntary transactions, numbers of organizations, amounts of knowledge, and diversity of culture for each unit of resource expended.* Increases in an index representing any one of these will be highly correlated with advances in other such indexes. One provision reflecting political realism must be added, however: most of the existing organization, knowledge, and culture will be stoutly defended and therefore will be preserved for a while, despite demonstrated inefficiencies.

New cities and the expansion of existing metropolises must grow in diverse directions. Admittedly that is not the trend today; we see instead imitative cosmopolitanism reinforced by the current accelerated expansion of international exchange. Primarily because the countries and cultures most in need of urban growth sent their sons to Great Britain, the United States, Canada, France, and Scandanavia to study the present crop of urban projects, whether transport, housing, environmental engineering, or offices, the wasteful standards and building forms of the West are repeated. The proposals of these overseas-trained members of the responsible elite set out to solve the problems of overcrowding and expansion in their own cities, but their proposals could not deviate very far from the conventional wisdom they were taught; otherwise they risked being criticized severely by their peers in the most developed countries. If they lost the support of fellow professionals overseas, they would then also lose the confidence of those associates at home who were unable to get away to study. Imitations of solutions learned in foreign schools are now all headed for crisis, however, because, in the long run, the resources are insufficient for the relatively wasteful Western technologies now being introduced into the cities of the Orient. Therefore a resource-conserving design must buck the mainstream styles, whether bureaucratic or idealistic, and yet discover a means for getting built.

The strategy to be employed in the course of applying this new outlook hinges upon the urgencies produced by

FUTURE DESIGNS

internal crisis. Imminent catastrophe narrowly averted provides the shock that overcomes conventional wisdom. Only then are alternative plans likely to be carried forward. In the future, each group taking this approach must consider prominent risks inherent in its own geographical and political setting. The possible catastrophes can be starvation, thirst, disease, inability to operate due to lack of energy, inability to compete due to lack of communications, revolution due to conflicting ideologies, and international war. The most promising technical and organizational potentials for avoiding such catastrophes are outlined below as an indication of the scope of change implied. Each policy is taken up in greater detail later.

1. Famine. The threat is threefold, the quickest being a shortage of caloric value in the diet, next that of protein, and lastly that of a continuing drain upon initiative and morale due to a lack of vitamins, minerals, and ritual foods. The foodstuffs rich in caloric values are the fats and carbohydrates, best stored in steel tanks, silos, and dry godowns. A metropolis should have access to buffer stocks of cereals, sugar, and oil sufficient to overcome the worst exigencies that might be encountered over a century or two. An alternative could be to design a food production scheme independent of weather and breakdowns in international trade, such as a nuclear-powered agro-industrial complex ("nuplex").[7]

Lack of protein-rich foods causes *kwashiorkor,* which afflicts the growing children and the sickly first and has been claimed to cause some permanent brain damage. The best solution is likely to be found in a number of prepared foods, which also meet the needs for vitamins and minerals, taking every edible form from soups and stews to beverages and snacks as well as sausages and vegetarian steaks without depending upon livestock. The underlying microbiological technology has been developed in Japan and America over the last two decades, but acceptance by the consuming public, although expanding 10-30% per year, is still extremely limited. In the future, livestock should be limited to the quantity needed for efficient recycling of organic wastes from the metropolis. In this case, livestock population is likely to be held at levels not very different from those presently found in poorer countries, which is about a third to a tenth of the man-animal ratios in North America, but the animals can be tolerated in much closer conjunction to the city. There should be enough meat on hand with that arrangement to maintain all the ritual occasions now defined as holidays and festivals.

2. Thirst. Cities will die very quickly of water supplies become exhausted. Fresh water can be obtained by distillation, recycling, or importation via tanker, but the requisite import and distributive facilities generally require more than a year to install. Crises can be postponed by paying careful attention to water-using urban processes and arranging for reuse. A pricing system that responds to the respective demands for different water qualities and faithfully reflects prospective as well as existing shortages may be required. Domesticated plants and stationary machine populations will be most affected by these economies. Much of the new urbanism should be able to function normally when consuming (i.e., converting to reject vapor and brine) only about fifty liters of water per capita per day for months at a time. This is less than a tenth of the demand created by new settlements in America and Europe.

3. Epidemic disease. Packing people more tightly together with each other, as well as with animals, plants, microorganisms, vehicles, and automata, increases the tendency for a given communicable disease to be transmitted to a larger population. The most effective counter-measures are based upon the removal of specific vectors from the environment and quick detection, followed by isolation, of the initial infection. Antibiotics serve as a last line of defense, though one that is still being extended in potency. The risks of illness must be low; otherwise key personnel that move between cities will avoid the area, and the city's sources of livelihood will dwindle away.

4. Critical supplies. Several nonferrous metals and phosphorus will become much scarcer in the foreseeable future. The large-scale urbanism anticipated will then need to depend upon improved salvage techniques and substitutes.

5. Energy. All the food, water, and material shortages now foreseen can, when known a few years in advance, be "solved" through the application of considerable amounts of imported energy. Fossil fuels have been drawn upon in the past to produce that energy, but soon only the expensively extracted reserves will remain, and insufficient quantities of those. Energy-conserving technologies are known but are little used. Energy, and the capital equipment producing and consuming it, is best economized by packing everything into a much smaller space and paying a great deal of detailed attention to the interfaces among the various urban species. When such approaches are fully employed, cities as effective as (and therefore competitive with) the leading American metropolises can get along on perhaps a tenth of the energy used by the latter, and most of the needed energy can be obtained from nuclear sources. Pollution effects must be designed out, and rejected heat and many wastes reused.[8] The overall flow envisioned is compared in figure 1.3.

6. **Physical catastrophe.** Large parts of a city have been known to burn, drown, blow away, or tumble down. Vulnerability to such extreme forces depends upon precautions taken in advance—controls on materials used in construction, the location of levees and dikes, the assembly of skeletal structures, and the design of foundations. The large crippling losses of the past are now preventable, although at a cost, of course. Spontaneous building of the physical city by family groups, speculators, and various associations must be brought under some centralized control; usually supervision requires licensed contractors whose work is regulated by regional or central government though, all too often, such controls proliferate and combine to prevent imaginative solutions to the problems of creating efficiently designed environments. Building codes, zoning provisions, and labor agreements in America together inhibit the application of the promising new ideas regarding structures, methods, and materials arising out of modern technological progress. The physical city can be lighter, stronger, and more transformable to other uses on short notice, yet still cost only half as much. The future approaches to building systems must incorporate self-help construction, cooperatives, and evolutionary building as well as factory prefabrication.[9]

7. **Breakdowns of public order.** Human communities are not infrequently riven by civil strife that not only destroys the participants but inflicts grave damage upon interdependent urban populations and their surroundings. New urbanization is far more vulnerable to such violence than older cities because many of the feuds and long-standing enmities of the countryside are swept in along with the new settlers; thus insurgencies among the peasantry can become explosions in the metropolis. A city must therefore have enforceable law, particularly regarding public property,

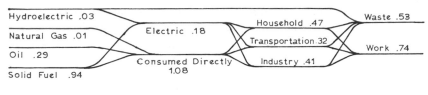

INDIAN ENERGY FLOW 1965
1.26 x 10⁶ Kcal / capita /year

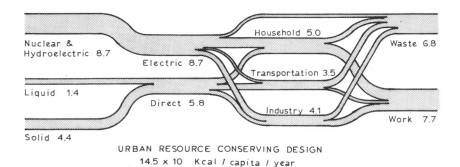

URBAN RESOURCE CONSERVING DESIGN
14.5 x 10   Kcal / capita / year

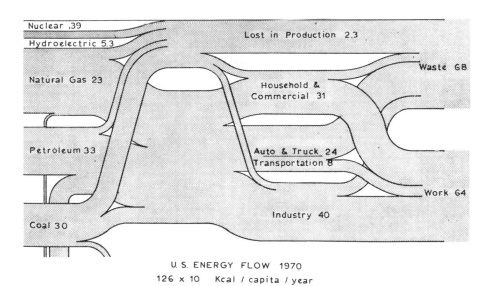

U. S. ENERGY FLOW 1970
126 x 10   Kcal / capita / year

Figure 1.3 Energy Economies
Over the long run it is anticipated that both the underdeveloped economies, as represented by the model for Indian energy flow, and the developed, as represented by the American version, must evolve in the direction of the resource-conserving pattern of flow. The design task is one of expediting as much social and cultural exchange as has been achieved in American cities with an infrastructure that saves energy. Health and security should not be impaired.

Redefining Urban Ecosystems   33

grievance procedures, arbitration, and political representation for all interest groups. It needs an effective police force. These legitimating institutions by themselves will not be able to prevent breakdowns in public order unless backed by large investments in an integrating infrastructure such as an education system that pushes most students well beyond literacy, accessible mass media with varied content, and active recreation. Such preventive agencies do not halt incidents, but losses can be kept small and localized, rather than catastrophic.

Designing new living arrangements and the physical backup systems to go along with them is a trivial exercise unless a continuing capacity to implement necessary change is incorporated in them. Since most of the catastrophes to be avoided are relatively unprecedented, prevention will make extraordinary demands upon human organization. Cities that overcome stresses and manage to move whole regions toward conditions supporting adequate levels of living are already discovering that their most creative effort is the work of fitting individuals and groups together to form organizations that get these complex jobs done. "Institution building" is a rather inadequate term applied to the process. The inventions and designs must be almost wholly indigenous; outsiders can only offer suggestive ideas based upon micro-level experience gained elsewhere in solving problems that seemed closely related.

Cities have until now done relatively badly in the job of organizing themselves so as to gain control of their destinies. The fact that surpluses have been accumulating most rapidly inside urban institutions should have given cities the freedom to act on their own behalf, but control of the new assets has usually been lost. In most instances the liquid funds are siphoned off by state and nation. If the nation fails in the attempt to capture control, the assets either flow out to other parts of the world where they are more secure or remain hidden in unproductive niches. The creation of suburbs often frustrates the ability to act as a coherent unit. If a metropolis should declare itself a sovereign city-state, it would normally cause greater overall losses than could be gained through comprehensive planning. Meanwhile the self-generated proposals for restructuring and for increased control of internal operations that have been repeatedly produced by city administra-

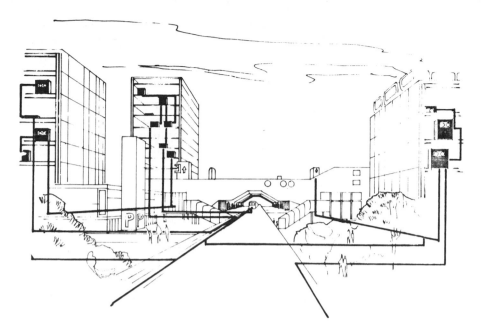

Figure 1.4 Networks of Automata in the New Urbanism
Programs within minicomputers are increasingly used for control systems in manufacturing and
commercial enterprises. Thus the most modern structures are designed for coaxial cables and
minimum interference between circuits as well as for the comfort of the human occupants.
These machines will carry on the routine functions of electronic data processing, but they will
also maintain catalogs, run diagnostic checks upon malfunctioning machinery, and monitor the
equipment introduced to maintain comfort, convenience, and safety in public buildings. Larger
computer centers quickly become a "neighborhood" of somewhat similar automata but also
handle much routine computation. Instruments at the interface with the environment are increasingly designed to exert some local control and continuously report back to a larger center
possessing some executive functions. The population of automata is estimated to be growing at
the rate of 20-30% per year, and almost all are in those activities that are simultaneously expanding their employment of people.

tions are timid and inadequate, mainly because small communities in the same state or the regions feel threatened, do their best to exert vetoes, and often succeed.

Yet a few great cities have accomplished wonders in some key sectors with only modest amounts of capital. Tokyo, Seoul, Nagoya, Hong Kong, and Singapore continue to improve their physical organization. A number of others, such as Sao Paulo, Caracas, New Delhi, and Teheran seem to have been keeping up with the huge rates of inmigration to which they have been subjected. One must ask how the relatively successful cities contrived to maintain and even improve physical as well as social conditions. Was the future borrowed from in some way to overcome stringencies? What was *their* formula for putting together an increasingly efficient apparatus for conducting commerce, industry, and public services? (See figure 1.4). Studies on the scene have thus far unraveled parts of the local strategies, but the inferences must wait for the exposition of a suitable theory.[10]

1. Jane Jacobs, *The Death and Life of American Cities* (New York: Random House, 1961); Lewis Mumford, *The Myth of the Machine* (New York: Harcourt, Brace & World, 1967, 1970), *The Urban Prospect* (New York: Harcourt, Brace & World, 1968).

2. Although not directly aimed at cities, a number of books arguing with ecological concepts have been concerned with the debacle of modern world society. They include Paul R. and Anne H. Ehrlich, *Population, Resources, Environment* (San Francisco: W. A. Freeman, 1970); Barry Commoner, *Science and Survival* (New York: Viking, 1966); and Max Nicolson, *The Environmental Revolution* (London: Hodder and Stoughton, 1970). A reply has now been addressed to such expositions by John Maddox, editor of *Nature* in his carefully argued *The Doomsday Syndrome* (New York: McGraw-Hill, 1972). Nothing is really settled, however, because two strikingly different viewpoints regarding the responsibility of scientists to society are embedded in the approaches taken. Critics of present trends feel that their duty lies in calling attention effectively to the hell into which the world is sliding. In order to be effective, they take the role of advocates and emphasize possibilities instead of probabilities, even though unlikely. Then the alerted activists and politicians must pick up the baton and effect the changes in policy. The counterview points out that unbalanced presentation of the trends and the vividness of the pictures of ecological collapse have induced the public and its usually reluctant representatives to choose inequitable and wasteful policies. In general I find both sides inadequate, so I shall start again from the data, using living-systems principles wherever they seem to apply and not bother to associate myself with one side or the other. An excellent foundation for treating the transition from bio-ecology to human ecology to urban organization has been formulated by Amos H. Hawley, "Ecology and Population," *Science,* 179 (1973), 1196-1201.

3. The concepts of human capital and of human resources were actively developed by economists during the early 1960s. They recognize that investments of attention and effort can be made in many individuals which produce expectations of earnings beyond the costs; a parallel observation is made for human associations, including corporations. For many human associations providing nonmarketed services, such as communities, some capital value may be attributed to the degree they prevent loss or wastage of other assets. The economic concepts are relatively straightforward and are admirably presented by Theodore W. Schultz, the man who contributed the most to launching the concept in the *International Encyclopedia of the Social Sciences,* II, 284-286. A more extensive review is provided by Melvin R. Levin and Alan Shank, eds., *Educational Investment in an Urban Society* (New York: Teachers College Press, 1972). The social psychological concepts are akin to morale and integration within a community or corporation, and the units of measurement are more subtle (Rensis Likert and David G. Bower, "Organization Theory and Human Resources Accounting," *American Psychologist,* 241 (1969), 585-592).

4. Defining the exact difference between automata and ordinary machines poses the same kinds of difficulties biologists have in distinguishing the living from the nonliving entities, and the chemist in separating organic from inorganic. Thus there are highly elaborated types, such as the autopilot in aviation, which are paralleled perhaps by the protozoa in microbiology. Incomplete, plug-in types, such as the battery-charging mechanism in a vehicle or a thermostat for a room, may be equated with the smallest crystalline viruses. A good standard example of an automaton is a weather-reporting station that collects environmental data, reduces them to a record, and transmits the stored information upon request to a center where world weather maps are assembled. It gives out periodic signals reporting that it is still operable, and may be designed to transmit an alarm if it detects a hurricane or a *tsunami.*

An excellent illustrated review of the functioning of automata in the manufacturing sector is found in *Business Week* (December 8, 1973), 68-78. It anticipates that 50% of the capital in North American industry will take a sophisticated approach to the use of automata by 1975, based on information obtained from Ford and IBM.

The theoretical formulation of the characteristics of automata is attributed to Türing. The concept has been important to philosophy, logic, decision theory, and computer science. A Türing machine has a finite tapelike input with discrete information, a set of transforming, adaptive criteria, and an output tape with similar characteristics. To operate in the real world, transducers are required at both ends. A number of such automata are likely to be maintained in a multipurpose computing installation. See J. McCarthy and C. E. Shannon, eds., *Automata Studies* (Princeton: Princeton University Press, 1956).

5. This model of the city was elaborated in R. L. Meier, *A Communications Theory of Urban Growth* (Cambridge: MIT Press, 1962). The importance of stimulating autonomous organizations was elaborated less formally in R. L. Meier, *Developmental Planning* (New York: McGraw-Hill, 1965).

6. Theodosius Dobzhanski, *Mankind Evolving: The Evolution of the Human Species* (New Haven: Yale University Press, 1962); Anne Roe and George G. Simpson, eds., *Behavior and Evolution* (New Haven: Yale University Press, 1958); Conrad H. Waddington, *The Ethical Animal* (London: Allen and Unwin, 1960); Leslie White, *The Evolution of Culture* (New York: McGraw-Hill, 1959).

7. The concept of a nuplex is simple: take a large coastal desert, add a large nuclear reactor which produces power, fertilizer, and desalinated water, irrigate several crops per year, manufacture electrochemicals and electrometallurgicals on site, then export power, crops, and semimanufactures to the metropolises requiring food and raw materials. Important economies of scale can be realized, so the first installations to be able to meet world prices will

be very large. Large-scale studies aimed at discovering the best technological mix have been carried out at the Oak Ridge National Laboratories, but only the preliminaries have been published (Oak Ridge National Laboratory, *Nuclear Energy Centers: Industrial and Agro-Industrial Complexes,* Summary Report, July 1968).

The Indian government is proceeding with a more modest scheme in the Indo-Gangetic plain where the nuclear reactor produces power for pumping water off of flooded land into canals one season and up from the aquifer most of the rest of the time, at the same time that fertilizer is produced and power for the metropolises is fed into the Regional Grid. Studies in both countries suggest that food scarcity must reach levels much more severe than in the 1960s and early 1970s before this approach becomes economic. A review of the applications to Israel is provided by David Vofsi in *Bulletin of the Atomic Scientists,* 28 (October 1972), 45-51.

8. R. L. Meier, "Technologies for Asian Urbanization," *Economic and Political Weekly,* 4 (July 1969), 1-7; "Resource-Conserving Urbanism: Progress and Potentials," in *Challenges from the Future,* Proceedings of the International Future Research Conference, Kyoto, 1970, vol. II, 385-408. See especially a series of reports from Environmental Engineering, Asian Institute of Technology, Bangkok, Thailand by Michael G. McGarry (1969 to 1973).

9. The literature in this field is simultaneously vast and nonexistent. A large number of case studies reporting on the construction of barriadas, favelas, bidonvilles, bustees, and hutments of satisfactory quality, and the few describing cooperative urban community redevelopment (as in Japan especially) are usually premature; personal experience has shown that most are not trustworthy. Generalizations arrived at by comparing experiences in various parts of the world reduce to a reiteration of common sense and cliches. What the field seems to need most is a handful of open-ended franchise operations fitted to specific building technologies based upon bricks, concrete, light panels, foam plastic, and possibly one other material. The users must be designers as well as builders. The provision of technical services accompanying the franchise is the real problem, and there seems to be no adequate descriptions in the literature of ways to organize it.

10. R. L. Meier and Ikumi Hoshino, "Adjustments to Metropolitan Growth in an Inner Tokyo Ward," *Journal of the American Planners,* 34 (July 1968), 210-222; "Cultural Growth and Urban Development in Inner Tokyo," *ibid.,* 35 (January 1969), 1-9. R. L. Meier, "Exploring Development in Great Asian Cities: Seoul," *ibid.,* 36 (1970), 378-392; "Singapore and Bangkok: Pacemakers for Southeast Asia," to appear in the second volume of a series edited by Leo Jakobsen and Ved Prakash as the South and Southeast Asia Urban Affairs Annuals, Sage Publications, Beverly Hills, "The Control of Central India from the Great Cities: Delhi, Cal-

cutta, Bombay," Institute of Urban and Regional Development, University of California, Berkeley, December 1970; "Developmental Features of Great Cities in Asia IV: Physical Expansion, Institution Building and Political Crisis in Karachi and Bangkok," *ibid.,* Working Paper no. 157, October 1971; "The Performance of Cities: An Assessment of Hong Kong and its Future," *ibid.,* January 1972.

The alarms of the past generation, one might say "since radio began," have been raised in sudden, sharp, and disconcerting ways. A border is invaded, an ultimatum announced, the value of currencies reshuffled over a weekend, massive strikes called, a great flood or a massive hurricane threatens. The scale of a crisis nowadays tends to be shaped by the properties of the media by which the progress of events is most closely followed; the size of the headlines and frequency of extra editions of the newspapers have been displaced by the amount of override assigned on telecommunications channels that can be discerned by audiences.

Crises arising from resource scarcity rarely demand public attention in such a fashion. Instead of quick breaks in the web of human arrangements, followed by a series of adaptations moving away from the fracturelike ripples on a surface, the Malthusian specters of famine and exhaustion of energy stocks nag and deter action; public announcements of depletion of stocks that would lead to hoarding tend to be postponed until it is too late, and price shifts that signal the shortage lead to price controls that diminish the release of added supplies. As a consequence, those who have relied on past experience rather than informed calculations of supply and demand are destroyed, their firms and agencies along with them. Malthusian-type crises seem likely to produce a great deal of suffering, but their causes will usually be attributed to more immediate causes, such as breakdowns in public order, conspiracies, or uncontrolled immigration.

One reason for this lack of imagination is the scarcity of premonitory events. There has not been a widely known and reported-upon crisis of this kind since the Irish Potato Famine, which occurred while Malthus was still alive. The famines in China, Bengal, and Russia since then may well have been more severe, as measured by loss of life, but they were difficult to reach and their victims out of contact with the world. Drama was lacking.

A specific attempt to forecast a likely sequence of events in one of the most overpopulated places of the world was undertaken in the 1950s as a part of an early instance of technology assessment. The prediction reflected the time it was made; this was a period in world history during which the population of many poor countries had stepped up growth to unprecedented rates. Marked improvement of public health had led to an extraordinary increase in survival—death rates were cut to a half or a third of former levels. Even persons without demographic sophistication could extrapolate trends and conclude that a critical situation would arise within two generations or less. However, the 1950s were also the period that saw the shock of the Korean War lead to a worldwide peaking of commodity prices, followed by expanded production and rapidly accumulating food surpluses, so that oversupplies soon caused distress among farmers in North America. Simultaneously, a strongly held belief prevailed in the capability of organized scientific research for solving long-range human problems. A combination of these factors implied that the first famines to appear would be alleviated by the food surpluses and that the knowledge resources of the sciences would be mobilized to meet middle-run shortages.

An adequately reported microcosm that seemed to be well advanced toward crisis was the island of Mauritius. A scenario for the transition to a new state of survival was elaborated to illustrate the implications of the existing conditions and fitted to the circumstances of Mauritius. It is most useful to review that projection and discover the reasons why catastrophe of the magnitude envisaged has not struck as yet, before undertaking a wider-ranging assessment. Such an exercise can tell us what kinds of events become significant when the margin of safety is very thin and a whole society teeters on the brink, becoming increasingly unstable as it makes more desperate efforts to survive.

SCENARIO TWO

Malthus in
Modern Dress:
Forecast versus
Outcome

The following is a direct quotation from <u>Modern Science and the Human Fertility Problem</u>, which drew upon sources available up to the middle of 1957:[1]

Mauritius: A Case of Imbalance in Welfare Measures

Mauritius is a remote island of volcanic origin in the Indian Ocean, containing altogether about a half million inhabitants. It has been a British possession for well over a century, but the basic culture remains French creole. It gains its livelihood mainly from sugar cane growing and the conversion of cane juice into raw sugar...[see figure 2.1.]. Not only was it among the most rapidly growing populations registered in the mid-1950s, but it is also one of the

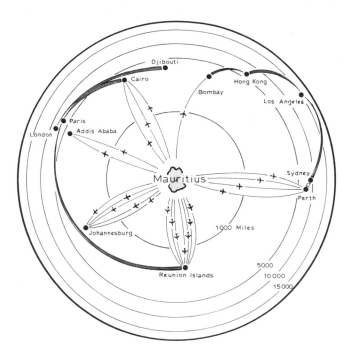

Figure 2.1 Mauritius and Its Links with the World
While isolated physically and politically from the ports of the
world, overpopulated Mauritius seemed more vulnerable to Malthusian-type disasters than any other place. Now that it has good
communications and retains a well-understood legal system, the
citizens of this former British colony can work productively for
multinational corporations. Mauritian labor can be fitted to whatever activities have begun to become too expensive in Hong Kong,
Singapore, Taiwan, or Korea, because of the onset of full employment in some of those places. Increased accessibility and opportunity greatly increase the capacity to resist disaster. Weekly airline
flights connecting Mauritius with overseas metropolises are suggestive of the interdependencies growing up between it and other
points. Distances of direct flights scheduled in 1973 are plotted
according to a logarithmic function that allows the eye to gauge
relative distances. Because air traffic in this part of the world is
still increasing very rapidly, access is bound to improve over time.

Crises of Resource Scarcity   43

most handicapped areas with respect to migration.[*] There are very few places its residents can go. For one reason or another the decanting of sizable numbers into other territories bordering on the Indian Ocean is likely to be unwelcome. South Africa has its apartheid policy, and most other territories do not wish to aggravate their minorities' problems. The costs of moving people to England or to British Honduras, or Brazil, are forbiddingly high. It is much easier for these territories to be supplied with immigrants from distressed societies closer to home.

The various racial stocks of Mauritius were assembled in the course of the slave trading of the eighteenth and nineteenth centuries, the importation of indentured servants when slavery was outlawed, and as a normal consequence of mercantile activities. In 1953 there were about 10,000 British, 10,000 French, 150,000 Creoles and Creolized Indians, 350,000 Indians, and about 20,000 Chinese. The rate of population growth had been fairly gradual before the end of World War II, seldom averaging more than 0.5% per year. But, thereafter the Welfare State arrived, bringing with it programs for the improvement of public health, particularly the elimination of malaria and the improvement of the water supplies. It also brought marked increases in education and various social services. At the same time, unemployment continued to increase, reaching 40% in the Indian sector of the population by 1952.[†]

The basis for manufacturing on Mauritius has been quite limited. There is sugar, of course, twelve plants in all, and a sack-making plant to supply their needs, matches, tobacco processing, shoes, and printing, if we include only those units which employ more than thirty workers. There are no valuable untapped natural resources, nor do geological surveys encourage any speculation in this direction. Transport and communications costs have precluded the establishment of many of the more mobile enterprises of the type which moved into Puerto Rico. Because of the great distances in the Indian Ocean area, and the lack of rich metropolitan centers on its periphery, the tourist trade has remained very small. There seems to be little hope that it will become an important way station. Mauritius has no hinterland like Singapore or Hong Kong, which would enable it to act as an entrepot. It is too far from the oil fields and the tanker routes to serve as another Bahrein or Aden.

[*]World Population and Resources: Political and Economic Planning (London, 1955), pp. 123-126.

[†] A large share of this material on Mauritius was drawn from the notes of Leo Silberman, who conducted a social survey in Port Louis, the Capital. His manuscript is to be published by van Hoeve, The Hague, Netherlands. The remainder of the information was drawn from various articles and documents that were available.

The power to plan for those things that are necessary to the society over the long run is out of the hands of the local leaders. For every major administrative change, for each unusual item in the budget, London must be consulted. Economic interests—sugar, banking, and shipping—are in the hands of absentee directors of companies, whose headquarters are also mainly in London. This fact means that each change in Mauritius must be considered in relation to the Barbados, Singapore, Guiana, and many other spots. Thus, change comes slowly unless initiated as general policy in London. Such a situation is not very suitable for making rapid internal adjustments.

The Breaking Point

The future livelihood of Mauritius depends upon sugar and allied industries. However, the amount of land on the island that can be used is limited and, for all practical purposes, that limit has been reached. If the world market improves there will be incentive to improve the irrigation systems and apply more fertilizer in order to increase the yield. These measures, combined with the spread of improved varieties of cane, should make it possible to increase production by 20 to 30%. Some advantage may be obtained by further processing a part of the sugar, molasses, and bagasse on the island. The establishment of tea plantations is a possibility. Paper and fermentation products are technically possible, but such plants are almost fully automatic, providing only a few jobs, so the returns are reaped mainly by the outsiders who provide the necessary capital. The best an industrial planner can see for Mauritius is a leveling off of primary income at a ceiling perhaps 30 to 40% greater than was obtained in 1953-55. This assumes that general world conditions are propitious, and that internal affairs remained relatively orderly. The time required for such industrial changes is one or two decades, with the latter more likely than the former.

Sixteen years later: The island economy has evolved very much as anticipated; although tea, tourism, and contract labor for international engineering firms working in that part of the world have been added, income remains almost 95% dependent upon sugar and its by-products. Sugar output seems now to have reached an irregular plateau. Per capita income also seems to be on a plateau but only because of the buoyancy of the world sugar market. Prices are higher than one would attribute to inflation, primarily because the major sugar producer, Cuba, has failed to meet either former production levels or present targets. Potentially lower cost producers, especially Brazil, Indonesia, and the Philippines, are expanding to enter the market so the relative price of sugar is expected to fall over the 1970s.

On the other hand, the population may be expected to expand more rapidly than 20% per decade, and no ceiling for it is in evidence. The birth rate cannot continue indefinitely at the level of the first half of the decade. Let us assume, as a first approximation, that it dropped rather rapidly to 35 per 1,000, which is roughly equivalent to the level observed in Jamaica. Of course, the death rate should also continue to drop, as an aftermath of the improvement of water systems and public health in general, probably to the neighborhood of 8 to 10 per 1,000. That would put the 1960 population at 610,000–630,000. Under these same conditions the 1970 population would reach the range of 800,000–850,000, an increase of 50 to 60% over the last census. Therefore, given even the best foreseeable use of local resources, a reduction in the level of living would become noticeable long before 1970.

The population growth rate did fall off over the interim, so that the estimated population in 1970 was 810,000. Between 1952 and 1968 the per capita income declined from U.S. $192 to $188. The level of crowding in urban areas exceeded 7.6 persons, or 1.6 families, per dwelling unit of one to three rooms.

Nevertheless, as long as no major disturbances are evident, this increasingly depressed kind of life should be expected to continue. There should still be a few odd jobs, or some months of work in the cane fields. These resources, along with the dole, and perhaps a bit of rocky land that can be gardened, will be enough to keep body and soul together in a tropical climate and to maintain the reproduction level. The daughters in families intent upon preserving respectability would have to wait longer for a suitable marriage, perhaps well into their thirties.

According to Christos Xenos, the level of employment, particularly of women, is still declining.[2] On the other hand, the literacy level is rising from 50% to close to 90%. A family planning program was initiated in 1964 and by 1970 20% of the married women of reproductive age were enrolled. The average age of women at the start of a union increased from 17.5 years in the 1950s to 18.5 in the mid-1960s, and indirect evidence suggests that it has been rising still more rapidly in recent years.

The society could not remain suspended in such a state indefinitely. Something is bound to give. It could be an earthquake that shatters the irrigation systems for the canefields and tumbles into rubble many of the more substantial structures in the cities. It might be a direct hit by the severe windstorms that move eastward on the Indian Ocean, or it could be a new disease, or pest, that devastates the sugar crop and requires a decade for the development and extension of a new strain. Since these are all relatively common disasters, one or more of them must be expected every generation. In addition, there is a much longer list, continuously being added to, of unusual catastrophes whose frequency is indeterminate. For the long run, one or more of these emergencies must be anticipated. What then might be the consequences for an overpopulated Mauritius?

The consequences of a disaster like this a century ago have often been recorded in diaries and official records. The initial destruction would very likely be followed by some epidemic which would erase 1%, 10% or even more of the population. Crops would be neglected, due to sickness and disorganization, and famine would ensue within a year. In the wake of the famine new epidemics would spread. Mortality would remain high for some years. Finally, some new equilibrium would be found, but in the meantime the population would have been reduced by 5 to 30%. It would then take a generation of reasonably good fortune to reach the former levels of prosperity.

However, the world has now become too much One World for a single disaster of this magnitude to change the face of Mauritius. The rest of the British association of peoples would lend a helping hand. The Catholic international charities would be of assistance. The United Nations agencies and the Red Cross might also take part. As a result, few lives would be lost.

Such a disaster hit in 1960. The island was visited by two cyclones, leveling most of the sugarcane and dropping production by 60%, but the total loss of life was less than 0.1%. Relief funds were collected in London, reorganization was rapid, and epidemics were not significant. The population pyramid remained intact.

It is true that a few more subventions from colonial funds would be required to keep the island's economic affairs in order. The liquid reserves of many households and firms would be exhausted by the reconstruction effort, and various private relief funds would no doubt keep funneling some of their charitable gratuities into respectable institutions for succoring the needy. As a consequence of such a disaster, Mauritius, like so many other territories, would become increasingly dependent upon gifts from the outside world, but in a manner so invisible it would hardly detract from the pride and independence of the inhabitants. The seesaw contest between population and resource limitations is thereupon resumed on virtually the same lines that it was carried on before, only the vulnerability to further disasters is markedly increased.

Mauritius was saved by a perfect season for cane-growing immediately after the cane had been replanted and the factories rebuilt. The 1962 record crop year exactly made up for the loss in production in 1960. Therefore the relief received actually provided a stimulus similar to investment from overseas.

Two or three disasters of differing kind and quality, when occurring in quick succession, would appear to have quite different consequences. Such a string of ill luck is not impossible—the odds are obviously longer—but it happens frequently enough to enable us to sketch out some of the implications for Mauritius.

In many instances the financial reserves are spent after the first disaster, so that the second completely wipes out a large share of the firms and households as independently functioning units. It might no longer be profitable to rebuild sugar production, so that insurance payments would then be spent elsewhere in the world. Life would become entirely disorganized. Martial law would be enforced but, since Mauritius is not an important military base, the forces available might be inadequate.[*]

If the world is not preoccupied with its own troubles the onset of critical conditions on the island of Mauritius would be noted in the major newspapers of many countries. The response would undoubtedly be generous and heartwarming. An airlift could probably be organized within a few days. A few hundred plane loads of cargo would be enough to prevent extreme suffering prior to the arrival of relief ships. The British Army and the Royal Navy would set up many emergency services such as electric power, water, telephone, and radio. The Red Cross would take care of extra needs for medical services. The Salvation Army might dispense food and good fellowship from their soup kitchens and canteens. CARE would route a stream of its packages to the destitute isle. Church relief organizations, Protestant and Catholic alike, would come in to help set family welfare problems in order. UNICEF might be brought in to

[*] Most scholarly analyses would stop at this stage. It is normally felt to be proper to leave to the reader's imagination the succession of events that would follow upon this situation. Experience shows, however, that reflecting upon catastrophe is painful for most readers, and they studiously avoid it unless the evaluation is made easy for them. The minority who are willing to study the anatomy of catastrophe—some say it is for masochistic reasons—very seldom make competent prophets. The few pages that follow present my own ideas as to the consequences. There are many possible outcomes, but this sequence seems to be the most likely. The advantage gained by carrying the arguments through to a conclusion is that serious value conflicts are discovered for the future which may be prevented, at least to some degree, through the use of foresight.

help with the orphans and the child feeding programs. There is little doubt that collectively these organizations would succeed at their self-appointed tasks. The loss of life would be limited to some thousands, and almost all the sick and injured could be expected to make a satisfactory recovery. The dimensions of the island, even with its expanded population, are small enough to be well within the means of the existing agencies.

Then what? In the catastrophes envisioned here, an important part of the subsistence was erased and the local sugar economy crippled. This leaves hundreds of thousands without a place in the productive system. Some will certainly retain their freedom, reconstruct their bidonvilles, and starve in easy stages. Most of the homeless and jobless are likely to find themselves in hastily assembled tent settlements, under semi-military discipline, where the conditions of living are not dissimilar to those presently experienced by the displaced Palestinian Arabs. They would become wards of world relief agencies, living out their days in meaningless, unproductive routine. The Arabs in the existing camps have at least a grand hate with which to illuminate their lives so that they can spend their time developing schemes for small-scale revenges. But postcrisis indigent Mauritians will have none of this; they will have to sustain themselves only on the occasional quick angry demonstrations directed at the procedures employed by their benefactors. Since such frictions are guilt-laden, and there are no other foreseeable outlets for action, the camps are likely to encounter extremely severe morale problems. The purposes of living would be lost; self-respect would be shattered.

If contemporary experience is at all typical, we must expect that the international civil servants in charge of the 100 to 200 thousands deprived of livelihood will actively seek arrangements for migration. But this way out has already been explored, and the prospects have been found to be dim indeed. Places might be discovered for a few thousands of the artisans and their families, but that is about the limit. The international civil servants will know from the start what to expect, but they will have to go through the motions anyway, in order to demonstrate that they are trying.

The absence of meaning and hope in the lives of their charges induces equally meaningless behavior on the part of the administrators. A routine of inspections, reports, and reorganizations will be created. This administrative job is a nasty one which must be accepted as a necessary step to more responsible and desirable posts higher in the hierarchy. The administrators are sent there to be representatives of the world's conscience, because these impoverished victims of disaster must not be permitted to die without a helping hand being extended. Once rescued, however, the world would prefer to forget the plight of those who were saved because there are other problems which demand attention. It is not easy for the respective nations to liberalize their immigration policies, particularly when there exists no readily apparent niche for immigrant Mauritians. The people who are surplus in Mauritius are, for the most part, surplus at any other point of the globe. They are not likely to be able to pay their own way. In fact, the cost of keeping them alive elsewhere would almost surely exceed the cost of maintaining them in Mauritius.

Thus, the camps for the indigent population, once they have been established, become a special kind of prison. It may take a few years, but it is inevitable that the inmates will discover they are really serving life terms. Problems of petty theft and policing will probably lead to demand by the independent residents of Mauritius that the camps be surrounded by barbed wire.* The decay of the fabric in the tents will lead to the construction of barracks-type buildings. By that time it will not only feel like a prison, it will also look like a prison.

The chain of events can be traced somewhat farther. For the convenience of administrators, the population which speaks Hindi would very likely be separated from the Creole-speaking elements. Much smaller camps might be organized for the Chinese-speaking element and perhaps even for the immigrant natives of Rodrigues. If that were the case, at least four distinct "indigent cultures" will be likely to develop. Each one, no doubt, would come to despise the others. Perhaps, to break the ennui, a kind of gang or guerilla warfare would break out between them. A decade or so of this will make it impossible to prevent general communal strife in Mauritius.

No nation has yet really faced the problem of "keeping people alive" in just the fashion that is likely to be encountered in overpopulated societies of the future, of which Mauritius is typical. The refugee and displaced persons camps in Europe were temporary establishments which, when left with a residue of persons that could not be placed, became, in effect, asylums for the defectives and the disabled. Because of age and other incapacities deaths exceeded births by a large margin. The problem therefore diminished with the passage of time. In Asia, the peasant households in refugee camps, whether they be Arab, Hindu, or Korean, seem to be as fertile as when they resided on the land. Indeed, there is usually present a strong feeling of having been done an injustice, that the land from which they were dispossessed belonged to them and it is the duty of the household to see that a line of legitimate claimants

* The present tendency is to set up camps complete with military guards and barbed wire within a month, but the breakout of the Hungarian refugees in France in December 1956 may change this approach in future emergencies.

continues to survive. For most of these Asian camps there is no end in sight. We see as yet no process by which they may wither away into non-existence.

Elsewhere in civilized countries a set of separate institutions, ranging from poorhouses and asylums to the dole, has been delegated special tasks and responsibilities for keeping persons alive who would otherwise be unable to do so on their own initiative. In the past, many limitations have been placed upon the behavior of such inmates and clients so as to reduce their demands upon society. One class of these restraints is directed to preventing reproduction. The measures that are used range from enforced separation of the sexes to sterilization. Yet, for reasons not easy to explain, it seems unlikely that international civil servants will demand that these same limitations upon fertility be applied to indigent populations supported in camps. Lacking any important constraints upon reproduction, it may be expected that the Moslem, Hindu, and Catholic elements will continue to grow in number by 2 or 3% per year; the relatively minor Protestant groups may or may not grow, depending upon the general morale, the sects represented, and other features.

Thus, once started, there would seem to be no conclusion to the problem. In event of a new world war, such camps would, of course, dissolve. Very likely the consequences would be tragic, but the scale would be small compared to the world tragedy brought on by war, so the disappearance of camps of indigents due to lack of supplies would amount to a small footnote in the chronicles of those times. But, if the world avoids war, the flow of supplies would continue and the two societies would live uneasily together. One of them, comprising the communities of paupers, will be contained by barbed wire fences and walls, while the other is independent, but fenced in by the Indian Ocean and the barriers to migration set up by the respective nations.

Within smaller societies these are, we may expect, the normal consequences in modern times of unrestrained fertility followed by a sequence of bad luck with respect to the behavior of the elements or the world markets. Very likely they apply to many parts of the world, but densely populated and fertile spots may be expected to experience such outcomes earlier than the others.

Over a fourteen-year period nothing happened to Mauritius or to related portions of the world that would have caused a change in this portrayal of Malthusian catastrophe in small countries. The situation was actually made more precarious because Mauritius was scheduled to become one of the mini-nations of the United Nations, and the United Kingdom was resolutely divesting itself of its colonial obliga-

tions. During that period a number of occasions arose
elsewhere in the world where large numbers of refugees
needed support, but no improvement in the administration
of relief evolved. The tendency for prolonged residence in
camps to lead to extreme ideologies and violence untem-
pered with mercy was re-emphasized by the feuds and civil
wars set off by encampments of Arab refugees in the period
from 1968 to 1973.   The violence engendered was so
bitter it triggered the tragedies of the 1972 Olympic Games
and those in a number of airports around the world.

In 1971, however, the prospects of Mauritius took a new
turn that seems to be a harbinger of the future, not only
for that flattened piece of volcanic rock but for many other
places. The original impetus began with the achivement
of full employment in Japan, which led to heavy subcon-
tracting in Hong Kong. Soon Hong Kong, too, reached full
employment, despite the turbulences of the 1960s. That
condition led to a round of raises in wages which put a
squeeze on margins in the garment industry. One of the
leading entrepreneurial groups of Hong Kong, a multinational conglomerate called Hutchisons International,
discovered the labor force of Mauritius. The island's
30,000 Chinese could communicate in detail with Hong
Kong, while the Indian component could work smoothly
with managers trained in Hong Kong garment operations,
which had always depended heavily upon local Indian labor.
Moreover, governmental processes in Mauritius were very
similar to those in Hong Kong. Thus Hong Kong textiles
could be flown or shipped to Mauritius and there fabricated
into garments, which could then be flown to markets in
Europe or America. Telecommunications between all three
points were due to be vastly improved in the 1970s so that
markets could be well served with low inventories in ready-
made clothing. Two competitors of Hutchison's were
forced to make the same move shortly thereafter.

A possible rescue for Mauritius, therefore, seems to depend
upon linking its increasingly accessible, literate labor force
to the mobile elements in international trade. The key institutional element in this diversion of destiny—the hero in the
melodrama—is the multinational corporation, which finds
free-trading societies and similar zones in coastal metropolises to be convenient sites from which to sell to the
world. By such means the unemployed of Mauritius and
similar mini-nations should be able to make a living some-

what above subsistence with long-run opportunities for "trading up" their skills in a manner pioneered by Puerto Rico in the postwar era.

This turn of events is indicative of one essential feature for the future design of cities—openness to international transactions. The range of economic and cultural opportunities is thereby increased, and effects of natural catastrophes can be greatly moderated. A price must be paid for these boons, however, in the form of speedy abandonment of externally resented traditions (but with the resurrection of others, equally old, that can be shared with visitors) and a loss in the feeling of autonomy. For example, when a metropolis is open to international transactions, the local officials are much less able to maintain wage stabilization programs and a stable currency simultaneously. Also, repression of dissident elements—a term employed by military men in high political or administrative posts—is made much more expensive for the financial elite, because when international traders become skittish many sources of livelihood for their members and dependents are cut off. Fortunately, Mauritius is subject to few such inhibitions to growth arising out of the international marketplace.

Meanwhile, the demographic transition for Mauritius is approximately only a quarter completed. The gloomy alternative for the future remains very much as depicted—it is still a real threat—but it no longer appears inevitable. The external contracts should reinforce the family planning programs, and factory employment should increase the independence of women. For economic security Mauritius should acquire dyeing and finishing, plastics, jewelry, paper, electronic assembly, watches, instruments, and other industries. Moreover, the next generation must move to parts of the island accessible to the airport and seaport. Hope for the million plus future residents comes from a projected evolution into a metropolitan satellite of the fully employed economies in Japan and the Common Market. With improved skills and connections Mauritian citizens should be able to gain the freedom to move and settle elsewhere in the world.

FAMINE IN ASIA

Larger societies living on major land masses add new dimensions to the Malthusian ordeal. Larger societies have more freedom than a bottled-up microcosm, and the responses to extreme stress are generated from a wider range of alternatives. When dealt a wicked blow by nature, for example, the immediate impact on a large society will be uneven. Some parts of its territory may initially emerge virtually unscathed, but then may become subject to an aftermath that could be more convulsive and inducive of change than the triggering catastrophe. The failure of a breadbasket region, for example, might lead to the breakdown of interdependent industrial areas when the local reserves of the latter are exhausted.

Since most of the world's population lives on and immediately around the Asian land mass, and the highest population densities are found there, the threat is most serious in Asia. But what are the specific conditions likely to produce disaster? A historical investigation yields some mild surprises. Shocks are perhaps most attributable to extreme variance in conditions affecting the society. The variables include temperature, precipitation, infestation, disease, earthquake, price of principal export, and cutoffs from principal imports. Thus the north and north-central regions of China, with their records of great droughts and floods, are more vulnerable than the southern provinces. An exclusively rice-eating population in Southeast Asia will be more vulnerable than one that eats maize, wheat, millet, or manioc as well. In order to gain some idea of *where* within Asia the next Malthusian catastrophe may occur and what form it will take, we are guided by a criterion of the intensity of shocks, rather than by the indices reflecting either existing population density or present rates of population growth, although these other indicators are obviously important. A fourth factor, which may be described as the quality of organization in public and private institutions, is exceedingly important but virtually impossible to appraise accurately in advance.

The last great test occurred in India so recently that appraisals of the response to it and to its aftershocks have only been journalistic or particularistic. The monsoon failed in the north of India in 1965, whereupon a great drought set in; moreover, it failed again in 1966, so that many of the ordinarily secure irrigated areas that drew their water from reservoirs also suffered crop failures. Some areas of India suffered from a lack of precipitation that, statistically speaking, is not likely to be repeated in a span of two hundred years. The food deficit had to be made up with imports from the surpluses of North America, but the demand was so great that it exceeded by a large measure what could be obtained and transported. The Indian civil service collected food locally and distributed these commodities along with the imports so as to spread rather evenly across the country the estimated 20% deficiency that still remained. At many points the margin beyond actual survival was very small indeed. In Calcutta at one time there was only enough food to meet minimal rations for eight days. It was also the season for the bore tides that affect the channel in the Hooghly River so that, as on many occasions in the past, the port of Calcutta had been cut off from the ships standing in offshore waters. Nevertheless, as with the other great cities of India and the relatively hard-hit agricultural areas as well, food was distributed with very few instances of interruption. As a result, the population of India did not suffer a detectable loss when viewed as a whole, although in scores of instances districts faced the prospect of massive starvation because they had eaten into their seed stock, and isolated incidents of extreme malnutrition were claimed to exist by the political opposition.

Again, in the deltas of the Ganges and the Brahmaputra, disaster threatened during 1972-73. Always a food deficit area in recent times, the east wing of Pakistan that became Bangladesh after a bloody revolt suffered from a greatly reduced capacity to plant and harvest crops. Distribution was hit even harder because bridges, railroads, ferries, and docks were incapacitated or destroyed in the conflict. The United Nations and other assisting groups were hindered by poor communications and a lack of clear authority, and they could not move quickly to aid a population that had been largely rendered homeless as well as deficient in food stocks. The odds were discouragingly high that Bangladesh would suffer the greatest famine since some of the poorly recorded instances associated with the fighting of World War II. Malnutrition was expected to bring on an unusual cholera epidemic in the following year since cholera has always been endemic in this region. (A new and relatively simple clinical treatment has been introduced for cholera, so it is not likely ever again to be the scourge of populations.[3] Future epidemics are expected to be restricted to the most isolated and disturbed districts.) The stress was therefore very great, and intensified because expectations

set off by the achievement of political independence were
so high. Famine and pestilence were overcome for the moment, but hopes for building up buffers and local reserves
to prevent similar crises are far from being realized. Outside help will be required in increasing amounts, but the
fact of aid generates resentments and xenophobic pressures,
and Bangladesh politics are expected to become very unstable.

These near catastrophes have demonstrated that the
bureaucratic apparatus in South Asian societies, *when
aided with free grain and some technical assistance from
surplus-producing countries,* is competent enough to cope
with the worst drought experienced in the course of a
hundred years. They can administer rationing systems and
keep hoarding under control. The armies of these countries
have sufficient discipline to enforce redistribution of food
stocks in an emergency.

Some observers may dispute this, arguing that the next
deficit in rainfall of this magnitude in monsoon Asia, the
fifty- or hundred-year drought for a major area, will have
an amplified effect. They might emphasize that the water
that is lost would have produced food, irrigation-based
grains in particular would register a sharper reduction in
supply. Most of the new production is based upon small-
scale irrigation systems that may be expected to go dry in
a catastrophic year and be out of use if a bad year follows.
At the same time the requirements for meeting the minimum rations will have expanded by 25-40% over those of
a decade earlier. India barely survived a 20% food deficit
in 1966-67; the absolute quantities of such a deficit would
roughly treble by 1980. The harbors were a constraint before; there is strong doubt that their capacity has been increasing rapidly enough. On the other hand, it must be
admitted that information about the seriousness of the
shortfall will be gathered and interpreted more quickly, so
the dock facilities would be in operation longer. Also the
LASH and SEABEE systems of shipment allow many smaller harbors to be served and the harbor bottlenecks now
appear to be of a kind that can be overcome within a year
after the decision to import. Growth in transport flexibility and capacity in and around the coastal metropolises
is now making as important a contribution to the postponement of famine as any of the river development programs

or the advances in fertilizer. A wholly independent factor has been the new capacity to draw upon water stored in aquifers, so tube wells plus electrification allowed India to hold down imports to four million tons in the severe drought year of 1972-73.

The year 1972-73 served inadvertently as another testing period for the existing capacity of facilities in the surplus areas to respond to needs elsewhere in the world, pointing up those specific bottlenecks, such as railroad car supply, which could not be overcome in times of crisis and would require long-term investment. Food stocks in exporting countries are maintained at lower levels now than in the 1960s because large carryovers depress prices to uneconomic levels. This response to market conditions is unfortunate because crop failures in the Soviet Union in 1972 resulted in purchases of close to 25,000,000 tons of grain, or enough to meet the caloric requirements of 60,000,000—80,000,000 people and the associated animal population in that climate. At the same time, China was importing several million tons of wheat though still exporting some rice. These grain movements strained the capacity of terminals in the exporting countries and created temporary shortages in the supply of shipping.

It might be possible that bottlenecks in food production and movement from the regions with throttled capacity could be overcome to the point where in 1980 the caloric needs of 150,000,000 people elsewhere in the world could be met on an emergency basis for the period of a year, but that would require coordinated international planning on agricultural and transport issues to a degree not yet achieved even among Common Market countries. Thus the expected capacity is somewhat short of that level, which means that the world could, by straining, respond to one famine threat at a time as severe as that experienced on the Indian subcontinent in the 1960s.[4] The requisite aid for overcoming hunger, when considering also the competence of internal distribution systems, should be forthcoming if the number of claimants does not exceed 100,000,000 persons.

In September 1972, the professional forecasters of Asia convened in Seoul and arrived unanimously at the conclusion that there will be a calamitous series of natural disasters in Asia in 1974.[5] Although their techniques are regarded as pseudo-scientific, since they depend primarily upon astrology and direction-finding with bamboo sticks (*haigaku*), these men are eminent in their profession. They have excellent networks for gathering a kind of information that does not flow into the channels tapped by journalists, and they use that background astutely by posing their own questions and framing the answers. It is well known that every year brings extraordinary natural events somewhere on a continent as large as Asia but that they become catastrophes only when societies are unable to respond appropriately, allowing amplification of the initial disruption of society. Therefore, one must interpret such a prediction to mean that the seers sense a reduced capacity in Asia to cope with adversities.

THE SEMANTICS OF FAMINE

This discussion of famine has been struggling against an inability on the part of any readily defined audience to perceive what a famine is and what it does to its victims. The principal reason that people in general, and scientists in particular, do not find the threat of famine credible is that the experience has never seemed real—being hungry for a day or perhaps even two or three, an experience many of us have had, is not enough, because the experience is private or familial and not collective. It represents a microscopic mistake in the working of a large system. Nor have the phenomena associated with famine been dramatized in the media in the way that concepts of justice or exhibitions of various forms of violence have been used to grab popular attention. In the short selections of film and text that have portrayed generalized hunger, only the concentration camps of World War II stand out in the memory, and they represent the inhumanity of fascism or a consequence of struggle against an authoritarian regime rather than a fundamental breakdown in the social processes that supply food.

Even William and Paul Paddock in their dire forecast, *Famine 1975*, which was committed to persuading Americans that a failure in food supply was imminent, did not spell out the attributes of the catastrophe they had in mind mind.[6] Moreover, their forecasts were faulty because they were simple and deterministic rather than probabilistic and interactive. The latter approach seems more realistic because it encompasses a range of the most likely responses. It includes the effects of the best societal responses to stress we can think of making at this time, but it is still certain to deviate from an actual sequence of events, because all the relevant facts are not available. The range of outcomes to be considered is suggested by an analysis of precedents, while the odds to be assigned to any alternative path into the future are strongly determined by the standard reactions to threat resorted to by affected institutions and are always influenced by local political circumstances. Human re-actions to the outcomes of famine may range from guilt to outrage, leaving long-lasting attitudes similar to those that recall the "bad old days" of unemployment in the 1920s and 1930s in regions that were seriously affected by the Depression. Famine and its aftermath could drag on for so long that institutions collapse; studies should identify the threatened areas as much as possible in advance and trace some of the structural changes to be anticipated in surviv-ing institutions. It is apparent that the social, political, economic, cultural, and urban effects of famine can be il-luminated by analytical research; but such work has yet to be done. No graded assessments exist equivalent to the de-scription of the effects of hydrogen bombs, nuclear radia-tion, and downwind fallout.[7] Historical precedents must be drawn upon to illuminate the range of effects of local-ized famine; and in order to obtain a complete picture we are forced to go all the way back to the Irish Potato Famine of 1846-47.

SCENARIO THREE

The Irish Potato Famine

Most bursts in population growth are brought about by sharp improvements in the efficiency of exploiting natural resources. For Ireland this was the adaptation of the po-tato, an exotic high-yielding vegetable from South America, by European plant fanciers to cultivation in bog soils. After its introduction in Ireland—a society that had lived upon barley, oats, some wheat, fish, and game—the potato quick-ly became a staple food for the common people. Hoe culti-vation of a small plot of marginal land planted to potatoes provided security from a hungry winter. Accordingly, the Irish population almost tripled in size during the 1779-1841 period, to a level of 8,175,000. Its agricultural density reached levels as high as any in Europe, with 800 persons per square mile being recorded in some instances.

The 1840s were years of grain panic throughout the world, and a major net importer, such as Great Britain, had reason for concern. Therefore the supply of wheat from Ireland

was carefully secured and much cheaper coarse grain, such as maize, was imported to meet the food requirements of the agricultural laborers.[8]

The blight on the potato appeared first in England in August 1845 and, within a month, in Ireland, where it spread over almost the whole island within a few months. Prompt action of the traditional sort was taken during this year by the English government. Relief ships loaded with maize (then called Indian corn) were brought from America, and the cargoes put on the market to depress food prices and minimize hoarding. Meanwhile, wheat was still being loaded for the British ports—a paradox that has been long remembered and decried. Bread was so highly valued that wheat brought several times its weight in cruder grains with roughly the same caloric content, so the poor could not afford to bake bread. Many despised corn bread, or were unable to prepare it, so they suffered. Nevertheless, by drawing upon sometimes invisible resources, as well as hastily organized assistance from the outside, no one starved in the 1845-46 season, as was admitted even by the political opposition. But the blight struck again in the autumn of 1846, so that almost all of the new potatoes putrified in the fields or in storage. All the recuperative activities, which had been mobilizing effort, in large part, by mortgaging future expectations, collapsed when those expectations became impossible to realize. Fatalism set in, and hundreds of thousands starved to death in a winter of misery.

The principal social consequence of famine, however, is not death but flight—if migration had previously been a means of dealing with stressful situations. In Ireland the pressure of population upon limited resources had been intensely felt in many households and districts much earlier than the 1840s. Migration of the Irish had built up to around 50,000 per year in the years immediately preceding the famine. Literate small farmers in the heavily Protestant Ulster area predominated in the flow before 1830, but after this, they were outnumbered by illiterate southern Irish. Women were more certain of employment in America than the men, since Irish maids had become a standard convenience maintained by the middle classes. Their migration was arranged mostly by families and did not receive any supervision until after the St. Vincent de Paul Society organized a committee in 1850. Seasonal harvest work in

England provided many contacts leading to emigration there, particularly into the expanding textile industry and for the crews needed to move cargo in the vicinity of the ports. The emigration of some paupers was aided with public funds and by landlords, but the mainstream depended on liquidation of the family assets or upon remittances transmitted until an immigrant was established and could begin repayment.[9]

In 1846 net migration doubled, and in 1847 it doubled again and then continued at an annual rate of 3-4% of the total population well beyond 1851. As a source of revenue, fares from the human cargo going West began to equal returns from cotton and lumber moving in the opposite direction. Eventually, specialized ships took over the trade, regulated by Passenger Acts that were aimed at reducing the hazards of ocean crossing. The Irish Poor Law of 1847 was the first legal response to the famine that affected migration. It included a "quarter acre" clause which deprived individuals farming more than that amount of land of the right to obtain dole. Tenants relinquished their leases and emigrated, leaving wives and children behind to come when it became possible. In addition, the Act initiated taxation on land rents that exceeded four pounds sterling (approximately $20, or a month's wage at a farm job), which caused a large number of small farmers just above this level to realize that they could not afford the tax for the dole provided to the truly indigent.[10] Migrants, therefore, were drawn most heavily from the middle groups of farmers and from the merchant class, to such an extent that these activities were virtually paralyzed for lack of managers and entrepreneurs. Thus, the casualties were heaviest among the very poor, and the channels of emigration carried away many of the more competent and independent individuals.

Both these pressures arising from the Act led to a rapid aggregation of small holdings into farms requiring greater capital and more planning. It also instituted an aversion to subdividing land into plots that provided less than subsistence. The prudent father thereafter designated which son would take over the farm or business, and the opportunities open to the others involved either going to the city or emigrating to foreign shores. Waiting for the chance to assume responsibility on the farm or to find a niche overseas led to postponement of marriage. Connell attributed the extraordinarily late age of marriage in Ireland, which has persisted for more than a century, to the shocks of the Potato Famine period.[11]

Institutions adjusted also. The Catholic church began to inveigh against irresponsible marriage and sexuality. With the aggregation of the land by people strongly connected by blood ties or social class to the clergy, the Church became a very potent institution within Ireland. Conditions of surplus combined with bonds of loyalty to their religion caused Irish nuns and priests to be willingly recruited in large numbers and dispatched to posts all over the world in a form of sponsored emigration.[12]

Over the course of a decade the population of Ireland was reduced to about half. An estimated two million people are known to have left Ireland altogether, and perhaps half that number died in the famine or in the epidemics that followed. A large number, amounting to almost a million, remain unaccounted for.[13]

Overseas the Irish fitted in where they could. They provided the labor for building the railroads and the extensions of the cities, they served as hired hands on farms, but a predominant portion settled in the cities. This was as true in Australia, Canada, and Argentina as it was in the United States. In many cities near the ports of entry the Irish settlers made it possible for the Catholics (then called Papists) to overturn power structures controlling local government; the Irish then took over management of the political apparatus, enabling them to monopolize employment in many urban services. Starting from shanty towns by the railroad tracks and tenements next to the harbor, they eventually joined the mainstream and moved to the suburbs.[14] In Ireland itself, however, the rural character was retained longer, and is still more strongly emphasized than elsewhere in the British Isles. Very likely the slowness to change can be traced in considerable part to the psychic scars left by the famine.

A MODERN MALTHUSIAN CATASTROPHE

The scattered arguments about vulnerability to famine and the scale of effects can now be pulled together and fitted to a most likely place and time. Meier and Meier suggest that famine potentials of the future be gauged in Irish Potato Famine Units (IPFUs).[15] Identification of a specific locale and its dimensions depends upon (1) current population-resources ratios; (2) the likelihood of interruption of local food production; (3) distance from stockpiles, measured in political as well as physical terms; (4) cultural limitations as to what is considered food; (5) prevalence of local customs and attitudes that maintain high fertility rates; and (6) precedence of military or geopolitical factors that delay or complicate responses to needs. The leading nominee is some large part of the Hwang Ho (Yellow) River watershed in northwest China.[16] It could easily reach a scale of 30 IPFUs, with odds estimated as one chance in three per decade.

Data from China itself are fragmentary, but from a post in the Chinese University of Hong Kong, Ching-Siang Chen has compiled relatively current estimates.[17] It appears that a combination of railroad building, water conservation, and mineral development has made possible enhanced urbanization and industrialization in the Hwang Ho basin, while residence in the coastal metropolises has been resolutely restrained. Cities like Lanchow (1,450,000 estimated for 1970), Sian (1,600,000), Taiyüan (1,350,000), Changchow (1,050,000), Paotow (920,000), Shihkiachwang (800,000), Loyang (580,000), Huhehot (530,000), and Sining (500,000) are showing remarkable increases. The total population in these provinces appears to have been growing, although at a declining rate, now very likely less than 2% per year. Therefore, despite the industrialization, the population on the land itself has been steadily increasing.

The frequency of famines in China is much better recorded than elsewhere in the world because they were occasions for intervention by the Imperial Government and the archives cover two millennia for the parts of this territory that lived under Han hegemony (some was not under Han control during the early part of the period). The provinces of Shansi, Honan, Anwhei, Hupeh, Shensi, and Kansu account for about half of all the famines due to drought in recorded history, but for a much higher proportion in the nineteenth century because their population had expanded very considerably. The reasons for the expansion are not clear, but in areas like this the human population usually expanded up to the level allowed by food production and health, so apparently significant innovations had been introduced. This area has also been the locus of the severest famines of the twentieth century (see figure 2.2). The population is now double to treble what is was at the time of the onset of the last famines, and the land has been very

Figure 2.2 China's Famine Bowl
Most counties in this region previously experienced famine once or twice each decade. Their vulnerability has since been reduced by a major water conservation program, but it is continually enhanced by a population growth rate of about 2% per year due to improved public health.

much changed by modified agricultural practice and mining.

A convincing account of the future that holds to some relevant track, avoiding sheer fantasy and fabrication and with the structure and shape produced by specification of detail, demands a thorough study of the rural background. The most complete of the village studies is by William Hinton, first an UNRRA relief worker and later an observer of the first land reform, who has provided us with a description of a village and its surrounding county in *Fanshen: A Documentary of Revolution in a Chinese Village.* In it he relates the organizational and political forces at work in the larger society to changes in life in the county of Lucheng, Shansi. This county is about six hundred kilometers southwest of Peking and contained about 120,000 people in the early 1950s. For a village in a nearby province to the west (Shensi) Jan Myrdal and Gun Kessle offer reports of changes from the villagers themselves.[18]

Hinton's community, called Long Bow (a translation of *chung chuang*), is beside the road leading through the foothills of the Taishang Mountains above the railhead of Changchih. The village consisted of 242 families with 943 acres (290 hectares) under cultivation. This is a region that depends upon maize intercropped with beans, wheat, millet, turnips, and cabbage, roughly in that order of significance. Orchards are being introduced in places, as is synthetic fertilizer. Animal husbandry as an occupation is limited to producing beasts of burden, which, along with agricultural implements, have always been exceedingly scarce, so they must be shared or put up for hire.

Long Bow possessed about forty different surnames, which is unusually high for China as a whole and is indicative of a history of ebb and flow of refugees from past disasters, in which a few from each wave found a means of obtaining land, an artisan's shop, or some other niche that allowed the family to stay indefinitely in the locale. Hinton reports that Long Bow is a place where the poor peasants frequently suffered from *ch'un huang* ("spring hunger"), so the margin of subsistence is very narrow. The mainstay of the diet is not rice or bread but *ke ta* (maize dumplings) and millet. Except for important people, pork and fowl are in the diet only on rare ritual occasions.

Weather is, of course, all-important. The monsoon rains normally arrive in July after a dry, windy spring in which the air masses flow down from frigid Manchuria. Hinton noted the effect of a July hailstorm which destroyed 50-60% of the crop yield. Help flowed in from outside in the form of extra turnip seed, buckwheat, and sixty-day maize for replanting. Recovery was apparently sufficient to prevent severe distress.

Some years earlier than most of China, Long Bow made the transition into a new era. The number of "middle peasants" operating two to seven acres per household was maximized, and many cultural impediments from the past were obliterated. Thereafter the interplay of politics, and perhaps indirectly the pressures of population, forced China to experiment with further reorganizations of the rural districts, of which Long Bow was one among a million, first with decentralized industrialization, then with reform of the government apparatus, with rural re-education of urban professionals, and with numerous less convulsive centrally directed changes.

SCENARIO FOUR

Malthusian
Outcomes
Modernized

The time is a full generation after the transition to Maoism. The county of Lucheng now has a population that is probably in excess of 200,000 people. The land under cultivation has reached 50,000 hectares, owing to strenuous efforts in building of small reservoirs higher in the hills and to land reclamation through terracing.

The people themselves are somewhat larger and more robust than before because many elements of public health were introduced that made a difference for this last generation. Water was boiled and fly-breeding areas were removed, so that dysentery was far less common during childhood and infant mortality declined astonishingly, Nutritional levels are better equalized among households and over the seasons than ever before. The midwives are now trained, and medical orderlies dispense miracle drugs along with acupuncture and bonesetting. As a result the amount of human energy that can be mobilized is much higher than in earlier generations.

The cities have grown proportionately more than the villages despite official intentions. Thus Long Bow has retained 360 families of somewhat smaller than average size clustered tightly together next to a road which has now been macadamized and has concrete bridges and culverts. The nearby coal mines have been greatly enlarged, and

scores of brutish black trucks rumble past on their way to
the railhead each day. Because of the road and the mine,
Long Bow has electricity, whereas most other villages in
the county still do not. It even has two factories, one making ceramic electric insulation parts with clay obtained from
a pit in the nearby hills. Preformed components are fired
in a small kiln next to the coal pile.

Last year the monsoon failed; the winds brought only
dust. When the clouds developed into blue-black cumulus,
only a sprinkle or rain fell before they dissolved. The labor
brigades drew down the reservoirs to save some of the
wheat. The maize and beans were a total loss, so the fields
were replanted to buckwheat and turnips. But still not
enough rain fell to hold down the dust, which in many of
the paths was now ankle deep. Late in the year an assessment was made of total stocks of food, and it was found
that only a third of what was needed to get through the
spring was on hand, so rations were reduced to half and an
appeal for help was agreed upon. The community officials
and Party members had been receiving repeated messages
regarding policy from headquarters, but none of them
seemed to apply to the local situation. Belatedly they discovered that the industrial workers would be sent rations
of about 1,800 calories per day per capita (one pound of
grain apiece) but that peasants would have to depend upon
hidden stores, roots, and other famine fare. Somehow, the
factory rations, which had apparently come all the way
from Canada, seemed to diffuse through the village.

Meanwhile, peasants from upland villages where the springs
and wells had failed were moving down the road by walking
beside bicycles loaded with household goods. Some had
carts pulled by sad-looking animals, but most merely balanced their loads on two ends of a sturdy pole. Many of
the "walking wounded" crowded onto the coal lorries,
which maintained, if anything, an increased frequency of
movement.

After an almost snowless winter the last of the locally held
seed stores were planted, but June arrived and passed with
no more than several centimeters of precipitation. The
ropes in the deep wells had to be lengthened, while the
shallower ones in the fields went dry. The Long Bow peasants who were unrelated to factory workers decided that
migration was the only hope remaining. The most vigorous

of them went over the pass into Honan, many headed north to Taiyüan, a metropolis of over a million people at the head of the valley, while the remainder hoped for transport by rail out of Changchih. Up to that time none had died and few were really emaciated. Hidden stocks from the good years had sustained them, though it was noted that most of the animals had disappeared, even those owned collectively.[19]

Long Bow families found the roads filled, and water was obtainable in some places only by barter or purchase. Dust was everywhere; the skies were an ominous gray. Huge crowds collected around the railroad stations. There they found railroad guards backed up by troops, hundreds of them at each station and thousands at junction points and yards where the trains were made up. The troops set up orderly procedures for those capable of purchasing tickets and supervised the loading of families on the roofs of cars. They also distributed relief rations of food, water, and fuel. The trains fell far behind their schedules, so they soon followed the rule of moving whenever they could. Trains arriving at intermediate stations were so full few could get on, so the refugees who were most mobile took to the roads again, heading for the starting points or destinations of the trains. Thus Taiyüan accumulated a million people beyond its previous million and a half, and Changchih doubled its original quarter million. Long Bow's hundreds in both places tried to stick together in separate encampments, but by the end of August they dissolved into the stream of humanity moving antlike across the face of China.

During August the pestilences began to appear; small children and old people were particularly common among those who succumbed. At first the causes were influenza and dysentery, but then cholera, smallpox, and typhus showed up, a few cases at a time, no doubt arriving from some out-of-the-way places in the mountains where they had remained endemic. As time went on, the toll accelerated, and the military was assigned the task of supervising mass burials.

In September cities at the end of the rail lines, such as Changchih, received no shipments of food. All the sealed cars designated for them had been raided by troops along the way—or were their contents sold by convoying troops? The rifled cars were filled with refugees before they returned to junction points in the plains, but that did not seem to diminish the numbers clamoring for relief. In mid-September the colonel in charge at Changchih took over a train and evacuated his troops, leaving the mayor and his council an impossible task. The Party cadre of Changchih (but not those of other locales in the hinterland) departed with the troops. In the days that followed, no more trains arrived. The factory-supported contingent in Long Bow was now cut off, as were the miners up the road. Their ration stocks were down to a matter of six weeks. So they shut down the factory and took to the roads also.

After the decision to halt production, each family began to fend for itself. Theft again became very common. The village loudspeaker radio still bleated, more shrilly than before, but it made no sense at all in the new context. Even those who once had rigidly conformed to the messages originating from Peking and Taiyüan paid no attention at all.

A hundred million people moved away in all directions. Traveling by road and train, most of them arrived in the humid plain and the great valleys of China, where rice was the staple of life. These plains still had green trees, but the fields at the end of the irrigation districts had turned yellow and brown. Rivers ran very low and were thick with algal bloom. However, the inland lakes and reservoirs of the rich Grand Canal area enabled it to combat the drought, so about 80% of the normal crop was being produced, mostly in the double-cropping areas. Yams appeared in the market-places much more than before, while pork went sky high in price in the black market.

Meanwhile, in Peking and Sian, some bitter decisions were being faced. The buffer stocks—nearly forty million tons of grain that China held in reserve—had dropped to less than ten million during the first year of drought.[20] At the most about eight million tons from overseas suppliers could be brought in through ports connecting with the famine area per year. Basic survival needs were estimated at fifteen million tons if carefully distributed. This would cause an average reduction in body weight of about 25%; any more would cause widespread loss of life. Who and where were the thirty to fifty million expendables? The Central Committee was at this time made up of individuals with managerial and military experience who had survived a number of occasions when supplies were grossly inadequate, and "amputations" of one kind or another were in

order. It appeared that the six provinces to the west of
the Taishang Mountains, the original breeding ground for
the Maoist version of communist revolutionary organization, would have to be abandoned temporarily to a fate
decided by a harsh Nature rather than by man. This meant
salvaging as much of the Army and of the Party organization as possible. It also meant pinching off the flow of
refugees into the still viable areas, lest the districts that
were still self-sufficient be overwhelmed with too many
mouths to feed. So orders went out to the Army to de-
camp to the green areas wherever transport existed; the Air
Force was to collect the Party organization.

Disappearance of the leaders who had been stalwart
figures, working indefatigably to alleviate the disastrous
effects of the famine, and sudden movements by crack
troops caused new rumors to fly. The commander at
Tatung, a rail junction city swollen with a million refugees
about two hundred kilometers north of Taiyüan and just
below the Great Wall, sensed that he had been chosen to be
sacrificed without having the chance to volunteer. A de-
votee of the classics, having memorized Sun Tzu's <u>Art of
War</u> among other things, he pondered upon what great
generals before him would have done.[21] The consensus
seemed to have been to accept fate, but owing to the circumstances, he was unwilling to do so. Overnight he constructed a desperate scheme and lost no time in acting
upon it.

He and his men were held in this trap by the Gobi Desert,
one of the deadliest and most fearsome terrains on earth.
Running through this desert was an invisible, often un-
marked line—the international boundary with Outer
Mongolia.[22] Far on the other side were the fat herds of
the Mongols; perhaps they were thinner this year because
of the shortage of grass, but they would be concentrated in
places where water was assured. The commander had been
on an official mission there years ago and remembered well
the desolate, sometimes rugged landscape. Only one way
into Mongolia remained—the rail line that stretched a thousand kilometers to the northwest. It presented an apparently inseparable barrier, however, because Mongolia retained
the broad gauge of the Russian system all the way down to
the border station, whereas his Chinese trains operated upon
upon standard gauge tracks. Yet the history of warfare has
many instances of the exploits of engineers who overcame

the track gauge incompatibility problem. Here it was only a matter of nine centimeters. He brought in his two top engineers, and laid out the alternatives. The men under his command could die on the spot without effect, or they could dissolve, allowing each group or man to use his weapons and survive through brigandage, but then each man remaining would live in shame of the acts committed in desperation. Could they somehow make a dash into Mongolia and try to live off the land? It would be another "Long March," but one that could not be negotiated on foot. Were there locomotives that could be refitted, rolling stock bogies that could be respaced, troop carriers that could be driven on the rails? He had six planes that could be flown for a while. Also, how much equipment could be seized at the border?

A desperate plan unfolded. Fifteen thousand men could cross the desert in three days if they left virtually all equipment and supplies behind. Should they arrive, perhaps an equal number would join them a week later. If they met serious opposition, they were lost. Fortunately the weather was on their side; the calm of autumn was giving way to the bluster of early winter, so the dust might offer cover. To be on the safe side, a diversion could be set up at the start to obscure their movement. There was no objective stated; once they arrived, they would diffuse into the Mongol population at company strength. Ten days later they would rendezvous in the rail yards.

By operating wholly at night, when reconnaissance by earth satellite was less effective, the border post was cut off and taken. There would only be pictures of dust clouds to the west, where trucks were sent to drag the dry desert floor with chains. The coordinated land-air lightning attack on the city of Ulan Bator drew upon an existing plan but was too feeble to have a real hope until the Russians began shelling the city where the Chinese troops had diffused into the population. Suddenly, pent-up frustrations were loosed; the Mongols turned their fire on the Russians. The situation became utterly confused and remained that way for four days while the civilian population disappeared into the countryside. Then more Chinese started arriving from the south.

In Mongolia there was meat and milk, but it could not be enjoyed for long. Russians and Mongol diplomats reestablished contact, and soon military representatives were disentangling the details, but the Chinese objective remained a mystery. Where were their remnants holed up, and what should be done about the newly approaching trains? The Mongols effectively had half the Russians as their prisoners and were not likely to give up this advantage without negotiating a bargain.

Meanwhile, the beleaguered Chinese commander, still alive, did what he could to reassess the situation. Their days in Ulan Bator would soon be numbered. What else could be done that would so surprise and confound the opposition that they could last a little while longer? Why not take the rail yard, hijack the trains, seize hostages, and move north? He had all the necessary skills with him. The really sizable stocks and supplies would be found at the Russian border.

Border clashes with the USSR had ceased some years before the famine, but the outcomes had been carefully studied by all the Chinese staff. Potential vulnerabilities of the Russians had been reviewed at length and discussed; the commander from Tatung was familiar with them, but in Ulan Bator he discovered that the Russians had almost stripped their bases and installations—while the Chinese were preoccupied with famine—and moved the troops to places cheaper to supply. The commander recognized that he could not go back, because the meat and rough grain available in a thinly populated country were insignificant as compared to the huge need to the south. Nor could he defend the city he had taken when the Russians were ready to move in. So he moved straight into their middle and advanced northwest along the rail line to Lake Baikal in anticipation of Soviet counterattacks.

Moscow received word of this most brazen border incursion to date and could not deduce the Chinese strategy. Photographs from reconnaissance aircraft and earth satellites showed masses of people moving up through Manchuria as well. Most were refugees, very likely, but were they also a disguise for troops? Troop movements had been unusual and mysterious for at least a week. There was a flurry of activity around nuclear operations at Paotou and Lanchow. The attempt to seize Mongolia without announcement or signal was very serious and demanded some response. Should they appeal to the Secretary General of the United Nations? That seemed silly. But nothing else made sense either. The Chinese had underemphasized the extent of the catastrophe partly because reports coming into Peking at first disguised the amount of disorder. The magnitude had to be comprehended there in a matter of weeks and during that period no public admissions of lack of control were possible. The rest of the world presumed China had an empty stomach, judging by the activity of its grain buyers, but it had no basis for suspecting an internal political crisis. One paranoid clique in the Russian Army argued, as expected, that a massive attempt on the part of overpopulated China to take over the empty spaces of Siberia had begun.[23] It did not make sense to start such an effort in September, but perhaps the intention was to disregard losses. There existed several fully elaborated plans to preempt China's nuclear capability while China possessed exceedingly limited long-range ballistic missile capability, but it would probably take sixty days to get fully set.[24] In the meantime, a nonnuclear response had to be prepared in the absence of any satisfactory intelligence except what could be seen from the air.

In Peking the disorders of the northwestern provinces were also viewed very gravely. A few isolated centers in the region with guaranteed food stocks were still in daily communication, but they had lost contact with the situation around them and had no hope of regaining control. The regular channels of communication were now operated by that splinter of the Red Army now on a rampage. Peking was worried also that two nuclear weapons being readied for testing at Lop Nor in the desert to the west might be seized. Measures had to be taken to double the safeguards. Fortunately the major nuclear production facilities had already been transferred to the Upper Yangtse region, an area hard hit by drought but not yet in motion and not in the pathway of the migrating hordes.

Pride in their own achievements, and to some extent the fear of dissension among a relatively new governing clique, prevented any public admission by Peking that China needed help from the world in a form other than imported cereals. Therefore they maintained silence, not even entering into discreet exploratory discussions at the United Nations in New York.

The scenario must end here, because what was a Malthusian crisis became an international crisis with strong effects upon the prospects for world peace owing to the presence of nuclear weapons and a background of mistrust. A different set of precedents applies; another category of experts must assemble the experience that establishes present expectations. How does the nuclear deterrent system respond to provocation by desperate adventurers?

Similar projections have been made in following out surprise-free sequences of events for other places in the world that will be vulnerable to Malthusian stresses by the 1980s, although significantly less so than northwest China. All of them lead to major international complications, although not necessarily affecting the nuclear standoff. A break in the precarious prospects of Java would affect Australia and Malaysia; Bangladesh involved India, an increasingly organized Muslim community of nations, also possibly Burma. Another famine threat in India would involve the Americans, Russians, and the new wheat bowl on the Indus in West Pakistan. The range of complications arising in the case of Egypt is immediately apparent to anyone reading the newspapers. For smaller places, it has already been suggested, the projections for Mauritius, in a form appropriately modified by climate, culture, and location, should apply. What the exercises teach is that the world has become an amazingly tight web of interests and responsibilities. If any one portion is really devastated by famine, the interactions quickly affect the security of others elsewhere in the world through relationships that go beyond the direct food exchange process, and most of them are indirect effects of the flow of refugees.

One last word on a possible sequel for Long Bow and Shansi, based upon insights from the Irish Potato Famine and the history of famine in China.

SCENARIO FOUR
SEQUEL

Three years later Long Bow looked green and prosperous. Farmers had higher incomes than they could ever remember, but that was mainly because only half of them were tilling more than 90% of the acreage. An additional reason is that the windrows of dust redistributed over the land added to the fertility of the soil. More marginal communities nearby, especially those heavily dependent upon grazing, were not reoccupied at all. The cities were surrounded by teeming squatter settlements, sometimes equal in population to the city itself. In them one found mainly people from Shansi, Hopei, and Honan who had somehow survived

**and now were fairly well established, just as Shansi people
had in earlier generations drifted to all corners of China to
settle in similar communities. The remainder had joined
their ancestors, but the graves were rarely found on ancest-
ral lands, if they could be found at all.**

We are faced with the inevitability of urbanization in our
era. Even if a prospective famine should reach a scale of
30 IPFUs, with loss of life exceeding all the wars of the
twentieth century, it would not halt the process. Cities
would become swollen with refugees who could be kept
alive there through the importation of food and water. The
population of China might pause for perhaps two years and
then regain the momentum that adds between 1% and 2%
per year to its. size. In China today we see the most vigorous
attempts to hold back urbanization, primarily through with-
drawal of rations and re-education in villages, but such
measures build up a pressure to urbanize that will make
itself felt when control is inadvertently lifted or when the
fabric of the society is torn by natural disaster. Thus China
seems likely to experience the same outcomes as other
societies even though it presently maintains much stronger
discipline.

A final insight is that the inhabitants of large cities, particularly those in coastal locations, are now more secure
against famine than most rural residents. They are now
more dependent upon the world rather than upon the immediate suppliers in the region. They have the most competent administrations for coping with rationing and for maintaining public order. They also have assets which can be
liquidated in order to buy food if credit is not available
immediately. The security of people living in the interior
will depend upon the capacity of such cities to transship
and deliver grain in emergencies. Thus the future for Shansi
depends upon Shanghai and Wuhan, just as Bihar must depend upon Calcutta and Haldia, and Bangladesh must maintain lifelines through Dacca and Chittagong.

Energy crises, unlike food shortages, rarely have natural
origins, and the responses to them are less primal.[25] Energy
requirements for large cities are strikingly high; they range
from perhaps twice the food and feed imports—measuring
both as calories—in the poorer Asian cities to as much as

**AN ENERGY
SHORTAGE**

30 to 40 times that figure in metropolises like Los Angeles and Houston. Energy is brought in mostly as fossil fuel, but increasingly it will take the form of electricity generated at a distance from sites with nuclear reactors using uranium as fuel. Both sources are nonrenewable, so the present metropolitan community lives off the expenditure of geological capital.

In the short run, war and other forms of international politics trigger modern energy crises. Since supply lines are usually quite long, they are vulnerable to disruption. Dependence upon external sources constitutes a source of defenselessness to actions taken by enemies or neutrals which can only be reduced by setting up alternate sources of supply. The last large crisis was caused by the closing of the Suez Canal. This event greatly extended the length of the route for oil tankers to Western Europe when no immediate means existed for increasing their number. The response was a quick reshuffling of routes and a significant rise in prices in and around most cities.

Rationing of fuel and restricting the end uses of electric power are both feasible. Cities under siege or blockade are forced to allocate fuels so as to maximize the likelihood of survival; when under these and other kinds of stress they may "brown out" many power-using but less than critical activities. Recreation, advertising, elaborate cooking, and household appliances are first to go, then the safety factors such as street lights. The stationary machine population, designed to produce capital equipment and exports, tends to be the next to be slowed down. Note that the activities of the machine population in the city are selectively affected, particularly the movements of the wheeled species when cutbacks are intense. The automata, such as telephone exchanges and computer centers, are now designed to be so independent that a reduction in their performance is barely detectable even when most machines are no longer operating. Plants and animals are affected indirectly, because of reductions in the transport of water and feed; their death rate mounts as the energy deficit continues. Man survives easily, but he may regress temporarily to what he conceives to be a more primitive state.

A new energy crisis began to be freely forecast in the spring of 1972. Experts could already identify a number of past actions which have consequences that are likely to converge. They included:

1. The OPEC (Oil Producers Economic Commission) was developing the cooperation and technical competence needed to raise the selling price of petroleum at the point of origin. They can make the price hold in the world market because together they possess a near monopoly in world trade.

2. In the largest continental energy consumer, North America, the strict limits set upon the levels of atmospheric sulfur dioxide, photochemical smog, and fly ash increased the scarcity of clean fuels throughout the world.

3. Excessive protection of the consumers of the cleanest fuel, natural gas, by holding the price at an arbitrarily low level, diminished the intensity of search for new reserves and led to a huge gap between demand and prospective supply. The scarcity will be felt at some times, and in some locales, even at prices four times as great at the point of origin as before.

4. A zealous environmentalist movement sprang up which objected to most of the locations of large energy-transforming facilities such as power plants, refineries, and chemical works, causing postponement or long delays in most projects. Thus energy conversion became more expensive and less able to maintain continuity of service, given the fluctuations in supply and demand.

5. Simultaneously, an appreciation of spacious life styles and of controlled living conditions inside buildings that emphasized thermal comfort created a demand for a greater energy use per capita.

6. The research and development effort, which is aimed at producing new knowledge about the sources of fuels and their conversion into forms usefully employed in cities, has been warped by institutional traditions. Much work has been carried out by oil company research and development organizations on liquid and gaseous fuels for which the supply must soon decline and very little on coal, their natural successor. Breeder reactor studies have been carried forward on too narrow a base. Therefore a new and more economical technology for conversion of fissile elements into power is not expected to be ready for large-scale installation until the mid 1980s.

A fair possibility existed that all these factors, and a few localized events as well, may have a simultaneous impact.

What were the prospective consequences for the living and future populations in a metropolis?

The signal for the shock would be a steep rise in the cost of fuel flowing through channels of international trade. An increase by a factor of three for clean fuel over the course of a year or so seems not impossible. Such a shift would cause abrogation of long-term contracts because they hold one party or the other in an untenable position. These breaks force new buyers onto a short market, pushing prices up still higher.

Large modern metropolises like New York would shout mightily but would swiftly tap all kinds of secondary supplies, so that most of its luxuries would still be retained. The prices of urban services would be selectively hit, but the average traceable solely to energy shortages should rise by no more than 5%. New York has the capacity to amplify its anguish, so the increase might seem like more (and indeed speculators may momentarily raise it higher), but that seems to be the maximum effect of the fuel component in New York's standard of living. Thereafter a number of relocation responses would be made by industries and organizations selectively hit by the rise in fuel cost. The installation of petroleum-fueled electric power plants, for example, is expected to be slowed down, and their design modified to improve fuel economy.

SCENARIO FIVE

Poor Cities
Subjected to
an Energy
Squeeze

It is useful to consider the shock upon a city like Bombay, whose population of eight or nine million by the end of the 1970s will be consuming three to four times as much fossil fuel energy as food and feed energy (as against New York at possibly twenty times). Assume a threefold rise in delivered price over a two-year period. Fertilizer production would be very seriously affected, because most of it is made from imported naphtha; the cost at the plant would perhaps double, while the cost to the farmer might rise by half, allowing for the steep jump in transport costs in between. Therefore, the Indian Fertilizer Corporation, after first appealing to the government for a greater subsidy, would be forced to adjust its prices to world prices, because no provision had been made for such a large extraordinary expense. World prices for grain, however, would also rise sharply in response to the increased costs of fertilizer; therefore, the controlled prices for grain within India could be raised to match the increased cost of production without adding to the apparent subsidy. The nationalized banks could give bigger loans without added risks. So the farmers find more cash flowing through their enterprises when they maintain the same formulas for production, but none of it can be saved. The agriculturists who find ways of saving on fertilizer and fuel, substituting labor, will make a profit, but they will constitute rare exceptions in the first two years after the price shift.

The Maharashtra and Gujarat electric power grids would find themselves in distress. Their fuel stocks are sufficient for only a few months' operations, and the funds on hand would be insufficient to replace them. Politicians would try desperately to postpone a general price increase for delivered power, but the rate of rise is too large for it to be absorbed. The New Delhi decision on fertilizer would apply immediately to power generation. Shortly thereafter, New Delhi would have to announce a bonus for adjusting government pay scales upward more rapidly than the anticipated inflationary spiral. Painfully battled out, this step might have to be taken twice within a year, and some politicians might destroy their careers by failing to hold the line. The ordinary, nonunion workers of Bombay would feel the effects where they hurt the most—perhaps a 10% increase in the cost of the daily ration and a lesser increase in the cost of perishables.

The most likely response is a surcharge that would be placed upon electric power, and provisions would be made simultaneously for cutting back upon its consumption. Marginal textile mills and energy-intensive operations such as glassmaking would then be forced to shut down, putting tens of thousands of workers out on the streets. The electric railways, buses, and trucks would raise the commuter fares. At the same time, the immediate demand within India for Bombay's output—machinery, garments, pharmaceuticals, fine chemicals, plastic ware, financial services, export services, publishing, and entertainment—is likely to increase less rapidly than before, since less income would be available for all of these after paying for higher-priced fuel.

Once the central government recognized that prices of imported energy were not likely to recede very much, it would be expected to act in four ways: (1) redirect its investment policy so as to produce more coal and oil internally; (2) accelerate the nuclear power program; (3) push exports still harder, particularly to Iran and the Arabian states, which would be collecting cash from higher prices and looking for ways to spend it; and (4) reduce the transport component in production by cutting back on the programs for decentralization of industry.

As the export program takes hold, Bombay's fortunes would shift. The new income would pour through the port, each middleman taking his percentage as fee for services, and the response of local producers to overseas markets would be more rapid in its vicinity. A few years after the shock it is reasonable to expect that Bombay would have been affected as if there had been a substantial increase in world trade and of Indian participation in it. There would be more jobs in the most modern activities and a wider range of opportunities for the educated classes. A larger share of the national investments program would be sited around Bombay in order to save energy-intensive overland haulage. The development of India as a whole might be set back considerably by a sharp increase in the cost of fuel, but the relative position of the coastal metropolis would be enhanced.

The market is a wonderful mechanism for distributing the shock of increased scarcity of a commodity, providing the law is effective in preventing hoarding and inhibits overreaction on the part of speculators. By developing marketing institutions as a kind of neuronal network, the metropolis is able to buffer itself against many external changes.

The principal result of a quick shift to a new energy cost plateau is a redistribution of the populations of machines in the city. Two-wheeled vehicles would grow in number at the expense of four-wheelers; machines attached to the electrical grid would speedily become more refined and mo more carefully designed. The need for prevention of waste through tighter controls and more complete information about operations causes an acceleration in the already rapid growth of the population of automata. As the rising flow of energy is dampened, the flow of information (negentropy) is multiplied many times over. A more integrated network of organizations is created as a result of meeting the challenge.

The foregoing exercise was played out in many alternative sequences during 1972, but as long as any fossil fuel at all remained available on the world market, each of them ends at a new equilibrium for urban operations. If breaks occurred, they would be brief and attributable to human error.* In the equilibrium situation the city would discard some of its energy-intensive machines, systematize better the use of its vehicles by allowing the inefficient to be scrapped with only partial replacement by other species, and it would introduce many more automata, since they consume so little energy.

The cities that most readily accomplish these internal transformations would gain a competitive advantage over the others, thus very likely experiencing growth in size. Those that develop a capacity to negotiate with sellers and obtain delivery of fuel from a great distance would gain a similar advantage. The advantages to industrial cities arising from proximity to a plentiful fuel source would be greatly reduced, because transport cost becomes a much smaller fraction of total cost of delivered energy.

Hardships created by an energy crisis are surprisingly mild—less heating and air-conditioning, less meat in the diet, fewer long recreational trips, and the like. The greatest impact would be felt in social and political relationships. Internationally, the oil and gas exporters would acquire huge amounts of capital that could not be invested locally due to lack of a labor force. Therefore it seems likely to flow into international banking. The foreign exchange required for the capital investment needed to economize on energy consumption should be available at reasonable interest rates, though the risk-minimizing nonfinancial terms attached to loans will appear to be onerous. Asceticism and consumptive restraints will be rewarded, political autonomy reduced, and interdependence strongly reinforced.

* Events caught up with this projection, since the rise in energy price did occur, and its effects were compounded by an extremely severe drought. The scenario was allowed to stand because it tried to isolate the pure effects of an energy crisis of the scale that occurred early in 1974.

1. Richard L. Meier, *Modern Science and the Human Fertility Problem* (New York: John Wiley & Sons, 1959). This book comprised a technology assessment of new, simple technologies of birth control then being considered at the experimental level or being introduced to the public for the first time. The Malthusian dilemma needed to be expressed in a new way, one that did not moralize or theorize and thus put heavy emphasis on fertility limitation.

2. Christos Xenos, "Mauritius," *Country Profile* (New York: Population Council, September 1970).

3. Cholera epidemics were once a significant hazard for cities receiving inmigrants from the countryside. They still gain a great deal of attention in the popular journals, but control of the disease has advanced to the point that it is a minor threat. This is one of the rare cases where "treating the symptoms" (acidosis, saline depletion, dehydration) saves the patient inexpensively and permits complete recovery in a few days. World Health Organization, *Principles and Practice of Cholera Control,* Public Health Papers No. 40, Geneva, 1970. A resident physician in Calcutta was heard to say that "The new approach to treating cholera makes a doctor feel worthwhile. A patient brought in without pulse, at death's door, revives very quickly and walks away the next day." The improvements are far more effective in cities than in rural areas.

4. These capabilities of the agricultural systems of North America and Australia to respond were incorporated into the projections of the O.E.C.D., Paris, 1968, *Agricultural Projections for 1975 and 1985.* The capacity to support external populations would increase by a factor of three over the 1961-1963 level of exports or about 600,000,000 people, if coarse grains such as maize were consumed directly by humans.

5. This item was reported in *Time,* September 25, 1972, p. 34. Political reporters in Asia say that a good deal of selection occurs among seers; therefore those that survive on the basis of performance demonstrate much wisdom. A great deal of "inside" information goes into a forecast, even if it is presented as a horoscope.

6. William and Paul Paddock, *Famine 1975! American Decision: Who Will Survive* (Boston: Little, Brown, 1967).

7. Most comprehensive by far, because it presents some of the politics and administration as well as the history and physiology, is Gunnar Blix, Yngve Hofvander, and Bo Vahlquist, *Famine: A Symposium Dealing with Nutrition and Relief Operations in Times of Disaster* (Stockholm: Almqvist and Wiksell, 1972). Modern society depends heavily upon novelists and script writers to illuminate the human effects of events. The subject of famine has been dealt with peripherally a number of times as part of history, but it has been taken up for modern times, as far as I can discover, only

by John Christopher in his small book *The Death of Grass* (London: Michael Joseph, 1956). It was later filmed under the title *No Blade of Grass* and republished by Penguin (1968, 1970) under that title in an effort to take advantage of the vogue in "environmental doom" building up at that time.

Christopher invoked a blight upon rice, which was later transformed into a disease that killed all grasses as the immediate cause of famine. In this speculation he is backed up by a recent assessment conducted by a committee of the United States National Academy of Sciences, *Genetic Vulnerability of Major Crops* (1972), which concludes that "most major crops are impressively uniform and impressively vulnerable to epidemics." The background is England of the 1960s or 1970s, and he conjectures speedy breakdown of the social order after food imports from elsewhere are cut off. He supposes that modern civilization would dissolve into a number of lawless bands preying upon each other and a resigned, fatalist population. Changes of character portrayed in that situation are interesting but not persuasive.

8. J. C. Beckett, *The Making of Modern Ireland: 1603-1923* (New York: Alfred A. Knopf, 1966).

9. S. H. Cousins "Emigration and Demographic Change in Ireland, 1851-61," *Economic History Review,* 14 (1961); Frances Morehouse, "The Irish Migrations of the Forties," *American Historical Review,* 33 (April 1928), 3.

10. G. T. Griffith, *Population Problems in the Age of Malthus,* 2d ed. (London: Cass, 1967); R. D. Edwards and T. D. Williams, *The Great Famine: Studies in Irish History, 1845-52* (New York: New York University Press, 1957).

11. K. H. Connell, "Peasant Marriage in Ireland," *Economic History Review,* 14 (April 1962), 3; "Catholicism and Marriage in the Century after the Famine," in *Irish Peasant Society* (Oxford: Clarendon Press, 1968).

12. Emmet Larkin, "Economic Growth, Capital Investment, and the Roman Catholic Church in Ireland in the 19th Century," *American Historical Review,* 72 (1967), 3; Oliver MacDonagh, "The Irish Catholic Clergy and Emigration During the Great Famine," *Irish Historical Studies,* 5 (September 1947), 20.

13. Cecil Woodham-Smith, *The Great Hunger: Ireland 1845-49* (London: Hamish Hamilton, 1962).

14. Andrew M. Greeley, *That Most Distressful Nation: The Taming of the American Irish* (Chicago: Quadrangle, 1972).

15. R. L. Meier and Gitta Meier, "New Directions: A Population Policy for the Future," in F. T. Brayer, ed., *World Population Policy and U.S. Government Policy and Programs* (Washington, D.C.: Georgetown University Press, 1968), pp. 103-116.

16. Ping-ti Ho presents a modern analysis of the statistical background to drought and famine in China in his *Studies on the Population of China, 1386-1953* (Cambridge, Mass.: Harvard University Press, 1959), pp. 230-236. This territory was stricken in 1876-1879 when a responsible official estimated that five to six million people were in desperate need of relief by 1877. The Foreign Relief Committee's estimate of loss of life was nine to thirteen million. Famine affected the same area in 1892-1894, 1900, 1920-1921, and 1927-1928. The introduction of railways greatly reduced the death toll in the last two of these, even though the severity of the last may have been greater than that of the late 1870s. Considerable loss of life was experienced in this area immediately before this series of catastrophes due to the annihilation of the Moslems and after this period during the Japanese wars.

17. Cheng-Sian Cheng, "Population Growth and Urbanization in China, 1953-1970," *Geographical Review*, 63 (January 1973), 55-72.

Number of Droughts in Different Provinces Observed during Historical Times in China[*] (by Centuries)

A.D.	0-100	100-200	200-300	300-400	400-500	500-600	600-700	700-800	800-900	900-1000	1000-1100	1100-1200	1200-1300	1300-1400	1400-1500	1500-1600	1600-1700	1700-1800	1800-1900	
Chihli	—	—	2	1	—	1	3	2	1	6	14	3	23	16	7	5	13	8	47	152
Shangtung	1	—	1	1	—	—	5	1	3	5	2	4	8	6	5	4	11	8	30	95
Shansi	—	1	1	1	—	1	4	1	5	5	1	1	12	10	7	8	17	3	12	90
Honan	5	14	—	—	2	1	3	1	8	30	23	2	12	12	4	3	9	2	20	151
Kiangsu	—	1	—	3	6	1	1	2	9	4	2	17	10	6	3	4	11	5	24	109
Anhwei	—	—	—	—	—	—	1	2	10	5	7	18	2	4	3	2	9	5	22	90
Kiangsi	—	—	—	—	—	—	—	—	5	1	1	5	6	2	2	9	21	—	12	64
Chekiang	—	—	—	1	—	—	—	1	8	2	4	19	7	6	14	22	20	8	15	127
Fukien	—	—	—	—	—	—	—	1	3	—	—	6	6	4	4	13	6	5	2	50
Hupeh	—	—	—	—	—	—	2	—	3	2	2	5	5	10	15	23	17	4	14	102
Hunan	—	—	—	—	—	—	—	1	4	2	2	7	2	5	9	4	11	—	11	58
Shensi	—	—	2	—	1	4	5	5	3	6	8	6	6	9	7	9	9	1	16	97
Kansu	—	—	—	1	—	—	—	1	—	—	—	4	—	5	1	1	1	6	9	29
Szechwan	—	—	2	—	—	—	5	—	—	—	2	10	4	2	2	2	—	1	—	30
Kwangtung	—	—	—	—	—	—	—	—	—	—	—	3	3	2	6	1	—	2	—	17
Kwangsi	—	—	—	—	—	—	—	—	—	1	—	—	—	5	2	7	3	1	4	23
Yunnan	—	—	—	—	—	—	—	—	—	—	—	—	—	—	2	10	6	—	1	19
Kweichow	—	—	—	—	—	—	—	—	—	—	—	—	—	—	—	—	2	1	—	3
Fengtien	—	—	—	—	—	—	—	—	—	—	2	1	1	—	—	—	—	1	4	9
Kirin	—	—	—	—	—	—	—	—	—	—	—	—	—	—	—	—	—	—	—	—
Helungkiang	—	—	—	—	—	—	—	—	—	—	—	—	—	—	—	—	—	1	2	3
Sinkiang	—	—	—	—	—	—	—	—	—	—	—	—	—	—	—	—	—	—	2	2
Mongolia	—	—	—	—	1	—	—	—	—	—	—	3	—	—	—	—	—	1	—	5
Kokonor	—	—	—	—	—	—	—	—	—	—	—	1	—	—	—	—	—	—	1	2
All China	25	35	24	41	37	41	43	41	43	64	69	58	77	60	54	84	82	36	70	984

[*]In some cases the phenomenon covers more than one province, while there are a few cases where location is not given; hence the sum for the different provinces in a century is not identical with the number given for the entire country.

18. William Hinton, *Fanshen: A Documentary of Revolution in a Chinese Village* (New York: Vintage Books, 1966); and Jan Myrdal and Gun Kessle, *Report from a Chinese Village* (New York: Pantheon Books, 1965); and *China: the Revolution Continued* (New York: Pantheon Books, 1970).

19. Walter H. Mallory, *China: Land of Famine* (New York: American Geographical Society, 1926). The author was chairman of the China International Famine Relief Commission; he reports on the normal disappearance of livestock during famine.

20. Surprisingly, the data on buffer stocks held were among the first to be released when China renewed its earlier policy of publishing statistics.

21. The most famous of these classics is that of Sun Tzu, *The Art of War,* which has a multitude of commentaries continuing to the present. Translations have utterly different styles; cf. those by Lionel Giles (London: Luzac, 1910); and Samuel B. Griffith (London: Oxford University Press, 1963).

22. Mongolia had been the locus for intense Russian-Chinese competition in the 1950s and 1960s, well before the ideological split between the two countries. It remains the key to military strategy for both armies. The scenario was written on the basis of scraps of information filtering out of the region before 1973, but no part of it had to be changed when a new body of detailed reports became available in 1974. See *Far East Economic Review,* 83 (January 28, 1974), 18 and 35; (February 18, 1974), 40-44. For example, the Mongolian livestock inventory was set at 24,000,000 head. The scheduled improvements in the railroad connecting Ulan Bator with China were presumed to have occurred.

23. Harrison Salisbury, *The Coming War Between Russia and China* (New York: W. W. Norton, 1969). Seymour Topping in *Report from Red China* (New York: Avon Books, 1971).

24. Charles H. Murphy, "Mainland China's Evolving Nuclear Deterrent," *Bulletin of the Atomic Scientists,* 28 (January 1972), 28-35.

25. In no society in the world today does the original cost of non-food energy consumed exceed 10% of total income. In many instances the cost of energy is, however, felt to be far more significant because quite considerable transport and distribution costs are added to minehead and wellhead prices, and governments then double or treble prices to consumers with excise and value added taxes.

A specialized method of argument has been used throughout
the discussion of urban crises. It has traced out futures for
cities should the poorest of a likely set of possibilities come
to pass. The method is often called "worst-case" analysis;
it provides the decision maker with some situations that
should be avoided, if at all possible, because of the undesirable outcomes. At the same time inputs are being mar-
shaled to maximize the value added by joint effort. If external forces had overwhelmed the defenses of the metropolis, however, and the worst happened, we imagined that
subsidiary groups and individual actors would draw upon
traditional routines of joint effort in order to cope with the
uncertainty and stress. The simile that comes to mind is
that of a skater on thin ice who crashes through the supporting surface and must discover how deep the water is as
well as use the standard lifesaving techniques learned earlier; but if the ice only bends, he makes almost as much
progress as if the surface were secure.

Preoccupation with worst-case analysis is not only morbid
and defensive; it can be hurtful. Society cannot afford to
become too concerned about all the unlikely sequences of
events that might lead into unexpected and unwelcome
futures. To be prepared for all of them would require infinite resources. Even the status quo could not be maintained. Our procedure intends to be prudent; it sets aside
relevant kinds of reserves for contingencies with precedents,
corresponding in many ways to insurable risks, with some
extra reserves for other contingencies. After that one hopes
for the best; the stocks held in reserve may for the most
part remain unspent. Beyond that, we must retain a streak
of fatalism which recognizes all the while that cities may be
long-lived but are not immortal.

Scores, if not hundreds, of large cities built up with generations of hard labor have disappeared altogether. Each
encountered a crisis it could not survive. The lesson that
might have been learned was usually lost because there have
been few reasonably unbiased records of the events that led
to their downfall; too often in the past the histories have
been written by successors, usually conquerors, who consistently attributed the destruction of the city to the significance of the omens, valor of the heroes among the
attackers, the strength of their prayers, or the rightness of

their cause. Occasionally, neutral third parties were on hand who did their best to render an objective account. More rarely still, teams of archaeologists, which are now made up of a variety of specialists, have pieced together explanations centuries, often millennia, after the fact. Classical scholarship has been able to deduce something about the specific underlying stresses brought about by resource scarcity at the time of catastrophe, but this is a very tentative kind of analysis.

Thus it is not surprising that ancient history provides us with no satisfying statistics or generalizations on the causes of the apocalyptic deaths of great cities, such as Carthage, Babylon, Nineveh, Antioch, Pataliputra, Baghdad, Ch'ang An, Teotihuacán, and the like. Nor is there an assessment of the reasons for abandoning such cities as Memphis, in the Nile Valley, Angkor Wat in the Mekong, the large Mayan centers in the Yucatán jungle, the ancient settlements in the Indo-Gangetic plain, or the early Yoruba aggregations in old Ghana, except that people appear to have become less numerous, less productive, and apparently not interested in urban life. Partial explanations do exist—quite frequently we can discover that a harbor was silted in, a water supply lost owing to the changing course of a river, the soils of a vital hinterland were worn out and eroded away, an ore body was depleted, or the population was destroyed by a great epidemic—but in few cases are they comprehensive enough to be persuasive.

In some instances, a chain of natural events may be triggered by customs and obsessions of the dominant classes. The patrician Romans in the villas of a reconstructed Olympia, the site of the world-famous quadrennial games, could hardly anticipate that their baths would cause them to be buried in sixty feet of mud and sand. The wood to fuel the hypocausts for heating the water was cut on the hilly flanks of Arcadia much faster than the forest could renew itself, and a record rain set off a huge landslide, thus preserving much of its integument for posterity. Similarly, the Romans did not understand the risks involved in building Pompeii, which was buried by the same vulcanism that produced the hot springs channeled into its famous baths.

The continued existence of cities has depended upon the maintenance of unified corporate organization, originally in the form of temples and royal households, later in associations of guilds of artisans and trading companies, and eventually in representative government.[1] When unity failed, the city dissolved or fell prey to the free-booters of the period. Factionalism in key sacred and political institutions sets loose the rumors that attract marauders the way that the odor of fresh meat draws hornets.

Recent history, however, has been very different. No large city has been extinguished by war, revolution, or natural disaster. Over time national social institutions have learned to apply modern technology and have synthesized a remarkable capability for healing urban wounds; the great destruction of World War II did not require more than a decade to overcome in most of the nations involved. Even Hiroshima and Nagasaki are larger and much more prosperous than before. The statistics suggest that we must be living in a fortunate era for cities because they not only survive but grow in number and size. Thirty or forty more urban centers are expected to move into the million size category over the next decade. Nevertheless, runs of good luck come to an end; we must seek cues or clues to the transition to some new state of danger well in advance.

One such set of disastrous futures that generate huge concern has arisen over the past several decades, but deliverance from them cannot be planned in detail. This set was encountered first in 1945 when the existence of nuclear weapons began to dominate action and reaction. Many major cities have their doom inscribed in the target setting of a multimegaton bomb in a second strike. Weapons aimed at enemy weapons have higher priority, and they will be targeted in early flight by enemy antiballistic missiles (ABM), but fallout radiation from these explosions would rain down on most other cities in the Northern Hemisphere. Some cities might be rendered uninhabitable, but much more likely the radiation would be distributed in some freakish way that would save a considerable number. Fallout over cities around the Equator and to the south would be more dilute. Nuclear warfare presents us with a discontinuous line into the future; all outlooks shrivel with the first release of nuclear weapons.

By my calculations and estimates most cities would survive an initial upset in the balance of terror that the present global system of government, based upon national sovereignty, has created. Some leading metropolises might be totally destroyed, some abandoned, and the remnants of the citizenry in others might be impelled to set up on a new site. In most instances, though, the city would be reoccupied if the cancerous effects of lingering radiation were less than those of cigarette smoking, because the surviving urban infrastructure would be much too valuable to abandon. Moreover, the chances for survival in cities improve over time as the ability accumulates to detect mutations, accept high abortion rates, construct elaborately instrumented systems of monitors that pick up the effects of radiation early, and cope with early forms of cancer. The attitudes of the surviving population toward human reproduction, processed foods, water supply, human injury, risk, and governmental authority, however, would have been transformed by the struggle to adapt to postholocaust conditions of life, and the changes are not now readily imaginable.

The chances of large-scale destruction are reduced even more because the controls over the weapons in the strike force are becoming more finely graduated, allowing last-minute retractions. The agreement on strategic arms limitation (SALT) between the United States and the USSR markedly reduces the principal source of risk buildup. Therefore, the longer a breakdown of the balance is averted, the better are the overall chances of the survival of the urban resident.

Curiously, although it is theoretically possible to design civilian defense systems that would greatly reduce casualties in the event of nuclear warfare, the very exercise of facing such a catastrophe seems to induce paralysis and disinterest. Normal people cannot contemplate gloomy and dismal futures very long. When their attention is deflected to more immediate concerns, any system tuned to respond to disaster tends to lose track of reality, each successive test encountering a greater disparity between its mobilization program and the needs of the then existing world; thus civil defense agencies become undependable and error prone as they sit and wait. For psychological reasons, then, an increase in the effort of nuclear disaster planning can no longer be viewed as productive.[2] Instead, organizations should be created that can react quickly to the unexpected, drawing upon active inventories and reserves, ready for any kind of contingency and opportunity.

An example of what is meant regarding constructive approaches to disaster planning would be helpful at this point. After the Managua earthquake of December 1972 (10,000 people buried in the rubble, 300,000 homeless or displaced),

American state-planning officials flew down to fill in an important gap in their information. How did their counterparts in Nicaragua survive during the first chaotic three to seven days after the shock? What sources of drinking water did they find? When did they recover enough from the shock to get hungry? Did they feel they had to loot grocery stores? What demands were made upon them for help, and to which did they respond? Knowing the confusion associated with the first twenty-four hours of relief operations, how did their counterparts find their way back into an organization with an integrated communications system? Personalized accounts of action at times of extraordinary stress are dramatic and much more easily recalled than the directions in a manual. Which of the individual histories would fit the requirements of a nuclear disaster?

Obviously, the best hope for avoiding destruction lies in finding a way to disarm. A joint process must be installed that not only prevents any further buildup of destructive capability but converts bomb materials into fuel for nuclear power plants. (Then their fuel value would be of the order of a hundredth of the cost of a bomb, but power production can nevertheless be a means of relatively safe disposal.)

This brief review of the very worst case for cities indicates that the need for unproductive contingency allocations is declining over time, and that they can gradually be replaced by support of those urban agencies and organizations with very short response times, such as police, fire, and medical emergency, linked with distributors of food, fuel, and other supplies by high-capacity wireless equipment. As this happens, the responsibility for civil defense shifts from national concerns to metropolitan functions; cities must increasingly take care of their contingencies as well as their progress.

Although experience with occasional catastrophic urban destruction has been lacking over the past two decades, one finds that the great cities have been going through repeated small-scale crises. These trials are worth reviewing because a catalog of "near misses" is as good a forecasting device as a series of well-reported failures. They point to many of the greatest hazards that urbanization faces in the future.

The idea that cities are being tested continually by small-to-medium threats of catastrophe, and that their responses to these emergencies set the precedents for the reaction to

GRAVE INJURY

great catastrophes, is an appealing one. Current world history might be assessed as if it were a gigantic natural experiment; great cities in various parts of the world must meet scores of threats that strike at essential operations over the course of only a decade. Information on the frequency and source of threat should enable city planners to prepare defenses against disasters that have yet to occur. Nevertheless, an attempt to carry out such a program of investigation of recent urban history very quickly reveals a number of inadequacies both in the concept and in the data.

It was thought, for example, that a list of potential urban catastrophes could be compiled in much the same way that the reports of wars and revolutions in the nineteenth and twentieth centuries have been identified and chronologically ordered. Human costs have also been quantitatively estimated in most instances.[3] However, catastrophes for cities were revealed to be different than for nations, primarily because the latter have legally defined occasions for waging war and citations for rebellion, while cities have precisely identified very few of the threats to their existence. The first "catastrophe list" that was compiled for world cities contained two classes of phenomena: one was a series of threats to survival which were completely averted (followed by sighs of relief); and the other designated events in which damages were sustained, but only by a dispensable precinct or ward. The final list resembled a batch of medical reports from a loosely interrelated population of patients, mentioning epidemic prevention, recommending antibiotic distribution, and reporting broken bones, fevers, digestive upsets, and expressions of pain (but no deaths) in the same context. The insight is important because the welfare of a city has properties closely parallel to the concept of the health of a group. On the basis of much study the health of a group is known to be measurable in many of its multitudinous dimensions, but not quantifiable as a single index number, so the analog simulates a comprehensive assessment. Employment of health-related terms is more descriptive than mere parable; it may well offer the most suitable paradigm.

Metropolitan Crises in the 1960s

A classified list of threats to functions (includes only million-size metropolitan regions)*

Water Hazards

Hong Kong, 1961; cut off from reservoir in China
Hamburg, 1962; North Sea flood tides
Bombay, 1963; drought
New York, 1963-1965; long drought
Madras, 1969; reservoir failure
Calcutta, 1969; works breakdown

Institutional Loss or Collapse

New Orleans, 1960; schools shut down
Rio de Janeiro, 1960; government moves out
Hong Kong, 1960; refugees overwhelm housing
Hong Kong, 1962; refugees overwhelm housing
Alexandria, 1962; loss of summer capital
Atlanta, 1962; elite die in air crash
St. Louis, 1962; metropolitan government rejected
New York, 1966; garbage and transit strike
Calcutta, 1966; university strikes
Singapore, 1966; U.K. Navy leaves
San Francisco, 1967; funds of council of governments stolen
Tokyo, 1968; universities shut down
Rome, 1969; strikes of service workers

Energy Failures

New York, 1965; power blackout
Belgrade, 1969; hydroelectric shutdown threat

Accidents and Natural Events

Tashkent, 1966; earthquake

Revolution and Rebellion

Dallas, 1963; Kennedy assassination
Singapore, 1965; separated from hinterland
Los Angeles, 1965; Watts "rebellion"
Jakarta, 1966; assassination and genocide
Cleveland, 1966; Hough riots

* The identifying descriptor serves only to focus attention on a complex set of events that is believed to have been associated with crisis behavior in million-size cities and has been reported in international news services to some degree.

Hong Kong, 1966; Maoist riots
Wuhan, 1968; Red Guard battles
Washington, 1968; riots and looting
Paris, 1968; student uprising and general strike

War

Berlin, 1961; a wall is built
Lahore, 1965; tank invasion threat
Prague, 1968; Russian takeover
Saigon, 1968; Tet offensive

News stories reveal great differences among cities. Some are loud hypochondriacs, while others are uncomplaining stoics. New York, for example, exhibits a long sequence of urban crisis headlines, but Shanghai's complaints, reduced to a few strings of characters by the time they reach nearby Hong Kong, are restrained. News of impending crises may be selective, since reports that entail loss of *face* may not be reported at all in Asian and African countries. Thus we are forced to discriminate between tub-thumping promotional cities that demand attention and the poor, ailing, powerless, undefended cities that seem unable to express what is happening to them in a comprehensible way. The former are consistently high-level transformers of resources, while the latter consume at a much lower intensity. Just as a doctor must appraise the effect of an injury upon "normal" human development, we are forced to specify an orderly development of million-size cities so as to amplify the laconic accounts of some cities and discount the dramatics of others.

Note that in the analogs the ecological framework has been temporarily abandoned and replaced with the organismic. The reason for this is the slow response time inherent in the organization of the populations in a community. The design of a living system possessing a heavy endowment of neural tissue inside a skin is nature's way of organizing biomass to get a quick response in averting a variety of threats. Natural communities suffer their losses and stubbornly regain their original state, but organisms are artful dodgers and can learn new evasive tactics without incurring damage.

These qualms about drawing inferences about the vulnerability of cities from the series of critical incidents which the largest of them face are raised primarily because the method does not seem likely to become improved by the expenditure of more research effort. What risk minimizers would like to do eventually is to make it possible to take out insurance with some gigantic successor to Lloyds of London. The insurance firms, using actuarial data available to them, would insist that cities take certain prudent measures to reduce potential losses; otherwise their insurance rates would be raised. Elected officials in such cities would find it much easier to persuade a public to undertake disaster prevention measures if they are clearly means of reducing the insurance component in operating costs. However, a first inspection of the information available on world cities indicates that it is not reported systematically enough to be subjected to actuarial analysis that will cover the full range of risks. Because the possibility of introducing the risk-reducing measures associated with insurance, along with the automatic provision of funds to restore normal conditions, seems not very workable, cities must depend instead upon altruism—the sacrifices people make to help others in distress. The technique of critical incidents remains, nevertheless, about the best available for balancing the attention paid to problems of prospective survival for cities with those of development.

The most serious difficulties with natural resources experienced by large metropolitan areas are those of water supply. As the population and the industry of a city continue to expand, whole new watersheds need to be dammed up. Their normal flow is then pipelined to the smaller reservoirs in the metropolitan area and from these points distributed through the urban grid. To do this, water authorities are formed to reach far out into the hinterland and purchase the rights to the runoff. If this acquisition is not undertaken well in advance of need, the occasional droughts that affect virtually every urbanized region and its water catchment areas will bring industries and sanitary systems to a halt.

The sequestration of water is most difficult in densely populated regions where rural communities have already established claims. Since the cities in many of these regions are relatively poor and cannot afford to build up a strong safety factor in the form of upcountry reservoirs, they are forced to find some way to ration limited water supplies about once every decade, and sometimes more often. When

**URBAN
WATER
HAZARDS**

this happens, announcements are made through the newspapers, and over radio and television, that there will be no
pressure in the pipes of the city water system except between specified hours. Meanwhile, water carriers and tank
trucks ply the streets selling water just as they might otherwise sell milk, kerosene, or vegetables. A shortage of food,
particularly the perishables that are usually grown close at
hand, is likely to follow the onset of drought. The combined difficulties are often sufficient to scare off potential
inmigrants and keep them out of the metropolis. If the
drought continues into a second or a third year, the parched
metropolis is likely to experience an inflation in food staple
prices as well, thus creating a condition that will drive poor
people back to their villages or set the stage for famine.

Large cities that have grown up near the headwaters of
river systems are most vulnerable. Examples are Mukden
and Sian in China, Delhi and Hyderabad in India, Addis
Ababa and Johannesburg in Africa, Bogotá and Caracas in
South America, Pittsburgh, Denver, and Dallas-Fort Worth
in North America. The upper watersheds they draw upon
tend to have a greater year-to-year variation in precipitation
than the full drainage basin. In dry years these cities are
likely to use the total flow available, draw down the reservoirs, and pump heavily from the aquifers underlying the
city itself. Many such aquifers rest on a base of dense
brine, so continued pumping from such strata results in
increasingly saline water.

There may be adequate supplies of fresh water a few hundred miles downstream, but it does not pay to build an up-
slope pipeline, especially since it could be rendered useless
for a decade or more by ordinary rainstorms. Further, since
at least two years would be required after the time of decision to put such an aqueduct into operation, the likelihood that the project would be regretted is exceedingly
high.

It is not at all easy for a metropolis to go into the countryside and buy up water rights. Inevitably, the political
leaders in the rural communities come to regard this action
as one that robs them of their future. The repercussions in
legislative assemblies and parliaments are highly undesirable.
Whenever dams and reservoirs are built, leaders at the state
or province level hear repeated stories, some true and many
false, illustrating the unfairness of the urban authorities to
"ordinary people." Often sizable villages are displaced from

their traditional sites. Naturally the rural representatives respond to the threat by forming coalitions to repel invasion from the metropolis, even if it is the dominant political center in their own state or province. Almost always the rural population is overrepresented in the legislature; it therefore possesses an unusually strong veto power.

The typical solution available to the growing metropolis is to pay for the same water two or three times. It must of course provide the scarce leadership and the capital for a regional water authority that has the power to collect the water at convenient points. This authority will find its actions bound by compromises in its charter which provide water for people in the vicinity of a constructed facility at rates a third to a tenth of those charged in the metropolis. Moreover, to obtain passage of legislation for such an authority with broad powers for water resource development, the metropolis must "bargain" for votes from smaller cities and some rural areas. It must promise to support independent legislation creating industrial estates, harbors, airports, technical colleges, and other installations at uneconomic sites purely because they are desired by the provincial elites. The metropolis creates the bulk of the taxable income and property, so the taxes applied to such projects derive from metropolitan production, and a water authority becomes a device for redistributing the added value created by urbanization to people who have thus far remained away from the cities.[4]

Woe be unto the metropolis that finds its water in an adjoining state or nation, because it is then not in a position to bargain for it directly. It is likely to pay much more without being sure of delivery even then, because extraneous issues due to strains in the relations between large political units can always be interjected. Everywhere in the world the subject of long-term water supply seems to be synonymous with political intrigue. Fortunately, large cities do not grow up in true deserts because in places like Arabia, as in the old Wild West, the occupants of the land go one step further and enforce their claims to water with private armament.

The normal effect of a great drought, such as that experienced by New York City during 1963-1965 and Hong Kong somewhat earlier, is to cause the water-using industries producing for customers outside the immediate region to locate their next plants in urban areas where water is more secure. For a river-based city, this is often down-stream. Estuary-based cities with shortages find themselves pushed into a flurry of water supply expansion activities by these same industrial interest groups.

Often high-cost substitutes are installed so as to reduce future vulnerability to drought. Thus, bottle washing and sterilization for reuse in milk, soft drinks, and beer distribution is displaced by disposable steel and aluminum cans and by plastic-coated paper. The new containers greatly exacerbate the solid waste collection and disposal problems faced by these cities, but those costs are seldom borne by the producer.

The large modern cities located on estuaries and shore-lines have one great advantage over those on rivers; they can draw upon the salt or brackish waters of the sea for the large-scale cooling requirements of power plants and energy-intensive manufacturing. If fresh water becomes dear enough, they are in the right position to fill a minor portion of their needs with desalinated water that can be produced as a by-product of these industries, though this is likely to happen only when the cost of adding extra water supply capacity equals the maximum experienced by a million-size city in the world today.

Much loose talk is heard about the ease of sabotage of the water supply lines to a city, including the introduction of some toxin into the water that would make it unfit for use. This is far more difficult than it appears. Even in Bombay, whose inner four millions are supplied by two large pipes, side by side, running above the surface for many miles (because the city rests on a rather narrow peninsula and its sources are inland), it would take the authorities only a few hours to replace a length or two of pipe or a valve that might be destroyed. Water requirements for several days are held in tanks and reservoirs within the city. Moreover, many of the poor get their daily water from the barrelmen who draw it from a few wells inside the city. The presence of contaminants would be detected hours or days before it reached the bulk of the city regardless of where it was introduced. Most inorganic contaminants would be he held back for a while by the sand filters that are routinely employed, while the biologically active materials are very likely to be fully inactivated by the chlorine that is routine-ly added. An extremely skilled and well-informed agent might overcome these difficulties, but such a person could probably have a greater impact by attempting to bring other departments of government to a halt, and it would take less physical effort as well.

It may seem bizarre to take up such eventualities, but the list of rebellions, riots, and strikes affecting great cities is longer than the "near misses" on water supply. Successful cities must be very open systems, so it is impossible for the city to prevent the entry of agents seeking their destruction. If the Bombay water system seems to be able to cope with foreseeable emergencies, then it must be possible for its counterparts elsewhere in the world.

A city that does not import energy sources for its internal **ENERGY** operations is dead. It can be shown that even the efficient **CRISIS** technologies for exploiting sunlight incident upon a city cannot support people at urban densities.[5] A large natural gas field immediately underground could support a small- to medium-size city, but it would be exhausted too quickly by a metropolis. Exploitation of a rich coal seam underneath the city is ruled out by the combination of the heap of spoil that would be produced at pit heads and by the settling of the surface caused by underground cave-ins. Thus, the larger cities must universally be fuel importers on a huge scale. Normally they bring in more than 99% of the fuel or electric power that is needed for their operation.

No metropolis has experienced a really serious failure in the importation of energy since World War II, unless one wishes to include Seoul and Athens when ravaged by the Cold War in 1950-51. At that time neither maintained a population exceeding a million. In the 1940s coal was still the predominant fuel, though oil often played a significant role, and the bulk of the imports, even in a relatively poor metropolis, was very sizable as compared to building materials and food. This meant that every time the rail lines and harbor came under attack, the inflows of fuel, food, and most reconstruction materials would be simultaneously cut off, and the respective stocks on hand would need to be rationed. Energy shortages were always accompanied by a lack of adequate shelter and by hunger; therefore, energy shortages are not an easily isolated threat to cities.

Since the construction of the autobahns, threats of invasion have almost always resulted in a military takeover of road transport, in addition to rails and harbors, and civilian needs have consistently been assigned low priorities in the allocation of transport equipment. Actual occupation of a metropolis by the enemy during wartime did not immediately result in improved access to food or fuel. Therefore, the great cities of Tokyo, Berlin, Leningrad, Manila, Hong Kong, and Athens suffered grievously during the 1940s.

Several predictable consequences were identified following those breakdowns in energy supplies. The most observable effect was the reduction in activity of all kinds— economic, cultural, and physical. Another was emigration, since the population of all the cities mentioned above was reduced by more than half within one to two years after the onset of attacks, and only a minor fraction of that loss was due to war casualties. Urban families with relatives or some kind of property holdings in the countryside thronged the escape routes. These refugees were joined by citizens on day trips who went foraging throughout the city's outskirts for food or lower-grade fuels. Bicyles became the most prized vehicles at such times. The forests in the parks and the green belts were almost totally removed, and even some of the peat bogs were dug up. Damaged buildings were scavenged for edibles and combustibles. At the same time, materials like paper became extraordinarily scarce.

Once hostilities ceased, however, supplies of kerosene and wheat flour were quickly moved in; technicians patched up the electric power distribution grid within weeks or, at most, a few months; electric power generating stations were put into operation even more speedily. All during this accelerated reconstruction period people flowed back. Indeed, the pace of resettlement proceeded to such an extent that each of these cities passed its former peak size within a decade of its nadir, even though housing and office space remained desperately scarce for more than another decade thereafter.

Never before have large cities recuperated so rapidly from such extensive destruction. This resilience in the face of great damage is attributed in part to the multipurpose diffusion of energy inherent in electrification, but the modern bureaucracies managing utilities and services in the metropolis should be given equal credit. In each case the organizational framework had not been totally destroyed, and the surviving elements retained the capability for recruiting and training individuals to fill the gaps. Bureaucracies heal wounds more quickly than the guilds of artisans and merchants that preceded them, and energy utilities such as electric power, gas, petroleum products distribution, and railroads ranked among the most advanced bureaucracies in each of these cities.

The ability to recoup damages to energy supplies has advanced even further over the past thirty to forty years. Power plants can now shift quickly from one fuel to another. Essential intracity traffic can be maintained with propane or even methane. Elaborate power grids have been constructed to provide back-up power for cities in case of the shutdown or loss of a captive generator. Many of the networks linking up the buildings in the metropolis have now been placed underground or underwater and are therefore not easily severed. Telephones are increasingly independent of the availability of electric current from the regional grid, so that systems of exchanges can work even when all the lights are out.

Presence of regional grids has, however, introduced a new and unexpected vulnerability. The Great Blackout of 1967 affected almost twenty million urbanites in the New York, New Jersey, Pennsylvania, and Ontario area for a whole night. Lesser failures have occurred since then in several metropolitan grids, and, in some cases, their origins remain totally inexplicable. Although in those instances subways and elevators stopped, trapping thousands, most buses and cars remained operational. Henceforth, too, a number of back-up generator units will be on hand in headquarters areas, thus greatly reducing the vulnerability of the large city to electrical energy supply failure.[6]

No other experience with threats of energy cutoff has come to hand that suggests large cities would be exposed to new disasters due to the inadequacy of the energy distribution systems. The planners of their public utilities have worked out a number of strategies that allow big cities to become relatively autonomous in the short run. In the long run a number of fuel substitutes can be mobilized, particularly if the population served includes a body of high-quality technicians—a condition that is at least 90% true for million-size cities today.

While persuasive evidence can be assembled to show that the physical fabric of the city is now mended more rapidly than ever before, there are some doubts that damage to the sociopolitical system can be as speedily repaired. Recent and widely publicized riots in American, French, and other

BREAKDOWNS IN PUBLIC ORDER

modern metropolitan areas caused much physical destruction, but they took an even greater toll from the amount of public cooperation that had been achieved outside of the firm and the workplace. Urban order is an ephemeral kind of human resource; it includes at least (1) tolerance of others different from one's ingroup, (2) consensus on the rules governing public behavior, (3) an acceptance of the legitimacy of the courts in the settlement of disputes, (4) admission that carefully constrained police powers are needed to enforce the authority of the courts, and (5) willingness to follow a responsible body of leaders. The resource is depleted when divisive issues are allowed to expand, causing polarization and breaking down the trust which is the basis of cooperation.

The characteristics of the urban social process enumerated above are all needed to expedite bargaining between individuals and groups without a recourse to threat or the use of violence. Coercion-free bargaining is the basis for urban order. Informal arrangements for completing social, cultural, and political transactions are almost always more efficient than the formal procedures; therefore the degree of utilization of informal social process appears to be an indicator of the order that has been achieved in that urban region. Among the great cities, Tokyo has organized itself most carefully to expedite visitation, consultation, negotiation, bargaining, and the closing of deals. Inside each organ organization, down to the smallest, is a formal visiting place, where each person sips tea at a low table and expresses subtle reactions produced by almost his whole body. The higher the status of the host, the higher the table and the stakes. Subsequent meetings are most often conducted on neutral ground in some restaurant, coffee house, bar, night club, golf course, or resort. The style of service of food and drink corresponds to the kind of arrangement to be produced from the meeting—with a foreigner one might choose a steak house or Chinese restaurant, possibly an eating place dedicated to an exotic specialty. With a provincial, one defers to his taste for the cuisine of his region; for a fellow professional, a bar traditionally frequented by other members of the profession may be most suitable—each place being designed to fit the needs of the man with the expense account. Each great city is famed for its expense account entertainment spending, but Tokyo easily surpasses others. The most complicated arrangements between multiple parties of different status, strength, cultural origin, age, and physical prowess can be bargained and closed more quickly in Tokyo than elsewhere. Business activities run on a higher proportion of credit than in other cities, so assessments of character are more important. Crime is moderate to low, racketeering and extortion are kept under control, corruption is not blatant, street violence is restricted to the university districts, and public officials pay respectful attention to complainants even if no action is likely to be taken. Reforms and improvements upon the public image are present everywhere. Therefore ad hoc organization is quicker and easier in Tokyo—if one starts with adequate cash and organizational connections and can handle unlimited quantities of tea, coffee, beer, whiskey, Scotch, sake, and then still more tea. Public life is so extensive and demanding that private lives are often starved and strained.

Calcutta is perhaps the prime contemporary example of a metropolis that has not developed this kind of human resource in a way that will contribute to its progress. Calcutta has always been a city of many ethnic and religious communities and large numbers of unattached men whose allegiances remain tightly bound to family and village somewhere in the accessible hinterland. Its severest trials, however, began at the time of the formation of Pakistan from 1947 to 1951. In the huge population exchange that resulted, Calcutta saw its educated and organized Muslims depart, while those that remained were the very poorest. The metropolis received many more Hindus than the Muslims it lost, so most of the refugees were forced to settle on the fringes of the existing metropolis outside the Corporation boundaries. The international boundary laid down at that time sliced off almost half of Calcutta's hinterland just at a time when it needed to support a big influx of settlers. The social fabric is only now, after the founding of Bangladesh, beginning to recover from these shocks.

The frustrations experienced by different elements in Calcutta's population led to strikes of several varieties, food riots, violent political demonstrations, local pogroms, student disturbances, and a sullen resistance to authority on issues that presented little difficulty elsewhere in India. Public life is normally dull, telephones work poorly, secretaries are inadequate, and expense accounts rare, so that much of the time on the job is spent on hobbies, family affairs, and gossip. Family life, when it is possible, is said to be rich and rewarding, or at least complex and puzzling.

Calcutta has only a handful of lunching places for business-men or public officials to get together—the old British clubs have been retained, but the transactions carried out in them are desultory. Alcohol is exorbitant in price, poor in quali-ty, and seems to be reserved for the military, who in turn are kept off center stage. There is a remarkably active world of make-believe—theater, films, music, poetry, intel-lectual circles, ideological groups, and religious associations—whose component parts interact on only rare occasions. The disinterest of most of these groups in British institu-tions and the architectural relics of that era is one of the reasons for the visible decay of the central districts, but the real sources of present civic disorder are much deeper. An established profit-minded clique has maintained its hold over the Corporation and the Improvement Trust. Cal-cutta's businessmen have extracted every rupee of profit possible from the urban milieu without promoting the new public services required for growth and development over the long run. Other great cities in India have produced some of the cooperative effort that was needed, but busi-nessmen and other community leaders in Calcutta have not bothered to defend themselves against charges of neglect; they can only say that they have been compelled to play the game of survival in a different way. The heads of lead-ing families have not been able to communicate with each other on development because each group, however it de-fined itself, aimed to obtain justice for itself first. Life has been conceived as a negative-sum game in Calcutta; a feeling of frustration and powerlessness has prevailed.

The concept of order in large cities is best visualized as a multidimensional web knit together in networks that have frequently reproduced distinctively patterned relationships. Under stress, the web is easily deformed, causing friction and perhaps even rupturing some bonds. In cities with gloomy prospects, bonds are being broken more rapidly than they are repaired or replaced, so that the overall order is dissipating.

New organizations and activities must be stimulated to halt the slide toward dissolution. They introduce new knots into the web; after some lag they produce new bonds in the networks. Even Calcutta generates a wide range of new organizations each year, particularly around its periphery. These include a number of new holding companies, small modern enterprises, still smaller traditional enterprises, private schools, government offices, political associations, sports clubs, dramatic societies, professional groups, religious missions, neighborhood organizations, and cooperatives. The difficulty is that more seem to become stultified, moribund, or pushed toward bankruptcy than are created. On balance, Calcutta has not been producing the new organizations that are needed to mobilize its human resources and produce expanding loci of order in its metropolitan area. A highly developmental metropolis, such as Tokyo, may have as severe a mortality rate for organizations as Calcutta, but Tokyo maintains a kind of civil order that greatly eases the task of starting and building new organizations. When the birth rate of organizations is greater than the death rate, the metropolis moves ahead—first in terms of increased social participation, then in economic efficiency, then in political stability, and finally in externally recognized cultural achievement.

The creation of new organizations presupposes a capacity to communicate. The city must install a variety of media that transmit information, preferably in an unbiased form. Thus information regarding a new opportunity and justification for forming a new organization most often arrives in specialized journals and catalogs, but it is reinforced by word-of-mouth reporting and perhaps with snapshots. Consider, for example, the establishment of a technical library, an art center, a housing cooperative, a private school, or a new manufacturing enterprise. The initiative is taken by a promoter, who through a series of face-to-face encounters persuades others that this project offers a profitable use of their time. He finds financial backing, chooses the operating site, and starts instructing others in the most efficient ways they can contribute. Then he must turn his attention to the consumer of the new goods or services he intends to supply. Potential users of the output must be found and then persuaded that this product is clearly superior to the existing alternatives. The most economic strategy for persuasion generally requires the use of several communications media in a way that allows them to reinforce each other.

When a formula for selling the product has been found, the organization must expand rapidly to fill the niche it has created. In doing this, the promoter must look for suitably educated or trained people in moribund or dying organizations and fit them into his organization. The dense settlement of a metropolis allows a promoter to draw from a large pool of potentially valuable preprogrammed (i.e., trained, educated, or experienced) individuals and in a matter of a few years construct a finely tuned and sensitive organization. The outcome for the metropolis is a new address where people have relatively stable long-range expectations and engage in orderly, integrated, productive action while depending much more heavily than ever before upon various communications channels for continuing operations. As long as most individuals and groups among the populations of men and automata can communicate with each other, the metropolis continues to be a self-repairing, self-renewing, ultra-stable living system.

The kind of catastrophe a modern metropolis most worries about is the failure of the organizations responsible for its major source of livelihood—the reason for its relatively elevated standing in the hierarchy of central places—but now with the advantage of hindsight we see that such fears are rarely justified. Thus Singapore imagined that it might lose its entrepôt status in Southeast Asia when the British Navy abandoned its installations. The organized efforts to compensate for the loss, however, caused Singapore to reach new new levels of civic achievement—including, quite unexpectedly, full employment. Similarly, Glasgow experienced a series of bankruptcies in its shipbuilding and engineering industries, yet unemployment has not reached levels that are normal in Canada, because the civic order was eroded very slowly. Now the availability of labor could bring it large new enterprises adapted to the expanded European Common Market. Bankruptcies of railroads and toll bridges, where complete shutdowns have frightening implications, almost always turn out to be more reorganizations than dissolutions, and the changes may show up in altered names, perhaps, but not in a significant loss of service. As a result of a wave of such crises, railroads all over the world have been nationalized, and the huge deficits are met out of the public funds. The precedent has now been extended, so that if a major organization, such as a Rolls Royce, Lockheed Aviation, or a Pirelli, founders, it is propped up by governments after minor slimming operations. Such transitions are agonizing; they reflect the collapse of a portion of the local leadership. Having paid much tribute to the national government to maintain the overhead costs of the nation, cities can put in claims for help in these times of emergency reorganizations, and they usually get what they need. Thus metropolises live through many headlined crises which bring about merely a loosening of commitments, greater dependence upon outsiders, new methods of accounting, a redirection of public attention, new leadership, and opportunities for new growth.

Therefore, despite cartoons depicting the precarious plight of the metropolis, wry satire on the fallibility of public services, waves of rumors predicting the breakdown of essential institutions, and the round of strikes that halt apparently necessary services, urban citizens lead a remarkably secure life. Viewed in the aggregate, the struggling metropolis can now maintain a steady state with scarcely a wobble, given any exigency short of nuclear warfare. In normal times, but particularly during the cautiously optimistic periods, the capacity to breed and import new highly productive organizations generates substantial growth. For world urbanism we can expect this growth to be relatively smooth, continuing over many decades.

Notes

1. E. A. Gutkind, *International History of City Development* (Glencoe: Free Press, 1964); Gideon Sjoberg, "The Rise and Fall of Cities," in Nels Anderson, ed., *Urbanism and Urbanization* (Leiden: Brill, 1964). Actually the literature is vast and features many viewpoints, but the line of development for city organization depicted briefly here is compatible with almost all of them.

2. Disaster studies received a fair amount of theoretical as well as practical attention in the decade after the first tests of hydrogen bombs. Interestingly, this interest fell off very rapidly, and there were relatively few reports of studies conducted during the 1960s. Repeatedly it was found that panic very rarely occurs under conditions of great damage, and that instead social relationships among the survivors were strengthened, even to the extent of causing remission in mental illness. A large share of immediate assistance is given by strangers who were also victims; but medical help, shelter, fresh water, and regular food after the immediate emergency must be brought in by rescue teams coordinated by a centralized ad hoc organization. Finally formal organizations complete the restoration of normal conditions through the payment of insurance claims, extension of loans, and restoration of services. Allen H. Barton, *Communities in Disaster* (Garden City, N.Y.: Doublday, 1969). The most impressive performance recorded thus far was for the coastal city of Niigata, where despite huge destruction due to earthquake and tsunami the loss of life was held to a very low level, and the city came back into operation with rapidity. R. R. Dynes, J. E. Haas, and E. L. Quarantelli, Research Report No. 11, Disaster Research Center, Ohio State University, Columbus, December 1964.

3. Joel David Singer and Melvin Small, *The Wages of War* (New York: John Wiley & Sons, 1972).

4. The political economy of water is very nicely handled by Bain *et al.* In their instance most of the water was to be used for export agriculture but the innovating institutional elements were backed by metropolitan water authorities. Joe S. Bain, Richard E. Caves, and Julius Margolis, *Northern California's Water Industry* (Baltimore: Johns Hopkins University Press, 1966). For the more technical aspects of metropolitan water planning, see M. L. Albertson, L. A. Tucker, and D. C. Taylor, eds., *Treatise on Urban Water Systems* (Fort Collins, Colo.: Colorado State University Press, 1971).

5. The calculations are made as follows: A hectare can produce under optimal conditions no more than ten tons of food and fiber, dry weight, per year. Some energy is needed for fertilizer and food processing, so the net yield is no more than eight tons. Each urban resident needs a million kilogram calories per year (250 kg) for food and about three times that much at a minimum to support transport, manufacturing, lighting, and other energy-using urban activities. With ideal technology that assumes the highest conversions and trivial amounts of waste, about one ton of organic matter could be converted to meet these requirements. Thus no more than eight

urban people could be supported by a hectare of rich land, and they would still need about a tenth of an acre or so for strictly urban activities not related to extraction of solar energy. The resulting density (maximally seven persons per hectare or 1,800 per square mile) is still too thin to be called urban. The typical conditions are, or course, more nearly half as productive or less, and the densities supportable thus become average rural densities. In the long-run future, however, the energy imports need not come along the sur- face—they could be concentrated by satellites and beamed down- ward.

6. The Northeast Power Failure, as it came to be called, led to a worldwide review of power grid design. In the United States the Federal Power Commission made a special report to the President of the United States: *Prevention of Power Failures* (Washington, D.C.: Government Printing Office, July 1967, Lee C. White, Chair- man). The occasion was marred somewhat by a similar failure covering an equally large region, in part overlapping the former one, with outages of one to ten hours, while the report was in press. Nevertheless in 1966 an equally large failure around Los Angeles had minimal effect because the Southern California Edison Company had installed automatic loadshedding triggered by relays that de- tected a reduction in the number of cycles per second of alterna- tion in the current. The experience led to much more compre- hensive planning at every level of service, apparently to the point where the irritation of the customer upon experiencing a failure is valued at many times more than the total economic loss. The un- availability of power to a customer is rated at less than one hour in about 20,000. The strategy now is to prevent cascading of failures in a network by isolating an increasingly small "island," which may require repair while the load is met by the extra capacity in the remainder of the network.

In developing countries lightning competes with human error and sabotage as a cause of failure. The reliability that is economic may well be in the 99.8 to 99.9% range. Cf. Proceedings of a conference on *The Economics of the Reliability Supply* held by the Institution of Electrical Engineers, London, October 1967, particularly papers by G. G. R. Argent, M. W. Kennedy, and A. B. Wood; H. J. Sheppard; and M. W. Gangel and R. J. Ringlee. A standard procedure hence- forth is the computer simulation of a network, subjecting it to all known forms of failure, so as to produce decision rules for power system managers.

Chapter 4

PROCESSES OF TRANSITIONAL URBANIZATION

The magnitude of the urbanization yet to be undertaken is hardly ever discussed. Contemporary urbanists do not see how such large aggregations of human population can function as cities. Although C. A. Doxiadis has shaken audiences when concluding that all the building so far completed comprises but a tenth or less of what must be accomplished by the next three generations of architects and engineers, his arguments deal much more with the dimensions and the implications of the challenge than with technical solutions.[1] Among most investigators and scholars one finds partial recognition of the significance of the urban transition at many points in discussions, but somewhere along the line the issues are ducked. Many take refuge in concluding that desperate, but still unspecified, measures will have to be undertaken.

One University of Wisconsin physicist-environmentalist, who preferred at the time to remain anonymous, reported upon the results of two years of subsidized exploration in search of suitable policies. They needed to be potent enough to cope with the population explosion that, with only a brief lag, creates the urban explosion. He found only one, given to him by an economist familiar with ecological principles, who shall also remain nameless. The policy leading to equity and reduced pressure upon resources was "Eat Rich People."

Anthropolologists claim to recall instances where it was the custom to sacrifice the chief when he reached a certain age; his organs would be ritually consumed, and his property distributed. Certainly the chief and members of the elite would have been relatively well fed and more succulent than the average tribesman, although the conversion efficiency (calories of feed into calories of flesh) would be very low at their age. Such a society should become equalitarian very rapidly, since the property holders could redistribute their wealth and avoid being sacrificed. The resultant lack of organization would cause the natural death rate to rise precipitately, sometimes to a level much greater than the birth rate. The population pyramid should then resemble that of the jackals, who still cannibalize their own kind on some occasions, although the victims appear to be strays from nearby bands.[2] A more likely resolution of such a rule is that powerful individuals would abjure private wealth but designate certain outgoup or ineffective persons to be nominal rich people who would be fattened for sacrifice, thus returning to conditions reported for the followers of Baal in the Bible and for a number of cities in both the Old and New Worlds before Christianity. The population pyramid may then become that of a species which is maintained at equilibrium because it is heavily preyed upon—in this case by a priesthood.[3]

Such policies, although they seem to have far-fetched precedents, are obviously not seriously proposed. They are used to illustrate the implications of extrapolating from the present to a future society that has both population equilibrium and equity in the distribution of income. The paradoxes encountered when applying this theory suggest inherent conflict between what is required by nature of the ecosystem for the long run and what is being demanded of the social and economic system by its members.

Better solutions than eating rich people can be offered for resolving the paradoxes but they violate other preconceptions and do not fit present preferences. In order to evolve an acceptable alternate proposal, it is necessary to review the human experience that lies behind the demographic statistics covering population growth. The data have anomalies in them that cause empirical investigators to be reluctant to do more than make cautious statements about what they are quite certain is true. Policy determinations cannot wait for certainty; they must be based upon what is most likely to be true. The task is to find a path for future urbanization that minimizes the frequency of disasters, and then invent or synthesize improvements that seem to add to the quality of life experienced.

An exceedingly significant effect of urbanization is its enhancement of control over population growth. Quite uniformly, but not quite unanimously, current evaluations find that contraceptives are more rapidly made available to users in urban regions. Also, the response to educational efforts about the superiority of small families is quicker than in rural areas, so the total cost per birth prevented is much lower in and around cities. Thus a simple policy for expediting urbanization should have the effect of reducing the rate of population growth in the society as a whole and a greatly diminished population size at the time of the completion of the demographic transition.[4]

Within the urban area the transition to small families will be much slower among certain inmigrant groups, particularly those who flee to the city at times of disaster. Over the past two decades the situations that have driven people to the metropolis have been small scale and local, so the proportion contributed to the total migration has been minor. When Malthusian type catastrophes occur, they are expected, as illustrated earlier, in the case of China, to *push* large numbers of people out of famine areas, leaving them squatting on land close to the transportation nodes which bring in relief from the outside. These well-connected points would become metropolises bloated with rural poor. Such poor do acquire urban characteristics over time, but the changes come slowly. Moreover, those families that have experienced great losses in members and proportions retain as a prime objective the recovery of their former dimensions—in numbers of members as well as social status and property. Small family size seems all right for others, but not for them. Thus it is quite logical that the longest lag times in acceptance and practice of birth control are expected to be encountered among these poorest refugees. Initially one should anticipate natural increases of 3-4% per year in this group. These rates are equivalent to those presently found in the poorer sections of Mexican, Brazilian, Philippine, and Indonesian metropolises, where cultural factors strongly encourage large family size. The exceptions to this rate that are reported would be happy findings that should be investigated in depth, because they would identify instances where social action in the near future could be undertaken to reduce the strain upon resources caused by population.

Migrants *pulled* to cities by the "bright lights" are quite different. They are drawn from the new generation in the villages, farmsteads, and towns, many of them expecting little opportunity at home beyond scratching out a submarginal existence. Therefore they consider known alternatives very seriously. The highest aspiration and wildest dream is a metropolis like Paris, London, or Madrid, or the cities of California, but all of those centers are exclusive and strictly enforce laws to prevent entry of poor alien immigrants. The most feasible course is to gamble upon a city that is open and accessible, preferably one which already contains kinfolk and former neighbors. There they have a hope of discovering a niche where life is better than back at the farmstead, village, or town.

A steady, infiltrating stream of these migrants moves into almost every city, and a counterstream carries them back to the towns and villages. The hard-pressed opportunity-seeking stratum from the hinterland in a region or nation in the first stages of urbanization exploits the city by a pattern illustrated in figure 4.1. For each of them the city is a boomtown where one plays the long shots, doing his best with education, relatives, friends, and a diligence reminiscent of Horatio Alger novels, to improve the odds of finding a place in society more secure than a grinding existence in the village. The typical migrant dreams of winning a stake which can be converted into land and status back home.

The behavior of an individual attracted to the city has many regular features. For example, since membership in the social circle in the home community to which he belongs must be kept secure, the bonds to kinfolk must be reinforced; the inmigrant to the city is therefore coerced to remit much of his hard-won surplus (typically 40% of cash income, if he is regularly employed and single) to his rural relations or sponsors. He is expected to make several visits a year on appropriate occasions, always bringing gifts to assure the significant others in his life that his loyalties remain with them. A large share of the population remaining in the village, and many towns in depressed areas as well, comes to be increasingly dependent upon the wages and salaries earned in the metropolises of the developing countries. At the same time a significant part of the non-working population of the rural community has been displaced to the city, many on short stays intended to introduce them to city life.

One of the most pervasive human dramas of our period in history is played out in many languages and dialects—the tentative preliminary visits as a gawking stranger, determinedly exploring a hazardous urban environment, searching for a livelihood, acquiring the art of self-defense, joining the gang or community offering collective security, discerning opportunities for improvement of status, and cannily grasping them. But our sympathies for the plight of the inmigrant should not be allowed to obscure the social mechanisms at work. Figure 4.1 represents a series of semiquantitative deductions and should be regarded as

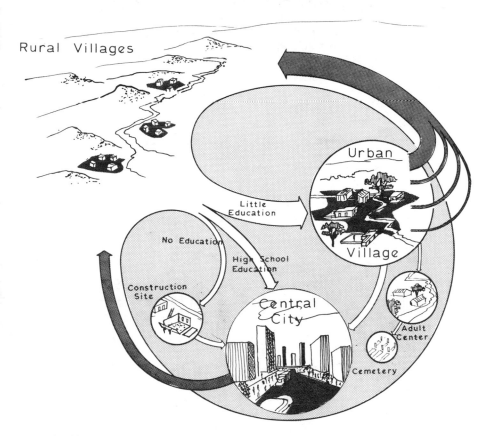

Figure 4.1 The Process of Urbanization in a Low-Income Society Develops Feedbacks
A growing metropolis attracts many ethnic groups, each representing a pool of culturally
homogeneous rural places. Streams to the city tend to diverge according to the amount of
schooling acquired before migration. The settlements may be a dense form of village—often a
squatter community—which modernizes migrants at their own pace, or temporary camps
associated with construction, which induce less adaptation. School graduates and skilled
workers often immerse themselves in the central city. The counterstream is made up of a few
successes and many failures, but mostly of persons called back to handle family affairs. An
exurban backflow arises in the second and succeeding generations; it seeks release from the
stresses of the metropolis. Breaking up families by migration creates the need for retirement
homes (adult centers) and for expanding provisions for cemeteries or cremation.

probably true in the aggregate, but for each metropolitan region it represents only a series of propositions which are to be tested through the collection of data before making major commitments.[5]

1. Source: The pools of culturally homogeneous rural dwellers potentially interested in going to cities. Each "pool" contains anywhere from a few thousand to a few million people who have adopted the same customs, practice the same religion, speak the same dialect, and have become closely interrelated through marriage. Even in China, where homogenization has perhaps gone furthest, a metropolis will be drawing inmigrants from scores of such pools; elsewhere it is often hundreds. The portion of the population potentially interested contains almost all the young in the 17-25 years of age range, others who become disengaged (because of death in the family, loss of employment, bankruptcy, feuding, and so on), and those who have a family that has already become established in the metropolis.

2. Streams. The main flow from each pool quickly finds the settlements in the city that speak the home dialect and maintain almost daily connections with the home district. Religious leaders in such settlements often spend almost full time expediting social contacts between the home district, its urban village, and the rest of the city. A secondary flow is made up of less educated, often illiterate, and landless people who go to construction sites and live in barracks, squatter areas, and similar supposedly temporary settlements with plural ethnic background. Such settlements often also contain individuals who were unfortunate in life, lost their position and status, and now quickly rise to leadership in these mixed lower-class communities, and may become celebrated figures. A stream that increases in dimension over time is the rural educated population that seeks white-collar employment in the city. It acculturates very rapidly, often choosing rooming houses in ethnically mixed central neighborhoods in the metropolis. Two other streams are sometimes significant—one of them being through military or merchant marine service, which produces self-confidence in pluralistic situations, and the other through cheap provincial colleges which generate aspirations for civil service and subprofessional work in the metropolis, while at the same time attenuating the bonds to family and the community of origin.

3. Settlement. To the inmigrant the urban parishes and districts are the nearest thing to a homelike village, even though they may be held together by no more than a church, coffee house, delicatessen, or tavern. To the long-term city dweller they appear to be a complex melange of foreigners whose behavior expresses the full range of assimilation into city life and where distinctly different types live virtually on top of each other. Lonely visitors and insecure inmigrants head for certain streets or intersections dominated by their own people—men who are known by name back home. These settlements are regarded as permanent by their inhabitants, as if they were county seats, but experience shows that they are often obliterated after two to five decades of existence owing to invasion by neighboring ethnic groups or by the need for metropolitan improvements. A few families flourish in such communities, often those with many sons, and they build new houses in the old areas to demonstrate that they have become established in the metropolis but do not wish to give up their close ethnic associations. These leading families often sponsor inmigrants, thus creating a following or constituency useful in politics.

4. Counterstream. A very mixed group decides to quit the city and return home. Land buyers strike it rich and use their stake to regain a status the family had previously lost, perhaps moving up a notch by building a grand house. Tradesmen take back a scarce skill (e.g., welder, electrician, diesel mechanic). Some return to become head of a household or a family enterprise; some merely to provide the labor needed to work land that is held by the family. Quite a few pensioners retire to the village, and they are joined by those who become nostalgic for country life. A high proportion go back defeated by the big city—having lost their employment, they could not pick up enough income to survive. They are often indistinguishable from those who become sick and cannot hold a full-time job. Finally there are some who are being hunted in the city, either by rival gangs or by police, and hope to find security among kinfolk and clansmen at home.

5. Exurban backflow. Some people have lived all their lives in the central city and suburb but find reasons to leave. The wealthier group migrates voluntarily, buying into the back country communities by setting up estates, villas, or reconditioning old residences. It initiates a largely urban life-style in the countryside, traveling frequently back and forth, and receiving much mail. Surplus graduates are unwilling emigrants from the city looking for employment in their occupation—school teaching, dentistry, managing an agency, sales. Finally there are the dropouts, often living in communes, who occupy aging villas or resorts as a healthier alternative to skid rows and lower bohemias in the metropolis.

6. Retirement centers. This phenomenon is a natural outgrowth of rapid metropolitan and political change, occurring coincidentally with the urban transition. Virtually every long-lived institution—church, labor union, lodge, burial society, or alumni group—is used to sponsor appropriate retirement centers in the metropolitan area. Decaying resorts and parklike areas are preferred. Because of rapidly increasing longevity, but lower than average education and income, these centers become a rapidly expanding welfare problem, which arises directly from the ways in which people are pensioned off and their incompatibility with the improvements installed by neighboring urbanites. The transition from an extended and joint family organization to nuclear families and a reduction in numbers of living children simultaneous with markedly improved health greatly increase the proportion of elderly, dependent, tradition-oriented women in particular.

7. Funerals and cemeteries. The city must complete the cycle that leads from birth or migration as entry, to death as exit by paying its respects to the departed. People's lives leave physical traces after them that last for decades, sometimes for centuries; In each society the living city seems to find a way of becoming a kind of monument to its departed citizens through preserving names, images, buildings, and gardens. Although death is a necessary feature of any living system, it bears a peculiar taboo for serious discussion in metropolitan culture, and little is written about its place in urban order. After death, the name must be removed from many registers, membership lists, and accounts; estates must be properly transferred to the living. When heirs cannot be found—a not unusual occurrence when inmigrants came from a distance or when the country was disturbed by famine or revolution—the title to land may be clouded, and further development of the surrounding block is inhibited. The disposal of bodies often presents problems.

In the growth of Western-style metropolises the place of final repose often becomes an embarrassment to succeeding generations; the municipal governments need to dig up old bones and rebury them in order to make way for transport improvements or denser housing. In India there are sometimes occasions when the fuel supply is insufficient for cremations, and partially burned corpses are found impeding navigation in channels. In China the amount of land dedicated to honoring ancestors became too great, so a quiet reform has been instituted by central direction.

Pressures created in the growing cities by human needs for living space are matched only by the demand for circulation space and parking areas on the part of the operators of vehicles. Drivers want their vehicle close at hand, yet they wish to move freely, unimpeded by other vehicles or by people, once a destination has been chosen. The relationship between a man and his automotive vehicle often becomes addictive, obsessive, and compulsive; therefore many apparently unreasonable behaviors and decisions must be anticipated. Several quite different urban problems arise directly from this love-hate relationship; they will be taken up later when we are searching for specific solutions for transport and land use relationships, but a systematic or ecological issue concerning an infiltration process that has become an integral part of the urban transition must be introduced at this point. Curiously, there seems never to have been a systematic presentation of the process, although it has been commented upon for at least a half a century.

SPACE PRESSURES FROM THE AUTOMOTIVE POPULATION

The niches in the urban community now occupied by the automotive vehicle population were previously held by animals—horses, donkeys, oxen—and by low-status human residents such as coolies, porters, and carters. Maintaining livestock in a densely populated area is often immensely inconvenient because of the bulk of the stored feed, its readiness to burn, and the diffusion of filth into the alleys, streets, and other public places. Yet they were absolutely necessary to the functioning of the city. It was recognized that the densities of the fly, flea, and lice populations were enormously increased by the presence of such animals, and the purity of the water was often threatened. Thus dysentery was endemic, and sporadic outbreaks of cholera and typhoid could be traced to this sector of the city. The humans competing with animal power, and often living in close proximity, were particularly subject to tuberculosis and venereal disease. The associated stockyards, slaughterhouses, and tanneries were a smelly, unhealthy abscess in a city, which everyone was glad to give up if transport services could be maintained.

As the trolley car, bus, and truck were introduced, the remainder of the metropolis expanded, while the precincts with large animal populations remained constant in size and were then redeveloped. The slaughterhouses were removed to peripheral sites, and the tanneries followed. This process of displacement occurred in America between 1890 and 1930, with relics surviving until 1970; cities in Western Europe, Latin America, and Japan followed, with a lag of a decade or two. The process is still under way in many metropolises of Asia and Africa. The fact that Indian cities leave cattle to roam the streets seems quaint to others, yet even there the policy of sequestering them in far suburban "cow colonies" is almost complete.

Infiltration of vehicles begins at the assembly plants, the places where vehicles come into existence, which are most often sited now not far from harbors in coastal metropolises. A huge amount of international trade has been generated in components, subassemblies, appliances, and plant machinery, so that each contemporary automobile is composed of manufactured products from a score or more metropolitan areas in perhaps a dozen countries, even if it is finally assembled in Detroit. The assembly plants for very light vehicles, including motorbikes, are not quite so restricted in siting, so that an isolated city with no better connections than a rail junction and a highway, but a tradition in fine metalworking, may be successful in such a business. Rarely will a coastal metropolis produce all classes of vehicle; it will specialize in some, producing for export, and it will import others.

Just off the assembly line, automotive vehicles are passively transported by ship, barge, or rail to the market where they are sold off to become slaves (in the technical sense of the word) of humans. Most of the vehicles introduced into the poorer metropolitan regions are public carriers or movers of freight. As per capita wealth grows, the proportion of private passenger cars also increases, eventually reaching a stage where autos are almost "symbiotic" with suburban households and the urbanized component in the exurbs.

Automotive vehicles, like people or animals or plants, may malfunction or be damaged in accidents. Most metropolitan areas evolve special districts for their repair. Some ethnic groups may specialize in that kind of work—in parts of India the Sikhs hold a near monopoly. Therefore certain urban villages adjoining the central city will create a complex of shops dedicated to salvage, repair, and maintenance. Thus the human ecology is strongly shifted, and the spatial structure of the total community is strongly revamped as the vehicular population expands and ages.

After automotive imports have proceeded for about two decades, the vehicular graveyards present a serious problem. Initially there are very few organizations or procedures for the decomposition of big pieces of a worn-out and abandoned vehicle, but sooner or later each major city installs a scrap furnace and rubber reprocessing plant, and scavengers soon can dispose of the larger pieces of scrap. However, as the road network into the interior improves, older and more obsolete vehicles that have escaped the high attrition caused by accidents in urban streets make up a large part of the counterstream that diffuses through various channels into the back country. There they may be incapacitated for lack of parts and eventually become inoperable. Salvage in those locales is casual and scrap collection does not pay; the skeletons of ten to fifty year old vehicles then tend to accumulate, creating a natural resource for rural inhabitants and an eyesore for tourists.

The rate of growth of the vehicular population (calculated by taking the output from assembly plants, adding the net difference between imports and exports, subtracting the retirement rate, and dividing by the number licensed for operation) greatly depends upon the growth of support systems. The cost of the street, highway, and bridge system tends to become more expensive per vehicle added as the population of vehicles increases. Their energy supply was experiencing constant or declining costs until about 1971 because large reserves of fossil fuels were opened up, but this situation is now changing sharply, and energy is expected to become relatively scarce. (The prospects for automotive fuels are taken up in the discussion of the total energy outlook in Chapter 7.)

This focus upon metropolitan vehicles has left out an account of other, more external modes of movement—rail, water, air, pipeline. Huge tie-ups are possible at points of interchange and break-of-bulk. Experience shows that the interfaces between the modes of movement require very sensitive planning, and since there are few, if any, precedents for such design efforts in developing metropolises, costly mistakes are likely. Truly serious error wastes more than human time and capital; it brings adaptive change to a slow, grinding halt and deflects growth to other metropolises. (The bottleneck at the Howrah bridge had this effect on Calcutta.) The questions about circulation in cities undergoing rapid growth require special attention; belatedly these matters are getting systematic review by international insitutions.

STANDARD INFRASTRUCTURE DEVELOPMENT

Early in 1972 the Asian Development Bank produced a report for a Southeast Asian region aimed at providing a rationale for future investments in transportation.[6] With the aid of American, European, and Asian consultants a systematic analysis of prospective development was prepared in such a way that competing and conflicting proposals for spatial integration could be judged for a part of the world that was somewhat more progressive than the average among the less-developed countries but separated physically by many barriers and also deeply troubled politically. The report provides an excellent up-to-date example of the huge intellectual momentum of Western technological and organizational concepts and introduces us to an easily pictured future involving automobile-oriented urban regions with central areas served by subways. The projected urban growth rates are respectably modest as compared to the recent past (table 2), yet by 1990, which is the far end of the slice of future being reviewed, Manila and Djakarta would have reached the dimensions and structure of Tokyo in the mid-1980s with Saigon not far behind. The normal expectation that their growth should be accelerating in the 1980s, because urbanization in their projection was not absorbing the population growth in the countryside, is not included, nor are the implications explored of their size surpassing that of contemporary Tokyo shortly thereafter, with many more inmigrants still to be added.

Although the defects are serious, overview studies such as this one more than pay their costs. They put into perspective the claims advanced by local political groups, and they illuminate an insufficiency of relatively productive proposals among those put forward by the longest-established bureaucracies such as the agencies concerned with harbors, railroads, and (sometimes) intercity roads. Also, when aggregate projections of the dimensions of growth for a multination region are prepared, and these are then compared with the projects for infrastructure which are actually being generated, it becomes apparent that no provisions are being made to install much of the infrastructure in greatest demand. In Southeast Asia the greatest shortfall in programmed expenditure clearly exists at the nodes in the transport network that are also bulk-breaking and transfer points. Coastal metropolises in particular need careful physical planning of public sector projects to match even huger investments in the private sector in trucks, cars, jitneys, and buses.

Anomalies begin to appear when projections are made according to presently accepted professional practices. An excellent illustration of unlikely outcomes is provided by the estimation of the growth of the vehicular population. The Asian Development Bank team expected the number of motor vehicles to expand as a function of income until it reached as a limit the level of 400 motor vehicles per 1,000 population, which is the approximate level for the

Table 2
Growth of Human and Vehicular Population in Southeast Asia (% per year)

	1960-1970			1970-1990		
	Urban Population	Intercity Traffic	Vehicle Stock[a]	Urban Population	Intercity Traffic	Vehicle Stock[a]
Indonesia	4.5	9.7	6.9	4.3	8.9	12.0
Singapore	2.1	7.3	9.7	1.8	7.6	7.6
Malaysia	5.1	10.4	9.8	4.4	10.1	10.1
Thailand	6.8	14.0	13.7	6.3	11.1	11.1
Laos	n.a.	n.a.	10.4	n.a.	10.9	10.9
Viet Nam (S)	n.a.	n.a.	9.1	n.a.	11.1	11.1
Philippines	4.5	9.1	11.5	8.5	10.1	10.1

Source: Southeast Asian Regional Transport Survey, Manila, 1972.
[a]Four or more wheels, self-propelled, using public roads.

Processes of Transitional Urbanization   123

more affluent portions of North America. As with a living population, the land-based motor vehicle "population explosion" was projected to follow a logistic curve, and the parameters for the logistic were derived from recent history in America, Europe, and Japan, where income, indeed, was the prime determinant. This procedure seemed to slight Indonesia; so the parameters were adjusted arbitrarily to allow that country to catch up to 60% of the Philippines. No adjustments were made for human population density in places like Singapore or Java, where parking space for vehicles would be competing actively with living space for humans. Street and highway investments were then estimated as a function of vehicular population, as were investments in petroleum refining and distribution.

As a forecast—an assessment of the forces of the present that shape human affairs in the future—this report of the Asian Development Bank is realistic for most of the time span it covers. Mimicry of Western modernization and urbanization dominates change in the region. Moreover, the major multinational firms in vehicle manufacturing began committing themselves to large investments for the production and assembly of automotives in the region shortly after the report was published. Competition between them for the Southeast Asian market will fit automobiles into every possible niche. Therefore, loans made by the Bank for the short-to-medium term that are based upon this projection are quite safe. Beyond 1985, however, the forces it ignores are likely to dominate the situation.

Taken as development policy the ADB report falls into a foreseeable trap; it fails to take into account the growing scarcity of fossil fuels and the foreign exchange problems introduced by a rising demand for gasoline. It also omits from consideration the backlash in public concern about air pollution, which will be directed at pollution caused by the auto supply industries almost as much as that arising out of exhaust from the cars. Finally, the capital expenditures made necessary to deal with the congestion brought about by the much-advertised "my car," that is, the privatization of the automotive vehicle population, would postpone completion of the urban transition on the part of the human population. Private cars accentuate the visible inequities in society that lead to political disruption. For densely populated regions the invasion of the private automobile is as much a prelude to disaster as a major epidemic, and addiction to automobile use can be as serious a reduction of future options as the compulsions brought about by drugs.

What would a balanced policy for vehicles look like? Their function during the transitional period is to serve man while he builds his urban habitat. Huge increases in the quantity of goods must be carried more efficiently than beasts of burden can manage, while human movements, needed to create and maintain organizations, must be facilitated. We assume from the beginning that public utilities moving water, gas, and fuel through grids in the city will function as effectively as they can, but where they fail to keep up with demand, the extra load must be borne by the vehicles.

Our attention is focused first on the activities of those vehicles that are most crucial to urban life, and therefore the highest prices would normally be paid for their services, should they remain scarce. The transport of food and essential raw materials falls into this category. Vehicles engaged in this service will be mostly based in the hinterland, integrating the movement of produce to market. In some parts of the world these vehicles displace oxen, buffalo, donkeys, and other beasts of burden, allowing land devoted to fodder to be switched to new crops. Mines and forests tend to support larger vehicles than farms. Where really heavy-duty movements are involved, an extension of the railroad network is called for, and behemoths capable of hauling thousands of tons are put into service. People often ride along with the cargo.

In irrigated, densely settled countryside, such as Java, Bangladesh, Ceylon, or Nigeria (generalizing now from the Asian Development Bank's exercise), the population of trucks, buses, jitneys, motorized carts, and scooters should rise to a ratio of one to every dozen or so humans. To these must be added variable numbers of off-the-road vehicles, such as tractors, bulldozers, and the like. The arteries assigned for the movement of these vehicles will need bridges, many widened routes, and controlled intersections, although they will hardly ever need to be advanced to the level of an American or Japanese-style limited-access freeway. Improvements for speeding flow are needed most for the routes that converge upon the metropolis.

Vehicles moving from countryside to city and back accommodate the movement of people into the city and bring bearers of modern ideas back to the countryside. Making trips to the city easier and cheaper brings more women into the passenger flow, which greatly assists social modernization, stimulates their education, and expedites many social adjustments, including the acceptance of family planning. After the harvest is in, the vehicular population is used for making pilgrimages, negotiating marriages, and performing other socially integrative functions that are important, although they do not contribute to solving the problems of completing the urban transition. Therefore the introduction of vehicles should be encouraged, mainly through the rural credit system. It can easily be kept from getting out of hand through the use of licensing and financial controls.

Within the borders of urban regions a much more careful and detailed overview is required. Congestion—the throttling of urban movements—remains a constant threat. At the growth rates expected for these metropolises congestion may spread from a few afflicted locales, such as are to be found even in the best of cities, and stultify a whole zone within a year or two. When the human density in a district is medium to high (greater than 20,000 per square mile or 800 per hectare), the population of privately held vehicles must be severely restricted. In part this can be done by requiring that each owner designate an off-street parking place that he has owned or rented. At these densities the land value for parking (even in a parking structure, if it should be made available) will usually exceed the cost of a new vehicle and act as a deterrent that is graduated according to the degree of crowding. The car craze is so strong, however, that it will usually be necessary to add a sizable registration or excise tax—whatever is most readily collectible. Part of the tax returns should go toward maintaining a relatively incorruptible enforcement and traffic police system. The remainder must be allocated to the stimulation of alternate modes of movement, especially bicycles (where very light three- and four-wheel vehicles can be accommodated along with the more common two wheelers), since they are particularly appropriate for the tropical metropolises under heavy pressure to grow. Another alternative is a dial-a-ride service ("demand-actuated" is one of the technical terms), which may need to be reinforced with portable telephone connections, because a standard-size vehicle can produce ten to a hundred times as many passenger trips per day as a privately owned car, with roughly equal convenience after one takes parking at the destination into account. When flows along certain channels become large, the system needs to be flexible enough to allow the passengers to be switched to bus or rail mass transit.

In such a transitional metropolis one visualizes as much as half the traffic on urban streets taking the form of light vans and passenger-or-cargo dual carriers. Traffic jams will be greatest around break-of-bulk points, such as harbors, produce markets, wholesaling areas, railway terminals, airports, printing plants, department stores, and breweries. Containerization would greatly speed goods movement operations; multiple-shift operation also helps. The investment in vehicles and associated infrastructure can be kept low, but greater demands are made upon human organization as a kind of trade-off. Organizations must be able to keep the inventory of containers low by preventing pile-ups, and they must be capable of managing work at odd hours.

Experience shows that transport is too valuable, and expensive, to be provided as a free good in the city. Prices are needed as signals to users of transport services, so that they will play the game of cost minimization. Prices must reflect not only the marginal costs of production for services, which vary by time of day and season, as well as benefits resulting from such factors as the creation of prestige locations, but also the costs that arise in the form of delays imposed upon others or resultant air pollution and noise nuisances. Excises have a very great potential for rectifying the social damage done by the attachment of a human to his car. Transport vices may be taxed through surcharges on normal selling prices in the same way that vices associated with tobacco, alcohol, or gambling are restricted. The effects of an outright ban are undesirable because they lead to a black market and a siphoning of funds into the pockets of risk-takers willing to work outside the law.

It should be noted that all these recommendations imply a unified overall transport policy-making institution for each metropolis, allowing it to take advantage of geography and special opportunities—a condition that is barely coming into existence anywhere in the world as yet and is certainly not found in poor countries. National planning and budget agencies, however, may reorganize themselves so as to achieve most of these rationalizations.

TERRITORIAL EXPANSION AT THE PERIPHERY

Growing cities have a way of transforming the environment as they occupy new territories. The visual features are modified step by step in a fairly predictable sequence. The natural history of a sizable parcel of land that is subject to overspill from a growing metropolis in a developing society reveals many situations familiar to Western urban residents, but some that are surprising. The following account picks up such an area, describes its recent past, and then pictures what is expected to happen, basing its projections on transformations being effected at the present time elsewhere on the urban periphery.

SCENARIO SIX

Metropolitan
Community
Achieved by
Ecological
Succession

After the disturbances of World War II a prototypical Southeast Asian community we shall call S . . . moved back to an agrarian equilibrium. The living system was dominated by man and buffalo, and the surface by rice paddy and carp ponds, with special fields set aside for sugarcane, yams, Chinese cabbage, tobacco, and minor crops. The skyline was broken by spreading mango trees, small stands of mixed forest, and, on the sandier strips, palm trees. The roads were usually raised several feet above the surrounding tilled land. Programs for the banishment of parasites causing malaria came along with the restoration of order; their success brought about increased alertness in the human population and markedly increased survival rates.

Closeness to a primate city distinguished S . . . from other such districts in only a few observable ways. There were more chickens and ducks, and citrus dominated many well-drained copses. Cottage roofs had more tile and, therefore, less thatch. The marketplace was relatively large. These differences were a matter of proportions, since the elements were the same as in other agrarian districts.

When change came, it was brought by the road. Some aged buses began to appear, providing service at convenient times and to preferred destinations. Oxcarts gave way to noisy three-wheel scooter vans, which were displaced in turn by marvelously decorated five-ton trucks. Pedicabs showed up around the marketplace instead of traditional rickshaws, and the bicycle population boomed. Shortly after the electric power highline was introduced, a string of shops appeared along the road on the edge of S . . . village, half of which were devoted to truck and bicycle repair and salvage, but where grimy boy-mechanics took on pumps and sewing machines as well. Because they had no adequate means for disposing of motor oil, nearby ponds and slow-moving canals acquired oil films. As vehicles came to be used for harvest, the embankments that separated fields were widened, and a lace network of tracks evolved, much better defined near the road than away from it. New houses for the master mechanics appeared in most quarters of the village, but some also went up at a distance, connected only by a bicycle track, and unshaded by trees. Very unusual!

The road was resurfaced and widened. Culverts were reconstructed. The normal speed of movement doubled. Man and beast were honked off to the side, forced often to create a relief track, and their presence on the road began to decline except during harvest periods. Jitney cars and light trucks appeared on the scene to pick up pedestrians when hailed.

A factory appeared on the edge of town (for that is what S . . . had become) nearest the city. It had corrugated asbestos concrete roofing and many more windows than a traditional structure, a fifty-foot brick chimney, a storage yard for drums, crates, spools, rejects, and a coke pile, all surrounded by a high wire fence. The low-lying lot next to it filled with rubble to expedite drainage, and then another factory appeared. The hillside quarry that had supplied the crushed rock for the road sprouted a plant that produced drainage tile and concrete blocks.

The land itself began to shrivel and die. Paddy fields were abandoned in many places and became dry weeds or swamp holes into which miscellaneous debris was being dumped. In some areas the skin was scraped from the soil by bulldozers, producing violently red rectangular wounds, which thereafter spawned large establishments with gatekeepers or guardposts and asphalted ways leading to the main road. Within walking distance of such places, sometimes immediately adjacent, a scramble of huts, puny obscene parodies of the local building styles, erupted simultaneously to house the antlike construction crews. Thereafter a new subpopulation of vehicles began to infiltrate the road network— jeeps, military command cars, cars with government insignia, chauffeur-driven limousines. On one large patch of land, a flock of airplanes distributed themselves behind revetments or clustered around a flimsy metal skin structure.

The road was widened again, and the strings of dingy shops, repair stations, and salvage piles that had accumulated on the roadside disappeared in the process. Occasional attempts at landscaped fronts were introduced in their stead, but most of the view from the road into the corridor of development created by it remained determinedly utilitarian, especially along the hivelike apartment blocks that occupied major tracts.

Now, on the sides of the corridor and away from the road, capillarylike lanes have sprouted walled or fenced plots, each of which has filled in over the course of a year or two with one or more houses displaying various middle-class characteristics. Simultaneously, market centers have expanded by spilling out into the streets and by converting nearby houses into offices and shops. Though the old village can be readily distinguished from the raw new development by its sturdy spreading trees, and because its cellulation is irregular as compared to the rectangular grid superimposed upon the land built upon most recently, S . . . , the old village name, is now assigned to a peripheral district of the metropolis containing ten to thirty times as many people as had tilled the soil before. Some of them came out from the city, but most are members of the literate surplus population from towns and villages in the interior.

Judged from the road, S . . . has become a solid new addition to the metropolis, and it is already 80-90% built up. The filling of the gaps will be determined by the neighbors, but raised quotations for land will affect the process. A view from the air at present shows that S . . . is part of a relatively thin psuedopod stretching out into the green countryside, supported by a black artery, which, in turn, is connected to a gridwork of thin black (shading off into brown and red) capillaries. The bypassed green blobs could remain as parks, but more likely they will be similarly transformed in the succeeding decade.

LANDSCAPES TO CITYSCAPES

Users of environments are guided about in them by cues and signs with which various sequential behaviors are connected. In an agrarian community like the S . . . of the scenario, children follow their parents and record the large forms of the familiar landscape in their memory. As they grow older, they are permitted to explore on their own initiative and, as they become adults, develop a personal repertory of signs much richer than is ever revealed by conversations about the environment. Domesticated animals develop such repertories also; for example, when their attention switches from generally familiar impressions of shape, smell, texture of soil under foot, and resonance to a unique configuration, known to be associated with a path to home and reward, they accelerate their pace quite noticeably.

In places that have been settled for many generations, the signs are also related to local history. Fields may be connected to former owners or past battles, and trees to recent incidents. Myths of long standing surround wells in such communities, and are frequently alluded to during conversations among villagers in the presence of visitors.

A few signs connect the village with a high tradition, such as the architecture of a temple, church, monastery, or school. Others, such as a policeman's uniform or a flagpole, will remind people of their relations with higher political or civil authority. The roadside will be much richer in such signs than the network of paths leading away from it because the diversity of travelers is greater.

The signs of change associated with modernization appear first on the road itself. Vehicles with new insignia, people in different dress, cargo with new shapes and different labels, together with unprecedented noises and smells. A practiced eye will discriminate among all the signs to discover those placed by urban-oriented distribution systems—from tobacco advertising to cooking oil, kerosene, matches, baby food, newspapers, bicycles, and sewing machines, all of which have brand names displayed in characteristic styles. Their containers have readily recognized shapes in paper, cloth, tin, glass, and rubber, even when reduced to salvage. Evidences of the introduction of beer and sweet carbonated fruit drinks are found in both the advertising and the discard heaps close to the road; they are followed by notices extolling exotic varieties of brandy and whiskey.

The arrival of widespread automotive vehicle usage introduces a myriad of indirect changes in the landscape. Many more alien artifacts diffuse into the community because the carrying capacity of a truck per year is a hundredfold greater than that of an oxcart. Since the urban eye notes most quickly the penetration of urban images and their destabilizing effect upon the more integrated background of traditional signs the visitor from the city is impelled to lament the decline of standards in the village. With dismay he notes that many of his urban vehicles spend their last days at the limits of their range, and are merely pushed aside after suffering a final breakdown, their skeletons rusting away for decades in full public view. The more matter-of-fact attitude of a local resident sees these signs as reminders of the follies of known personalities or of memorable events. He also sees them as indicators to resources much superior to those available before, which can be drawn upon as needed. The battered, blown-out truck tire, for example, can be converted into several sturdy, long-lasting pairs of sandals with only a few hours of effort.

Another big transition occurs with the stringing of live wires—telegraph, telephone, and electric power. Radio used to to follow right behind (except for battery sets possessed by people of high status), but with transistors the diffusion of radio precedes invasion by the power grid and the telephone. Now the television antenna is recognized by everyone as a sign of the local frontier for modern metropolitan culture.

Access to nonindigenous materials of construction via truck delivery and the opportunities provided by electricity for lighting, entertainment, and production bring about changes in the architecture. Many adaptations are merely stuck onto old forms, but elsewhere a direct borrowing from the city is evident, as at the cinema house. A few instances of new construction show serious attempts to rationalize a life that uses modern artifacts for continuing old routines of production and distribution.

The appearance of instances of modern cosmopolitan architecture constitutes a declaration that the city has arrived to stay. A bank, a vigorous department in the government, or the new generation in a commercial family might opt for these images in an attempt to establish a claim for leadership during the transition to city life. Much greater attention is paid to public appearance where street boundaries are marked by curbs, drains, and sidewalks, especially where various other middle-class images (as in clothing and furniture) are displayed.

Eventually, the fields of S . . . are filled with a mixture of incrementally planned settlements, some stimulated by separate government and corporate entities and a much larger number by small enterprises engaged in producing dwellings. Whatever was sacred, whether shrine or burial place, becomes a relic or ruin and often leaves behind no more than a name on the land reproduced in street signs and maps. A few sturdy trees survive, but their outlines have been changed by the need to pass wires through or around them.

This invasion of the countryside by the shapes, signs, and images of urban society is a natural process that reflects the dominance of cities in our era. Politically powerful forces install their images at points suited to imposing control over public movements and flows of information. Economically effective organizations take over both marketplaces and industries, and they set up competitive eye-catching signs along the paths to the market. Culturally influential associations enter through the school, cinema, newspaper, and telephone to introduce approved images. (Note that the graffiti produced by the underground counterculture rarely ever penetrates to the periphery, and when it does, the locale had previously not been wholly rural but had served as a resort for intellectuals or as an urban colony.) Outcomes of the invasion from the metropolis have a localized semipermanence—wherever colonizing-type development such as tracts of standardized small homes has emerged—but in most places a succession process is underway. Although this process keeps the urban system in flux, it continuously accumulates a greater density of signs and images over time. If one maintained a reasonably exhaustive list of all the kinds of images present in the cityscape (conceptually equivalent to species in the ecosystem), he would find that some become extinct, a much larger number are imported, and a few evolve *de novo*.[7] Thus the *information* present in the cityscape (the sum of the probabilities of finding a specific kind of image or sign multiplied by the logarithm of that probability for the total population of signs and images) not only will have expanded manyfold in the transition to cityscape but, short of catastrophe, will continue to increase as one cityscape succeeds another on the same site.

As the metropolis grows, what was once unspoiled countryside first becomes outskirts, then fringe, periphery, and finally interior, or fully consolidated urban development. Soon afterward it densifies and reorganizes to handle the flows that go through it, always adapting to the total mass of the surrounding metropolis. Houses are rebuilt to

CATCHING UP TO TOKYO

accommodate roomers, and small food shops are set up in the side streets and alleys. When the streets become torrents of buses, cabs, jitneys, vans, and motorbikes, pedestrian overpasses are constructed at key intersections. Each community in the metropolis takes on one or more metropolitan functions—here it may be wholesaling, there it may be music publishing, and down the street it might be the formulation and packaging of medicinals—each of them a cluster of related activities. It was noted earlier that restrained extrapolations of urbanization in Southeast Asia implied a Djakarta at Tokyo scale in two decades, with Saigon's dimensions not much less. What does this mean for such cities and their populations? Tokyo appears to be close to the limit that this kind of incremental urbanization can reach. Commuters from the fringes now travel about a hundred minutes each way by bus and train so that home to work and return consumes four hours a day, with perhaps half of it spent straphanging in a tightly packed aisle—if a strap can be reached! Out of every ten persons added to the growing edge of Tokyo, one or more will have to pay at least that price in order to obtain work at high enough pay to enable the others to live at a reasonably adequate level. Anyone analyzing the crowds of the city in the afternoon rush can spot the long-distance commuter by the amount of fatigue that is showing; it is equaled only by that of working mothers on full-time jobs.

An alternative for the urban resident is that of paying a higher rent so as to live closer to his employment. There he competes for space with small families containing two or more workers, which bid up rents to levels equal to half a paycheck or greater. In a family with one salary this leaves very little for other necessities. It may also be possible to find a place to live in a highly polluted manufacturing district, with drifts of fly ash during dry periods and eye irritation a hundred nights per year. There are better places to live in the metropolis, but they are predominantly tied to one's job and acquired after accumulating seniority, acting as a side payment for bondage to a large bureaucratic organization. One is required to leave the neighborhood if one leaves the organization, and sometimes upon promotion within the hierarchy as well. Most people feel trapped by the metropolis, almost to the same extent that they might have felt trapped leasing a parcel of land and living in a village a generation or two earlier, since each of the apparent alternatives for improvement of conditions of life is closed off by intolerably high costs or insufficient social status. They cannot even "get away" during their leisure time. On regular holidays all the accessible parks, beaches, and stadia are filled to overflowing; life is spent moving from one queue to the next.

MEGALOPOLIS AND ECUMENOPOLIS

As a result of these conditions, a large number of Tokyo residents, from executives to manual workers, are actively plotting their escape. In doing so, however, they want to bring education, health, transport, electric power service, television connections, and similar amenities with them. Thus metropolitan Tokyo will invade the peripheral countryside, and exurbs, later to be satellites, will crystal-ize, alleviating some but not all of the problems the refugees had fled. Metropolitan Tokyo will probably start losing population very soon, and towns or cities around the hundred-kilometer circumference line will begin to sprout modern eight-story apartment houses and walk-up garden apartments at a rapid rate. New transport lines on the standards of the Tokaido express will have to be installed at tremendous capital cost. VSTOL aircraft will serve a net-work of centers in the Kanto plain and beyond. For rea-sons elaborated later, important portions of the surface of Tokyo Bay will be occupied.

In the course of the next generation the Tokyo resident will find that he is still trapped but that the cage is much larger and more individuals are given freedom to roam the whole zoo—perhaps thirty million people will be sharing an area ten times as large, as against the present twenty-four million within commuting range. Perhaps half the land area will still be in intensive gardens, orchards, golf courses, parks, and newly established mariculture in depolluted waters, though only ritual quantities of rice paddy will be retained. The rest of the Japanese archipelago will be reached by many millions of people annually, while many hundreds of thousands will take trips overseas.

A higher level of organization is already imposing itself upon Tokyo—a Tokaido megalopolis is coming into being. It is already far more integrated and matured than the special agglomeration in the northeastern United States that impelled Gottmann to use the term. The same four hours of daily commuting that has seemed to set absolute spatial limits for the extent of the metropolis can now be spent in getting to an airport, flying to another, and getting to some nexus of organization on the other end, while still putting in a full day's work and returning to home at the end of the day. With air space becoming congested, a means for expediting this kind of urban movement has been found in the superspeeds of the Tokaido express. Thus, centers of large cities are becoming linked, usually in a corridor along a coastline.

Only 1 or 2% of the labor force of Tokyo is directly affected by the growth of daily intermetropolitan, or megalopolitan, movements,[8] and in the long run the proportion does not seem likely to exceed 3 to 5%. Other cities along the corridor are even less affected. Usually it is the coordinative occupations—executive, sales manager, buyer, broker, consultant, public administrator, labor union secretary, journalist, and the member of nationwide committees— that take to regular metropolis-hopping. Extreme specialists in medicine, technology, education, and cultural activities will be shared. The evolution of the megalopolis is much more evident to the visitor from outside who must use these bustling channels for the purposes of his visit than it is to the resident urban population. The bulk of the population does use the intermetropolitan transport lines for social and recreational purposes—and makes up a not inconsiderable share of the total flow—but this use is not enough to interest people in an overall picture of their changing environment and does not justify the high standards of performance.

Megalopolitan channels of transport and communication are important for understanding future urbanization in another way—they promote equalization of the growth forces. Land rents in Tokyo are kept from rising even higher than they have by the existence of significantly lower levels in accessible centers down the corridor. Cramped activities will often decentralize through redistribution to many points accessible to the megalopolitan main line rather than move to an enlarged site in a suburb. Improvement of telecommunications service through microwave relays greatly enhances the possibilities for coordination at a distance as soon as the underlying legal arrangements have been made and promise to be repeatedly renewed.

As cities almost everywhere in the world expand in population and area, the channels that connect them grow disproportionately. Moreover, the population pressures against local resources encountered in a few centers may very well be relieved by exporting people to where the jobs are, or, on a few occasions, by importing the jobs to the places where the people live. With these and other equilibrating assumptions, the team led by Doxiadis and Papaioannou could consider the theoretical implications of the completion of the urban transition on a global scale in their City of the Future study; after the megalopolis, and larger by far in scale, comes the Ecumenopolis, linked by the newest technologies—communications satellites, long range jets, and containerized, computerized shipping.[9] They could identify where urbanized people are expected to live once everyone has had a chance to move to the city. For these urban regions to survive, they have to assume that adequate resource substitutes will be found promptly in virtually all growing metropolises. Their work in this vision of the future was inspired by their awareness of the phenomena exhibited by Athens and its overspill on the Attican plain (Athens being close to the median among world urban centers in its access to raw materials, level of development of human resources, and the income levels being achieved) as contrasted with the predominant share of the urban analysis in the world which emanates from the affluent centers of North America, the United Kingdom, and Scandinavia and bears imprints of that cultural bias.

The Doxiadis team used a simple model that allowed rural people and townspeople yet to be born to escape living at subsistence, semiemployed at best, and to take up the struggle for existence in cities where life had greater variety and more hope for the long run. Taking into account the physical requirements for future urbanization, and reviewing the characteristics of available territory, the team sees the web of urbanism spreading across the world by the second half of the twenty-first century (see figure 4.2). Much more detailed analyses of current urbanizing forces, based upon extensive field work, were undertaken for specific regions, such as Greece itself, the Great Lakes area in North America, and Pakistan, so that the overall projection was informed by some analyses in depth. Many critical tests of such an outcome of the urbanization process need to be made; thus far only a few have been undertaken. Most important are those that deal with limits in scale.

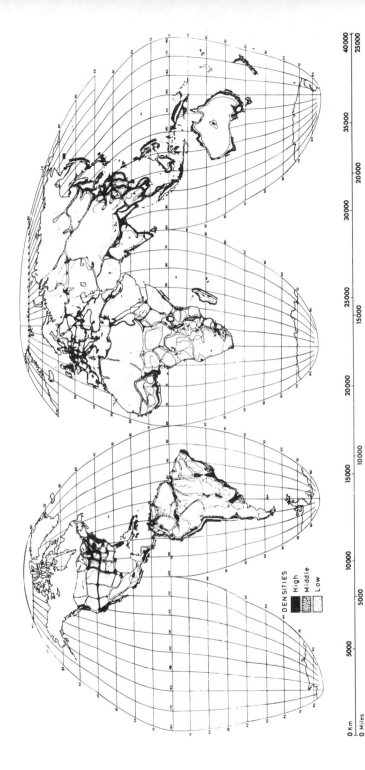

Figure 4.2 Ecumenopolis at the End of the Twenty-First Century

The land areas of the world were reviewed according to suitability for urbanization. The principal criteria for settlement were water supply, flatness, equable climate, and prior history of urbanization. This is a conservative allocation because no allowance has been made for the impact of new technology. For example, it will be argued later that some of the most densely settled areas have the opportunity of spilling out onto the sea. Reappraisal of the implicit energy costs suggests that future urbanization may be denser than visualized here, thus creating much more open space. (Map courtesy of C. A. Doxiadis and the Athens Center for Ekistics.)

The extreme case for long-run demand for urbanization is presented by China. Interesting as it might be for its own sake, however, China does not offer the best test of the problems associated with urban scale. It lacks a complete current census, and the available maps of urbanized and urbanizable areas are neither consistent nor comprehensive; in addition, economic, social, and health data are fragmentary at best.[10]

In every respect, India provides a better laboratory for analysis of future urban scale. Its problems are almost as difficult as those of China, because land, water, and other natural resources are equally scarce, but data covering every aspect of the society are available and are becoming increasingly reliable over time.

An estimate of India's equilibrium level population is 1.2 billion persons (this corresponds to an ultra-optimistic set of assumptions regarding population control, with Doxiadis's "low" estimate set at 1.5 billion). These levels would become fixed three or four generations hence, with only slow growth remaining. The other populations on the Indian subcontinent that speak the same or closely related language (Bengali, Urdu, Sinhalese, and Tamil) are expected to reach 0.5 to 0.8 billion persons. About a tenth of the overall number would be sufficient to manage the countryside, and in an era of common markets and transnational development projects, it may be expected that significant amounts of mixing of urban populations would occur, much as is presently taking place in Western Europe. Therefore, somewhere on the Indian subcontinent potentially urbanizable space must be found which will harbor at least 1.5 billion (but more likely as many as 2.0 billion) heterogeneous people (see figure 4.3).

The standard demographic transition already seems to be taking hold. Estimates prepared in 1972 for India itself suggest that the birth rate had begun to decline in 1971 for the first time since it had become a nation. Evidence of increasing acceptance of family planning was appearing throughout the country, but especially in the urbanized regions, and projections that were conjectural in the 1960s are beginning to be borne out in the 1970s.[11] Pakistan, Bangladesh, and Ceylon are changing more slowly because of less education and urbanization, particularly of women. The present total in the four countries of 770 millions may no more than triple in size before it reaches

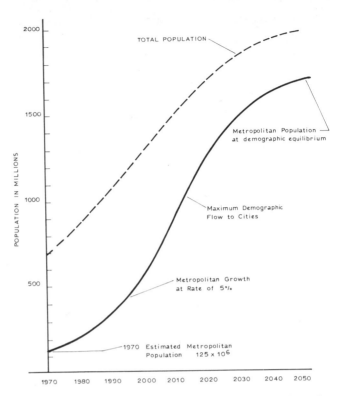

Figure 4.3 Projection of Future Metropolitan Growth on the Indian Subcontinent

If avoidance of overwhelming catastrophe is assumed and reasonable rates of urban growth are achieved, the projections show that villages must expand about 40% before coming to a peak. The extra population is almost wholly unproductive while residing in the agricultural areas. It is anticipated that increased investment will bring about a reorganization of the countryside that adds exurban settlers who can no longer tolerate the city but loses a somewhat larger number of rural migrants to the city.

the zero growth stage, but this ultimate number represents a fifteenfold increase in the total population now living in cities!

After projections of these less gloomy population estimates had been made, we prepared a new model which assumed that the Indian subcontinent would manage to achieve economic development as well as feed itself. These assumptions seemed to require that the urban population would grow by approximately 5% per year (it has been almost 4% in the past) after 1980 until the surplus population in the villages and towns had been exhausted and counterstream migration equaled the flow to the cities, with urbanization completed about a century hence. Then, decade by decade, underemployed population in the villages was transferred to the nearest available cities.

It was conveniently assumed that satellite cities equivalent to Tokyo in size (i.e., 10-20 million population) would be formed to take up the new growth. It was obvious that at least three to four decades were needed to form such a city but that the bulk of the growth would probably occur over the course of one decade. Tokyo was chosen as a prototype urban unit because it was originally built around a rail network that conserved energy, and it generated a rate of social and economic growth even greater than that required by this development model. Tokyo's experience indicates that city building at this scale and at this rate is feasible, and a closer scrutiny of its recent history and metropolitan operations suggests that many shortcuts in the installation of infrastructure can be proposed.[12] The gross density, including surrounded floodplain, reservoir, park, intensive gardens, and wasteland areas, is expected to average around 20,000 persons per square mile (800 per hectare) and can be represented by a hexagon about 15 miles (25 kilometers) in diameter. Where steep slopes and floodplain prevent economical urbanization on this scale but fractional metropolises fit, they are set down as such on the map.

Each decade the new growth is allocated to the remaining prime urbanizable land, taking into account (1) the availability of fresh water in drought years, (2) access to raw materials and world trade, (3) proximity to the territories generating the urban migrants, and (4) the desirability of postponing the formation of a congestion-creating megalopolis (i.e., continuous, overlapping strings of major centers) as long as possible. The outcome is shown in figures 4.4 and 4.5; the major megalopolitan string along the coastline bordering on the Bay of Bangal was evolved primarily because the water supply was more secure at the same time that freight costs were minimal.

A review of the proposals for high-speed surface or tunnel transport suggests that the Japanese concepts for a second New Tokaido line should be able to meet the demand for intercenter travel as the Indian standard of living continues to improve.[13] Food, energy, and raw material requirements were compared to known capacities for production over this period and found to be quite feasible. Water supply presented certain local problems in times of great drought, but fresh water could be delivered from estuaries with surplus to the deficit area, and it was believed that this could be done more cheaply by means of tugs towing large plastic tubes filled with fresh water or with the large supertankers now being built than by large pipelines that are seldom used to capacity. Therefore, once capital becomes available, the appearance of continuous urbanization is no longer troublesome.

Most of the housing would average about two stories in height at these densities, so its construction and use present few complications. The operation of central business districts raised serious questions because in Tokyo's mass transit and elevator systems perilous levels of crowding during peak periods are sometimes observed. The solution that seems to be indicated is one that has been long advocated for Western metropolises but never more than 25% achieved—the flattening of peak flows through multiple-shift operations. A review of the implications suggested no reason why such a system could not be effected in the 1980s, since telecommunications and computer capacity should be sufficient by then.

Outdoor recreation, especially the kind involving complete escape from the urban milieu, introduced much greater difficulty. In Tokyo, as many as a hundred thousand people queue up on weekends at the train stations with their rucksacks, hoping to get out to the mountains, forests, beaches, and bays. Educated people and newly urbanized populations feel this need most strongly. City people elsewhere in Asia prefer to use their time for recreation in different ways. G. W. S. Robinson has surveyed recreational reasons for getting out of the metropolises in South Asia.[14]

He found that the seaside held a strong attraction everywhere except in areas with swampy coastlines which, not
long ago, were malarial, and in inland metropolises such as
Delhi, where the cost of reaching a true beach was pro-
hibitive. The historic "hill stations," scenes of many ro-
mances and settings for many movies, are refuges from the
heat, humidity, and many of the tropical illnesses and have
retained their appeal in most instances, even after the disappearance of colonial rulers. Mountain spas are prized in
a few societies for health reasons as well. In Bengal, and
not a few places elsewhere, holidays are spent visiting distant relatives. However, the really large-scale movements
among Hindus, Buddhists, and Muslims are pilgrimages to
temple towns and other holy places, with the educated
among them adding historic sites to their itineraries.

These patterns will change, mostly through the addition
of new activities. Visitors note the rising popularity of hik-
ing, camping, mountain climbing, swimming, boating, and
the cosmopolitan outdoor team sports among the young.
As the volume of recreation demand rises, the mountain and
hill areas will become congested, so the masses must look
to the sea for open spaces and contact with the wilderness.
Fortunately this area seems more than capable of meeting
new demands. Prototype resorts that are, in effect, floating parks are now being designed for Okinawa and Hawaii
and appear to be not only technically feasible but also
economic.[15] There could be many such floating platforms,
differentiated by purpose and style, in a complex.

Storms during the monsoon season have always posed a
threat, but research has recently shown that circular or
hexagonal slabs more than a thousand feet in diameter with
cylindrical spar buoys extending three hundred feet below
the surface are ultrastable in the face of extreme wave
motion. Therefore, it appears that recreational complexes
can be built out at sea with excellent access, up to the
scale that the population in the nearby cluster of metropolises finds desirable. They are shown as lozenge-shaped
settlements offshore.

To sum up, every concrete objection that could be raised
by urban specialists against urbanization at this rate or at
this scale was investigated. In almost all cases an economical and socially feasible solution to the proposed problem
could be found using existing practice in some part of the
world, if not in India. For the remainder a solution which

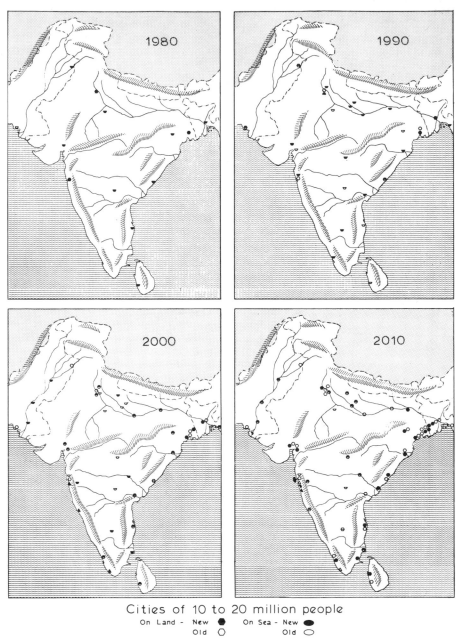

Cities of 10 to 20 million people

On Land - New ●   On Sea - New ◖

       Old ○   Old ◔

Figure 4.4 Metropolis Distribution for Maximum Economic Growth, 1980-2010
For each successive decade the movements of surplus villagers to the urban districts near to
them (or those that are easiest to build because of their location) are mapped. The cities are of
a size that is known to work with ordinary technology. Offshore complexes begin as recreational centers. A common market arrangement was also assumed for the long run. The bulk of a
metropolis is built up over a period of thirty years; the decade of most rapid construction is
shown in black.

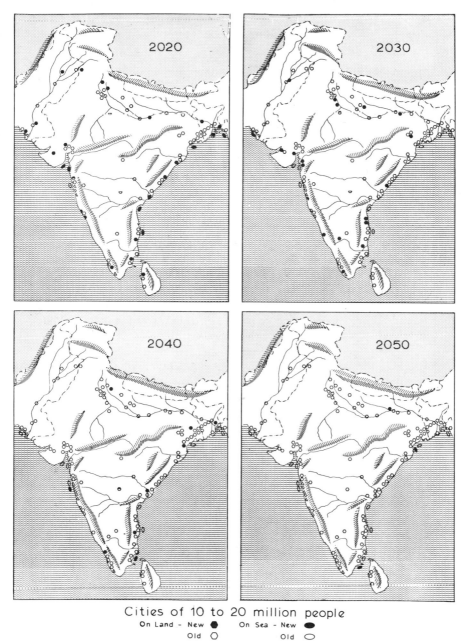

Cities of 10 to 20 million people

On Land - New ●   On Sea - New ◖

Old ○   Old ◯

Figure 4.5 Metropolis Distribution for Maximum Economic Growth, 2020-2050
The availability of secure sources of water supply are a major determinant of the location of
large clusters of metropolises. Adjacency of metropolitan areas does not seem to generate
extraordinary crowding, except in the areas of very highest access. Operating these centers
around the clock seems likely to obviate the difficulties. The offshore settlements begin as
recreational centers, but the life-style attracts other activities.

Processes of Transitional Urbanization   145

promised to become economic during the 1980s had already been shown to be technically feasible. The implied social change is not drastic. Therefore, we can say with a fair amount of confidence that the capacity for urbanization of the subcontinent of India is upward from two billion human population. Numbers in that magnitude are not desirable, because higher levels of living could be achieved if numbers of consumers were less, but living standards could be made far more acceptable than in Asia at present, and they could be at least as comfortable, convenient, and intellectually challenging as in Western European and Japanese cities today.

These conclusions are particularly significant when compared to the failures not reported here. Whenever a path was sought through the demographic and urban transitions using Western standards of urbanization (American, West European, or Russian), but limited to Asian demography, geography, and hydrology, no way at all could be found. Some clearly impossible or highly improbable intermediate step was encountered. The new steady state could be reached only by the invocation of magic or by assuming scientific and technological discoveries that had not yet been made. Similarly, if one follows through the typical advice being given to governments by Western advisors, or Western-trained Asian consultants, equivalent difficulties emerge—the transitions in a reasonably realistic model cannot be completed. The path outlined here was found by reviewing recent Asian partial successes, using Asian urban densities, refusing to be trapped by the American views about adequacy in water quality and sanitation, finding an acceptable relationship with the automobile, and introducing Asian responses to the use of discretionary time. These and other strategies for conserving resources are discussed in the following chapters.

The importance of finding a path for the very difficult case of the Indian subcontinent that still allows a number of trade-offs is that the conflicting issues of equity and efficiency introduced at the beginning of this chapter have some relevance. Room for political maneuver exists, thus increasing the likelihood that acceptable compromises can be found before the onset of many multimegadeath catastrophes. The policy implications will be considered after reviewing the resource-conserving technologies.

1. Constantinos A. Doxiades, *Architecture in Transition* (London:
Hutchinson, 1964).

2. Hugo and Jane van Lawick-Goodall, *Innocent Killers* (Boston:
Houghton Mifflin, 1971); Hans Kruuk, *The Spotted Hyena* (Chicago:
University of Chicago Press, 1972).

3. The equilibration problem for a human society, if the birth rate
cannot be reduced to replacement levels, reduces to a search for
some legitimate self-induced source of mortality. War and the
associated pestilences have often increased mortality in the past,
but selectively affected young males. The necessary number
of deaths required to sustain equilibrium would be relatively high,
because a loss of young males would not affect the birth rate as
directly as would the loss of a corresponding number of young fe-
males.
   Predation normally has a limited effect upon reproduction also.
The sick, the aged, and the least protected among the infants are
caught by predators, but healthy individuals in the prime of life are
able to evade the attack or to defend themselves successfully. As a
result, loss of life due to predation must be quite heavy if population
equilibrium is to be maintained. If the object is to achieve equilibrium with the least loss of life, the choice would be virgins at mar-
riageable age. At one time the Turkish overlords held down the
East Mediterranean populations of infidels by collecting such blood
tribute.

4. "Completion of the demographic transition" assumes that the
society has found some way of feeding back information about
overall changes in population size to individuals so that an appropriate fraction of the couples postpone the birth they planned. Explicit mechanisms of this sort do not yet exist, but informal processes that set styles and fashions in age of marriage and family formation seem to have an equilibrating effect. These styles and
fashions originate in the largest cities and diffuse to lesser ones.

5. The terminology used here is drawn from a prepositional inventory on migration prepared by Everett S. Lee, "A Theory of Migration," *Demography,* 3 (1966), 47-57. Additional features regarding settlement of migrants was drawn from E. B. Brody, ed.,
*Behavior in New Environments: Adaptation of Migrant Popula-
tions* (Beverly Hills, Calif.: Sage, 1970).

6. Asian Development Bank, *Southeast Asian Regional Transport
Survey,* prepared by Arthur D. Little, Inc., and associated consultants (Manila: Philippine Republic, 1972).

7. I have found no study that systematically analyzes the economies
of the rural-urban transition. The method of linking change in signs
and images to the changes in the language, particularly the addition
of neologisms, is described in R. L. Meier and Ikumi Hoshino,

"Cultural Growth and Urban Development in Inner Tokyo,"
Journal of the American Institute of Planners, 35 (January 1969),
1-9.

8. R. L. Meier, "Notes on the Creation of an Efficient Megalopolis" in Gwen Bell and Jaqueline Tyrwhitt, eds., *Human Identity in
the Urban Environment* (Harmondsworth, Eng.: Penguin Books,
1972).

9. Special issue of *Ekistics,* 35 (March 1973), "City of the Future."

10. Chen Cheng-sian, "Population Growth and Urbanization in
China, 1953-1970," *Geographical Review,* 63 (January 1973), 55-
72.

11. Some of the most interesting experiments in the introduction
of family planning occurred while the intra-uterine device (IUD)
was a medical novelty. Jae-Mo Yang and Sook Bang, "Improving
Access to the IUD: Experiments in Koyang, Korea," *Studies in
Family Planning,* no. 27 (March 1968), pp. 4-12. The diffusion of
the techniques throughout the world was reviewed by the Advisory
Committee on Obstetrics and Gynecology, U.S. Food and Drug
Administration, *ibid.,* pp. 12-15.

12. R. L. Meier, *Resource Conserving Urbanism for South Asia,*
Regional Development Studies VII, School of Natural Resources,
University of Michigan (Ann Arbor: University Microfilm—Xerox,
January 1968).

13. "Airborne Future for Tomorrow's Trains," *New Scientist,* 49
(February 25, 1971), 424.

14. The information about resorts was collected in the 1968-1970
period: G. W. S. Robinson, "The Recreation Geography of South
Asia," *Geographical Review,* 62 (October 1972), 561-572.
Also *Ekistics,* 35 (March 1973), 139-144.

15. John Lear, "Cities on the Sea?" *Saturday Review of Science,*
December 4, 1971.

FARSIGHTED STRATEGIES FOR ORGANIZATION

What has been depicted thus far can be called urbanization-out-of-desperation. Because societies far out of demographic balance are producing many more people in rural areas than can be supported by the locally available resources, the biological, physical, and social supports necessary to survival are sought in readily accessible places—the large cities. Despite this largely uncontrolled influx, cities have learned to respond to basic human needs quite effectively, and the frequency of crippling disasters has been sharply declining in recent decades. The capacity of much larger cities to cope with the foreseeable future stresses remains to be demonstrated. New demands, it will be shown in considerable detail, can be met if a city is allowed to borrow promising ideas from elsewhere in the world and to use the borrowed capital that often follows them, for adapting those ideas to local applications.

Urban policy since the nineteenth century has been determined predominantly by *national* politicians, administrators, and planners, and by special interest groups represented by those professions—firms, religious groups, and cultural organizations, which have become accustomed to introducing their own proposals and exerting vetos over others. In less-developed countries the emphasis is upon national interests, often at the expense of development in the cities. There the politicians have predominantly rural constituencies, and top administrators often originated among the landed gentry or were recruited by the military services, in which their talents were first recognized. In the period of incremental urbanization cities have rarely been organized well enough to become corporate actors on the national scene; they have been parts of the economy, and more recently the ecosystem, which have been acted upon. The cities have responded by adaptation, but occasionally there are also sharp backlashes in the form of urban riots. This period is coming to an end and is portended by the growing size and effectiveness of cities. If the Indian subcontinent develops as projected, for instance, the urban population will become a numerical majority about the year 2000, a transition that was experienced by many large Latin American countries in the 1960s and by Japan before World War II.

As the urban transition progresses, a few metropolises have found ways to serve national interests and at the same time take control of their own destinies. They have become "engines for development" that build up marketable skills, generate income, attract outside capital, and diffuse modern ideas into the remainder of the society. Their success stories need to be critically analyzed in order to discover the crucial policies that seem likely to become effective elsewhere. The experiences of Tokyo and Nagoya, and most recently those of Seoul, Singapore, and Hong Kong, are relevant.

Within rules laid down at the national capital, which may often be one of its own precincts, the metropolis of a developing nation must compete with other metropolises. Inside tariff and immigration barriers cities compete for income-generating facilities such as factories, and for public services in transport, telecommunications, and education, to mention only the leading sectors. They also try to attract private sector investment either by improving physical conditions needed for installations or by providing an "atmosphere" conducive to the starting of new enterprises. On a world scale, each metropolis finds itself competing for export markets and for capital.

Two metropolises have had a relatively free hand in organizing for intermetropolitan competition because they have not been hindered politically by a rural hinterland—Singapore and Hong Kong.[1] Their strategies illuminate very clearly the existence of quasi markets within which all metropolises—whether postindustrial, industrializing, or otherwise—must compete for a share. The scarce commodities are loan capital, mobile entrepreneurs, technologists, tourists, firms, government offices, and the like. The need to attract them is a fact of urban life that is often ignored, but as size increases and the numbers of metropolitan centers increase (there are now over 140 of the million-size metropolitan areas, and several more are being added every year), the cost of being oblivious to the nature of this competition increases more than proportionately.

One of the newest phenomena affecting cities is the expanded capacity of the multinational corporations and nonprofit associations to manage operations in many locales simultaneously and to transfer both resources and personnel among them. The strong propensity of these organizations to grow and mobilize more and more resources sharpens intermetropolitan competition, but it also introduces major new opportunities for overall growth. By becoming a host for them, the open metropolis—a city that lowers the barriers to the flow of ideas, people, institutions, investment-seeking funds, and cultural values—has many more chances to balance its expansion and integrate its growth. Because they represent a major power outside the normal controls of the nation-state-city system, the multinational organizations are feared and resented by many urban leaders (in part because the multinationals are less willing to be corrupt in the traditional ways), and their entry is opposed before an understanding of their potential contributions emerges. (The full argument is presented in Chapter 11.)

When the issues of metropolitan development are carefully considered, it becomes apparent that the maximization of the gross domestic product is already an inadequate rule for designing and choosing new projects and programs. The goals for cities have become much broader, because they must take into account fair nonmarket values along with those to which some kind of price is attributed. Indices that combine market and nonmarket values are needed at the aggregate level, so that it becomes possible to discover the impact of policies intended to lead to improvement in the overall quality of life. The measurement problem is a classic one that cannot be resolved for the general case, yet it should be possible to identify the phenomena that are now worth propagating by means of urban environments. Quantitative indicators of their presence may be an indirect by-product of special traditions of public administration, such as reports upon who pays how much tax for what reasons—in some cultures they could be brought out into the open by means of standardized methods of printing the language or presenting messages through the mass media and counting the output. In such ways we receive indications of the growth of the *social transactions* and the *cultural transmission* in a metropolitan area. These are broad concepts and can include regional domestic product growth as a special component. Income potentials themselves represent a dwindling share of the information needed to make effective metropolitan decisions.

The presentation that follows, therefore, proceeds from the best existing case of accelerated urbanization to the nature of the present and future competition for scarce resources between great cities. It then takes up the issue of what represents "improved performance" over the long run and reviews the strategies that appear to organize activity in a city so as to get this performance.

A PROTOTYPE OF ACCELERATED URBANIZATION: SEOUL

Nowhere else in the world today are the processes of urbanization so intense, so compressed in time, as in the capital and primary city of South Korea. The flow of people into the metropolis has been at flood stage since 1953. Its nearest equivalent in recent history is in Japan, where the surge began eight years earlier and has by now transformed almost all remaining rural people into urbanites. Japan had, however, started with a relatively high degree of indigenous industrialization; predominantly rural South Korea emerged from subsistence levels usually associated with China, Indonesia, and South Asia. Because it had been a colony, a common experience in Asia and Africa, industry had been discouraged before World War II.

The process by which Seoul added to its population has been quite normal; it is only the pace that is unusual. During the first three years after the Korean War refugees returned and began to rebuild what had been destroyed. Seoul was supporting its prewar population. At the same time refugees from North Korea continued to move from camps and makeshift housing to the metropolis, assisted by massive reconstruction financed by foreign aid in the manner of the Marshall Plan. Seoul's rate of population growth was 9-10% a year, and about an extra million people were added in the course of four years. In 1961, national development planning began, and it decentralized the investment of capital, distributing it around the country. Immigrants continued to prefer Seoul, however, and at a 7-8% growth rate a year another million people were added. Since 1966 people in the lesser cities have been moving up to Seoul, opening up niches for their successors from the countryside; still, most rural dwellers migrated directly to Seoul. In the early 1970s Seoul continued to grow by 8-10% per year, which, after allowance is made for natural increase, means that it was absorbing upward of 400,000 persons a year; only after 1972 strong signs of diminished demand for entry began to appear.

What brings them? No longer are their urgencies compounded by homelessness or incompatibility with an alien administration as in the 1950s. When they are surveyed, more than 80% of the immigrants indicate economic motives, and the remainder generally mention educational opportunities and medical facilities. Land reform in the villages was successful, but it does not hold the population down on the farm. The second and succeeding sons volunteer for the army, or work on contract, even if this means going to Japan or to German coal mines. They emerge with skills they feel equip them for Seoul; if there is an uncle or cousin who might help find employment that offered better prospects than the village, so much the better.

The level of per capita income in Seoul remains almost twice that of the rest of the country including Pusan, Taejon, and other large cities; it is about three times that of the villages and towns in the post-Korean War period. This means that, on the whole, the city has managed to produce jobs for immigrants about as rapidly as they have been arriving. Like other cities in developing countries, Seoul maintains a dualistic society. It has many hundreds of thousands of people living in areas just outside the old city walls who are delegated dirty and undesirable jobs in the city and live at levels interchangeable with those expected from agriculture. This substratum does not seem to be growing as rapidly as the city as a whole, however. When these people are counted in the total, the extraordinary differential in earning power between metropolis and village becomes all the more remarkable. A partial explanation is to be found in the observation that projects in Seoul are often completed ahead of schedule, and that output tends to fit the market closely, whether at home or overseas, so that Seoul-based projects consistently generate the best benefit-cost ratios. Seoul has accumulated the best organizers, the greatest range of skills, the fullest set of urban services, and the readiest sources of short-term capital in the country. The extremely helpful and well-informed national policy explains much more.[2]

Surprisingly, the capacity of the schools in Seoul has been keeping up with the population growth, although perhaps at the expense of quality in education for the rest of the nation since teachers scheme to be appointed in Seoul even though the cost of living is so much higher. Seoul's average class size has been slowly declining. An interesting excess of enrollment of boys can be identified; apparently they are in Seoul living with relatives or in boarding school in order to gain a headstart on the path that will take them into a leading university.

Throughout Korea, recent successes in family planning and expanded teacher education are about to pass on a dividend that will probably be spent raising the quality of the school system. Teachers will be better trained, and classes can be smaller. School buildings need to be reconstructed in any case because improvements in health and nutrition have been significantly increasing the body size of the student population, achieving almost European rates of growth in stature in the present generation. Also the raise in standards of educational performance on the part of the facilities will require a reduction in noise levels, more playing field space, better heating, and especially some books. The curriculum content has already been reformed along lines familiar to advanced countries, with goals being worked out in continuous consultation with principals and classroom teachers so that they were widely accepted when adopted. Identification of students with high scientific aptitude and creative ability was made the goal of educational research, and much emphasis has been given to taking the abnormal stress off of the prepuberty tests. High levels of early achievement had been associated traditionally with subsequent academic success in Korea but caused an abnormal number of mental breakdowns and diminished physiological capacity. Foreign languages—English and some Japanese—are taught so as to achieve a pragmatic, wide-ranging view of high culture, popular culture, and modern science, rather than the emphasis upon classical literature commonly adopted elsewhere.

It is clear then why international firms in precision electronics could build up production so rapidly in the Seoul area. The required infrastructure was installed, first in the vicinity of the modern airport and toll road according to carefully drawn up plans, and the quality of the available labor, due to prior attention to investment in human resources, made Seoul enterprises strikingly successful. The Koreans at that time already believed that open social and economic systems offered a formula for success that could not be surpassed, although how they reached such conclusions, given their history, is a mystery.

Everywhere in the documents on urban planning in Seoul one sees comparisons with Western European countries and sometimes the United States—the standards of performance, consumption levels, organizational framework, evaluative systems. This is the way both the advisors to Korea, which were provided by the United Nations, and Korea's overseas-trained students had been taught. The approach does not lead to error at the project and program level of planning because by now this road to development has been heavily traveled, and previously encountered traps can be bypassed. However, any tendency to follow such leads without strong questioning results in a serious problem for the 1970s—a Western-oriented consumption has extended to unsupportable levels. The demand for "my car," a Japanese neologism introduced through advertising about 1964, reflects the intense feeling of a materialistic society for the prize possession of all, a private automobile, and presents the problem in the most acute form. A major program of land readjustment in the city, which will raise circulation space to 20% or more from 7.2% of urban land area in 1970, is designed to accommodate the coming "my car" days. Moreover, Korea has no petroleum of its own, and its coal is quite expensive to convert to liquid fuels, so the shortage of foreign exchange is expected to be a continual frustration to these dreams.

One factor that spiraled out of control for a while was the land price level. Speculators seem to have already discounted the values implicit in a metropolitan area of 15,000,000 population. By 1972 the price of commercial land passed $5,000 per square meter, top residential land $800 per square meter, and both were still rising. Some land readjustment remained feasible because a plot that has access to side streets is worth more than twice as much as a plot reached through lanes, so owners will gladly give up 20% of their area to be able to park at the curb while unloading. The cost of acquisition of land for public purposes ran so high that the government refused in 1973 to pay any more than the 1972 level price.

Another significant scarcity is found in the water and sanitation service. Planners talk of installing flush toilets in 30-50% of all buildings by 1986, despite supply difficulties in dry seasons. According to the third five-year plan, Seoul is scheduled to get a sewer system in the late 1970s mainly because (according to public arguments given) the city would lose self-respect if it did not have one. However, there are also some fairly persuasive arguments on hand to back up the case for sewers. The night-soil collection system, for example, is breaking down because of the superiority of synthetic fertilizers for growing Korean crops. Night soil must be sterilized rather than distributed raw to farmers, and the sewage treatment plant is the modern way. A comprehensive watershed study of the Han River was undertaken to discover the most economical means of combating the effects of water scarcity and stream pollution at times of low flow.[3]

A variety of independent indicators provides evidence of fundamental changes. Previous improvements in water supplies were largely responsible for the spectacular reduction in the prevalence of illness in Korea during the 1960s (23% reported themselves ill in 1964 but only 10% in 1968, and the crude death rate dropped from 22 per thousand to 9 per thousand over a somewhat longer span of time). Mental health also seemed to be improving as the city grew, with the sensitive indicator of juvenile delinquency falling off in a significant way. There was no strong resort to "retreat from reality," as is sometimes induced by the shock of urbanization; and the gradual increase in licensed witches, diviners, palmists, physiognomists, graveyard selectors, and sutra-chanters reflected, if anything, a proportional decline in attention. Nor was there any serious narcotics problem. Therefore, the striking disappearance of illness cannot be explained by the changing of statistical categories, it is a real improvement.

The improvements registered in health and welfare will probably be advanced further through subtle changes induced by a major program in the construction of low-cost housing. Simple five-story walk-up reinforced concrete unfinished apartments were made available to displaced squatters, who could either occupy them or sell the option to households with capital. Thus large developments attracting a mixture of white-collar, commercial, and factory workers were finished off with self-help or with the assistance of artisan-contractors. The program was virtually unsubsidized and was at the same time notably popular with voters.[4]

As a whole the consumption patterns considered as a function of income seem to follow those of Taiwan and Japan after adjustments are made for the climate. Both of them preceded South Korea in the development process by five to twenty years, but the Koreans are rapidly closing the gap.

Seoul's success seems to have stemmed from an early emphasis upon investment in human resources, in the form of education and health services, and upon an open society capable of receiving financial and technical assistance from elsewhere in the world. An increasingly vigorous and educated population was encouraged to talk about and promote business, social, religious, and cultural enterprises, while the government retained authority and a willingness to use it, even if somewhat arbitrarily. A huge increase in social communication occurred at the onset of this self-organizing process. It was followed by an equally surprising spurt in the creation of neophyte government agencies, new firms, professional associations, and novel sociocultural groups. The real acceleration in economic growth followed, starting about 1966, when the rate of expansion of a regional gross domestic product seems to have exceeded 25% a year in real terms, and it appears to have remained at that level for most years since.[5]

Perhaps the most important feature of the South Korean formula for metropolitan development has been the creation of a special variety of assets. They are a kind upon which it is impossible to take out a mortgage but which will nevertheless enhance Korea's credit. These assets take the form of an almost universally literate background in the population at large, quick-acting, hardworking government offices, aggressive firms capable of putting foreign licenses to work, high professional standards of competence, and a growing network of contacts and relationships with individuals and organizations all over the world. Whenever quick shifts occur in world politics and international markets, cities with assets like these are likely to be able to take advantage of the opportunities that are generated. Therefore, although quite a few small-scale mistakes in the creation of its urban infrastructure can be discovered if one looks closely, the momentum that has been generated allows Seoul to write off these errors and redirect itself toward less constricting lines of development more readily than competing metropolises. To a large extent, this momentum has been achieved because it has swept so many people into contexts suited to organized, productive activity and has left out very few. Also because of this, only a minimal number is willing to support one or another form of active resentment. In other words, the imbalances and inequities that remain in the different levels of physical development have small behavioral consequences when compared to the effects of efforts in the areas of education, health, family planning, and land reform.

The greatest immediate risk for Seoul, deriving from its policy of maintaining an open economy, was its dependence upon an increasing inflow of foreign capital. The principal sources for South Korea were Japan and the United States. A stable and steadily growing international system of trade and payments is required to maintain Korean (or, "Korea's kind of") strategy for accelerated growth. The sources of credit seemed to be expanding even more rapidly than trade, because of rapidly accumulating savings in Japan and new financial devices for moving dollars across international boundaries (the Euro-dollar short-term notes), and the interest of holders of capital was also stimulated by the extraordinary returns that were being generated in and around Seoul. The resultant inflow of easy money, followed by overextensions by leading firms and government authorities, could have led to some kind of a collapse. Plans to overcome such crises necessarily evolved in back rooms, because rumors alone could break a market. That they had been prepared became evident only with the onset of the international financial crisis that led to the devaluation of the dollar (referred to as "the Nixon shock" in the Orient). The crisis was used to institute credit reforms inside Korea itself by funneling money at reasonable rates (using government backup) to small-to-medium operations instead of to the larger syndicates directly engaged in export promotion. Very few reorganizations to prevent business failure resulted from the sharp change in the external financial climate, and there was a welcome reduction in urban land speculation. The tendency of large firms to conspire and restrain internal competition was reduced by this reinforcement of the small-to-medium firm. Thus the government used the crisis to improve equity in opportunity, while allowing economic growth to slow down, though it stabilized at levels that remained very strong as compared to the rest of the world.

Phenomenal growth in organization followed by an even more remarkable expansion of economic output seems to have created many intergroup tensions in the society. Democratization of politics accompanied by noisy demonstrations of university students quite obviously raised fears in the military-oriented elite that the previous conditions of notorious political indiscipline would return.[6] The response of the government was to demand a change in the constitution which would allow it to remain in control beyond its scheduled term in office. These troubles in liberalizing the national government are largely independent, however, of the socioeconomic functions of the Seoul metropolis, even if it is the national capital.

This introduction to a recent star performer among great cities has been phenomenological. It has dealt with explanations in a manner one would be forced to use when introducing an unusual person—say, an innovative businessman possessing a flair that could lead to great success in the kind of future that was generally anticipated. Such a person could be explained in part by the circumstances which allowed him to get a start, in part by his education and prior experience, and also by the assets he inherited. Account would need to be taken of the special risks and uncertainties existing at that time. One could emphasize present style of operations as well—pace, determination, attitude toward risk, ability to improvise, affectations in dress and speech, and the like. Underlying the expression of psychic style, it is evident that the state of physical health, age, vigor, and physiological limitation may explain a great deal. Such a person would need to be introduced as well through his exploits—the ways in which he dealt with crisis and came out on top. If one wished to decide whether to trust him with a responsible post, one would prepare a checklist of a few hundred such items, collecting information on virtually all of them but reporting only the highlights. Even an extraordinary star will have traits that are predominantly normal and not worth describing. Most of the information so collected is partial and unsupported with hard evidence, yet it is more useful than his bank account, university grade average, income tax report, or the miles he has driven his car—each of them a statistic that may have significance in a special context.

This mode of description of the more complex phenomena exhibited by a metropolis is intended to communicate at the third level of familiarity. It is deeper and more economical than the first two methods of assessment, but it produces skepticism among professionals on the scene and

ASSESSING OVERALL PERFORMANCE

among social scientists. Therefore, it is worth reviewing at this point the other levels at which one can judge and compare metropolises.

The first is that of the tourist who collects mental images the way a photographer collects slides. They are always personal impressions. Cities are then distinguished according to whether they are exciting, stylish, congenial, colorful, noisy, decadent, pushy, stingy, dangerous, or intimidating. The validity of such impressions cannot be contested because they are personal and they are widely shared. To a large extent they are created through the successes and failures of the tourist organizations, their publicists, and the multitude of entrepreneurs (legitimate and otherwise) that live off the bounty of strangers. The mosaic of mental images of a city is first created by expectations before arrival, then by the experiences while there, followed by matching the highlights with the impressions of others; it creates a reality that film makers and novelists are expected to catch and epitomize. As a result, educated people feel confident that they can rank cities according to the quality of life they provide without working out a technique of asking the residents themselves. Architects are expected to maintain or restore the positive features of such images—also to redress the negative—while in quite a different way Chambers of Commerce do their best to build up and sustain such images with the aid of public relations and advertising techniques.

At the second level stands the journalist who has worked in several cities and is assigned the task of reporting and explaining the events that take place. Often he finds himself contrasting the tourists's image with states of affairs that are revealed by asking questions in depth. The stories pieced together deal with immediate causes, such as administrative decisions or political choices. From these reports and observations the competent urban journalist will infer an underlying structure of power and influence, which in turn explains the overt decision. Such a reporter from America would quickly identify in Seoul a collusion between its city hall and the large contractors that would remind him of unsavory conditions in Boston or Chicago at their worst. Moving on to the universities, he would find a vociferous, documented, statistically backed criticism of the government. When he assembles his picture of Seoul, it is made up of a list of wrong-headed decision makers influenced by certain greedy firms or ideologically founded groups. When presented with evidence of extraordinary rates of economic development and improvements in health, he is likely to regard the data as evidence of profiteering and a body of official lies. That evidence also seems to be borne out by the information that his methods of research pry out of the urban scene. The remarkable flow of immigrants sustained by the metropolis is interpreted as a predictable breakdown of the deconcentration policy designed to bring capital investment to the hinterland—it was intended to provide services for people close to where they were born, but it ends up being installed in Seoul. The cynic can even explain why civil servants work so hard—they are raiding the government treasury while they can. A Japanese urban journalist would see much more that is familiar. He sees little harm in the collusion between contractors and city hall, since it is needed to get work done quickly. He would deplore the loss of faith in tradition and the erosion of standards brought about by such rapid social change. The structure of society that provided meaning to human existence was dissolving away; his interviews find some people turning to new religions in order to cope with the lack of anchorage in Seoul public life. The work of others like themselves, using the same techniques, tends to confirm the image most Korean intellectuals hold regarding themselves and conditions in their city, which a tourist is rarely able to tap because of the loss of self-respect incurred in the exchange.

The third level of familiarity, as may be expected, is quite suspicious of both the tourist's and the journalist's approach. It searches for objective bases for comparison, such as uninflated measures of income and wealth, distinguishing differences appearing from one year to the next and between metropolises. It suspends belief in potentially self-serving reports from bureaucratic offices but acquires information in a roundabout way by discovering advances which their clients or competitors admit have been made. This mode of analysis is preferred by the public policy analyst, the planner, and the top manager when appraising health, education, and social progress. They ask what amounts of investment must have preceded the instances of growth detected and what kinds of policies were effective, in order to get explanations for constructive change. For them Seoul presents many substantiated successes, including lessons that might contribute to improved performance in other metropolises. The time scale for their assessments— the connections between causes and effects—is five to ten years, as against the journalist-intellectual outlook that ranges from two to a hundred weeks, and the immediate impressions of the tourist who thinks of causes being simultaneous with effects since he must see them that way.

There are a surprising number of people who try to get at the urban milieu on a fourth level. They worry about the longer term, because five-year plans warp the social data in such a way as to make the planners, politicians, and administrators look good. They might very well be borrowing from the future in order to be popular now. The behavior shows up most clearly in the exploitation of resources. Is the knowledge about improved efficiency of utilization and substitution being introduced more rapidly than the reserves disappear? The natural resources themselves are distributed over the hinterland, but the knowledge enters through the metropolis and is transmitted through its educational and technical consulting institutions. For the foreseeable scarcities is there an ever widening circle of people acquainted with the most advanced relevant knowledge available anywhere in the world? Thus, at this deeper level, the city is judged by its ability to acquire and distribute the knowledge needed to sustain a future for itself.

In this respect also, Seoul's performance is outstanding. Outside of Japan no other Asian metropolis has been able to bring back and use such a high proportion of the internationally trained scientists and scholars that it had originally launched. Moreover, in the Korea Institute of Science and Technology (KIST), smaller parallel institutions, and the spinoffs from KIST, the holders of these advanced intellectual skills are put to work on strictly utilitarian projects aimed at applying knowledge from elsewhere in the world to recognized Korean problems, even though they might have been participating in pure research when abroad. Seoul's institutions of higher education have modernized rapidly, in many ways passing the metropolises of Japan except for Tokyo. In the government new plans and administrations have been quickly formulated for conserving resources not highly valued by villagers and townsmen; their programs are far in advance of those adopted elsewhere in

Asia. Only in the sphere of political development have there been setbacks, where the future has been borrowed from in order to produce the appearance of public order in the present. In that regard Seoul is no different from Singapore, Athens, Buenos Aires, Rio de Janeiro, and Ankara.

In Seoul and its nearest rivals (Hong Kong, Singapore, Taipei, Pusan, Bangkok) the data demonstrate repeatedly that the individual urban resident and his family have continuing improvement of welfare, despite an increasing openness to events in the outside world, over which neither the metropolis itself nor the nation of which it is part can have any control. Dependable indicators of welfare are difficult to obtain, because metropolitan changes are diluted by the slower change of surrounding regions when statistics are assembled. However, we can get pure metropolitan performance in a few instances.

Among cities in the Orient, Hong Kong, a city that has recently passed the four million mark, has demonstrated unusually strong performance. It is also one of the very few examples where relatively comprehensive data have been collected for a pure metropolis, unmixed with the surrounding region. Analysis of the local information for the 1960s revealed the following greatly differentiated growth.[7] Although the official physical dimensions of Hong Kong have remained unchanged since 1861, the amount of land, including fresh water reservoirs, actually increased 0.1-0.2% per year because of reclamation from the sea. At the end of the 1960s the human population was expanding about 1.5% a year, and the rate was moving toward zero population growth. The number of vehicular trips was expanding at the same time by 2-3% yearly, the number of dwelling units by about 3-4%, and the amount of roadway by the same proportion. The number of school places increased by 4% a year, and the number of jobs by about 5-6%. The amount of water consumed rose by 7-9% a year, the amount of income in real terms available for consumption by about 8-11%, and the amount of solid waste by 10-12%. The number of vehicles licensed increased by 10-13% a year, the electric power produced by 14-16%, and telephones installed by 17-20%. At the same time the value of checks cleared increased by 25-30% a year, and additions to capital stock were also 25-30% larger each year. Each of these dimensions of internal growth is a relatively independent indicator; those mentioned earlier and exhibiting more gradual growth comprise physical resources, along with basic commodities and structure dependent upon them, while the intermediate growth rates involve transfers of consumer goods and services with a marked style, quality, or informational component. The last three indexes possess the symbolic values associated with increasing power and control. The last group make minimal demands for space; they exhibit little friction with the physical environment.

All the foregoing indicators reflect vigorous activity and increasing levels of organization. Have they been obtained at the price of health or some other aspect of welfare? Indications of misfits with the biological and physical environment or of incompatibilities with the social environment need to be reviewed. On the health side dysentery rates were decreasing by about 12% a year during the 1960s, deaths from measles and chicken pox were severe as late as 1967 but then became negligible, and the incidence of the big killer, tuberculosis, was falling steadily at a rate of about 3% a year. Cases of crime reported were decreasing by 11% a year, though narcotic offenses have been increasing by 1%. Vehicle accidents are increasing by about 1% a year per thousand potential victims but have been declining by about 10% a year per thousand vehicles. On the housing front, the population living in substandard units, mainly squatter settlements, was declining by 10-12% a year.

Data like these demonstrate quite uniformly that in Hong Kong the individual resident and his family have growing security against disaster, despite an increasing intensity of public interaction, which could transmit epidemics or result in injuries from accident. Even the narcotics offense trend appears to be healthy when the sizes of the cohorts entering susceptible ages are taken into account. An objective observer is forced to conclude that the Hong Kong of today, as compared to the Hong Kong of last year or earlier, has significantly fewer bad things happening. The evidence suggests that the increasing investment in education and the growing experience with modern government synchronize to diminish unwanted features of city life at the same time that they enhance, in a much less measurable way, the positive qualities of the environment. Very substantial progress has been made since the heavy distress flow of migrants from the hinterland halted in 1962.

Singapore's internal development was equally dramatic

over this same decade, but because of its political separation from Malaysia in 1965 the statistics are more difficult
to assemble. With only two million population, on land
that is much flatter, Singapore is less crowded than Hong
Kong. It has also consistently paid more attention to housing, physical planning, and external appearances.

In 1972 a transformation occurred within Hong Kong that
reduced the capacity of the external onlooker to interpret
its life through observation. Responding to repeated comments upon the contrast between the dinginess and filth
evident in the precincts of this entrepôt and the almost
sterile cleanliness of the cities of the People's Republic of
China or the garden city aspect imposed upon Singapore
by its own government, accumulated litter was cleared away
by a combination of the colonial authorities using police
powers and cooperating community groups. With posters
and television, using singing exhortations and dramatic skits,
they inveighed against *lap sap chung* ("litter worms").
Visual evidence of the inner workings of a city is more difficult to collect when the city shows a scrubbed and freshly
painted face.

Although Hong Kong, Singapore, and Seoul are poles
apart in ideology, with Hong Kong expressing an uninhib-
ited laissez-faire philosophy, Singapore taking a strongly
socialist position, and Seoul adopting a fiercely anticom-
munist, capitalist-planning stand, all profited from an overspill of Japanese economic growth. The rapid expansion
of international trade effected by multinational firms and
backed by nonprofit professional organizations provided
an extra set of opportunities that aided each of them.
Local savings were matched several times over by outside
resources available to the corporations and their financial
backers.

This approach to development seems to be much less
painful and far more rewarding for the great bulk of population than the autarchic, nationalist strategy strongly advocated by a large body of intellectuals throughout the
developing countries. (The most significant exception to
general improvement in the quality of life, following this
formula for participating in international trade and intellectual exchange, is the deprivation felt by a tiny well-
educated, established elite, much weakened by war and
ideological dissension, which is losing its sense of leadership

and control over society. Now it is forced to consult with many outside groups, many of them not yet legitimated, before making what was previously an internal or local decision. They recall the good old days when a *tai pan* or a colonial administrator would have the last word.) Therefore the formula that draws upon multinational resources in the manner of Seoul, Hong Kong, and Singapore seems likely to be imitated in the future and applied to the development of dozens of growing metropolitan areas. As a result much greater intermetropolitan competition for mobile capital is expected henceforth than has occurred at any time in the past.

In addition there are many citizens with an enterprising outlook—in total perhaps a number equal to 5-15% of the metropolitan population—who undertake to compare opportunities in other cities with their own and are willing to make a move to someplace better. Should they take themselves and their liquid assets to Hong Kong, Singapore, or Sydney? Or should they drop to a lower division and consider Kaohsiung, Penang, or Saigon? What about London, New York, or San Francisco? Whatever cities are chosen will acquire capital and new export industries that will enable the firm to compete better.

It is important for city managers and planners to know what kind of expertise should be attracted in order to compete better. That will require a careful investigation of the potential solutions to forthcoming resource scarcities, which will be discussed in the following chapters. In Chapter 11 it will then be possible to fit all the pieces together and propose a strategy for coping with immigration forces, on the one hand, and productive employment, on the other. It will often entail the immigration of various kinds of promoters and entrepreneurs.

Inside each metropolis public officials recognize that each distinctive feature must be presented in its most favorable light, yet they must remain honest so as to prevent misunderstandings and backlash in the next round of locational decisions. To illustrate what these strategies imply, a scenario has been prepared for Singapore. Because it is a city-state and does not have to curtail its ambitions in order to satisfy a rural-dominated parliament, the policies and issues appear in their purest and most uncomplicated form.

In the year 197— the illness of someone at the top of the
political hierarchy, combined with the exodus of a number
of promising young Singaporeans, created a crisis. Government by troika was instituted, and in order to keep pace
between strong, independent planning and development
agencies, the three who shared the executive brought in a
firm of international planning consultants for a thorough,
future-oriented review. They hoped that a review would
reveal what Singapore was doing well and where its performance was likely to lag behind the competition if present policies were continued—as claimed by those who
voluntarily went into exile. Also it would suggest what
could be done in policy realignment to maintain Singapore's
ranking among world metropolises and perhaps raise it
higher.

The planning consultants (according to a recent tradition,
a mix from East and West was dispatched to the scene)
quickly sensed the strong feelings aroused by measures for
accelerating integration and population equilibrium in its
multiracial society that could not be reported in the newspapers or the mass media. Additional problems had been
encountered in the course of creating a viable and defensible
small nation. They sympathized with the ends even if they
did not understand the justifications for the means. Therefore they eschewed review of political matters of the kind
that largely occupied Dick Wilson's attention in his book
The Future Role of Singapore.[8]

They also separated their appraisals of internal management, which are of immediate interest to local citizens but
not to others who judge the long-term capabilities of cities.
The conclusions they reached were a reaffirmation of Singapore's current development strategy, but they were reached
by taking into account more than ever before the experiences and prospects of other metropolises of the world.
The following points are highlights of the findings:

1. Tourists remain a key component in Singapore's development strategy. This means that the airport and the airline, which provide the channels by which virtually all
tourists arrive, must have sufficient capacity to handle the
tourist flow comfortably. The comments of the airline
pilots' association and the airlines themselves about terminal
facilities must be heeded to prevent the costly shock of an
accident. More efforts will be needed to fill in the future

SCENARIO SEVEN

A Planner's
Program for
Improving
Singapore's
Performance

seasonal slumps—by means of exhibits, promotions, shopping expeditions, and sporting events that are publicized elsewhere in the world. Further hotel building should not be curbed until a wide choice in rooms and service becomes available. This will mean that a number of bankruptcies must be anticipated and plans must be made in advance for alternative uses for hotel and resort facilities. Strenuous efforts by the Ministry of the Environment should continue to be made, despite escalating costs, to keep clean and presentable all parts of the city likely to be visited. A continuing issue will be the economic collection and disposal of solid waste, where the long-term solution might be combustion in the nearby electric power plants, with salvage to follow.

2. Singapore will become increasingly attractive to many kinds of potential immigrants. For some time it has gone to rather extreme lengths to establish a puritanical image and thereby prevent an invasion of dropouts such as was experienced by Nepal, which would threaten to divert the mainstream tourist flow. Singapore can use highly educated refugees and sojourners to leaven its still sparse intellectual circles, but that will require more careful management of its exclusion policies. More important yet is the problem of overfull employment, which, in a society like Singapore can lead to job-hopping and wage inflation. It can be avoided, or at least reduced, by adopting a policy like that of Germany, with the wholesale importaion of Gastarbeiter, or that of Japan, which contracted out to other countries in order to meet its delivery commitments. If Singapore is prepared to do both, it gains extra competitive advantage.

The overspill of Singapore's prosperity will increasingly affect Bataam and Medan in Sumatra, creating many jobs there that depend upon prime contracts made with Singapore organizations, while the southern tip of the Malay Peninsula has already felt the first surges of induced acceleration. Exchanges in residence will be needed to expedite transfers of scarce competences. The extension of work permits must be made increasingly flexible in order to assure the availability of a more diverse set of skills.

3. Capital movements into Singapore were once the result of confidence on the part of investors with an "El Dorado mentality" (Goh Keng Swee's term), but by 1970 they had already been displaced in importance by multinational corporations. While the former were attracted by low taxes,

docile labor, and minimal government intervention, the multinationals are more interested in the availability of land and of information that permit them to minimize risk. The rapid expansion of the security market will also go a long way to expedite the joint venture arrangements with multinational corporations. Joint ventures are normally preferred because they introduce new skills into the local society at the same time that a larger share of the profits are retained.

Huge sums will be risked in the search for petroleum and natural gas in the vicinity of Singapore. The attention of speculators trying for big winnings is almost totally engaged by the explorations for oil; nowadays they think of little else. Singapore is already the preferred base of operations or involved one way or another, but the other metropolises are quickly becoming more sophisticated. Malaysia is adding new harbors and shipbuilding, creating its own commodities and securities markets, and now actively encouraging Malays to get into the operation of large enterprises. Singapore has built up an engineering school with training programs to assist these enterprises, and again Malaysia has followed quickly to develop equivalent institutions. Therefore Singapore must look for still other services that stabilize the operations of the multinationals, such as the evolution of Asian dollar financing, parallel to the Eurodollar markets for short-term obligations and competitive with the Euroyen. It has also installed containerized cargo handling that allows ships to turn around in three days or less. The major multinationals are likely to operate in all countries in Southeast Asia, but they will prefer to locate their most complex and advanced efforts in the environment that provides the greatest range of services.

4. Professionals such as doctors, engineers, architects, accountants, psychologists, and other top-rank consultants make fine discriminations regarding the places they can set up their offices. They appreciate support services, such as dependable electricity, power, and transport (for which planners are responsible), but they also demand civic order and civil liberties up to the levels maintained in the more developed areas of the world. Licensing policies must be based upon evidence of competence, and not upon racial, cultural, or national origins. In many instances the openness of the professions, and the attractiveness to top professionals, can be maintained by appointing external mem-

bers to the examining boards, much as is already done in the University, so that Singapore becomes a full member of the international community. This will mean greater independence from the United Kingdom and more connections with Japan and North America.

5. Urban administration is a particular pride of Singapore, and its quality is matched by other departments of government and many sectors of business administration. However, times are changing, and the standards of performance in administration with them. For example, rehousing parts of the population was undertaken with vigor and imagination, so that the entire image of the city has been changed. However, there is little evidence that the families who had to move feel that they are better off or that their lives are richer as a result of the demolition of the slums. Henceforth, housing administrators must be pressed to fulfill both objectives simultaneously. Singapore has been emphasizing speed and economy of production and not the quality of "fit" to various needs; it badly needs a great variety of housing and educational services. If administrative procedures are evolved that fit diverse consumers as well as production technologies, Singapore should find that this know-how would become an export industry.

6. Planners have a way of judging other planners on the basis of the constructive changes being wrought in a society. Singapore planners, therefore, have a high reputation, and other societies looking for help are likely to come to Singapore and try to hire away its best young planners. If political or budgetary frustrations accumulate at home, the planners will be tempted to go where their expertise seems to be needed. A city is interesting to planners if its planning agencies can complete developmental tasks, but it is more attractive when political and economic forces are ready and willing to allow innovative projects. Cities planned in a mediocre way find innovation extremely difficult.

7. Executives judge cities not only by the ease with which they can do business in customary styles (i.e., with telephones, computers, multilingual secretaries, multicolor brochures, and accessibility to an international airport) but also by the ease with which they can indulge in such avocations as golf, tennis, swimming, sailing, and gourmet dining. The community must have cosmopolitan clubs, comfortable houses and apartments, modern clinics and

hospitals, English-language private schools for the children, department stores, clean environments, and pleasant public parks. Singapore has done well in those respects, so it remains a first choice for branch headquarters of multinational firms in that part of the world. When its own firms go overseas, they are likely to retain their headquarters in Singapore.

8. Singapore's thinking is extraordinarily market-oriented, even in the public sector, and so it has not considered the kind of asset nongovernmental agencies and international associations can be. Such agencies need the same urban services as major business firms, but they rarely can pay as much. Their sites will most often be found adjacent to universities, rather than in the central business districts, because they are as dependent upon libraries and museums as businesses are upon banks and securities markets. Cultural organizations and professional associations, however, along with the international foundations, are extremely sensitive to infringements of civil liberties, including any form of censorship or coercion, and are willing to move the innovative commissions they sponsor to another center that is more open-minded and more strongly committed to social justice. Capacities of this sort place a city in a class with Paris, London, and San Francisco—one to which Singapore might well aspire.

9. Intergovernmental agency directors, such as ECAFE, UNESCO, and the World Bank are interested in sponsoring successful programs for urban development. The city that appears to manage its own affairs well should find it easy to get their support. Often the agencies try to assign transport, health, or educational projects to the city that do not interest Singaporeans; the unneeded projects are intended primarily to test the general economic feasibility of an idea.

A kind of international civil service is evolving in these agencies, and the high-status people normally are granted a choice as to where they wish to operate from. In that case, their judgments should parallel those of the directors of nongovernmental organizations mentioned above. Singapore is already often preferred over Montreal and Bangkok.

10. Finally, to attract ambitious students and recognized scholars, a city needs to maintain an intellectual community. The universities must be able to offer positions to eminent refugees from other countries and to hold on to citizens who have gained worldwide respect. The libraries must be

comprehensive and up to date in all the relevant subjects and cultures; museums must be willing and able to present displays from all over the world; scientific laboratories and experiment stations must be able to maintain an active interchange of people and ideas with equivalent institutions elsewhere in the world. The Japanese set out to do this many decades ago in Tokyo, and still set the pace in the Orient, though the most remarkable institutions created recently have been in Seoul. Israel has demonstrated that a small country can become internationally significant in scientific and cultural affairs (as well as military prowess), a phenomenon that has not gone unnoticed in Singapore.

If Singapore's performance in all these arenas were to be compared with neighbors, such as Bangkok, Djakarta, or Saigon, it would be assigned very high marks. Its strongest competition is found thousands of miles away in Japan, Hong Kong, and perhaps Australia, but the performance of the whole group is rapidly improving, in part from analyzing the success of Singapore. As a result, all may be able to acquire resources, build up infrastructure, generate productive jobs, and manage their internal environment more rapidly than was possible in the recent history of cities, but the pace of growth still will be very slow as compared to the demand for places in the city arising from excess population in the countryside. Since Singapore people feel they could be swamped by squatters if they opened the gates to everyone (a proposition that has not been tested and may not be true), this emphasis upon openness as a prerequisite for high performance has some limits.

Smaller metropolises may excel in only a few arenas and still do well in attracting their share of the mobile resources, but as they grow larger, their efforts must be better balanced. Penang, the Malaysian free port, is engaged in such a process. It takes one to two decades of effort to establish competence in a new arena, so planning and promotion must be started very much in advance of need. The planners must first identify an internal political constituency that will back up their recommendations for reallocation of metropolitan investments. Together with such a group a search is made for short-to-middle-run opportunities, and a program of institution-building is laid out. Progress is initially judged by the respect generated in the minds of neighboring competitors and the ratio of outside resources mobilized to internal resources committed. Later the achievements are assessed by worldwide impact and the capacity to extend help to upcoming metropolises inside and outside the home country. The mature metropolis teaches as much as it learns from others.

Many Western metropolises have rapidly expanded their populations in the period since World War II while also improving their internal organization and increasing the overall level of welfare. São Paulo, for example, is a pacemaker in the production of a new, effective organized urban population, and Mexico City is another. (If we relied only on interpretations obtained from indexes, Johannesberg, South Africa, scores very high; nevertheless, the rest of the world believes, it perseveres in moving toward a future with a dead end.) Athens and Madrid have not done at all badly when the long term is taken into accounts. In another economic system, closed off from continuing review, spectacular growth and development has been registered in places like Moscow, Tashkent, Warsaw, Bucharest, and a number of other centers that have now advanced well beyond the million mark in population. Why has not this argument drawn as heavily from their successes as those from Southeast Asia?

On the basis of farsighted strategy for world development (thus raising the debate to the highest level of discourse), we see that these Western or westernized metropolises represent an agglomeration of societies that have progressed at least halfway through the urban transition. Less than half their labor force is engaged in primary production, and that share continues to decline. Somehow, with assistance from a number of innovations yet to be tested, they should be able to obtain the resource inputs and borrow the techniques needed to complete the urban transition, reaching the climax stage in the not-too-distant future. For South and Southeast Asia this reliance upon momentum seems unrealistic, because it is doubtful there that the societies have moved even a quarter of the way through the urbanization process. They could even be pushed back again to an agrarian equilibrium, 15-25% urbanized, through the intervention of worldwide Malthusian catastrophe; but the exploration of those outcomes in some detail in Chapter 2 made that kind of future seem a long way off. According to evidence offered in Chapter 3, since all of these cities are

CONTRIBUTIONS FROM THE WEST

becoming tougher and better able to cope with challenges posed by nature (but more vulnerable to weapons designed by man), they are not going to give up easily. In Chapter 4 a pathway into the future was sketched out, using Aisan precedents to a large extent, that seemed feasible if the food, energy, and minerals could be found, while here it has been shown that a few (less than 10%) of the Asian metropolises possessed unsuspected organizing capacities. They can bring into being "social reactors" that are competitive on the world scene, and organize a society more rapidly than the best instances known in the West, but this is still not good enough in relation to the dimensions of the task. Even more powerful techniques for organization are needed. Because of the background in social technology built up through research and experiment in advanced Western metropolises, the principal hope of these Asian cities seems to rest in the further development, transfer, and adaptation of these organizing concepts. The search uncovers some likely prospects.

New York offers the multinational corporation. It has no monopoly upon them, but the firms holding about three-quarters of the assets do have headquarters in New York. As a class they have demonstrated the capacity to install modern technologies in city, town, and country. If necessary, they sponsor the construction of their own New Towns. Modern methods of management are transferred along with the technology. Corporate personnel can be moved to a new enterprise in a new locale, thus infusing it with life. Capital is acquired through multinational banks, and personnel come from internationalized universities, particularly their schools of business administration, engineering, and chemistry. The legal relationship of an affiliated entity may be that of a branch, a subsidiary, a joint enterprise with one or more firms, a spinoff, a franchise, a nonprofit association of firms or individuals, or even a cooperative. The external form represents a good fit with the political system on the local scene.

The significance of the multinational firm is enhanced by its ability to draw upon the services of other organizations in a city in a way that reduces frequency of failure and growing pains, though at the same time it is often inhibited from grasping obvious opportunities by its own standard operating procedures. When that is the case, many local organizations can be spawned by individuals (often refugees)

who serve as middlemen and live off of the external economies created by the imported technology. Much more will
be said about the future functions of the multinational
corporation after the key technologies for building resource-
conserving cities are identified.

The other highly significant growth stimulus identifiable
in Western metropolises, but not yet elsewhere, is the modern use of the university. The old idea of the university
still dominates its public image so that the "multiversity"
concept is still debated long after it has been permanently
installed and further evolution has begun.[9] In standard
thinking the university puts a four-to-eight-year veneer of
"know-what" on an entrant, which later can be partly
transformed into organizational "know-how" when the
student enters the labor force. In this thinking, the university also has another lesser output in the form of books
and research papers, which make knowledge more accessible
to its graduates.

Around Boston and the metropolises of California a more
advanced form has evolved and is ready for transplantation.[10] An attempt to put what has happened into ecological language may generate some shock of recognition. In
ecological terms, the university community is a dumping
area for the fruits and husks of organized effort elsewhere.
Reports, concepts, ideas, images, forms, and patterns are
stacked in ordered heaps. There decomposing organisms
go to work, comparing, criticizing, analyzing, reducing.
The students are paralleled by the larvae that wriggle
through this fermenting mass, picking up nutrients as they
go, emerging from their chrysalis to seek niches in outside
communities. The richness of the compost increases with
the range of species drawn upon. It provides a base for the
sustenance of vigorous communities when transported elsewhere, and around the fringes of the compost heap itself a
mix of extraordinarily exotic species are supported.

Massachusetts Institute of Technology evolved a means of
encouraging productive new ideas, working with banks and
promotional groups, on the one hand, and in the councils
of national policy formation, on the other. These ideas
propagated hundreds of innovative organizations, mainly
in the area of technology, which clustered nearby. Harvard
also became deeply involved in national councils in medicine, business organization, and international relations in
such a way that the new organizations stimulated by it

more often than not settled down on distant metropolitan sites.[11] Between the two universities almost all of contemporary civilization was critically reviewed, partially decomposed, and sometimes recombined on the spot.

In California, Stanford University demonstrated that variants of this formula would work elsewhere. It provided the focus for the quickest-acting technological complex (solid-state electronics, plasmas, pharmacologicals, biotics, applied systems) that the world has yet seen. Berkeley and U.C.L.A. have demonstrated that equal power can be generated within the public sector. In their case, the resources mobilized are an order of magnitude larger, and the effects reach greater distances, but the time that they take to become visible is also greater. They have found a way to establish contact in depth with most of the world. The resulting cultural explosion is marked by bouts of silliness (which happens when every new channel of communication and each new freedom to explore new relationships is first exploited), but a technique of "instant organization" (ad hocism) seems to be evolving faster in the milieu dominated by this university than elsewhere. Only there, for example, could the streams of innovation in popular culture become interwoven so thoroughly with high culture, commercial culture, and counterculture. Excellent examples exist elsewhere (particularly London and New York); otherwise the phenomena of instant organization would be considered merely a provincial aberration, but nowhere are they found in such a high-proof distillate as in the vicinity of the Berkeley-Stanford-San Francisco axis and its satellite communities in the hills and redwood canyons.

The University of California has found a means for producing graduate and professional teaching and research that generates high respect among its competitors, both private and public. At the same time it is in the vanguard of a system that mass-produces higher education, gaining a higher penetration of society than is achieved elsewhere. Despite necessary standardization, it promotes the greatest diversity. The great cities of the future will have to foster urban institutions still more elaborate than these leaders on the American East and West Coasts. They will have to allocate whole quarters of the city to these cultural reactors and the spinoff organizations they make possible. The expected structural impact will be discussed after the practical issues of sufficient food, shelter, and mobility are resolved.

1. W. H. L. Wheaton highlights the lag in political representation of metropolitan areas in national councils. The loyalties of new immigrants lie with the home province for most of their life. Many of their children identify with a ghetto within the city or a suburban community, so it is difficult for a metropolitan politician to mobilize a large plurality. Add to that the defenses devised by politicians who represent much more land than people; they hold on to committee chairmanships, judgeships, and other posts of real power long after their constituencies have been outnumbered by metropolitan growth. Thus cities are milked of the surpluses and savings they generate not only in order to maintain the apparatus of the nation but also to subsidize rural activities. What would happen if cities were in control of their destinies? The potentials are put together very succinctly in his "Singkong: A Parable on Regional Planning," *Proceedings of the Third International Conference on Regional Development,* Japan Center for Area Development Research, Tokyo, 1970, pp. 257-260.

2. It is evident from earlier mentions as well as this eulogy that I have been greatly impressed by what is being achieved in Seoul. A participant in the scene sees primarily the buzzing, wasteful confusion; the situation is barely held together by ad hoc coordinating efforts stimulated by the need for direction felt by both the top executive and by the business and professional sector. An outsider notes the astonishing leaps and short cuts taken as compared to elsewhere or when contrasted with history. A more complete report is given in R. L. Meier, "Exploring Development in Great Asian Cities: Seoul," *Journal of the American Institute of Planners,* 36 (November 1970) 378-392.

3. A thoroughgoing study of the hydrology of the region surrounding Seoul was published by the Ministry of Construction and the Korea Water Resources Development Corporation in cooperation with the United States Bureau of Reclamation and the Geological Survey, *Han River Basin,* 3 vols. (Washington, D.C. 1971).

4. Several programs for housing have been under way in Seoul, with many being overpriced and hard to fill, but the "Shi-Min" low-cost apartments produced by Seoul City Hall were the most interesting. Although decried by professional housing people as too cheap (about $60 per square meter including very high land prices), they were rented out in "sevenths" of an apartment to boarders, thus allowing many squatters to occupy housing in the same general neighborhood as their original hut. The interiors were completed by themselves or by artisans. Institute of Urban Studies and Development, Yonsei University, *A Survey of the Housing Market in Urban Korea* (Seoul, August 1972).

5. These deductions are based upon reports of overall growth of output in South Korea, of 12-17% per year, combined with the observation that this development rate was being paced by a metropolis that was gaining in population by 10% or more per year. D. C. Cole and P. C. Lyman, *Korean Development: The Interplay of*

Politics and Economics (Cambridge, Mass.: Harvard University Press, 1971); also Irma Adelman, ed., *Practical Approaches to Development Planning* (Baltimore: Johns Hopkins Press, 1969).

6. Gregory Henderson, *Korea: The Politics of the Vortex* (Cambridge, Mass.: Harvard University Press 1968); Pyong-Choom Hahm, *The Korean Political Tradition and Law* (Seoul: Hollym, 1967).

7. This analysis of the mechanism of intermetropolitan competition arose out of a study undertaken in an effort to understand the relatively unexpected success experienced by Hong Kong, particularly during the 1960s. The model needed to be one in which laissez-faire behavior works as well as any other strategy. The study remains unpublished, because I could not discover empirically the political behavior in Hong Kong associated with the choices; therefore, the mechanism of allocation remained obscure.

8. Dick Wilson, *The Future of Singapore* (London: Oxford University Press, 1972).

9. The concept of the multiversity, an institution that provides every form of higher education in the sciences, humanities and the professions, has been evolving over the past decade. Clark Kerr in his *Uses of the University* (Cambridge, Mass.: Harvard University Press, 1963) introduced the idea in conjunction with his view of the future of the "city of intellect." These grandiose ideas encountered budgetary restraints and were reconsidered in his work with the Commission on Higher Education, Carnegie Foundation, *New Challenges to the College and University* (Berkeley: University of California Press, 1969). I have considered the university in its urban context, having a function similar to that of a medical center, but with many more externalities.

10. The most enterprising real estate and private banking firm engaged in creating the right services for advanced technology is Cabot, Cabot, and Forbes; originally from Boston. See Freeman Lincoln, "After the Cabots—Jerry Blakely," *Fortune,* 62 (November 1960), 71-84; "Looking like New," *Nation's Business,* 58 (October 1970), 93-96.

11. Perhaps two out of ten projects arising from academic research can be marketed successfully, but one or two out of thirty become big winners that pay off all the losses and still yield unusual profits. Anon. "The Golden Touch of American Research and Development," *Dunn's Review,* November 1968, pp. 40-45.

THE GREEN REVOLUTION AND
ITS AFTERMATH

Raising the achievements of a few metropolises to the status of "heroism in production and modernization" while approving their efforts to evade the conservative vetoes of politicians in the provinces has meant underplaying the significance of the simultaneous transformation of the countryside. In Asia and Africa, particularly, because the urban transition is only now under way, most of the reorganization of outlook must occur in the countryside. Without the Green Revolution urban heroes could not have broken records for growth and development very long; if they had pursued their aims without increased inputs from the rural areas, they would have gone down in history as fools. Building a new urbanism requires an assurance that urban markets can attract rapidly increasing supplies of food.

The Green Revolution is a complex agricultural transition—so much so that the closer one gets to the phenomenon, the more dubious becomes the term *revolution*. [1] At any given place or time where it is said to have occurred, one discovers that progressive modernization has been under way for decades. A sharp jump ahead, however, gave rise to the term; in the period since 1967, the end of the double failure of the monsoon in most of India and Pakistan, modernization took the form of sharply increased yields of wheat associated with the introduction of a new dwarf strain. The Food Research Institute of Stanford University called it a "seed-fertilizer" revolution. [2] The term was extended to rice and maize, where dwarf strains, evolved through similar strategies of plant breeding, were also becoming available, though increases in yield were less certain. Once Green Revolution became a journalistic term, and one with generally favorable connotations, many other modernizing forces claimed to be a part of it, often without evidence of any contribution to overall output.

For the city dweller in Asia who must be satisfied with juxtaposing reports he can read in the newspaper and hear from landowning relatives in the countryside, with the prices he pays for staples in the market place, it is at least a revolution in thinking. In the mid-1960s the chill threat of famine was felt. The large-scale, sometimes heroic, efforts that brought about the transfer of grain, mostly surplus wheat, from North America to needy populations in the Orient were obviously temporary expedients. The crisis was postponed, and families hoarded against the bitter season. Then quite suddenly—in some metropolises it was only a matter of a few months—attention shifted to the equally heroic efforts of modernization in agriculture, which were beginning to bear fruit in the form of higher and more dependable yields (see figure 6.1).

Six separate procedures for improved output—better seed, reliable irrigation, synthetic fertilizer, control of pests, de-centralized technical assistance, and convenient credit—were so tied together that they were introduced virtually simul-taneously and in the correct proportion. Before-and-after comparisons from fields lying side by side were then very striking—and also easily reportable with photographs.[3] After the first spectacular instances of application were ac-complished, the output gain to be expected from soil types available to the farmers might not really pay for the added costs of production, but many modernized never-theless. Most such people profited in the long run because they began to pay close attention to optimization, and they eventually found a kind of advice that paid off consistently. The first surpluses were usually stored in the farmer's house-hold; but production soon went beyond that, and strenu-ous efforts were needed to build a farm-to-market infra-structure that would accommodate the new yields. The collectable grain in a district undergoing the transition was increased by factors of three, five, or even more. Silos and grain elevators had to be built for efficient storage, trucks acquired for shipping grain out of the collection area, and roads improved so as to move the trucks. Rolling equip-ment had to be ordered for the railroads, and adjustments made in the mills so they could cope with the new compo-sition of the crop.[4] Administrators in the cities, who had been scraping bottom to meet the minimum demands set by ration cards distributed to their citizens, were then able to build up some reserves. Thereafter they could turn their attention to problems of maldistribution and to improving the quality of nutrition.

Thus the outlook changes swiftly from one of worsening recurrent food crises to a state of relative optimism and back to reports of food riots. Black market operators in the cities switch from the necessities of life to contraband luxuries in order to stay in business, but a few years later

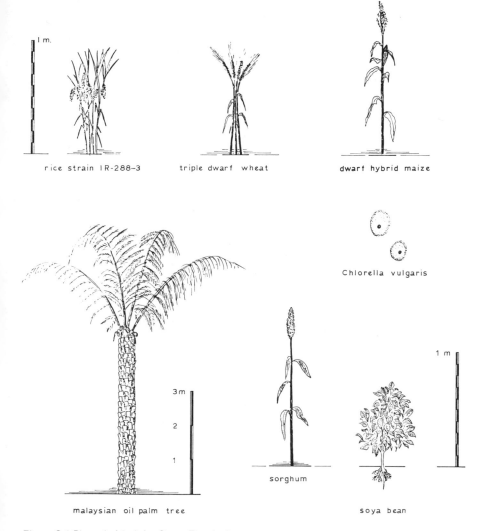

rice strain IR-288-3 triple dwarf wheat dwarf hybrid maize

Chlorella vulgaris

malaysian oil palm tree sorghum soya bean

Figure 6.1 Plants behind the Green Revolution
Most of the increase in production over the past decade has been stimulated by new strains of wheat, maize, and oil palm. Rice expansion requires a great deal more preparation than the others, while sorghum is expected to grow rapidly during this decade. The increases in soya beans are due, not to strikingly improved yield, but to extended range. *Chlorella vulgaris* is a strong nominee as a soybean substitute, but cultivation was only begun in the 1960s. New plants better adapted to high-intensity cultivation in the tropics, using the four-carbon intermediate path for photosynthesis (similar to sugarcane and maize), are now under active development but may take more than a decade to become important.

they find themselves peddling the bag of rice or the carcass of lamb that will permit a proper wedding celebration during a period of rationing. For a short period the spread of the technique of the Green Revolution appeared to be so inevitable that politicians and top administrators became overconfident. They had hoped that the attention of the public could be directed to pressing matters beyond that of food. Investments needed to supply the expanded populations of the 1980s and beyond were being diverted.[5] However, the unusual weather of 1972-73 that affected the granary area of Russia most strongly, followed by a very severe drought in Western India and Pakistan, wiped out virtually all of the world's buffer stocks of grain and cooking oil. World cereal prices temporarily soared to record levels in 1973-74 as governments and food processors scrambled to assure themselves of adequate stocks. Cost-cutting procedures had earlier resulted in a reduction of inventories to levels required for a few months of production. In times of uncertain supply the stocks maintained close to the points of distribution should be increased—if it is possible to do so.

FERMENT IN THE COUNTRYSIDE

The Green Revolution is generally agreed to be a quick transition to a more highly organized production system for food and fiber. Readiness to make the shift may be attributed to predispositions in parts of the rural populations that were created by prior contact with cities. The manner in which they have come to modernize has been given a great deal of attention by scholars, who have reached much consensus about a body of doctrine regarding rural change and its antecedents.[6] Most of these studies, however, have historical foundations, since they are based upon reports of transformations wrought between the 1940s and the early 1960s. They were conducted in the context of a dismantled colonial administration in most parts of the developing world and were accompanied by rising nationalistic feelings. The doctrine for agricultural output expansion emphasized the importance of literacy and book learning, political reports arriving by newspaper and radio, the work that could be done by chemicals and machines, and the significance of banking services for the medium-to-small operators. The countryside will need much more of these services than it has had until now, and it will need others as well.

Expediting the Green Revolution requires that attention must be given to the increase in strength of the outwardly directed forces from the metropolis. The city-based bureaucracies are now much larger and can provide many more services in the hinterland, sometimes with quite comprehensive and dependable coverage. In other instances unplanned, haphazard influences such as weather, insect depredations, and epidemics in livestock are becoming controllable and may be amenable to some central direction. The information collected and distributed can be of greater value to agriculturists.

The method of analysis to be employed here is to identify the known transactions between city and countryside that could affect outputs in rural areas. How might they best be used to stimulate the needed changes in social organization? In these arguments it is possible to be most explicit about anticipated conditions in non-Communist Asia, but occasional references will be made regarding how such phenomena may change when rural populations in Africa and Latin America are considered. We shall have to rely on the experiences of pacemakers for hints regarding future policy for getting greater advantage from the Green Revolution.

1. The counterstream of migrants.[7] Nowadays most rural communities contain more than one person who has "been to" the city and survived there for a while. A fair fraction of these are not failures but were recalled to head a household or to take advantage of an opportunity at home, while many others feel they were "not lucky," rather than dealt with unjustly. Urban concepts therefore are not automatically discounted as alien modes of thought, but are put forward by a potent minority within the rural community in face-to-face interaction with others as desirable ways of doing things.

When reinforced by returned migrants, it is possible for government not only to bring from the city specific information about tools, machines, catalogs, and dealers but also to find some resources already at hand. Repair skills, operating knowhow, routine maintenance experience, quality control, accounting techniques, and pricing sophistication are all behavioral innovations essential to good management. The counterstream from the city brings back capital in many instances and prospects of a continuing capacity to invest, because there are kinfolk or fellow clan members of the counterstream left behind in the city. In this way newly perceived opportunities and a capacity to implement them are simultaneously brought into being.

Therefore, in the current wave of modernization one sees hastily constructed roadside shops for such things as the repair of diesel engines, installation of mechanical pumps and electrical equipment, and tire retreading. In and around the villages one sees evidence of agents who distribute materials and equipment for home manufactures (displacing the traditional handicraft industries), the harvest of specialty crops, and the fencing associated with advanced animal husbandry. These indicators are superimposed upon earlier changes wrought by special producers for urban patrons, shopkeepers with added lines of merchandise, trucks-for-hire operators, and jitney drivers. When in close touch with the urban market, producer's cooperatives are easier to organize; they are also more likely to survive feuds and financial crises. Since electrification is already common but far from universal, the politics of bringing in power, along with the opportunities generated by its introduction, will remain a major preoccupation of the counterstream.

Governments will resist rapid rural mechanization because it creates unemployment and exacerbates political problems. Partly because of its forbidden features, enterprising youth with no personal contact with the city will become obsessed with machines. Black markets will develop not only for tractors and harvesters but also for motorized bicycles and other consumption-oriented machinery. An important basis for status in these changing rural areas is to become a master of machines instead of bullocks.

Interestingly, the rural areas that are most marginal, where decades ago a population increase in combination with periodic droughts or other catastrophes caused desperate families to encourage their sons to volunteer for the army, go to sea, or join a construction gang, are often affected earliest by the counterstream. As a result their schools are better, their water supply is more highly engineered, their animals receive the benefits of veterinary medicine, and their homes have access to radios, despite their normally poor access to the urban centers. Others, in similarly marginal areas, have inexplicably remained thoroughly traditional and fatalistic, even though threatened with extinction. Communities with intermediate access to cities and less stringent environments are less likely to be influenced by returned emigrants unless urban ideas are reinforced by the construction of a road, electrification, or the provision of irrigation water.

2. Political ideas. The politics of forces that vie for control in rural areas of developing countries have a foundation in the competition among modernizing and revitalizing ideologies. The fanatic core of an ideology is organized like a priesthood that recruits and trains missionaries. Often, as with indigenous versions of communism, a component of the urban population is an essential element in the strategy for coming to power, but programmatically it is discovered that this is hardly likely to be necessary when a countryside is in ferment. Population growth alone is sufficient cause for fundamental change in the relationship of man to land, but usually there are other more proximate causes that provide content for speeches and propaganda about social justice and the need for a new social order.

Land reform, which means not only a reallocation of the control over soil resources but also a reformulation of the legitimate bonds that tie a household or a community to a place in the environment, is needed now for all those districts where population growth has been sizable. In almost all instances rural districts have been strongly affected by the counterstream from the cities, so land reform policies must take a body of readily absorbed urban ideas into account. If the reform is to expedite agricultural techniques leading to increased production, it must be made popular among the majority of rural residents, yet such attempts can lead to the negation of the reform as the urban transition proceeds and excess rural population finds niches in the city. The land reforms needed to expedite the introduction of the Green Revolution could become a strong deterrent to development in the foreseeable future—only one or two generations distant.

The example provided by Japan deserves close study. The "MacArthur Constitution" brought about a widely respected land reform and permitted the achievement of the highest rice yields in the world. Yet within two decades, during which rapid economic development and urbanization occurred, the plot sizes and guarantees given the farmers became an acute embarrassment. Subsidies for traditional crops like rice were elevated to levels much higher than needed for optimal land use, which resulted in a great deal of waste from the application of fertilizer and other inputs to the wrong land and the wrong crops. An insistence upon preventing the reaggregation of parcels (and thereby allowing an apparent return to "landlordism") is particularly inappropriate for the future the world must face in the next three generations.

At least one feature that will differentiate most of Asia and Africa of the 1970s from Japan's experience is the "overproduction" in Asia and Africa of secondary school—later, university—graduates in the cities and towns. Positions in governmental and business bureaucracies do not open up as rapidly as schools produce diploma holders. Young men who started in the countryside and who hope to make their way in town on the basis of their investment in education very often are forced to return to the parental household. They bring with them a capability for reading technical materials and writing fair accounts of the local situation, even if little else of their training is relevant. This decentralized capability makes it possible for many small nonfarm enterprises to be launched. Typically, returnees will be commission agents of large organizations that operate in the modern sector, but they will also find it possible to create cooperatives and commercial groups with their roots in the countryside. Some promoters of modern organization will also operate in the political, social, and cultural spheres.

Five or ten years after the surplus graduates have returned from the city, one should see a crop of new firms, cooperatives, dealerships, clubs, sports, agricultural specialities, and political party cells within the villages, all of them tentative and unsteady unless subsidized from the outside. The organizations that survive will provide new channels for modernization that extend beyond the school system and radio or television. They will have a metropolitan base, including headquarters and membership, but will maintain a strong loyalty to the land.

In India, an overwhelming surplus of graduates accumulated when the monsoons failed in the 1965-1967 period and industry could not expand. The surplus has continued to grow since then. In Latin America a general oversupply became evident shortly thereafter, while in Africa the surplus is most often still at the secondary school level. Since none of these societies now possesses sensitive feedback loops to anticipate future surpluses and close off entry to the colleges, thus stabilizing the rate of social change (a widely practiced colonial policy, although for quite different purposes), we must expect a kind of ferment to arise in the 1970s that is better organized than any that preceded it, but no less radical in outlook.

Meanwhile, Calcutta University has passed 150,000 enrollment and is forced, by popular demand, to continue expanding. Other large metropolitan universities, there and elsewhere, are in similar situations. At this stage credentials seem to be more important than demonstrated competence, and standards are debased. The ferment is being fueled by academics; no one in government knows how to turn off the spigot.[8]

3. Tax revenue and capital mobilization. Since the bulk of the tax revenue is collected in the cities, the government share of development programs in the countryside depends upon urban success. An acceleration of economic growth in the large cities tends to pump funds into services directed at villagers. Cynics point out that national and state capitals bloat with functionaries "getting their share" before any services are delivered, but this may be a necessary evil. If the growth process is to continue, the government must funnel teachers, nurses, village development assistance, road construction projects, relief in emergencies, technical assistance, and much else into the countryside in order to expedite the extension of the Green Revolution. Agents of change must be collected and trained in centers before being diffused to accessible locales. It is becoming uneconomic for middle landowners to put their savings into gold and silver because the supply of bullion is inadequate; the surplus income is collected through branch banks set up in all the market towns and, later on, even in some central villages. A large part of these funds can then be invested in small-scale irrigation projects and in connections to the electrical grids moving out from either the large city or some upcountry hydroelectric facility. Quite a few non-urban, white-collar employment opportunities are generated by the accumulation of bank deposits, the writing of insurance, electrification, installation of water distribution systems, and maintenance of mail order agencies. Almost always a different training is normally required for these than is provided now to students in the colleges. Some of the funds are wasted because of the inevitable mismatch between the education of the man on the spot and the skill that is actually required. These mismatches must be more common in the countryside because of attachments to the land according to family and community and a social structure that is more rigid than nearby cities—thus allowing a post to be filled from only a few nominees.

The rules for extending credit, the evidence to be used for appraising risk, and the interest rates to be charged are all set in the finance centers of the metropolis. Thus the bank branches and agencies in the countryside become part of an apparatus of effectors, and policy is adjusted according to the exigencies of international markets, national tax potentials, and the preconceptions or felt needs of urbanites. The rural areas will be more responsive to aggregate economic changes than in the past.

4. Mass media. Ferment is sensed more by the young than the old; they voice their as yet contentless feelings in popular culture—songs, music, dances, hairstyles, sport clothing, games, new words, and new gestures. The mass media, television more than radio, and radio much more than magazines, distribute youth culture, because they must search continually for novel content or be ignored. The media sources in large cities must build up a community of talented contributors, each of whom is rewarded with cash and glory if he manages to catch the attention of a significant fraction of the public.

This system for creating popular culture quickly finds itself pressing politically as well as culturally against norms set by the society for social communication. Inevitably censors move in and try to set standards to keep outrage created in powerful people at tolerable levels. Limits for decency, as marked out by the constituency behind the censors, immediately create a situation that encourages an underground culture to proliferate in the cities—it cannot survive in the countryside because of too low an intensity of interaction. Taboos constraining the content of the media allow artists and writers to create new materials recognized as sinful; they are occasionally whispered about in the countryside, but they are made available in urban black markets by the underworld and the counterculture and therefore provide an extra attraction for rural visitors. Even strict censorship, as in many Muslim countries, or an emphasis upon collective self-censorship, as in the Soviet Union, cannot prevent the infiltration of contraband popular culture into the cities. Among the youth in these countries, especially in the underemployed rural areas, part of the ferment is attributable to a desire to participate in the sampling of new cultural efforts that take off in disapproved directions. Recognizing this continual pressure of the market, censors may relax standards, but within months the creators of illicit material will have identified a new boundary and will continue to stimulate this dissatisfaction with the present state of affairs in society.

In various ways the Japanese experience with mass media over the course of its urban transition seems likely to be repeated. Despite exceedingly diligent enterprise in newspaper and magazine journalism, the attention of the general public moved to cinema and radio, and then to television. Television first reinforced the official standard culture; its poignant serial drama reinterpreted the recent past and provided a shared tradition. The feedback came in an increasing proportion from youth, however; according to the polls made by the producers, their enthusiasm was directed to performances from Hollywood, Madison Avenue, and London. Thereafter Japanese television proceeded to transmit predominantly international popular culture.[9] Japan's ferment resulted in an extraordinarily rapid reduction of parochialism. Some of it might have been because the old elite, which would have put up strong resistance, had lost its power after World War II, but most was due to the ease with which popular sentiments flowed into the countryside and provided the necessary idiom for propagating social change, especially modifications in diet and in the organization of the family.

Many will argue that a rural population living close to subsistence will not be able to spend $100-$200 for a television set, but experience in Southeast Asia and Latin America demonstrates that the poor will gain access to the medium as rapidly as the middle class. Unexpected receipts of cash, whether from a lottery, from some price squeeze or an illegitimate transaction, are not uncommon in the lowest income group, and the conversion of such money into a television set generates a huge amount of prestige in the neighborhood. New gift-giving patterns tend to be established, with the household having the television set on the receiving end. Such a household receives samples of all the best dishes prepared and the finest fruits that are harvested. Small change is collected when repairs are needed. The arrival of a television among the poor creates a new sense of community at the scale of a subneighborhood, and the ideas stimulated and discussed can lead to marked changes in social behavior.

5. Family organization. Through these media, concepts of a new way of life based upon a small family size must be transmitted to the overcrowded countryside. Confidence in a low mortality rate must be established so that parents do not have to produce two or three sons to be sure that one of them will survive to care for them in old age. Substitutes for all the services provided by children in a given culture must be found and glamorized, or at least explained in infinite detail, over radio or television channels. Without any overall plan or direction, but responding to a conscious awareness of the population problem, the media have been presenting the superior opportunities open to smaller-size families in South Korea and the Chinese communities in Southeast Asia in such a way that an important segment of the nonurban population does respond.

Exceedingly little is known about the acculturation stimulated by television, yet it offers perhaps the most potent means by which metropolitan areas can influence the countryside. Television is likely to be particularly important in Muslim society, where cinema has especially high prestige (especially where it is forbidden), because the image of the city penetrates the privacy of the home without requiring any deviancy in public behavior. The use of detergents, baby food formulas, dehydrated soups, electric cookers, simple household remedies, and government services are all depicted effectively on the screen and might be used to reinforce positive images of life-styles involving small families.

If the metropolitan areas fail to transmit messages that introduce fertility reduction effectively (it should be noted that the schools—the only real alternative—are far too traditional and too slow), they will be swamped by an influx of uncultured inmigrants when the latter are forced to leave their homes because of food shortage or political crisis. India was very fortunate in having a sizable buffer stock on hand when Calcutta had its population almost doubled by refugees from East Bengal in 1971. If the political crisis had erupted a year or two later, when food had to be moved to the drought-stricken west, the loss of life could have run up into the many millions.

This discussion of the kind of rural change induced by urban growth and improved organization moves from describing what *has been* happening to what will *probably* happen next and then to what *needs* to happen. The transformation, or buildup of ferment, is proceeding much too slowly in most countries; the Green Revolution has not yet been harnessed to push along the demographic transition, except to some extent in Taiwan.

The success of the Green Revolution particularly introduces a capability for planning ahead. It should lead to locally evolved strategies in each region in which the agricultural transformation is felt. The truly creative and constructive work in family size adjustment is as likely to be initiated by voluntary groups as by designated official agencies, although the volunteers rarely have either adequate resources or continuity of effort. A variety of sponsors and programs will be needed if the methods of introducing contraception are to fit the multicultural societies of India, Pakistan, the Republic of the Philippines, Viet Nam, and Indonesia, where the Green Revolution has had some effect already, and promises much more in the future. The multitribal states of Africa, where population pressures are not quite so intense but the need for enhanced food production by modern approaches is equally great, similarly deserve detailed attention. Egypt, Thailand, and Bangladesh are populous nations with relatively homogeneous cultures that present less complicated problems. Thus far, despite the opportunities presented by both the Green Revolution and the ferment it induces, less than a tenth of the effort now devoted to the health of the farmers has been mobilized for the purpose of limiting population growth. In the next few decades that ratio may need to be reversed. The task will be one of discovering the proper set of arguments, medical supports, and incentives.

IMPACT ON URBAN SOCIETY

The most significant and direct contribution of the Green Revolution to the cities is the buffer stock of foodstuffs that it makes possible. When increased supplies are transported to storage points readily accessible to the large cities, the authorities are able to release more ration cards, allowing more people to live legitimately in the metropolis. The emphasis on legitimacy is important because all cities that restrict residence through internal passport or food-rationing systems tend to harbor a greater population than is officially recognized. The authorities must make allowances for travelers, visitors, students, and seasonal workers in the distribution of the food supply, as well as write off as lost a certain percentage for petty pilferage, consumption by rats, and spoilage. Through various devices a moderate share of these allowances are channeled to the illegitimate residents. When buffer stocks are low, black market prices rise significantly. They serve as an indicator of distress for this illegitimate segment of the residents. The larger the buffer, the lower is the differential between the black market price and the controlled price.

Cities much prefer legitimate workers. They are formally employed by corporate units—public, private, and cooperative—or belong to syndicates of crafts working in small establishments. Since they become steady customers of nearby established shopkeepers, they can obtain credit in a pinch. They are visible, countable, predictable. A number of them, however, in search of additional income create a shady stratum by joining those who live wholly by their wits. These people have a legitimate function in that they fulfill needs overlooked by planners and administrators, and they add spice as well as variety to life in the city. They are quite willing to handle contraband and some will resort to the redistribution of wealth through organized theft. They support street hawkers, tea shops, and cafés catering to workingmen in the older and poorer portions of the metropolis that are independent of the formal food distribution system. The steadier the supply of food, the larger is this versatile, underemployed underclass of urbanites.

This substratum is reinforced by rural people who are unable to take advantage of the Green Revolution; taken together, they will probably constitute a majority of the whole population. The distress of the rural contingent will actually increase, because the many small farms operated at subsistence levels produce only a small portion of the output that enters the market. Each of them must first buy whatever is necessary for producing the next crop—such as seed, containers, fuel, and tools that cannot be saved or made at home. The little cash they have left must be spent for clothing, household supplies, and rituals such as marriages. Irrigation, fertilizer, pesticides, and special seeds require capital, but credit in small sums is expensive at the same time that returns from small plots of land are more risky. The low prices brought into being by the presence of the buffer stocks leaves even less for the marginal household, which thereupon goes into debt and, if it lacks remittances from the city, loses its land.[10] At least as strong an influence is the higher survival rate of children in most households, which means that there are more mouths to feed with the output from the same fields. In most cases the addition of labor alone does not raise production, so the extra hands do not contribute enough for their own support. People with insufficient land will take to the highways as migratory labor, much as the Okies, Arkies, blacks, Appalachians, and Mexicans have done in North American agriculture. For rice, at least, the achievement of maximum yields on farms of less than two hectares is labor intensive. Many eventually find a small place to settle down to sharecrop, some will participate in land reform schemes, but most will end up in metropolitan slums. Thus much of the labor surplus freed by increased agricultural productivity and reduced commodity prices reappears as substratum population in the city.

As a rule of thumb we think of the Green Revolution bringing about a quick (i.e., in five to eight years) doubling of yields wherever it is fully installed, with an additional 50% that can be realized after huge investments are made to improve control over irrigation water and experience is gained in combating pests and other hazards. Thus, over the course of a generation the unevenness in production would be reduced and the overall average yield enhanced, but not to the degree that the nearby cities have been accumulating surplus villagers. The Green Revolution by itself is an inadequate, interim solution. Very soon, in less than a decade, some new heroic measures must be planned for the densely populated societies which can be installed in the succeeding decades.[11] At the time that the increases to be obtained from the present developments in improved genetics and management are expected to be encountering the law of diminishing returns a way must still be found to double, and redouble, the flow of food supplies to the rapidly expanding cities.

Three such successor revolutions can be detected in the course of reviewing scientific and technological reports.

The first of these represents an extension of the Green Revolution type of organized agriculture into thinly populated, coastal desert regions with the assistance of nuclear energy. It would initiate a number of nuclear-powered agro-industrial complexes that promote food production which is partly labor-intensive but will depend increasingly upon large tractor techniques needed for multicropping. The second recycles urban organic wastes, preserving most of the phosphorus and nitrogen by microbiological conversions, and uses water to maximum advantage through labor-intensive measures applied within the urban environs. High-valued perishable commodities are produced from multicrop gardening and aquaculture close to the point of consumption. The consumer, with all of his wastes and wants, is intimately linked into a production system for two-thirds or more of the food tonnage moving within the city. The third revolution would aim at optimizing the conversion of sunlight to organic matter with the aid of virtually automatic continuous flow technology. Introducible almost simultaneously with the intensive gardening techniques, it would bring water surfaces into production instead of marginal land, so that the potential output is greater than the others combined. The prospective timing and relative shares of each is shown in figure 6.2.

THE NUCLEAR-POWERED AGRO-INDUSTRIAL COMPLEX

If the present agricultural trends are projected into the 1980s, the production of food will become increasingly specialized and market-oriented. Partially irrigated plains and rain-watered prairies will be allocated the task of producing cereals and legumes (heavily favoring soybeans and peanuts). The wet estuaries and flood plains will grow rice and sugarcane. Tropical sandy and hilly soils will produce palm oil and bananas. Mountainous areas will grow fruit, coffee, tea, and many spices. These staples will arrive at the environs of the city as bulk or containerized commodities; the subsequent processing into edible foods is expected to be continually refined and elaborated. Not only must these fit the taste and convenience of the consumers, but efforts will be made to extract a bit more sustenance from progressively scarcer water, soil, fertilizer, and fossil fuel resources.

Machinery, especially pumps for wells and tractors for the fields, will very often be able to add to yields by accomplish-

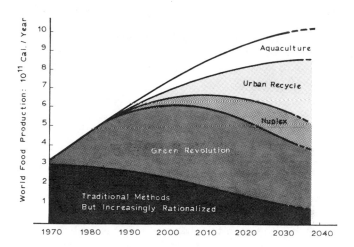

Figure 6.2 Future Sources of Food Production
Traditional methods are being displaced by high-yield strains and
by the more systematic use of fertilizer, water, insecticide, and
crop storage now more often associated with the Green Revolution.
Industrial farming techniques will be elaborated in the 1970s, and
can then be employed to advantage in the 1980s using natural gas
supplies in many instances as precursors to large nuclear reactors
energizing the cultivation of coastal deserts. Urban recycle gardening has existed in and around traditional cities, but public health
needs require a drastic reform; vegetables, tubers, and other
perishables will be grown intensively in new areas added to cities.
The aquaculture phase becomes significant first as mariculture,
producing high-valued domesticated fish, but it can later utilize
swampy areas to produce vegetable protein with algal culture.
The costs of production over time must increase, but the cost of
distribution of an adequate diet could diminish, because of economies of scale.

The Green Revolution and Its Aftermath   195

ing tasks that are impossible to carry out with labor-intensive techniques. More machinery will be added, for example, to enable farm operators to harvest, clear the land, plow, sow, and irrigate within a week, so that a second crop, or even a third intercrop, has a chance to mature. Therefore, agriculture in the lowlands is expected to exhibit increasing capital-intensity, even in countries with increasing rural underemployment. The most capital-intensive projects would be expected when reclaiming waste lands in unsettled and thinly settled parts of the world, among these the "nuclear-powered agro-industrial complex" presses the foreseeable limit.

The underlying idea for such a complex is readily understandable. It rests on the observation that a number of highly accessible coastal deserts throughout the world could produce food on a virtual factory-in-the-field basis, if water was made available. The heat from nuclear energy could be converted into the electric power needed to fix the nitrogen and reduce the phosphorus for fertilizers. Extra power could be employed in electrochemical industries backing up synthetic fertilizer production and the production of polyvinyl resin for irrigation pipe, using as a raw material the low cost sea salt offered by such a site. Electrometallurgicals would also be economical since magnesium salts can be obtained from the sea water and bauxite for aluminum could be readily imported through the port built to export agricultural commodities. Extra power would be available to be delivered to a metropolitan grid allowing the scale of the nuclear power plant, which would be by far the most expensive unit in the complex, to be set at a size that would get the best unit cost. A series of by-products would round out a complex that depends upon power and its by-products, but produces food, fiber, and industrial commodities to be delivered directly to a growing metropolis (see figure 6.3).

A survey of world climates and soils suggests such sites as (1) northern Mexico, adjacent to the Gulf of Lower California, (2) the coast of Peru and Chile, (3) western Australia, (4) the Gulf of Kutch coastline in India and Pakistan, (5) much of the coasts of Iran, Arabia, Egypt, and Sudan, (6) Somalia, (7) Morocco, Algeria, and neighboring arid coastal plains. Some of these may not need nuclear energy because they are endowed with low cost, often by-product, fossil fuels that are even more conveniently adaptable to "food

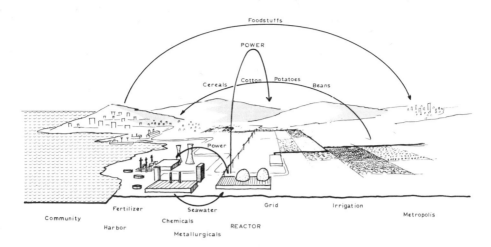

Figure 6.3 Nuclear-Powered Agro-Industrial Complex (Nuplex)
The Oak Ridge designs assume nuclear reactors with 1,000 MW (electric) or more capacity placed on an arid coastline. The bulky imports are ores and hydrocarbon feedstocks for chemical synthesis; the high-valued inputs are uranium, seeds, breeding livestock, and equipment for farming and industry. The reactor at the heart of the complex provides economical heat for the distillation of sea water. The fresh water is used for supplementary irrigation. Fertilizers are produced both for local use and for export. Extra power is consumed by the manufacture of plastics, insecticides, electrochemicals, and nonferrous metals. Large amounts are transported to a metropolitan grid. Typical agro-industrial output would include wheat flour, corn meal, potatoes, beans, cotton, fish, milk, meat, hydrogenated oil, and paper. For a unit farming 100,000 hectares (400 square miles) of desert, a city of over 100,000 population is expected to form back of the harbor.

The Green Revolution and Its Aftermath   197

factory" types of production, where machines and automata would carry on almost all operations. Among the remaining sites the principal problem preventing early utilization is the lack of a nearby metropolis to use the electric power produced by the nuclear plant and to connect it to other metropolitan areas. The most promising sites for early development are in Mexico, India, and Egypt. Careful technological studies have explored the possibilities in each of these instances.[12] They were conducted before the upward shift in the price of fossil fuels had begun, or the rise in world food prices, so the conclusions regarding economics require major readjustments.

The following procedure is recommended by technologists: Build a medium size nuclear reactor (300 MWe) with a high-efficiency desalination unit and a brine electrolysis plant. Sea water treatment to control scaling in the desalination unit is accomplished with sodium hydroxide and/or with hydrogen chloride obtainable from the electrolysis unit, depending upon local markets for chlorine and caustic soda. Build an electrolytic hydrogen producer and combine its output with nitrogen obtained from air to produce ammonia for fertilizer.[13] Add an electric furnace phosphorus unit that would produce the phosphate component for the fertilizer. Build pipelines to about a hundred thousand hectares of low, gently sloping desert soils, and sprinkle them with distilled water until the salt is removed from the surface. Add fertilizer and grow wheat, beans, cotton, oil seeds, potatoes, and specialized crops, depending upon world market prices and regional demand. Export the extra fertilizer with the agricultural produce through a sizable new harbor that may need to be dredged out. Incorporate as many power-intensive electrochemical and electrometallurgical plants as one can find markets for, and export as much power as possible by high-voltage cables. Add another power reactor with two or three times the capacity and repeat the previous steps where possible. By 1978 it is anticipated that even the two most advanced component facilities could be purchased "off the shelf," that is, requiring no risky research and development. They would be replicas of existing plants, slightly modified to fit the intended site, so that the operating characteristics are known, the delivery time is minimal, and risk of technological failure or major cost overrun is small.

Complications appear, however, as soon as the human element is added.[14] Planners discover this as soon as they map out a program intended to bring the "nuplex," as it came to be called in the Oak Ridge National Laboratories, into being. A modern organization of major dimensions must come into operation within a matter of months to make such a project feasible; it cannot take a decade to accumulate staff and experience because the smaller sizes of such a complex are uneconomic unless a sufficient supply of cheap fossil fuel is available initially—a condition that may exist in the Red Sea and Arabian Sea area but not elsewhere. Necessarily capable of administering advanced technology, this entity must spring from existing organizations—it could be, for instance, a joint venture between a government corporation with production responsibilities, a local marketing organization specializing in food, and an international group that understands both construction and commercial agriculture. The minimum capital for a food-producing nuplex based upon unoccupied coastal desert was estimated at a billion dollars (equivalent to a very large hydroelectric dam project) in 1968, and the amount of credit required before the first crops are harvested is about 40% of the total. Thus, an international financing agency, such as the Asian Development Bank or the World Bank, is likely to be involved.

The basic organization responsible for management must be programmed to come into being in the same fashion as the design of the technological facilities, with each step incorporating reasonable time lags. When such an exercise was carried out in 1968, it was discovered that the critical time-consuming stage was the local experiment station that developed appropriate seed stock for the farms, started the trees for the townsites (a coastal desert without shade is a most unattractive place to live), and built up breeding stocks of the animals and fish that would be used to consume by-products. Some of the best talent in the world must be attracted to the first nuplexes at this very early stage in order to minimize risks. Full operation probably could not be achieved in less than seven to eight years after taking over the land, and the systematic use of internally generated by-products could not be installed before another ten years. Full profitability could be achieved only about two decades after initiation.

One of the most surprising outcomes of this organizational calculation is the size of the projected population settled around the nuplex. In a developing country (which means any of the potential sites except Australia) a range of 250,000-400,000 persons seems most probable when assuming a 1,000 MWe nuclear capacity. The poorest countries would be found on the high side of that range, on the basis of an estimate of the demand for labor, which is substituted for capital as much as possible.

The expected structure of the new settlement would include (1) a "harbor city" that conducts manufacturing, shipping, and provision of services of about 100,000 population, (2) up to a score of "farm-factory villages" with 5,000-12,000 apiece, (3) smaller villages to settle the nomadic people in the region who prefer to manage livestock, and (4) several thousand independent farmsteads operating as "small-holders." Such a structure was arrived at in a pre-design exercise for a nuplex adjoining the Gulf of Kutch in western India (table 3).

The best use of nuplexes in Indian economic development would be as a substitute for the buffer stock of cereals and oil seeds required for the growth of large cities. Instead of holding a half ton or so of staples in storage for each permanent resident of the city, a nuclear reactor could produce desalinated water independent of the vagaries of the monsoon producing crops in all years and seasons with equal dependability and offering greater capacity to shift to alternative outputs in periods of more abundant supplies. The upper and lower shores of the Rann of Kutch alone, using presently known technology and obtaining yields already achieved under well-managed conditions could supply enough foodstuffs and fiber to support at least 150,000,000 people in cities at an adequate standard of nutrition. Pakistan has an equal number of satisfactory sites. The nuclear reactors could export enough electrical power to support all the nonindustrial needs of the urbanized populations as well.

The nuplex should be regarded in most developing countries as an urban satellite that could be launched by a metropolis to assure its survival when the Green Revolution encounters rapidly increasing marginal costs. Such a food-factory satellite could produce a fairly high percentage of profitable specialty foods in normal years but would revert to maximal production of cereals and legumes in times of

food scarcity. The coastal location, required for the desalination plant, suggests that the output could be barged
to coastal metropolises of the same society most economically, although some metropolises in China and Java may
have to rent parts of the Australian shoreline in order to
assure survival in times of world food shortage. There is
enough coastal desert in the world to enable billions of new
urban dwellers to consume traditional foods while they
are learning to live in the city. The nuplex is properly
understood as a highly rationalized, but perfectly obvious,
next step that carries current ideas about agriculture to new,
otherwise inaccessible soils using high-cost distilled water
to maximum effect, with revolutionary optimization and
elaborate linear programming approaches for achieving
economic levels of output.

  As a result of a careful comparative evaluation of alternatives the Indian Department of Atomic Energy rejected the
coastal agro-industrial complex at this stage but embraced
another scheme that should add to the effectiveness of the
Green Revolution in India. Its members identified the

Table 3
Operations of a Nuplex on a Coastal Desert Integrated with a Growing Metropolis (ca. 1995 A.D.)

Dimensions

Distilled water:	approximately	1,000 million gallons/day (3.6 million tons)
Electrical power:		1,000 megawatts (2 reactors at 300 and 700 MWe)
Cultivated land:		320,000 acres fully irrigated (130,000 ha)
Marginal land:		100,000 acres rain watered (40,000 ha)
Mariculture:		70,000 acres of fisheries (30,000 ha)

Management

100,000 acres (40,000 ha) corporation operated
50,000 acres (20,000 ha) smallholders (many under contract)
20,000 acres (10,000 ha) urban settlement, gardens, etc.
170,000 acres (70,000 ha) livestock, orchards, specialties

Typical Annual Crop Output

200,000 acres (80,000 ha) cotton (1,900 kg/ha)
400,000 acres (160,000 ha) wheat, millet, or maize (6,500 kg/ha)
120,00 acres (50,000 ha) legumes (3,300 kg/ha)
60,000 acres (25,000 ha) safflower (4,500 kg/ha)
60,000 acres (25,000 ha) potatoes, sweet potatoes, and yams (50,000 kg/ha)
70,000 acres (30,000 ha) fish and fish food (1,100 kg/ha)
100,000 acres (40,000 ha) forage crops
120,000 acres (50,000 ha) vegetables and small fruits (35,000 kg/ha)

challenge as being that of utilizing an efficient nuclear-powered generator of electric current at near capacity levels around the calendar. The energy would be used for food production, decentralized industry, and domestic purposes. They found that much land in the Indo-Gangetic plain, that is presently single-cropped with an occasional failure, could be double-cropped with little chance of failure if water were to be pumped off the land into canals during flood stage, then pumped up from the lowered water table during the dry period. Power would be required about eleven months of the year. Fertilizer applications would be increased, perhaps by a factor of three, and pest control would become a serious problem, but the yield per unit of land would be increased by more than a factor of two and the reliability of the agricultural output would be greatly enhanced. By drilling tube wells, digging canals and embankments, and laying pipelines for this kind of irrigation, much more land can be influenced by the Green Revolution (see figures 6.4 and 6.5).

The greatest problem in such a proposal lies in getting the people already settled upon this land to adopt complex new approaches to agriculture. The Indo-Gangetic plain contains some of the most conservative village populations of India, many of which have retained very high levels of illiteracy. If the rate of social change at the local level is the critical step, a very expensive nuclear reactor installed to pump the water might remain largely idle. The Indian proposal for getting around this difficulty is to establish a number of small temporary generating stations in thoroughly surveyed rural areas; these facilities have low capital cost but relatively high operating costs. Gas turbine generators fitted to several railroad cars could be put onto a railway siding near a market town, and from it a low voltage grid could be developed which served not only the pumps of scattered tube wells already drilled by enterprising groups of farmers but also a systematic network of new wells designed to get the greatest value from the geological structure of the aquifer.

The temporary generating plant would be supplied with fuel by railroad car. The same trains could bring in fertilizer ingredients for local mixing, insecticides, cement, pipe, and other supplies: a central supply station for producers' cooperatives would be a natural outgrowth of the installation. Some formula for mixing state direction (only the

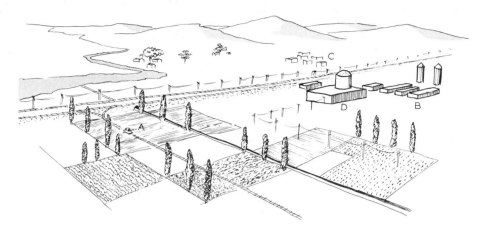

Figure 6.4 Nuclear-Powered Agro-Industrial Complex for India
The Atomic Energy Commission in Bombay has designed an evolutionary form suited to the Indo-Gangetic plain. Rural districts are electrified with mobile gas turbine power plants that can be used to operate pumps of several kinds eleven months of the year. Precision water control would allow multiple-cropping instead of the growing of an uncertain single crop. The district center also mixes and distributes fertilizer, fuels, and insecticide. In addition, materials, seed, technical advice, and credit are made available. When sufficient tube wells and drainage have been installed, the nuclear reactor should come into operation and provide the required energy. The displaced gas turbines move farther down the rail lines and start new districts, thereby justifying expanded nuclear production. One calorie of energy from fission can thus produce, with the aid of sunlight and the proper amount of water, about three calories of food.

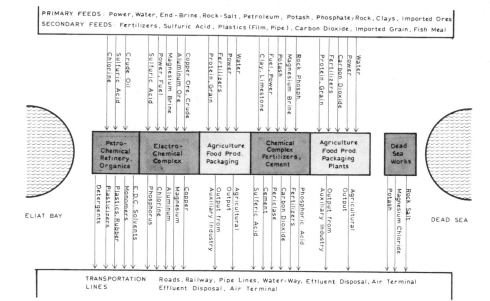

Figure 6.5 Israeli Version of the Nuplex Concept
Installations are proposed for the most desolate part of the country, a corridor between the
Dead Sea and an extension of the Red Sea. The distilled water is intended to make the Negev
region bloom. (Reprinted from David Vofsi, "An Agro-industrial Complex in the Arava,"
Bulletin of the Atomic Scientists, 28, no. 8 (October 1972), 45-51.)

state could install the levees, canals, and bunds) with local cooperation needs to be found, and each village will pose different problems. The motivating force is the prospect of doubling earned income in the community within a few years, with the potentiality for more as greater skill in irrigation technique is acquired. When enough of the villagers adopt organized agriculture of this type and electrify their households, the expense of a nuclear reactor that can produce electric power at half the price (or less) can be justified. Then the portable gas turbine generator can be moved on to another district in Uttar Pradesh or Bihar and repeat the transformation process for another several hundred villages out of the hundred thousand that await such change.

Thus far the concern expressed about the feeding of cities has been quite standard; we have assumed, as almost all others have done, that human taste is relatively fixed. However, the ferment in the countryside and the even more rapidly changing life-styles in the city suggest that more radical possibilities, those involving the dissolution of tradition in diet, should also be explored.

ESCAPE FROM TRADITION

When people live at subsistence levels and are immersed in a single tradition, they will eat only items that have been previously defined by family, peers, and community as food. Taste is virtually invariant. Because cities bring about a mixing of people, and the cuisine of one society is made available to others, dietary customs are challenged. Another challenge comes from science, which accumulates rather comprehensive objective information about the nutritional needs of the average man. Once the propriety of tradition in diet is no longer binding, radical changes in production become possible, including the domestication of new species of crop plants, which would add to output in critical places and at critical times.

At present the preparation of food according to habit or ritual in the countryside is being displaced by the practice of an art in the metropolitan tradition. In urban areas one encounters many degrees of quality in cooking—the rare, high-level achievement, the competent performance by a disciplined artisan, the faddish popular presentations, and the miscellaneous morsels offered by hawkers in the streets. Style of presentation is the basis of most popular discussion about the adequacy of food, rather than nutrition of the

body. If the arts of cooking and eating could be rationalized to the point where people ate a nutritionally balanced
combination of what was most economically produced, the
outcome would be equivalent to a doubling of the yield in
agricultural production. This kind of revolution in consumer behavior is very likely part of the sequel that is needed
when the Green Revolution loses its momentum.

Freeing the human diet from ancient customs has proceeded the farthest in the United States; the process has been
vastly accelerated by the way in which television commercials have exploited every possible association with traditions and past preferences. Tradition has been made
cliché, so the consumer welcomes new ideas in eating even
if he must pay for the cost of innovation and for the design of the imagery which dresses it up. As a consequence,
hundreds of new products made from low-cost but nutritious materials and branded with carefully selected names
have invaded the American supermarkets, and an increasing number of them maintain their niche on the shelves in
competition with all other household products. A significant proportion of them are convenient snacks and beverages designed to be consumed in front of a television set
and in other areas in the home not specifically set aside for
dining, but they also make up a good share of children's
school lunches and appease the appetites of travelers.

Using demonstrations and adapted advertising techniques,
most of these specialty foods could be readily sold in Asian
and African cities. Sometimes one or another will become
a craze. For the best nutritional results this line of products
will need public supervision, a counterpart of the United
States Food and Drug Administration, so that vitamin and
mineral enrichment of the vegetable foodstuffs is assured.
Packaging should also be continually reviewed by some
responsible public body because cities have rapidly changing problems with the disposal of their litter. A large proportion of income from sales of food specialties goes to
"middlemen" rather than agriculture; this trend fits the
pattern expected of cities in the future, where new jobs are
predominantly in the service sector.

Developing countries very much need protein foods in
ready-to-eat packaging and a few products are now appearing. ProNutro is a powder sold in Africa for soup, beverage,
or cereal. Vitasoy is a popular soybean-based bottled drink

in Hong Kong; Singapore and Malaysia have a Vitabean; Bangkok has a Vitamilk; and Guayana in South America has Puma. Though all have the same basic ingredients, each has a different taste. Protein-enriched breakfast cereals and packaged soups offer other modes of entry into the diets of developing countries.[15]

One trend in dietary change, the gravity of which cannot be overemphasized because it markedly increases the likelihood of a Malthusian crisis and reduces the effectiveness of the Green Revolution, is the spread of the consumption of meat. Chapter 1 described how modern cities have evolved an ecosystem that maintains quite large populations of domesticated animals for meat production. Most of these animals are raised at distant points, slaughtered there, and the refrigerated carcasses are transported and stored before they are cut to meal-size portions. Every calorie of nutrition obtained from this meat consumption requires five to ten calories of vegetable feed, and the feed is produced by the same soil resources that would grow staples for a low-income human diet. Thus, the meat is produced at the expense of food supplies for the poor. The modern, affluent cities of the world have already contracted for much of the world's high potential soil resources in order to support the livestock their inhabitants eat; now the elites in the cities of developing countries are acquiring the same enthusiasm for meat with similar consequences for agriculture. Beefsteaks and French cuisine are spreading out of the intercontinental hotels into the restaurants of business districts. Hamburgers, sausages, fried chicken, and kebabs are now being franchised for mass sales. If the typical consumption levels reported in meat-eating urban areas (around 200 lbs, or 90 kg, per capita per year) were applied to the world, it would double production requirements for original calories and overwhelm all possible economies to be obtained in the course of rationalizing nutrition.

At the other extreme, a strict vegetarian diet, sentimentally denying man's role as a predator species in nature, is also notably inefficient. By-products of farm crops and yields of inferior grade should be consumed close to the point of origin so that their phosphate and nitrogen can be recycled effectively. Some kind of biological converter can almost always be found that is efficient in carrying out such a function. Therefore, a maximal output from the land farmed by well-organized agricultural enterprises should contain a significant fraction of animal meat and fat.

The urban resident whose social status is improving tends to eat more meat, and he resents government efforts to prevent him from doing so. If the government makes strenuous attempts to force a reduction in meat consumption (usually done by developing a rationing system), a black market in meat is likely to result. This means that the developmental metropolis in densely populated countries needs a substitute for meat almost as badly as it needs a substitute for the automobile—both are expensive tastes that cannot be afforded except in small amounts. This would be true even in a future associated with the smallest of the projected global population increases.

Fortunately for the societies approaching complete use of their soil resources, the scientific work on proteins and tissues has progressed to the point where economical meat substitutes can be prepared. The fact that the pioneering technological and marketing developments are being carried out in the United States, where the taste for meat is highly elaborated, is likely to increase the rate of acceptance overseas. It is reassuring to read an item, such as the following, in a recent technological journal:

Meat substitutes from plant sources

By the 1980's many Americans will be eating ersatz "ham" made from soy protein, boneless "chicken" from cottonseed protein, and "hamburgers" from peanut protein, according to Dr. Herbert Stone, director of Stanford Research Institute's food sciences department. He forecasts that consumption of protein concentrates in the U.S. will increase from about 500 million pounds today to 5 billion pounds by 1985. A few years ago, he says, high-protein meat substitutes made from low-cost plant sources retained an aftertaste of the original plant flavor, but now their taste and texture can be made indistinguishable from that of meat.
Chemical and Engineering News, 50 (April 24, 1972), 17.

In the United States, both Worthington Foods and General Mills have been active in developing and marketing textured foods produced by either spinning or extrusion of vegetable proteins. They report a "new level of sophistication in producing textured animal food analogs," which allow the food manufacturer to synthesize a product that is more nutritious than meat, since it does not contain cholesterol.

In Japan, flavor is far more important than texture, and a much larger variety of proteinaceous, processed foods such as *shoyu, tofu, miso,* and various noodles are made with plant proteins, mainly soy.

Acceptance of such processed protein in America received its first strong impetus when the Food and Nutrition Service of the Department of Agriculture allowed textured vegetable protein (now often referred to as TVP) to be used as an extender for ground beef, poultry dishes, and sausages in school lunches. Another push came when supermarkets began to use a 30% blend in hamburger to keep it from rising as rapidly as other beef prices during the 1973 Phase Four price control efforts. TVP is required by regulation to have a protein efficiency ratio of 1.8, as compared to 2.5 for standard milk casein. The actual levels of protein efficiency have been around 2.0, but the level can be raised further through the addition of some fish protein concentrate, which is mostly produced from the rich anchovy fisheries off Peru and Ecuador. Up to 30% fat is added to the spun fiber, as well as vitamins and minerals of types and concentrations characteristic for meat.

One difficulty to be anticipated is that the preferred sources of protein—soy, peanut, and cottonseed—have not been very susceptible to the attempts to increase crop yields. Whereas maize yields increased 4% per year in the 1950s and 1960s in the American Midwest, on the same soils and in the hands of the same farmers soybean yields increased no more than 1% per year. Nor do the experiment stations promise any new genetic strains with remarkably higher productivity. Increases in production will come at the expense of acreages in maize and wheat, much of it in South America and Africa. Experiments covering the acceptance of TVP were already under way in at least ten developing countries, and the reports have been good, mainly because of a compatibility with indigenous spices.

It is quite possible that protein "requirements" for adequate nutrition have been too large; the standards set by medically trained Westerners in the World Health Organization and the Food and Agricultural Organization are repeatedly revealed to be overgenerous on the basis of field surveys. Perhaps too much of a safety factor has been incorporated in the caloric and protein requirements to obtain a fair distribution of food when it is scarce.[16] Reductions of the order of 10-20% may be possible as the distribution system incorporates vitamins and other nutritional additives. As will be argued later, since this improved nutrition leads to significant increases in body size in the next generation beyond subsistence agriculture, the potential saving in food may have an effect primarily in the generation of urban migrants themselves and very little thereafter.

Fish occupies the role of a meat substitute in the diets of many cultures. Although nutritionally the equal of meat (a little less protein per unit weight, due to higher water content), fish are less highly valued in world markets. The relative price (about half that of meat) will probably increase over time because the hunted species of fish will not sustain much higher yields, and many of the wild populations are being reduced because of overfishing. Thus far only a few edible fish species have been fully domesticated; of these carp and tilapia are the most popular among the fish-farming specialists. The highest yields are obtained in tropical ponds where fish serve as converters of vegetable by-products and animal wastes, as well as consumers of plankton.[17] The production of shellfish along the coasts, the most active branch of mariculture, offers an efficient means of harvesting nutrients. Most species of fish grow faster and more efficiently in warm water, so the low-grade energy delivered to the rivers and seas by power plant cooling systems in the future can be put to productive use.

Therefore, the diet of most people living in cities a generation or two hence is likely to be based upon many convenience foods and labor-intensive delicacies made from plant proteins and fats, with fish filling in for the more formal regular meals. Meat will be reserved for special occasions. Beverages would have a wider range of flavors, with the new ones being as carefully synthesized as Coca-Cola or the latest "wines" designed for the youth market, but still contributing to balanced nutrition. Taste is so conservative, however, that even the new entries will probably remind the consumer of the familiar spices, flavors, and condiments discovered by various cultures before the dawn of history. The remarkable feature about the future diet in normal (non-famine) times is the extended range of choice that will be offered to the underemployed poor as well as the salaried man; it serves as a significant attraction for some rural migrants.

Attention has been focused thus far upon regional situations over the next four decades or so, in part because the crystallizations of large-scale urbanism is a regional phenomenon but also because the stresses of meteorological extremes, ideological excesses, and of human conflicts focus upon regions. The first nutritional crises are likely to arise under conditions when a region either has become disconnected from the global system or else has been so loosely coupled with it that the rest of the world is unable to transmit sufficient assistance.

Technological and social forces combine to integrate the cities of the world. Improved telecommunications bring markets, interest rates, and knowledge into equilibrium. Vastly increased capacities for air and water transport will permit quick redistribution of inventories of commodities and semimanufactures, so that the scenario for famine in northwest China would have been halted through the delivery of food from the outside if droughts of the same severity had occurred two decades later (and global transport capacities would be estimated four times greater). An integrated world system, through a market, would take on the problems associated with the supply of food in a somewhat more organized way.

As we now envision it, the rationalized food production systems associated with the nuplex and the reformed agrarian societies will be moving their surpluses to burgeoning metropolises in the early twenty-first century. These commodities will be converted in the cities into a wide variety of standardized, graded, labeled packages in sizes convenient to the consumer, but less wasteful of paper, plastic, and sheet metal than today. Traditional foods, without the packaging, would still be widely served in public and in the home. The additions of the coastal deserts, and of mariculture, to presently surveyed soil resources promise to open up sufficient capacity to meet the requirements of the growing cities. Moreover, the production should be more dependable, season to season, than at present. A large share of the improvement in efficiency would be met by addressing attention to patterns of consumption, changing them by means of product design, education, demonstration, and advertising through the mass media. The dietary requirements for ten billion urban residents do not constitute a very difficult challenge to planners even for the contemporary state of knowledge about food technology, if approached incrementally. Later additions to capacity are highly capital intensive, thus they must be preceded by the achievement of enhanced efficiency and mobilization of savings within the cities themselves. Food production becomes much more like other industries, though in this instance the technology is regulated by the availability of sunlight and the cost of the energy going into fertilizer and transport.

One often overlooked feature of improved dependability and quality of nutrition is the increase in a human body size—about 20% in the first generation of escape from subsistence level food intake and another 10 or 20% in succeeding generations.[18] North Americans saw this happen to the children and grandchildren of their immigrants; gains in stature and body size were particularly marked among those from the tropics. In the last stages of its urban transition, Japan now finds that its school furniture is too small to be used, and classes in old buildings must be reduced in size. The need for protein is increased proportional to weight, while the need for calories is proportional to skin surface (or the two-thirds power of body volume or mass) and also to the amount of extraordinary physical work done. This factor is expected to add a demand during the twenty-first century above and beyond population increases roughly equal to the present total food production. It can be avoided only if scientific techniques could be developed for reducing new generations to pygmies (not impossible) and, much more important, the social system attributed high status to smallness (very few precedents).

Part of the changes in food production that follow upon the Green Revolution and will be strongly responsible for the diet improvement that results in the anticipated increase in body size of urban residents are the developments in very intensive gardening, a large share of which can be conducted in the zones of the metropolis yet to be constructed. The basic scientific knowledge underlying the creation of an efficient food web within metropolitan boundaries is already at hand. Gardens, whether operated with soil or dispensing with it, as in aquaculture, offer a natural part-time occupation for rural inmigrants. In the beginning traditional high-yielding tubers, vegetables, and small fruits would be grown for consumption inside the neighborhood and among relatives. This is a labor-intensive activity suited to the marginal workers in urban households—women, juveniles, handicapped, and aging—at least as well as any work available in the home villages.

The first stages of food processing, cleaning, preparing, grading, and crating the new output, are equally labor intensive. They must be done promptly, as well as carefully; otherwise expensive, energy-intensive refrigeration is needed to prevent spoilage. Much of the delivery to customers can be expedited with hand-carts, scooters, and small vans. This is an industry that might well use as much as 5% of the total labor, and 10% of the citizens in the labor force, at a time when half or more of the population is already living at the minimum adequate standard of living. Availability of water is the limiting factor so the possibilities will be discussed in detail in that connection in Chapter 7.

For the long run, an intricate, highly capitalized web of biological interdependencies is envisioned. It would emphasize those higher plants that incorporate both means of fixing carbon dioxide (i.e., the oxaloacetate as well as the 3-phosphoglycerate intermediate).[19] (See figure 6.6.) The ambient temperatures associated with this optimal synthesis will be in the 20-35°C range.[20] Perhaps a third of the caloric value of the diet, and more than three-quarters of its economic value, would be produced in the urban community, with the remainder being grown at a distance. The specialization should continue to a point where several thousands of species and varieties of higher plants are regularly marketed, as compared to a few hundred at present.

The fourth revolution in food production—application of the continuous-flow methods for promoting synthesis of foodstuffs—has already entered the preliminary stage in a small way. Continuous-flow processes require much more detailed measurements, but they conserve capital and labor and are far more susceptible to control by automata. The technique has already been used extensively in fermentation processes, and so the synthesis of protein by the mass culturing of food yeast was accomplished rather easily. In that instance the raw material was molasses or hydrolyzed cellulose from paper mill waste. In the past few years engineers have been able to extend these technologies to bacteria which utilize methane and wax for their metabolism. The organisms are then precipitated and centrifuged to be sold as "single-cell protein." The amino acid balance in such protein allows it to compete with soy and cottonseed

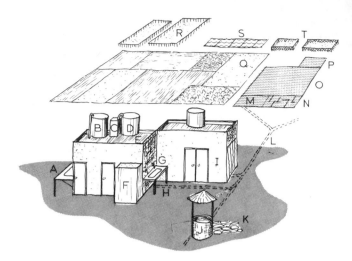

Figure 6.6 Recycle Systems for Urban Villages in a Tropical
Environment

The above arrangement fits life-styles found in Java. The facilities
shown in the lower half of the illustration should be constructed
by a neighborhood to fit its own needs. When the well or the urban
supply is suspected of contamination—a not infrequent condition—
potable water may be imported by truck and sold in plastic bags for
household use. Sewage from several urban villages would be combined, with the water and algae later supporting gardens, dairy,
chickens, and fish to be consumed by the human population in the
vicinity.

Key

A   Food preparation table
B   Second-quality water
C   Filter
D   Waste water from bathing
E   Solar water heater
F   Pumphouse, electric and manuel
G   Laundry area
H   Waste water from laundry
I   Toilets
J   Water-watcher's kiosk
K   Plastic bags of drinking water
L   Sewer line
M   Anaerobic digestion
N   Aerobic digestion
O   Oxidation pond
P   Algae harvest
Q   Intensive garden
R   Dairy cattle
S   Fish ponds
T   Chicken battery

products used for cattle feed. As with soy, it may eventually enter the textured vegetable protein industry for human consumption. The amino acid deficiencies in the original product can be balanced out by blending or by adding pure amino acids such as lysine and methionine.

Present production of single-cell protein fits into petrochemical complexes very handily. Into large chemostats, which maintain constant chemical and thermal ($\sim 45°C$) environments, are fed (1) pure methane or wax, (2) oxygen gas, and (3) an aqueous solution containing amino compounds, and salts taken up by the cells, while out of it is extracted cell mass. Although the British, German, Italian, and Japanese firms are quite secretive, it appears that the principal bacterium that is being domesticated in this fashion is *Methylococcus capsulatus.* It converts 30-50% of the caloric content of methane into calories of protein. By 1980 facilities culturing yeasts, molds, and bacteria should be producing new protein at a rate that equals millions of acres of new land being brought under the plow.

Producing protein from fossil fuel is a temporary expedient for the world. It is likely to remain economical over the lifetime of the production facilities now being built or planned, but not much longer. The obvious succeeding step is that of reducing the mass culture of single-cell photosynthesizing plants to continuous flow processes. The underlying science for that development was reviewed in my book *Science and Economic Development* (2nd ed., 1966), but since then the approach has been industrialized in Japan, with very little attention being paid to the achievements in the West because the product went into a Japanese form of yogurt consumed solely in local markets or into materials suited for the practice of Chinese homeopathic medicine on Taiwan. The cost of the *Chlorella* algae was too great to be competitive then for protein production, but the product was desired for its "growth factors." By the end of 1972 the plant capacity was in excess of 300 tons per year; the yields were typically 7-8 metric tons per hectare of pond of dry green product that is more than 50% protein.[21] If the 1973 prices for soybean meal ($250-350 per metric ton) persist, it appears that *Chlorella* could make an interesting substitute. The ponds could be located in areas that are otherwise unproductive and would thus constitute a net gain to food production capacity. They are usually built immediately outside cities.

The Japanese and Taiwan facilities use synthetic fertilizer mixes admitted to shallow, stirred, concrete ponds. The mixing and harvesting costs are not reported, but must be quite large. Their greatest success has been the control of airborne infection, but the methods used remain a trade secret. The largest facility is 200 hectares, but the dimensions have probably not yet reached a size that takes full advantage of economies of scale. Although production in Japan itself is seasonal, the annual yield closer to the tropics is not significantly increased, probably because of the haze usually present in the humid tropics that reduces incident sunlight.

In the long run it seems likely that cells of the leaves of higher species of plants will be cultivated by continuous-flow techniques. They would provide variety in compositions and flavors. Protein promises to be most cheaply produced by using nitrogen-fixing blue-green algae (perhaps the most primitive plants still alive), particularly the thermophilic varieties, which convert sunlight more efficiently and are not easily infected by bacteria. Enough scientific research has been completed to render any of these processes technically feasible, but the opportunities have been too little explored to determine which combinations are competitive. It is expected that yields should eventually exceed 10 tons per hectare of a product that is 50-60% protein.[22]

At that time, protein may well become the cheapest component of the diet, and, at least on a caloric basis, carbohydrate would be most prized. Fat, too, can be produced microbiologically, although the processes are much more difficult to control, but thus far there have not even been any serious suggestions for producing starches and other digestible carbohydrate polymers. If those conditions are maintained, much of the tropical regions may need to be assigned to the production of sugarcane and various roots and tubers.

What do these new approaches to the feeding of cities imply when they have become tightly integrated into a community in the ecosystem? What is the space economy that results? It is proper to ask about the peak densities of population that the foregoing provisions for conserving essential inputs will allow. An upper limit is set by the utilization of photosynthesis under controlled conditions. In the tropics and subtropics plants should produce with an efficiency of

2-8% of the radiant energy incident upon them, if we take into account all the kinds of energy stored in the protoplasm or in its immediate environment. The processes involved are relatively continuous and do not require heavy investments or elaborate equipment for stockpiling and the prevention of losses through spoilage. Safety factors can (and should) be large, and wastage of nutrients would be eliminated through design.

This kind of thinking harks back to the classical "man-land ratio" that one finds in older textbooks and still fits the ecology of agrarian settlements. For resettlements in primitive areas a fairly secure subsistence can be assured for a family size averaging five persons along with a cow or some goats, chickens, or pigs, and a cat or dog from two hectares of adequately irrigated land. If one allows for the extra space dedicated to reservoir (which yields some fish), and to roads for transferring surpluses to markets, the total space required comes to about 5,000 square kilometers for each million people to be settled. However, the various combinations of soil, water, and topography suited to such schemes are far from sufficient to provide niches for the households already in existence, not to consider the much larger numbers to be accumulated before zero population growth is achieved.

Cities can be more efficient in the utilization of sunlight because they can manage many more feedback loops, or techniques for optimization, and can draw upon many different kinds of supporting surface for the photosynthesis that provides for their nutrition. However, cities also create a demand for a higher standard of living than that of mere subsistence as a semiliterate peasant. City life creates an urge to participate in a flowering civilization as complex as any already in existence. A higher culture means that a much more varied diet will be demanded. Granting this aim to be legitimate, we can argue that the urban residents should be able to approach the presently calculated optimum conditions for photosynthesis when using fertilizer, genetic adaptation, and recycled by-products, along with balanced and economical nutritional behavior on the part of the public. Such designs commit only about 500 square kilometers to tropical agriculture and intensive aquaculture for the support of a million people and their associated livestock. Of this about a half could be at a distance from the principal concentrations of urbanites.

In twenty-first century designs, which would not yet be at steady state or climax conditions, decision makers will find it economic to draw upon coal, shale, tar sand, and uranium deposits for basic energy supplies. The cities themselves will then be producing a predominant share of their perishable foodstuffs. For the same million people it now appears that about 40 square kilometers or more could economically be devoted to intensive gardens and hydroponic style aquaculture carried on within walking distance of urban dwellings. An approximately equal amount of area is required for algae culture, both for recycling and for the production of foodstuffs made from plant proteins.

These dimensions should be compared to 6-8 square kilometers of sheltered living space per million human population, and an equal amount for their public space, plus some structure for storing and protecting artifacts. Not all of the floor space needs to be at the ground level. A common compromise would allow 20 square kilometers to structures (half or so multistory), an equal amount to circulation, twice that to garden, twice again to pond, something like this also to reservoirs upstream, some mariculture nearby, and the remainder to agriculture at a distance. This newly balanced ecosystem established by stepwise design should be able to evolve toward a true steady state.

1. Morton C. Grossman argues that this transition should be called the "Green Evolution," because the overall effects upon food production amounted to only 2.5% per year in national food production.

2. John Cownie, Bruce F. Johnston, and Bart Duff, "The Quantitative Impact of the Seed Fertilizer Revolution in West Pakistan: An Exploratory Study," *Food Research Institute Studies in Agricultural Economics, Trade, and Development,* 9, no. 1 (1970).

3. A popular account with excellent technical foundations has been provided by Lester R. Brown, *Seeds of Change* (New York: Praeger, 1970). This was followed by *Social Impact of the Green Revolution* (New York: Carnegie Endowment, 1971) and a view from a global perspective which prescribes measures of international integration, *World Without Borders* (New York: Random House, 1972).

4. A multitude of stories has appeared, each recounting a few of the unplanned consequences. An organized analysis is provided by Walter P. Falcon, "The Green Revolution: Generations of Problems," *American Journal of Agricultural Economics,* 52, (December 1970), 698-715.

5. This warning was the message of Norman E. Borlaug, who received the Nobel Peace Prize for his organizational, scientific, and technological contributions leading to the Green Revolution, in his Coromandel Lecture in New Delhi in March 1971. See *Fertilizer News,* 16 (June 1971), 21-28.

6. One body of literature is assessed by T. G. McGee in his "Catalysts or Cancers? The Role of Cities in Asian Society," in Leo Jakobson and Ved Prakash, eds., *Urbanization and National Development* Beverly Hills, Calif.: Sage, 1971), pp. 157-182. An approach arising from the concepts of political system has been contributed by David E. Apter, *The Politics of Modernization* (Chicago: University of Chicago Press, 1965). McGee identified the connection between the traditional rural society and the bazaar society of the metropolis, and capitalist industrial-type firm with the modern bureaucracy. Apter is concerned with the ways in which modern roles are spread through a traditional society from the centers of power and how they mobilize individuals through a combination of information and coercion.

7. Reallocating land so as to emphasize family farms quickly encounters innovations that would be labor-saving or yield-enhancing if farms were larger. As economic development proceeds, small farms require increasing subsidy.

8. None of the states of India has found it possible to cut back the admissions into colleges, despite the wave of disturbances. It was

thought for a while that the spread of extreme radicalism, particularly the Naxalite ultra-Maoist movement in Eastern India, which was accompanied by alienation of students and graduates from their families, might act as a deterrent. However, police repression in West Bengal detained thousands, and scores died in a fratricidal phase during 1971-72, so the extreme features of the expression of protest have not diverted the channels that deliver the youth to the cities, there to become disenchanted. Academic administrators report that rural youth are more likely to become involved in violent protests than those with urban origins, although the latter are more competent at demonstrations, which are noted by the press.

9. Background music provides one of the simplest tests. In 1966 I noted that Japanese television advertising already used at least half international themes, with Western classical music for high prestige modern artifacts, and Japanese music for programmatic material. Five years later only about a tenth of the themes were Japanese, and most listeners in Tokyo were unable to discriminate between West and East.

10. World prices for wheat, maize, and rice declined markedly after the famine threats of 1966, while food prices as a whole tended to increase and industrial prices increased more rapidly. Thus in the 1968-1972 period the subsidy programs aimed at holding down the production of unwanted foodstuffs became very expensive. The poorest rural producers were normally selling the lowest grades of output, and these exhibited greater than average weakness. Many were not helped when prices reached their peaks in 1973 because they experienced severe floods. Excesses of natural phenomena produce inequities in the rural community, and the Green Revolution seems to exacerbate them. Those that are able to practice modern agriculture can take measures to minimize the cost of disasters.

11. The impact of the new agricultural technology in wheat will have subsided by the 1980s, according to Cownie, Johnston, and Duff (see note 2), but rice will take longer to reach its zenith, while millet and oilseeds would help the food supply enough to move into the 1990s. The expected onset of regional inequalities and income disparities, particularly among small cultivators, sharecroppers, and landless agricultural laborers, has been discussed repeatedly. See Montague Yudelman, *OECD Observer,* June 1971, pp. 15-30; Z. M. Ahmad, *International Labor Review,* 105 (January 1972), 9-34.

12. Much of the Oak Ridge investigations of the technology and economics of the nuplex have not been published, largely because of political sensitivities. Such studies could be interpreted by citizens of the country concerned to be acts of imperialism, even if (as was always the case) engineers and agronomists from the country itself participated in the investigation with full approval of their governments. Opinions change only when food is critical, but fitting into public approval in this fashion makes it impossible to plan

in advance. The last report to appear was ORNL-4293, T. Tamura, W. J. Young, M. M. Yarosh, *Possible Locales for the Agro-Industrial Complexes* (Oak Ridge National Laboratory, February 1971). The first was ORNL-4290, *Nuclear Energy Centers: Industrial and Agro-Industrial Complexes* (Oak Ridge National Laboratory, 1968). The urban effects of the use of this technology on an economic scale are outlined in R. L. Meier, "The Social Impact of a Nuplex," *Bulletin of the Atomic Scientists,* 25 (March 1969), 16-21. The major Indian report followed: see K. T. Thomas, Chmn. Working Committee, *The Nuclear-Powered Agro-Industrial Complex* (Bhabha Atomic Research Centre, Atomic Energy Commission, Government of India, Bombay, June 1970). A number of unpublished analyses have been prepared elsewhere, particularly for Mexico and Israel.

The uniform conclusion seems to have been that with 1972 commodity prices the effort would be marginal at best; at 1973 prices it would be profitable, even when allowing for the high interest rates. One or two instances of the coastal desert model seem likely to be started in the 1970s in order to expedite political as well as welfare goals.

13. At this point the industrial chemist, knowing about the need for using up intermediates as well as that of balancing outputs, will note that this proposal thus far generates a huge amount of oxidizing agent at the site—oxygen in both liquid or gaseous forms from electolysis of water and the production of nitrogen for fertilizer. This surplus opens up the site to a variety of other industrial processes not specified here; they depend upon access to mineral resources in the community. However, it is not expected that they will add any more to the value-added-in-manufacture than the miniscule amounts generated by access to sea salt.

14. A detailed analysis of the organizational implications and some of the impact upon urbanization is provided in R. L. Meier, "Resource-Conserving Urbanism in South Asia III: Two Nuclear-Powered Agro-Industrial Complexes," Working Paper No. 85, Institute of Urban and Regional Development, University of California, Berkeley, October 1968.

15. The promotion of protein-rich foods with a balanced distribution of amino acids has often been undertaken by the nutritional scientists themselves, consulting with private entrepreneurs. Elsewhere they work with governments. It is virtually impossible for ordinary citizens to distinguish science-based contributions to the diet from those of food faddists who borrow much of the terminology but add many unnecessary injunctions which may be harmless physiologically to the consumer but add to the cost of production. A useful source of information about dietary improvement programs elsewhere in the world has been the newsletters of the League for International Food Education in Washington, D.C., an organization founded by food scientists, with Samuel M. Weisberg as director.

16. Nicholas Wade "World Food Situation: Pessimism Comes Back into Vogue," *Science,* 181 (August 17, 1973), 634-638. This is a good recapitulation of various kinds of expert opinion interacting with itself through the press. Since the press emphasizes highlights that the public wants to believe, an irregular oscillation of mood is built up that operates almost independently of objective forecasts, such as provided by the futures markets and estimates of products potentials.

17. The experience with growing various domesticated fish has long pointed up the advantages of a warm habitat; J. E. Bardach, John H. Ryther, and W. O. McLarney, *Aquaculture* (New York: Wiley-Interscience, 1972). Arrangements have been reached for establishing a mariculture facility on the effluent of the Moss Landing power station at the mouth of the Salinas valley in California, but production is not likely before 1975.

18. Gabriel W. Lasher, "Human Biological Adaptability," *Science,* 166 (December 19, 1969), 1480-1486. Also, Japan Ministry of Health and Welfare, *Nutrition in Japan, 1959* (Tokyo, December 1959).

19. The four-carbon pathway to the fixation of carbon dioxide in photosynthesis is a relatively new and important finding. Maximum efficiency for these plants is achieved when the leaf surface is at 35-47°C, instead of about 25° for the plants limited to the three carbon route. Jean L. Marx, "Photorespiration: Key to Increasing Plant Productivity?" *Science,* 179, (January 26, 1973), 365-367; I. Zelitch, *Photosynthesis, Photorespiration, and Plant Productivity* (New York: Academic Press, 1971). An excellent report illustrating the sources of the enhanced efficiency and describing genetic experiments aimed at extending the range of this discovery is provided by Olle Bjorkman and Joseph Barry, *Scientific American,* 229 (October 1973), 80-93.

20. R. I. Mateles and S. R. Tannenbaum, eds., *Single-Cell Protein* (Cambridge, Mass.: MIT Press, 1968). This is a very balanced review of the state of knowledge in 1967. The contributions and potentials of algal culture are fully reviewed by William J. Oswald and Clarence G. Golueke, pp. 271-306 with hints of things to come arriving from Africa via France reported by Genevieve Clement.

21. The only major publication on the modern mass culture technology of *Chlorella* is a book in Japanese by Takachi Yoshiro, *Chlorella: Fundamental Knowledge and Application* (Tokyo: Gakushukenkyosha, 1971). I am grateful to Professor Michael C. McGarry of the Asian Institute of Technology, Bangkok, for providing me with a partial translation.

22. Much higher yields of algal biomass have been reported in the literature and most reviewers are far more optimistic, the latest of them being T. R. Schneider, "Efficiency of Photosynthesis as a Solar Energy Converter," *Energy Conversion,* 13 (July 1973), 77-85. Careful inspection shows that most calculations do not take into account losses due to plant disease, the energy costs of stirring or of harvesting the crop, the special stimulus of organic substrates, as from digested sewage, and other such factors. My calculations use an estimate that represents only a slight improvement in net yield from what has been obtained commercially during an early stage of the art in facilities on Okinawa and Taiwan, thus representing a precaution against overoptimism.

ENERGY AND WATER SUPPLY Chapter 7

Almost everyone raised in an urban setting takes energy and
water for granted. They are obtained with the flick of a
switch or the turn of a tap. The supply is set up in such a
way that there can be no thought of strict economizing,
such as occasionally occurs with food, because bills come
a month or two later, or are hidden within the rent. Only
in the very poorest metropolises does one still find that the
conspicuous consumption of energy and water are involved
in the maintenance of social status, the provision of education, and the resolution of conflicts. Even there, citizens
naturally assign greater importance to other matters.
On the rare occurrences of prospective failure in supply
one does not restrict use, but puts in a stock of candles,
flashlights, and charcoal, or stores up reserve water in tubs,
buckets, and bottles. Often more energy and water are expended on the substitutes than are withheld by the utility
system during the breakdown, so that per capita consumption levels may not decrease even though the quality of
service does. When an interruption is over, the automatic
behavior characteristic of previous use is resumed.

Such conditioning is not conducive to the future economizing that appears to be required of cities. Therefore the
actual economizing must be done *for* people, not by them,
just as the supply was arranged for them in advance of felt
needs. The economies will have to be as automatic as the
use, with the shifts that recondition habits of life in cities
being widely debated as alternative public policies so that
residents understand the reasons for changes before they
are forced to adapt. Future programs of economizing must
fit into a context comprising all other issues at the community and metropolitan level. Plans must be formulated in
terms of the long-range commitments—contracts, bond
issues, and capital investments in general. They must be
set up on the basis of planned improvement programs or
capital budgets, and participated in to some extent by a
population that votes for a whole development package.

Since energy and water make up part of the physical environment of the city, we must revert for a moment to an
analysis of the urban ecosystem and consider the functions
of these two essential inputs. Although at present they
are quite separate services, they do create parallel problems,

and in the very long run trade-offs between them must be calculated.

ENERGY DISTRIBUTION IN THE URBAN ECOSYSTEM

Fossil and fissile fuels energize the machine populations in urban settlements. Imported fuels are delivered primarily to mechanized complexes—electric power plants and refineries—which convert them into electrical power or clean hydrocarbon or carbon fuels. The electrical power is distributed by means of a grid that is tapped by sessile motorized machines throughout the urban settlement. The purified liquid fuels are delivered to the motile machines because each vehicle must carry a reserve of fuel with it that adds as little as possible to total weight, and liquid hydrocarbons contain a higher concentration of energy per unit weight than any of the other chemical compounds that are readily handled. Electrical power, hydrocarbons, and coke are all used for the manufacture of such energy-intensive construction materials as light metals, iron and steel, concrete, glass, and plastics. Therefore, construction and repair of the physical environment in a modern city is increasingly energy-rich. Finally, the energy is used to moderate uncomfortable micro-environments by changing temperature, humidity, or air velocity in the vicinity, and it reduces inconvenience by generating light, precipitating dust, and performing similar tasks. To summarize, the energy (1) activates the machine populations, (2) produces the stuff from which machines and shelters are made, and (3) keeps environmental conditions of man and machines within a tolerable range. Tiny amounts are also used to (4) process food and water required by humans, and (5) activate the telecommunications circuits that extend the spatial range of both human and man-machine interactions.

The principal threat to long-run stability of energy flow and allocation within the urban ecosystem is the lack of natural replenishment of stocks of fuels. More than 95% of the energy is drawn from irreplaceable reserves. Within several hundred years cities will need to depend upon sunlight and geothermal energy with some help from hydroelectric power generation, in the manner of the other ecosystems that manage to maintain themselves for very long periods of time.

Living organisms require larger amounts of water than food, and the biomass in photosynthesizing plants demands more water by far than the protoplasm in man in most of the animals. The uses of water inside the organisms differ markedly from those outside. The primary function of water inside the cell is that of a medium for biochemical reactions that has the dielectric strength to bring together ions, metabolites, and organic polymers; second, water acts as a coolant by evaporating through the cell wall and must be continually replaced; third, water is needed to dissolve wastes excreted from cells. The daily intake of water by humans amounts to 5-10% of the body weight. More water is excreted by a human than is ingested because water is one of the oxidation products of food, but the differential is not great.

Much more water is used in human habitats for washing the skins of organisms and the surfaces in the environment than is consumed internally. The interfaces between organism and environment must be kept clean and sensitive, free from irritation. In cities, much huger amounts of water are also used to entrain wastes from organisms and machines, flushing them out of the settled area in underground sewers. Most cities add another use for water, flotation, when they build canals and waterways for the movement of bulk cargo and for recreational use.[1] The machine populations in cities, particularly the nonmotile types, also use water as a coolant.

Cities take on a different character as their ambiance shifts from moist to sere. A wet city will flush itself out through verdant tidal canals; its motorboat population approximates the auto population. Many of the dwellings are on boats, and much of the drinking water is collected off roofs from the rain. The runoff rate is kept high, because floods and mud can be a problem. Bangkok was a city of this type, but it is now burying its canals to accommodate the exploding automotive population. On the other hand, a dry city must fight dust, and its plant population is highly restricted—this result, in turn, limits local wildlife, especially birds. Much of the protection from oppressive solar radiation must be built into the city physically, while at night people sleep on the rooftops for comfort. Fountains, parks, and tree-lined avenues are highly valued, if judged by the proportion of water and energy

WATER DISTRIBUTION IN THE URBAN ECOSYSTEM

expended to support them. Teheran is such a metropolis, but it is reaching for still more water, laying the dust with asphalt, and accommodating a busy automotive population like the others.

Successful cities have been founded in estuaries and deserts, but quite surprisingly no sizable settlement has been established in a rain forest, and none has been maintained on pack ice. (Antarctica and Greenland have only camps, not cities.) The reason for surprise is that cities are most vulnerable to *variability* in water supply, yet both of these environments have water in abundant supply. Drought is the greatest threat to a city, and its implications have already been reviewed. Thus far pack ice and rain forest have been rejected for sites not only because they are uncomfortable but also because they required too much energy to provide year-round access and circulation for residents.

It was thought, when desalinization became commercialized, that many modern cities would establish themselves along desert strands. Producing fresh water from salt water, however, is an energy-intensive business, particularly when it is not a by-product of heavy industry. Therefore, proposals for new cities in these otherwise attractive sites have been shown to be exorbitantly expensive, and unable to compete with growth on the fringes of existing cities, unless the new sites serve as winter havens for well-off tourists.

FUTURE DECISIONS IN POWER GENERATION

Policy decisions with respect to the provision of added electrical power do not ordinarily raise political controversy in the developing areas. The decisions are said to be made on the basis of economic analysis. This means that the choices with respect to the site of operations, the scale of a facility, the technology employed, the quality of service, and pricing of the product have been analyzed with respect to each other in order to obtain the greatest possible social return. Yet, in apparent contradiction, some of the major policies affecting power production are actually arrived at by means of guidelines set in labor negotiations by precedents set by the courts, and by the standards for what are considered to be acceptable risks by insurance companies and government safety inspectors. The interactions between technology and social order encountered in planning a future urban society are worth careful scrutiny.

In general, one approach exists for countries endowed with sufficient petroleum potentials and another for those that must look elsewhere. Cities like Teheran, Baghdad, and Djakarta are able to get sufficient energy for future growth by converting the lowest-grade petroleum into electric power. The technology involved has barely changed in almost thirty years, and all of the equipment can be ordered "off the shelf" from any of a dozen sharply competing firms located all over the world. Foreign exchange for the power plant can be obtained from the sale of the naphtha, gasoline, or liquified gas fractions of the petroleum to other countries. The gravest problems faced by the public utilities firms supplying power in these countries are those affecting the price they get for their service, which may be warped by inflation, currency controls, or provisions for subsidy, and affect their capacity to sell bonds in the security markets. The requirements set by banks and institutional investors, however, have now become almost as standardized as the technology. The methods used are sufficient to force countries to sell power at economic rates so that one can have confidence in the ability of the public utility to finance the installation of new capacity and meet increases in demand even if they should reach 12% per year. Because such countries have been following directly in a path that has been taken repeatedly by many expanding Western countries since World War II, no crises were anticipated as long as the petroleum supply lasted. The power for transport is handled as easily because the fuel is generally available at low marginal prices and the transport systems are served by the standard vehicles used in the West. Thus Caracas, the primate city of Venezuela, does not really sense the need for an energy-economizing policy, nor does Lagos, since Nigeria has become an important exporter of petroleum.

As a result of the quick shift of the price of petroleum in late 1973 to what appears to be a new plateau, even the populous oil-exporting countries, such as Indonesia, will have sufficient capital to finance their own development. The constraint that most limits their growth henceforth is the greatly inadequate capacity of the local modern institutions. The rate of development will depend heavily upon the extent that the society can tolerate the foreigners needed to install the new infrastructure and supply the scarce technical skills. Serious friction must be anticipated because the imposition of their upper-middle-class suburban life-style upon a developing area looks like rank exploitation. Many of those consumption habits are likely to be transferred to the local people they train. These are the countries most likely to adopt the Western automobile-oriented urbanism.

The other 90% of the developing world will have to learn how to live with much higher petroleum prices. They are forced to pay close attention to systems for energy conservation, as well as substitute fuels. Coal and lignite, where those minerals are available, will again be given high priority. China and India, for example, have significant quantities of coal and the labor force to exploit it, but it takes close to five years to get new pit mines into full production. Therefore, even in countries with reserves of fossil fuels, the metropolises will experience strong measures for energy economy until well into the 1980s.

Surface mining has quite different implications for miners and consumers. First, the quality of the coal is poorer when it is so close to the surface; its primary use, therefore, is for electric power production, and very little will get into metallurgy or even into domestic use. Second, labor is of necessity associated with gigantic earth-moving machinery, and the miners associate with their machines more than with each other—a man and a machine make up a work team, rather than a band of men with hand equipment and a machine or two as in the underground mines. Third, the community of miners is so small, and so temporary, that it is likely to become regarded as a very high-status, very well-paying occupation by the agricultural community within which the mining goes on. The miners are envied rather than pitied, basically because they have so much horsepower at their disposal and are rewarded for the responsibility of keeping the equipment in operating condition. The principal drawback in open-pit mining is the reaction of the rest of the community to the step-by-step destruction of their environment. The cost of restoring the land to its original state or a near approximation is many times greater than its market value for agricultural or forest purposes. Emotions are not reduced by cold, dry statements of costs, however; so local political opposition to open-pit mining is easily aroused. Appeals for the preser-

vation of the land often have religious undertones. Therefore, the capital-intensive alternative for mining coal could,
depending greatly on site, encounter great troubles and be
no more dependable than pit mining even when its output
is most needed in the cities.

A further difficulty with coal is that it contains 16-30%
noncombustible minerals, which are converted to cinder
and ash when the coal is burned. The fly ash causes air pollution, and cinders make a major contribution to the solid
waste in a city. Thus cities with as low a consumption level
as Calcutta can (with some contribution from foundries
and steam engines on the railroads) accumulate a smoke
pall equal to any in the world from burning low-grade coal
for domestic purposes, though the temperature never falls
below freezing. The soil in central Calcutta has become an
ashy clay. Urban citizens have begun to rebel, however; so
it appears that electrification and gasification of coal will
be introduced along with more modern technologies for
energy use. Already the railroads are largely electrified or
dieselized, and new power plants are backing up an extended electrical grid. Smaller metropolises in the Indo-Gangetic
Plain will tend to follow the Calcutta metropolitan district,
even though the problems of pollution they face have never
been as serious. Bombay, being so far from the mines,
developed hydroelectric power and depended much more
upon imported petroleum products.

In Indian metropolises, as elsewhere in the developing
world, energy sources have evolved independently, so that
a variety of specific product-middleman-consumer relationships have grown up with relatively little change from one
source to another. The next set of development decisions
concerned with energy must strongly enhance interchange-
ability among fuels so that powerplants could use most
grades of coal, residuum from oil refining, or even switch
to liquified natural gas on a few months' notice if it should
become economical. Chemical processes may switch to
gasified coal to drive reactions to completion. Thus integration of the energy industries seems to be a key policy,
and in this step it appears that some of the space age technology offers promising shortcuts compared to the path
the West was forced to take in building its industrial cities
on a coal-steam-steel technology.

**Integrated
Coal
Development**

The United States is facing an energy pinch in the period from 1974 to 1985 because of the coincidence of several independent factors, all stemming from policies adopted in the past and none related to overall United States reserves of fossil fuels. The technological solutions we will introduce for the United States are expected to be applicable in part to developing economies that have access to moderate quantities of coal.[2] The set of fuel technologies that are to be fitted together and placed upon a coal field exist already but only at the level of small, isolated units or as advanced pilot plants. Pilot plants are likely to be licensed by the patent holders for installation elsewhere after they have been proved economical in the United States. The information on these processes now exists in technical reports and designs. Publications of the formal variety are not plentiful, but energy technology has an excellent reporting service, which can be depended upon to transmit important technological advances within months after they have been proved to work safely and efficiently; it is this technological journalism that will be drawn upon in preparing the following program for coal resource development. In laboratories and design offices the outcome is occasionally referred to as a "coalplex," comparable in many ways to the nuplex described earlier.[3]

The present recipe for a future (1980s and beyond) coalplex (see figure 7.1) in countries like Colombia, Korea, India, China, Mexico, Tanzania, Turkey, Chile, Brazil, and Mexico is as follows, if it is to be economical: Take a coal deposit that is guaranteed from information obtained by drilling from the surface to contain at least 20,000,000 tons of coal that can be mined, or preferably much more, and plot out a strategy for the lowest-cost extraction if forty years of production or more are anticipated. Find a source of cooling water, preferably fresh, that will dry up less frequently than once in a hundred years. Build an electric power plant to suit a demand for power projected three to four years after its start, but leave room for a twin- or a double-size plant immediately adjacent. Maintain a coalpile that serves as a buffer stock or reserve for the power plant, and set up a coal gasification unit on the other side of it. Send gas of high thermal value, mainly methane, to the industrial estates of the nearest metropolitan areas, primarily for chemical and metallurgical processing. Convert gas of low thermal value into hydrogen, concentrate

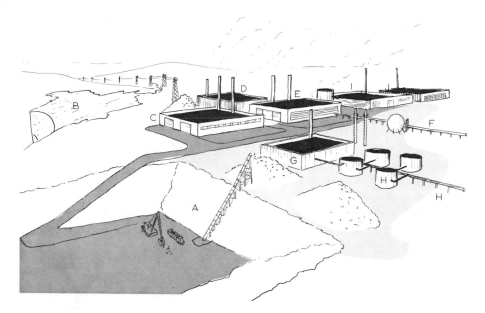

Figure 7.1 Simple Version of a Coalplex
Low-grade coal is now economically converted into gas, liquid hydrocarbons, and aromatic chemicals. With the aid of locally generated electric power a number of niches are created for fertilizer, resins, plastics, synthetic rubber, and a number of other manufacturing enterprises. By-product ash, combined with clay and lime, yields cement, cinder block, concrete pipe, and ceramic products. The most valuable products are gasoline, diesel fuel, jet fuel, and city gas.
Key
A Coal mining with spoil heap accumulation
B Reservoir of water for cooling and process stream
C Electric power generation
D Calcination of ash and clay
E Coal gasification
F Synthetic methane pipeline
G Coal liquefaction
H Hydrocarbon products pipeline
I Ammonia fertilizer plant
J Aromatic chemicals and resins. The chemicals and resins plant has barrels stacked next to it, preferably close to the railroad.

it, and deliver it to facilities in the vicinity that use either hydrogen or direct current (chemical syntheses, heavy-duty machines, nonferrous metals reduction).[4] If the demand for hydrogen rises, as a number of engineers now anticipate, a special capital-intensive high-yield reactor should be installed and much of the added hydrogen used onsite to convert coal into liquid hydrocarbons for a petroleum substitute. A new mining technique is being considered which would dissolve coal from the bed in the presence of hydrogen using bore holes similar to sulfur mining. It would expedite the reduction to liquid hydrocarbons.

With this recipe the industrial units at or on the coalfield would be exporting energy via (1) high-voltage cable, (2) gas pipeline, (3) liquid pipeline, and perhaps (4) railroad for the transmission of coal and coke. Downstream from the hydrogen plant most of the countries named earlier would find it advantageous to locate an ammonia plant, which draws the nitrogen input from air. The process absorbs quite a bit of power, which obviously can be produced more economically on this site than elsewhere. These additions would require a railroad to carry tanks of ammonia out to the irrigated fields in surrounding valleys.

Very likely the ash from the coal, which will be collected rather than belched into the air, will have a claylike composition that can be compounded with another clay and with lime. The mix can then be calcined with the aid of powdered coal or gas to make portland cement, cement pipe, cinder block, and other prefabricated building components. These products move by rail, primarily to the metropolis.

A few years after the coal hydrogenation and liquefaction plant has been operating, other opportunities will arise from the existence of certain fractions in the output that appear to be too valuable to be used as fuel; distillation towers and absorption columns would thus be installed. These steps will extract up to a tenth of the mass from the output. Benzene would be taken out for polystyrene production, toluene for the TDI (toluene di-isocyanate) component of polyurethane, orthoxylene and naphthalene for the phthalic anhydride that goes into paint resins and fiberglass laminate resins, paraxylene, which ends up in the popular polyester fibers, and perhaps a few others. Most of these intermediates will be shipped to the metropolis for further processing, but if one of the procedures requires pure oxygen, dilute hydrogen, carbon dioxide, off-peak electric power, or similar by-product potentials provided by the coalplex site, it will more likely take place in its immediate vicinity. Thus a miscellaneous set of small-to-medium-size chemical plants is likely to spring up as soon as the output mix of the basic production units is relatively standardized. They will be distributed among facilities based upon whatever other mineral resources are found in the region; a few of them will be attracted to the location by its superior transport connections.[5]

The mining community in the coalplex will be diluted by workers in the chemical and transportation industries. The result is a small industrial city that is dependent upon coal but might operate for a while off the stockpile; it is therefore not so vulnerable to the politics of negotiation with the miners.

After Coal, What?

When coal is depleted, a wasteland is left behind. The pit mine leaves a mound of spoil and an area that cannot be built upon because the ceilings of the abandoned drift tunnels will fall in. Hollows and holes appear at the surface to disturb drainage, tip structures, and kill many of the trees. Strands of broken wire cable emerge from the ground, and remnants of old foundations can be discerned in bush-covered hummocks. The settlements are old, shabby, disorganized, and show little attempt at decoration except for plots of flowers. The people who live in them have dedicated their lives to the mines or working for the community of miners. They prefer to spend their pensions at home, where the cost of living is low, while the next generation moves on to the metropolis.

An open cast mine (in a developing country that cannot afford the luxury of restoring the land completely) creates an incredible, corrugated landscape with grassy slopes, forested ridgelets, shallow ponds with deep greenish or reddish mud, at least one deep "fishing hole," and occasional piles of jumbled sedimentary rocks. The minimum size is about 300 hectares; usually a working mine is several times that scale. The best use of such land is for noisy activities—engine test centers, race tracks, motorcycle cross-country competition—but inevitably the demand is insufficient to match the supply, and the remainder becomes low-grade forest and pasture.

The urban energy users are forced to look elsewhere when the mines are closed. If extra geothermal energy is not available, they may have to depend upon nuclear energy for electric power. It could come from nuclear-powered agro-industrial complexes, from floating energy centers that stand offshore, or from nuclear power facilities built very much as at present, on isolated tracts of land adjoining the metropolis. The liquid hydrocarbon fuels so necessary for independent vehicles will be more problematic. The principal sources remaining fifty years or more from now will be oil shales, tar sands, and lower-grade coals, mainly in North America, Siberia, and the Near East. The world market will be larger than today, and the extraction process pushed to a gigantism in engineering on a scale not yet experienced. Many implications of that scale of operations are not yet evident. Most of the sites will produce methane and hydrogen gas that could be moved to the coast by pipeline, liquefied, and taken by tanker to coastal metropolises.

Since Earth Day was initiated (1970) and the environmentalist ideology became fashionable, many avant-garde space science engineers have come to regard liquid hydrogen technology as one of their major contributions to the cities of the future. They see the transfer of hydrogen as a very natural means of moving clean energy into metropolitan areas. There, with the aid of a fuel cell and solid-state devices, it can be converted into domestic voltages. A small bank of fuel cells and devices similar to those developed to produce alternating current for automobiles would supply an apartment house, a neighborhood, or a small-to-medium-size industrial establishment. The thermal efficiency is very high, and the equipment cost appears competitive with alternatives if, as is expected, the lifetime of the fuel cell can be extended severalfold.[6] Probably the heaviest cost will be for the nickel kept immobilized in these cells. The by-product is distilled water—a product that presumably has high value in the metropolis. The yield would be something in the neighborhood of three tons of such water per capita per year if energy were produced at the level of the minimum adequate standard of living. If a city were starved for water and paying the highest prices for distilled water, the water produced in this way would be about 10% of the minimum required. Thus hydrogen transmission represents a significant, but not a substantial, contribution to water inputs.

A completely different approach to energy generation draws upon sunlight and photosynthesis. After projecting a relative cost of hydrocarbons that has risen threefold or more, the conversion of waste organic matter into methane (or into hydrogen) using mixed cultures of anaerobic bacteria begins to be of interest. The methane as generated contains some carbon dioxide, and the constituents of the gas can be catalytically reformed to produce hydrocarbons that fulfill present liquid fuel specifications.[7]

The first production of methane in significant quantities is likely to be based upon substandard food products. Foodstuffs that spoil or become contaminated by invading organisms would be routed along with other biological waste products to an anaerobic fermenter unit, which would convert 80-90% of the caloric value to methane; the remainder would be lost in sludge and volatile fatty acids.[8] It should be possible to use the by-product ammonium and phosphate salts for fertilizer, because the price of fertilizer will rise almost proportionally to fuel prices. Crude versions of this process have been employed for sewage treatment for almost a century, but by-products have rarely been salvaged.

The demand for fuel in cities is expected to be at least several times the total caloric value of food and feed, even in the most energy-economizing modes of organization; therefore, an energy supply based upon by-products of food and feed cannot possibly meet the eventual demand. Facilities specifically designed to produce urban fuels will have to be created. Economies of scale would be sought in carefully integrated microbiological photosynthetic facilities. If they were to be built from the present knowledge, it appears that a hexagonal network of ponds would be constructed with a plastic film separating the culture medium from the sea water.[9] Mild wave action is useful for stirring, but storms with big waves must be damped as much as possible so that much of the capital cost of the facility would be directed at assuring its security in the face of foul weather. One option would be to pump the culture medium for algae into underwater tanks to ride out the storm, since yields would be poor in the absence of strong sunlight. The area of water surface needed to run a typical small refinery would be twelve to fifteen kilometers in diameter. This would produce a thousand tons of liquid hydrocarbon per day, enough for several hundred thousand vehicles to carry on normal operations. One such refinery could supply the minimum fuel requirements of a million-size city located on flat coastal plains in the tropics. The dimensions appear to be quite reasonable, since the micro-biological solar energy collector and refinery would require only a little more area than the city itself.[10]

THE ENERGY FUTURE

On the basis of estimates of solar, nuclear, and geothermal technologies, the world has more than enough energy to urbanize ten billion people, maintain them at adequate standards of living, and still have some left over. The critical period will be the next half century, since huge capital investments must be made out of limited incomes in order to introduce the energy utilization systems.

Electric power seems likely to become the cheapest form of energy available in cities. Some categories of costs in the production of electricity will rise significantly—increased concerns about changing physical environments in the vicinity of power plants will add a variable amount, and costs of construction seem to have a built-in escalator that causes them to move upward, often even more rapidly than price inflation.[11] Some properties of the system will have a downward thrust, however—the introduction of prospective breeder technology should decrease the cost of nuclear fuel after about 1990. The shift to larger power-producing units, particularly on sites outside North America, will introduce significant economies of scale. Some cities will experience an actual reduction in the real cost of a delivered kilowatt hour because the power plants and distribution systems under construction are of a size that will markedly reduce the cost of an installed kilowatt. Most electrical grids, however, will experience relatively constant or slowly rising costs at a time when incomes are rising strongly. Given the high elasticity of demand for power in developing societies, economists expect a very rapid rise in power consumption—if past power uses continue into the future. Although still cheaper now, the prime hydrocarbon fuels useful for transport will be catching up to, perhaps passing, the cost of electric energy in bulk quantities.

Fossil fuels, particularly petroleum and natural gas, and accessible coal very soon thereafter, will rise very substantially in price to the plateau set by the costs of gasifying and liquefying coal. Before the coal has been exhausted, the price is expected to rise further—enough to allow the most economical locations for converting sunlight into hydrogen or hydrocarbons to start producing. A variable mix between underground and solar sources comprises the energy production picture at the time the urban transition is virtually complete—about a century hence. That would be at a time when a majority of the population will have reached the minimum adequate standard of living and the remainder will be struggling to achieve it.

Energy consumption could thereafter continue to rise. As the accumulation of wealth proceeded, people would find excuses for visiting sites at a distance from the megalopolitan clusters. Mobile life-styles require more vehicles covering more difficult terrain, causing the demand for liquid hydrocarbons to rise disproportionately. The extra demand could be met by taking over portions of the open sea for the manufacture of hydrocarbons.

The sun alone provides enough energy to allow at least ten billion people to live like North Americans today, if they wish to pay the price of being regarded as "peculiar." There is a fair possibility that the capacity of the world at this level of per capita expenditure could reach fifteen billion. That scale of energy utilization should markedly change the environment, however. The surface of the sea would become warmer because high yields of algae require the separation of a thin layer at the surface for ideal growth conditions, preventing mixing or extensive heat transfer with the water below and thus raising the surface temperature during the daytime. Whether this warming is bad or good depends upon an ability to reorganize structures and habitats in the ecosystem; at present the models of meteorologists and sociologists are not good enough to predict outcomes without building a number of large prototype facilities and observing the actual environmental impact. Since something like ten years would be required to find the optimum annual cycle for energy production (the problem is not dissimilar to the situation encountered in a valley with newly reclaimed agricultural land where crops, soils, water, and machinery must be fitted together to maximize the yield), the effects on the environment could not be estimated until some years thereafter.[12] The slow rates at which such knowledge is acquired suggest that the likelihood of wasted effort is high. The rest of the world will look carefully at alternatives to North American energy consumption, because the huge amounts of capital involved could be directed to other, more valuable ends.

The very long-range future for electrical energy production looks more promising. Power from fusion reactions may become feasible as knowledge about the containment of plasma advances; the present state of the art misses proposing a technologically feasible process by a large margin, and so we cannot prudently take into account the earth's stocks of lithium and deuterium as energy resources. If cities are limited to known technologies, the low-grade ores of uranium and thorium (containing only a few tenths of a percent of these heavy metals) will not be drawn upon for almost a century. The scale of the mining (mostly open pit) should be no greater than for the copper that makes this future possible, the fuel cost should remain small as compared to the capital service costs of big power generation facilities and the costs of maintaining high-level safety both for personnel and for the environment.[13] The long-term availability of this energy at reasonable prices assures us that urban regions will continue to be populated with large numbers of immobile machines, providing supports for accelerated cultural activity in the cities.

Consumer Behavior Rationalized

Energy-intensive urban systems are quite new, being wholly a product of the twentieth century, yet they are overlaid and permeated with anachronisms. The old-fashioned, long-way-around methods of producing convenience for humans use up far more energy than is necessary; they also delay construction of cities that will accommodate those who are poorly served. Finding short-cuts in energy-consuming steps through modifying either human behavior or man-environment relationships offers an exciting approach to substantial economies. The kinds of rationalization that have become exceedingly refined when dealing with industrial uses of fuel and power have not yet been applied to man's most immediate environment.

An analysis of the human energy consumer can begin at the skin and more outward. The skin itself is a mild emitter of heat energy at variable rates—it ranges from 50 to 400 cal/hr per capita but averages a little over 100 cal/hr. The loss takes the form of low-grade radiation and water vapor. The environment for the human body must have a heat sink at a temperature lower than 38° C in order to receive this energy; otherwise thermal stress builds up in the body. The ambient atmosphere should be moderately dry, to aid evaporation, and between the temperatures of 15-30° C. The low end of this range is determined by the tendency of muscles to stiffen after sitting still when they lose too much heat to the immediate environment, but the range is readily extended through insulating the body with one or more layers of clothing. At temperatures below 10°C, a covering is also needed for the extremities; otherwise the ability to operate levers, such as the keys on a typewriter, is reduced. Ideally, temperatures and humidities inside a dwelling unit should moderate the much larger variations occurring outside and permit full use of the body at all times.

Technological calculations can be made to show that it is most economical to condition the atmosphere in the immediate vicinity of the skin rather than regulate all the air in a room and the walls. Thus, in temperate and cold climates, it pays in terms of money as well as energy expenditure to design carefully fitted clothes with adjustable insulation and ventilation to cope with the different amounts of heat a body generates as a result of exercise.[14] In hot climates, it pays to circulate air, dehumidified if necessary, for cooling body surfaces; otherwise performance is not dependable.

Equally important is the design of the surroundings outside of the clothing—beds, furniture, floors, doors, communications devices, memorabilia. When cities are limited predominantly to the pedestrian mode of movement, the best balance between access and living space yielded an average of six to seven square meters of floor space (60-70 square feet) per capita.[15] In advanced Western societies the floor space requirements have been expanded to about thirty square meters, to which must be added another ten to help accommodate the private vehicle attached to the household. The extra space is occupied by the bulky furniture and appliances brought in to equip the house and facilitate a contemporary urban life-style. Inside a room all the space above and below the relatively inert and occasionally used furnishing must be heated or air-conditioned; this requirement results in a high maintenance cost in an extreme climate. Extra energy is also expended to produce the materials incorporated in the enlarged Western-style structure and for its furnishing. There seems to be no reason for expanding the normal human habitat beyond what it has been in the most comfortable rural dwellings; almost all over the world this falls within the five to eight square meter range (per person). Increased privacy and control of human contact can be designed into the structure and, especially, into codes of behavior that function well without this waste of space.

Many solutions exist, each of them fitting certain social class and cultural expectations. One such design is presented here as suited to the educated classes of a wide range of cultures, especially the new generation, since it was constructed and lived in by an inventive designer of Berkeley, California.[16] The size is fitted to a couple but could accommodate occasional overnight visitors or an infant. Let us enter:

The door is of standard dimensions, well fitted, secure against simple attempts at break-in, but in color and imagery introduces the residents. A tiny foyer is stocked with outdoor clothing, boots, shoes, miscellaneous storage, switches, and a foam-filled cushion in the corner for putting on complex shoe wear. A kitchenette-bath is ahead, partly curtained off; it contains a down-jutting film projector above head height, but the biggest furnishing is an accommodation to American supermarkets—the refrigerator. (A more universal solution would be to cook Oriental style with hot plate and steam pressure cooker, with the addition of a small microwave oven, while seated on a low stool and working from surfaces and cabinets that fold up to the wall, while refrigeration is made communal (one rents a locker). A shower-watercloset solution similar to shipboard would have been most economical, but this was only slightly expanded.)

The main living room, 3 X 3.5 meters in size, serves also as a bedroom. The floor is padded and covered with a tough coated fabric somewhat thickened underneath, and a sturdy double-size built-in bunk is placed on one side of the room. Each bunk can be separately lit and curtained; each is equipped with cushions that can be shaped in a minute to fit body size, and more cushions are on the floor. This particular room has a window looking out onto a miniature garden (it could have been a bubbling, lit aquarium, if this were an interior wall), equipped with a screen for filming to be pulled down over it. The stereo sound amplifier is a dodecahedron suspended from the ceiling. A master switch panel controls light, sound, ventilation, and projector. Corners are used for storage of bedding, tape library, books, and the like, so that a spherical appearance results. Enough room is thereby provided, on one and a half levels with the contribution of the bunk, to have parties of up to fourteen people, with all given a chance to see cinematic material or view television from a favorable angle. Food and drinks are served on trays, and cleanup is accomplished with a wet cloth. Floor covering, wall surfaces, bed pads, pillow covers, and drapes are all white or figured with white background to allow changes in light color according to mood. They are readily detached for cleaning or replacement. Thus the time required for housekeeping is minimal, while comfort and convenience equal anything today. Most significantly, the energy expenditure for space heating and cooling is reduced by two-thirds or more. The aim of such a life-style is full participation in the urban media—sight, sound, print—under conditions that are comfortable, sociable, undisturbed, and secure.

The same designer has a model of what a living unit could be like in the future when urbanites expect to use the media to enable them to live many lives compressed into one. Interfaces with communications channels would be far more complete, since the whole back wall can be engineered for the admission of colored light that is programmed in advance (or modified continuously through brain-controlled feedback systems). Locations of switches, thermostats, and knobs are illuminated by points of light provided by fiber optics. Because the added equipment, including computer terminal, uses solid-state electronic microcircuits and fiber optics, the actual energy requirement will decline slightly. All the intermediates for such a future design for dwelling are already on the market, and the prices are declining rapidly, but they remain to be adapted to normal domestic life in cities. It should be emphasized that totally different approaches can be equally convenient and economical; these will all require a certain amount of adjustment, fitting, and perhaps skill development in order to extract the potential savings.[17] About a tenth of the youth in Western societies would like to live this way, and the proportion is increasing over time; thus cultural resistance is not as strong as most middle-class, middle-aged people would imagine.

Inside the dwelling the key to energy conservation is to (1) eliminate mass, (2) exploit properties of materials to best advantage, and (3) organize space for multipurpose use. We should also admit the widest possible range of information useful for both personal and automatic control of the environment. Usually this involved the manipulation of solid-state components sensing environmental changes. At the cultural level, an exposure to educational, training, and gaming materials in the various media can introduce alternative behaviors suited to increasing scarcity (e.g., conditioning exercises, bathing, musical instrument playing, writing). Most of the energy required for manufacturing nonmilitary consumer goods (about a third of the total in affluent countries) can be conserved ultimately through conscious decisions about domestic life-style, which is basically a cultural matter. Waste over the long run is traced to the habits of consumers, but they are malleable and so it is reducible. Many of the strongest objectors, in principle, to this kind of compression, or densification, of living spaces find that they can adjust to life aboard ship (which usually has stricter standards of space economy) within a matter of days.

Urban Movements at Human Scale

Households must be connected to urban services. One can plot inputs of food, clothing, equipment, and utilities, and identify the output of wastes in a relatively formal fashion, then propose a network of transport services which should optimize the satisfaction of perceived requirements. But these are static solutions and quickly become obsolete for some very interesting reasons.

People try to reserve a certain amount of discretionary time for themselves, which is spent either inside or outside the dwelling, according to the rewards offered.[18] The superior urban life makes accessible a greater range of opportunities for finding such rewards within whatever time is available. This means that a new set of addresses, independent of those providing standard goods and services, tends to be drawn upon for voluntary participation, stimulus, and interest-generation. An accumulation of these voluntarily undertaken experiences may bring about a change in values, a focus on certain religious, avocational, or second job commitments, and a redefinition of patterns of consumption. Therefore the capacity to make trips to places outside the dwelling should remain ad hoc and extremely flexible with respect to destinations and scheduling. It is this demand for flexibility that has made the automobile the pre-eminent solution to modern metropolitan transportation. The auto's capacity to generate freedom of choice in the use of discretionary time dominates our thinking to such an extent that it is easier to communicate about the search for alternatives by describing various "partial substitutes for the automobile" rather than the specific operating characteristics of the proposed new arrangements for movement in cities.

Energy enters the picture as soon as an effort is made to speed movement, thereby saving time; the greater the acceleration applied in a physical sense, the greater is the expenditure of energy. Wherever human effort is programmed, as is the case in almost all places of work or study, time and money usually become interchangeable. Thus calculations are possible, based upon wage rates and energy costs, and time lost in passenger movement is added to the cost of transportation. The value of a man's time going to work, school, or an organized activity where the clock dictates his pace must be close to the value his employer agrees it is worth. The higher the pay scale, therefore, the more energy it is reasonable to spend when traveling to workplaces.

However, the values assigned to discretionary time are extremely variable and unstable as well, since value depends upon context. Moreover, "going along for the ride" is often an important part of the reward; so travel time may not represent a cost at all in some circumstances but be a reward in the form of tourism. Competition in the sale of automobiles has caused them to be designed to be used as an end in themselves—an object upon which or with which one's free time is expended and by which one's ego is expanded—rather than a means for reaching destinations. In many middle-class communities spread all over the world, the Sunday morning car wash has replaced going to church, temple, or mosque.

For pure transportation, defined here as a technology by which people and cargoes of various sizes get from here to there and/or back, the cycle mode appears to be highly efficient. Its advantages stand out clearly for populations living at medium density and with low levels of capital available on a per capita basis. In table 4 the bicycle comes out as the most energy-conserving, capital-conserving, and space-saving mode of movement for distances up to ten kilometers, though it rapidly loses its superiority as the trip is lengthened.

We should note that mechanical transport is a necessity in a modern urban environment. Any society living above subsistence and predominantly at the minimum adequate standard cannot afford to spend time on more than short

Table 4

Costs of Urban Transport Typical of Densely Populated Metropolitan Regions, 1973 (Example: South Asia)

Mode	Energy Cost	Capital Cost	Operating Costs	Time Cost	Total Cost
	Passenger-kilometer	Passenger-at peak	Passenger-kilometer	Per kilometer	Passenger kilometer
Walking[a]	60 cal	Rs. 100	Rs. 0.02	18 min	Rs. 0.75
Bicycle[b]	15	250	0.03	5.0	0.03
Motor scooter[c]	120	1,000	0.12	3.0	0.32
Bus[d]	60	1,000	0.06	6.0	0.27
Rapid transit[e]	60	6,000	0.03	2.0	0.27
Automobile[f]	500	20,000	0.70	1.5	1.03

Source: Adapted from R. L. Meier, "Resource-Conserving Urbanism: Progress and Potentials," *Challenges from the Future, Proceedings of the International Future Research Conference* (Kyoto: Japan Society of Futurology, 1970), p. 396.

[a] Walks with drainage are assumed, as well as flat terrain, and frequent halts at intersection. Progress is at 3-4 km per hour, and the average value of time is Rs. 2 per hour ($0.20-0.27).

[b] A second-hand bicycle that will operate for several more years will need tires, repairs, and drained paths or roads to average this speed.

[c] A used light motorbike or scooter is assigned a 1.5 passenger capacity for the peak periods. Value of time is set at Rs. 3 per hour because they are used primarily by the young in the middle class.

[d] Allows for delays equal to the riding time, but the value of time is the same as for pedestrians and bicyclists.

[e] Waiting time is half the riding time, but the average value of time is equal to motor scooter users.

[f] Whether taxi or private, an auto averages about two passengers at peak. Costs of extra roadway and parking space are included in estimate. Average value of passenger time is set at Rs. 5 per hour since autos are used for higher-priority movement.

trips (half a kilometer or so) as a pedestrian, unless the walking is being used as part of the individual's discretionary time. This principle of economizing on one's productive time is practiced, often unconsciously, by all people with adequate income expectations living at urban densities.

The bicycle takes a path about 1.25 meters in width and a 5-6 centimeter depth of surfacing (2 meters if three wheeled and four-wheeled cycles are common) as compared to an automobile lane of 4.0 meters and a 15-20 centimeter roadbed. The capacity of the bicycle channel is 1,500-2,500 vehicles per hour at velocities of 15-20 km/hr during peak periods.[19] An automobile in the less affluent city is usually held to an average of 25 km/hr, so the larger lane conveys perhaps 750 vehicles per hour, each containing on the average about two persons. Thus the bicycle uses urban circulation space three to five times more efficiently than the auto, and for parking or storage it is close to ten times more efficient. Potentially then, if the total urban system were to be designed around it, the bicycle would allow more people in the active age brackets to reach a greater number of alternative destinations in a given amount of time. Cities dependent on bicycles have evolved in South and Southeast Asia, but their land use has not been systematically elaborated to take full advantage of the properties of the cycle mode of movement. Such a system could include the following kinds of vehicles in large-scale use besides the standard two wheeler:

1. A two-wheel, push-pull dump cart with reinforced bearings and rims to carry 500 kilograms, which can be stacked when space is scarce (as in Japan and Korea).
2. A four-wheel display cart, flat top, up to a 50 kilogram capacity, for temporary markets and hawking (as in north India).
3. A tricycle frame suited to passengers or light delivery, carrying up to 200 kilograms (as in Chinese societies and elsewhere).
4. A small-wheeled multiple-geared bicycle for moving in and through heavy pedestrian flows (so far only seen in America).
5. A folding wheelchair, pushed or self-propelled, for infirm people (hospitals and airlines).
6. A pedicar with flywheel that enables one to accelerate from a traffic stop and to move briskly up moderate hills,

even when carrying a load (an American invention inspired by the environmentalist movement).

By themselves the vehicles are not adequate until equipped with appurtences for riding at night, carrying children, carrying baggage, quick repair, frustration of theft, motorized assistance for mild grades, protection from the weather, and so on. All of these accessories are available in some major metropolitan societies, although often still in astonishingly clumsy forms.

What seems to be least developed in the cycle mode of transport is the design of terminals and standard services. Careful studies need to be made for an efficient means of stacking and storing cycles, preferably in some containerized form that could be transshipped on railroads, trucks, and ferries. In addition, the rental system, conducted now only on a personal appraisal of credit basis in some cities of India, needs to be improved along the lines of automobile rentals in the United States. Bicycle lanes need to be even more carefully maintained than highways and preferably designed so as to produce short cuts to the arterial flows used by bus and rail. All cycle networks should allow for an increased use of low-powered motorization, mostly in the form of scooters, which come into greater use as income increases and density diminishes. Repair and maintenance services need to be dispersed as systematically as service stations for autos are distributed in Western cities, rather than concentrated in a specialized district of the metropolis as is so common in the Orient. Standardized signs are presently being developed for cyclists, but these are mostly for outdoor sports in affluent societies and may not be sufficiently utilitarian for developing countries.

Bicycles are just now regaining high status in developed countries. The business has expanded greatly in the 1970s (more sold now than cars in the United States), and an increased amount of advanced engineering design is moving into the field, though only scattered results are evident thus far. The total effort is estimated at being less than 1% of the technical design inputs for automotives; so the independent inventor still remains important.

The task of systematizing the cycle mode is difficult to organize for a quite unexpected reason. The repair, maintenance, and use of cycles seem to be a first step out for the landless population engaged in subsistence agriculture;

therefore, in any dual economy, bicycle-mode jobs will be held down to the lowest levels of pay and very low social status. Bicycle maintenance is readily learned by apprentices, while both the vehicles themselves and the tools by which they are formed and repaired are at a scale that makes them easily comprehensible. Young men who master the bicycle are teased intellectually by the possibility of increased complexity associated with increased power, greater precision, or massive size, usually represented by the automobile and the truck. The best bicycle mechanics graduate to engines, motors, and sophisticated automatic gear assemblies. Therefore, because the cycle industry is regarded first as an escape from rural insecurity, and then as a stepping stone to a real mechanics job, it will not be able to retain the best minds and will continue to be regarded as a relatively low-class industry and repair service activity. Cut-rate prices will prevail because of continuous entry of cycle mechanics from the countryside. Under such conditions the overhead costs of quality control and stable management cannot be afforded, and an overall bad image results. Yet any struggling government interested in producing urban services with minimal capital investment should assign high priority to stimulating the growth and elaboration of the cycle industry. Widespread acceptance of cycle use is of highest priority in energy-importing developing countries, since automotives, the next step up in mechanical complexity, are known to make a huge drain upon scarce capital and foreign exchange.

The puzzle is a managerial one which is not readily resolved with sociological precedents. How is high status to be accorded to occupations so easily entered from below? Only one strategy can be suggested; it is a result of casting about widely in search of solutions, and it applies only to societies with large internal markets with potential economies of scale. The cycle mode may be regarded as a fruitful direction for export promotion. The Italians and the Japanese are about at the stage where they could be displaced from world markets by innovative low-cost producers. The new major entrant into the American market is Taiwan. Mass production of wheels, frames, small engines, and accessories, however, has already been initiated in China and South Asia, though very little capability for advanced design and marketing has accompanied it. The prestige export market in America and Europe, where new cycles are used for sport and minor convenience, demands a sophisticated approach. If Asia and Africa can fill these demands, the same skills, once evolved, should make possible a better fit to local needs.

One major design opportunity exists in Asia that could add hugely to the social status of the cycle in the future. It is now possible to construct, in Asia more cheaply than elsewhere, quite elaborate solid-state electronic devices with remarkable short-range signaling and automatic control capabilities weighing only a few hundred grams. They will soon be used, for example, for monitoring and adjusting the performance of working parts in automobiles. A cycle-mode vehicle is too simple to require monitoring that cannot be done as well by human senses, but these devices could be used for building "responsive environments" along the network of paths set aside for cycles and at important destinations. In such an environment automata stand ready to open gates, turn on lights, light up direction-finding signs, search out destinations for which latitude and longitude are known, trigger traffic control devices with the onset of congestion, and allow entry into small selective locations (equivalent to Peking's inner courtyards). Thus a man with a cycle in which a computer and short-range two-way radio had been installed could go almost anywhere without being stopped. A man's social status in future bureaucracies and clubs might depend heavily upon the number of electronic automata he was allowed to control by himself rather than by the fact that he was allowed a car and driver by his agency or corporation. Such a modest outlook is much more compatible with public behavior in China than elsewhere in developing countries; so it appears that some kind of revolutionary discipline may also be required before this highly energy-saving mode of transport finds its proper place in urban design.

It will be noted that the small electric car has not been mentioned even though it can be made highly compatible with cycles, particularly when an important fraction of the vehicles have acquired mo-ped engines. The reason is the capital cost, which seems not likely to be reduced. Though there have been technological optimists for many decades, and despite the expenditure of hundreds of millions of dollars, little advance has been made in design. The compo-

nents of all foreseeable batteries (the Mendeleef table of
atomic elements and the electromotive series allow only a
limited number of cell compositions) involve nonferrous
metals, which will become increasingly scarce and expensive
to mine and refine. Continuous takeoff of electric power,
or even repeated quick injections of energy into flywheel
storage inside a vehicle, puts the vehicle into another category, class or mode that is generally termed "mass transit,"
because cost per use declines rapidly with scale until one
reaches trolleybus or streetcar dimensions.

While the cycle mode is uniquely fitted to servicing the **Urban**
household, for the face-to-face network of relationships **Mass**
and the less-capitalized modern enterprises and agencies, **Transit**
mass transit serves the big private and public bureaucracies
and provides access to the unique, one-in-a-million acquisi-
tions of goods and services. Bicycles may take people to
cinemas, but buses and subways get them to the theater.
Whereas urban movements employing a well-organized cycle
mode would, when plotted on a map, show up as a fine
cobweb that thins out in the center, the mass transit movements made up of bus and rail trips show a strong radial
tendency, with the main corridors serving as spokes. Very
large cities would develop strong subcenters in the corridors
with similar radial flows converging upon them. Pedestrian
movements dominate the cores of these centers and subcenters, taking people to the foot of elevators and escalators.

Large-scale organization is needed to assemble and control
large aggregations of capital. Therefore it seems quite appropriate that some of this capital be applied to improving
access to the organizations for workers and clients or customers. Mass transit by rail is potentially cheaper (see table
4) than bicycle when programmed human time becomes
several times more valuable than it is around subsistence
levels; those economies, however, are bought with very
heavy investment of a kind that can easily be miscalculated.

As with bicyles, mass transit has become faddish among
intellectuals, yet it is very poorly supported by the middle
class. While an increasing number of bicycles are bought
and used for sport and convenience, at least by the youths
in the household, mass transit in Western society and Japan
has been abandoned gradually in favor of the "anti-ecolog-
ical" automobile, which has supplied almost all the expansion of land-based trips. The reason seems to be that the

real service provided by a bus or electric train misses what is believed to be ideal by a large measure. The auto approaches the ideal of personalized transport much more often ("I go when I am ready, not when the schedule says I can, and I arrive in the style I wish to appear"); therefore people will spend three to ten times as much money on necessary trips and save little, if any, personal time, but gain real satisfaction from remaining in control of their movements.

Now we can turn to the planning of a transport system for a growing metropolis. The best strategy is to postpone investment in heavy fixed-route transport as long as possible. This policy implies finding temporary substitutes for freeways and subways. During the early period of growth, coincident with the initial settlement of neighborhoods, the necessary trips are to the sources of employment, such as an industrial estate, a major installation, or a marketplace. Education at that time emphasizes part-time instruction related to employment prospects. School facilities must work multiple shifts. Therefore the bulk of work and educational trips can be served by pedestrian, cycle, and bus modes on a street grid. Improvement of roadbeds needs to be brought up to the requirements for a five-ton truck on the most heavily used routes. As a variety of services is added, however, this distribution of trips shifts rapidly to a more diffuse set of movements. The amount of discretionary time increases; people change their jobs but not their neighborhoods.

With a decade or so of infill into empty lots and with second jobs or school places being found for members in established households, the destinations for programmed trips begin to be widely scattered. The transportation systems then experience a demand for much more cross traffic. If that demand is met with installed public transport capacity, the neighborhood is allowed to become truly metropolitan.

How long can a growing metropolitan area postpone developing underground or elevated mass transit systems? Much will depend on whether it can flatten peak loads over a long time period. It will depend even more upon the ability of the government to deflect demand away from private autos into the various substitutes offered. General Motors can show that two lanes for buses at the surface will, when carefully platooned for movements through a central grid, handle as many passengers per hour as a subway and distribute them more efficiently in the periphery, although the system is very vulnerable to invasion and degradation by autos.[20] Let us suppose that these disciplines of timing, spacing, and allocation of lanes are strict and can be maintained over time. Then it appears that cities on flat land could exceed ten million people before they are forced to introduce electric mass transit on other than the intercity rail lines with which the city was endowed from the beginning.

An idealized urban village mode of growth, in which the metropolis produces most of its own perishable foods through intensive gardening, would depend much more than present developing metropolises do upon radial lines of transport. Passengers would move into centers and subcenters by an orderly hierarchic process—by foot or bicycle to a station, by bus to subcenter, by express bus or train to center, with volume of flow at each stage increasing by a factor of a hundred or so.

Consider the evolution of such an urban village with rational transport planning: when a piece of territory (say, a block ranging from 0.5 to 2.5 square miles, or very roughly 100-500 hectares) is designated to become a "site and services" settlement with associated intensive gardening and is not served by an intercity road or railroad, the first developed transport link should be by bicycle mode. It should be quickly followed by an improved road to handle light vans and jitneys. The vehicles may be either scooter or minivan scale (up to five passengers), as in South Asia, or minibus (up to sixteen seats). When the movement becomes large enough (say, five hundred round trips per day), private enterprise buses will be willing to go out of their way to pick up passengers. When settlement is complete, and two to ten thousand trips per day to the city at large are generated, a few bus loads may make direct connections, though most buses must serve a string of urban villages and urban communities in order to provide frequent service. Thus, as far as the user is concerned, no innovations or major adjustment in standard patterns of service is implied by the urban village proposals for metropolitan evolution. Their intensive gardens can be harvested by means of hand-carts and minivans, and the packing sheds or processing areas should be at locations where containers can be put on trucks or buses for distribution in the vicinity.

Energy and Water Supply   253

If any system redesign at all is indicated, it should take the form of adding telecommunications systems that link up station masters, central headquarters, and groups of users. For passengers this continuous flow of messages along the communications channels would mean that they wait shorter periods for a seat and that connections between lines are more frequently made rather than missed. The result would be more trips completed successfully per capita, thus enabling more participation in organizations outside of the family. In the case of goods shipments, an expanded communications capability associated with containerization results in greater use of back-haul capacity, so that fewer trains and vehicles are needed for the transport system. The movements are expedited, so smaller inventories are required for manufactured goods. For transport, as elsewhere in the urban economy, the communications system saves both energy and capital for expansion of capacity in industries with less sophisticated technologies, but it accomplishes the improvement indirectly and almost invisibly. The contributions to efficiency made by communications are part of a general phenomenon of great importance in resource conservation, which will be taken up later at a more theoretical level.

Water Supply Systems

The provision of water to cities is also a matter of transport, but the system utilizes flow rather than bulk packages moving on wheels across the land surface with significant amounts of rolling friction. From thirty to two hundred tons of water per year per capita is delivered to homes and factories under present conditions, but in the future it must be less in most locations.

The strategy introduced here for economizing on water consumption starts from very different assumptions from those employed in the handbooks and textbooks on water supply. Most thinking up to the present time has been dominated by the vulnerability of the city to waterborne epidemics, but now an assortment of economical techniques exists which assures control over disease. The emphasis needs to change to ways of stretching the water supply equitably when it is short. The method of supply in developing metropolises must also fit the life-styles of ordinary people, most of them initially very poor.

The best indication of features inherent in a non-Western approach to water supply is obtained from close observation of current adaptations. The traditional water carrier,

who either provided a daily service like the Western milk-
man or hawked his product on the street, drew his stock
from a fountain or a well and carried it in a goatskin or in
a barrel on a cart. If the water seemed impure, he would
warn his steady customers so that they would be sure to
strain it before boiling it. A family could not live long in
such a city if it could not pay its water carrier, since public
sources were available only at extremely inconvenient times.
As the reservoirs have been expanded and taps provided in
increasing numbers, the task of carrying water has been
relegated to young women and children, but one also sees
an increasing number of garden hoses and clear plastic tubes.
These are strung down to the public tap and lead to private
tanks on the roof that are set up by families with some
capital. They are attached in off-peak periods. Often there
will be a second tank or cistern for lower-quality runoff
water used for washing clothes and also for bathing. Many
cities still provide this second-quality water with canal
systems, which, ideally, are flushed out by tidal action;
otherwise a waterkeeper releases a surge of water from a
reservoir, and the householder fills a tank underneath the
house. Usually there is a tax or a charge for the service.
Only in government-supplied housing, or subsidized slum
redevelopments, is potable water supplied free. However,
those taps are poorly maintained and often muddy or un-
sanitary. So the portions of the population with steady
work and improving prospects are likely to purchase hot
tea, soft drinks, beer, and other drinking water substitutes
from nearby shops, send their clothes out for washing, and
regularly attend the local bathhouse.

If such a background is used as a base rather than an idealized Western experience, it becomes possible to plan for
several water qualities. The top quality is potable and used
both for drinking and food preparation. The second quality
may be of varying constitution according to season and
locale but can be depended upon for washing, bathing, and
watering plants and animals, while a third is industrial water
containing high levels of dissolved solids, which can be used
for cooling purposes and for flushing away inorganic wastes.
Coastal metropolises may circulate seawater for this lowest
grade, treated to reduce scaling of heat transfer surfaces,
while during the dry season inland metropolises would reuse water until nothing more than a salty sludge remained.
Many American power plants, metallurgical works, and

chemical facilities in the Western states have perfected these techniques while achieving competitive costs of production, so the often-quoted industry norms for water use no longer can be offered as compelling arguments against installing industry in such water-limited areas.

A variety of technologies already exists for converting a lower quality of water into a higher quality. They all require energy, which is employed with increasing efficiency as the size of the water-processing unit is increased. New technologies in water processing have had such an enthusiastic popular press that many marvelous things have been promised and are expected; once a full assessment of costs for a nonsubsidized process is assembled, however, the degree of progress seems disappointingly small or nonexistent. Nevertheless, the range of contaminants that can be removed has been expanded, and virtually any impurity can be removed at a price that is not totally unreasonable.[21] The existence of this postwar technology with its relatively predictable set of costs indicates that the water planner should think in terms of the relative value, or price, of the respective grades of water. In other words, a water market with real prices for the commodities appears desirable; it would cause consumers to modify their demand for water so as to conform more closely to the volume that can be supplied. Without it many public and private decision makers will be forced to set up a quasi market with shadow prices.

Thus if it is assumed that a water market exists in the future metropolis, how might it work? The highest-quality water might be retailed in plastic bags, bottles, and standard tanks at a rate around U.S. $1.00 per ton plus charges for the container. This is a small cost for a typical family of five using about 25 liters per capita per day; in India it would be a little more than a rupee per day, or about half what is paid now to the water carrier.

The second supply would be piped to water stations, at the end of a hall in an apartment house or in an inner courtyard, which supply from one to thirty families. These water stations provide fresh water for baths with an opportunity to filter and reuse it for washing clothes. This dirtier water might be reused again, if the price reflected shortages, for flushing away wastes. Each culture has developed its own rituals and preferences for bathing which need to be respected if the water centers are to be used and not bypassed, but the washing of clothes in the city is expected to progress rapidly to the use of automatic washing machines, so that some variant of the American "laundromat" could be installed. However, the variable water price would probably frustrate direct coin-in-slot payment and replace it with variable-price tokens. An automaton doing the laundry might charge 10 cents when reservoirs are full, but 30 cents at the end of the dry season. The maintenance of such a group facility suggests that a special occupation or service is likely to evolve to replace the original water-carrier and washerman, but the new job will require training in sanitation and the maintenance of simple water-recycling equipment. It would use the human in a role that maintains and advances social integration rather than as a beast of burden or menial servant.

The third quality of water would be delivered to industrial installations. It would require continuous analysis and occasionally rather high-grade technology for treatment to prevent polluting the environment with dangerous wastes. The detoxification of waste products is now an intrinsic feature for each new technology and is quickly being added to older ones where it has been neglected, so that experiences with visible water pollution, so common today in developing metropolises, need not be magnified or even continued.

It will often happen that this third grade of water is warm, since one of its principal uses is as a coolant. Wherever the heating is dependable as in a power plant, a steel mill,, or a refinery, the warmed water can be vacuum-distilled using the reject heat to produce a smaller quantity of top-quality water. Thus a power plant could provide the pure water requirements for a brewery, a soft drinks bottler (this function seems likely to last even though the container of choice may eventually be neither glass nor a bottle), and other potables producers. By-product industrial heat, now often regarded as "thermal pollution," is actually a special urban resource for the conversion of low-grade water into high-grade water.[22]

Wherever the price of water reaches high levels, it will appear desirable to use electric power for desalination purposes. However, the seasonal cycles in the scarcity of water in locations where it seems at all possible to build cities call into question the heavy capital investments that would be required. It does not pay to desalinate sea water, even using off-peak power, only four months a year or thereabouts. It is cheaper to invest in extra storage facilities in conventional locations.

A sometimes superior alternative to constructing extra storage is to hire a large tanker. It could fill up with raw water from the nearest estuary with a surplus and pump it into the reservoir backing up a city's water works. The cost varies with the size of the tanker but should rarely exceed $1.00 per ton. A competing possibility is the Greek *dragone* (sea dragon), which is a long sausagelike plastic bag pulled by a tug. The tug's pumps are used to fill the bag in some estuary with surplus fresh water and again to empty it. This solution is particularly advantageous because a major drought should slow down local coastal trade, thus rendering some tugs redundant in their day-to-day functions. Also, dry periods occur when there are no storms, and so tugs are not likely to be called upon to cope with emergencies at sea when needed to tow dragones.

Inland metropolises have fewer options. They would, as a matter of course, set up a pipeline system that would allow them to draw upon more than one watershed. Neighboring watersheds, however, are usually affected by common drought. One partial solution has been proposed: the inland metropolis is likely to feel the need for a pipeline to the sea to dispose of difficult wastes, but such a pipeline can be reversed (while the flow of wastes, reduced in amount by the drought, could be ponded) and fresh water supplied by the same means a coastal metropolis obtains its emergency water. The cost is obviously quite a bit greater, and would reflect itself in prices. Problems like this occurring every few years are sufficient to cause people to prefer coastal metropolises in the long run; so the latter must anticipate the brunt of the inmigration during the period of massive urbanization.

Water for the Urban Village

Considerations of food economy suggested that perishable foods be produced very close to the points of consumption. Perishable foods have high water content, and vegetables and small fruits normally require, up to the time of harvest, between ten to a hundred times the weight of the crop in water for growth. Therefore the incorporation of intensive gardening into the metropolis simultaneously introduces the largest single water consumer.

Allowing for a kilogram of perishable foods per person per day (including milk and soybean curd), on the order of ten times as much second-quality water, is required for the individual as he consumes in the household in the form of first-quality water. Perhaps a quarter to a half of all this water could come from waste waters in the city itself (greatly depending upon prices and the level of maintenance of the sewerage system), an important fraction from rain and runoff, while the remainder must be imported from reservoirs higher up in the watershed. The water in gardening is lost primarily through transpiration—cooling of the leaf by vaporization as it absorbs solar energy and converts it into protoplasmic raw materials—and from percolation through subsoils down to the water table. All cities pump this water from the water-bearing strata upon which they rest. Often the rate of extraction of water from subsoils is so great that the land settles on the seaward side, thus requiring a raising of dikes. Intrusion of seawater into wells dug miles away from the coastline is often a threat. Tokyo has had a perennial problem with "sinking lands," while the Israeli costal cities have consciously developed what are believed to be the most delicate subsurface balances known in the world.

Experience shows that heavily fertilized gardens and orchards, even fields of maize, will create a buildup of nitrate ion as well as chloride and sulfate in the ground water which will prevent well water from being used directly as first-quality water. The nitrate ion can cause blindness in infants, while chloride and sulfate reduce the respiration efficiency of the roots of many plants. Therefore gardening is likely to bring with it detailed attention to deionization facilities to maintain water quality. Deionization is needed to increase the amount of water recycled by percolation through the soil within the metropolitan area.

The proper approach to minimize water requirements for foodstuffs, discovered through laboratory studies, is to optimize growing conditions for the plants—by providing all required inputs at their respective optima—and to reuse any surplus water. The scientific prescriptions are best met by imposing the following conditions:[23] (1) replace soil with a coarse sand or gravel, which serves as an adequate support for rootlets and a source of trace elements; (2) wet the gravel with a fertilizer solution and then pull away the liquid, allowing cool air to get at the roots; (3) humidify the air and circulate it past the leaves, making sure that sufficient carbon dioxide is available without dehydration of the plant; (4) provide extra supports for the aerial portion of the plant so that as much of the incident sunlight as possible can be intercepted and the flow of sap is not restricted; (5) maintain leaf temperature in the optimum range—this usually requires some shade to protect from overhead sunlight; (6) pay close attention to the possibility of virus infection, taking action ranging from the abolition of smoking tobacco (a source of tobacco masaic virus, one of the most devastating epidemic agents of this type) to the speedy removal of any abnormal plants, the incorporation of antibiotic compounds in the plant nutrient solution, and the prevention of insect infestations. As a result the plants grow much faster than in soil and the output is more uniform— the best the genetic endowment of the plant permits it to do. These techniques are already employed in the United States and some other developed countries for the production of luxury vegetables, particularly tomatoes, and flowers to be cut for the market. Experience shows that the process as presently practiced is both capital- and labor-intensive, and therefore the produce sells at premium prices. However, these designs have been improved and have now been made available for franchise; moreover, it appears they can be improved upon still further by adaptation to local conditions, such as the following description of the aquaculture that is presently visualized for a relatively dry part of tropical monsoon Asia.

The tanks are filled with water from (1) the last stage of the conversion of human and animal wastes into protein, (2) runoff from urbanized areas, and (3) raw water imports. About fifteen tons per hectare per day, on the average, is the total requirement, but part will be supplied by the natural precipitation. About two or three kilograms of fertilizers will be dissolved in this water—urea, potassium, phosphate, and a bit of iron and magnesium salts, and an antibiotic. The actual amount added will depend upon chemical analysis of the contents of the separate tanks.

Each day after dawn the nutrient solution is released into the sand, reaches a level just short of the surface, and then is allowed to drain away into a sump. A pump returns it to the tank so that the wetting process can be repeated an hour or two later. The roots take up this nutrient solution at a rate determined by the strength of sunlight and the temperature.

Plants grow in raised meter-width trays that are actually made of vitreous clay sewer pipe, molded into more convenient shapes. Elsewhere it may be more economical to form channels out of soil. The channels' berms are covered with black polypropylene sheets, with coarse sand placed upon them in the channel. The paths between the channels are wide enough to allow easy walking and the movement of narrow carts.

Vegetables like broadbeans, tomatoes, brinjals (elongated eggplant), and sweet corn are supported by string from a superstructure raised above the trays, or with sticks stuck into the sand. Melons are treated similarly, but strawberries do not normally require this support. Therefore an aquaculture facility normally has an overhead lattice work fabricated with tied bamboo. Above this framework are plastic shades that convert light to the proper wavelengths reflecting the excess away. These arrangements must always be adapted to local winds and rain, so the design of the superstructure may vary even within a given metropolitan area.

Workers pace the rows overseeing the growing process, tying up new branches and pulling out weeds. They also cull deformed plants and those with a few drooping leaves. Elsewhere they are transplanting, and further on a harvest is under way. The produce is collected in strong, light, plastic containers (holding about twenty kilograms so that they can be easily handled by women or older men) on carts. These boxes are delivered to a packing facility, where the pesticide is washed off and the bulk of the output exported.

Potatoes and root crops are different. The investment will be less since fewer overhead supports are needed. Work is done by men lying prone and moving over the plants on a frame on four cycle wheels. The crop is harvested with a lightly powered digger and taken away in half-ton handcarts. The yield is very high—upward of two hundred tons per hectare—therefore the harvest replanting must be sequenced carefully.

Night work is common. After a late afternoon harvest old plants may be ripped out and replanting undertaken at night so that not a single day's growth is missed. (The principal incentive may be to catch the metropolitan market before the price is depressed by truck gardens that are less highly capitalized and start producing a week or so later.) In other instances the sand needs to be sterilized, or pumps replaced. The fight against disease and insect infestation is a continuous one; that is why each hectare is divided into ten to twenty separate units.

American experience has shown that about 90% of the work is accomplished very well by barely literate or illiterate laborers. The remainder requires technical expertise up to technical college level. From one to five workers per hectare are needed, depending upon the crops raised. More labor is involved in processing and packing the output. Other workers must prepare waste vines, stalks, and roots for animal feed and composting.

After a number of cycles of releasing and draining the nutrient solution, salt concentration builds up. Some plants, such as beans or asparagus, can tolerate a surprising amount of salt, so they may be used for the last few cycles of the solution. When the water is discarded, it must be either de-ionized or sold off as third-quality water, though an alternative is to use it for humidification of the air during dry spells. Usually the quantity of waste water will be a third to a tenth of the original intake. The only losses to the water table and runoff would be attributable to leaks and accidental spills and the occasional floods that occur even in dry climates.

Anyone who has walked in the intensively gardened sections of the Kanto plain around Tokyo, the Han basin around Seoul, or the vegetable plots of Singapore Island will recognize that what is lacking in the above description is the ingenious application of plastic film used by peasants to get desired quality. Missing also is an account of the dexterous use of curiously shaped hand tools and the forming of plants so as to expedite harvest. Once aquaculture of garden plants starts up, it is likely to become highly differentiated by specialized skills and cultural background. Since some of the labor is periodically surplus, it will be expended upon the overall structure of the facilities, so they will often become a medium for the expression of folk art, just as tea gardens, hop fields, orchards, and vineyards commonly are today.

In closing, it must be pointed out that this vision of the efficient metropolis, capable of saving more than 90% of the energy and water expended per capita in American and European cities but producing as much in the way of sustenance and human services, presents itself as a garden city. Roughly half the area is given over to labor-intensive propagation of green plants. On paper it would seem to fit utopian ideals laid down at the beginning of the twentieth century. From the point of view of the sophisticated resident, however, it fails to please because when it is viewed from roof tops, bus windows, or the bikeways, it appears densely settled. The gardens, with their tinted plastic panel covers and the supporting structures, resemble cheap industrial sheds. Therefore the urbanized population will plant trees in private plots, public areas, and odd protected corners. Since trees transpire in sunlight and tap ground water to make up their losses, thus reducing the metropolitan reserves, a price must be paid for a pleasant and humane settlement; it is taken out of the aquifer upon which the city rests. Each full-sized tree in a dry climate expends as much water as a whole household; where population pressure is great, it may be economical to build insulated structures for the provision of shade and coolness as substitutes for trees.

What is important is that the energy and water accounts be kept open for inspection and analysis, so that the adaptations to scarcity can be made promptly on a decentralized bases. That takes a different kind of planning than is done for today's cities.

Notes

1. In the United States metropolitan areas 41% of the domestic water consumption (which typically averages 50 gallons or 0.2 tons per capita per day) was accounted for by flushing toilets, 37% by washing and bathing, 6% to kitchen use, 5% to drinking, 4% to clothes washing, 3% to watering the garden, and 1% to washing the car. C. N. Durfor and Edith Becker, "Public Water Supplies of the 100 Largest Cities in the United States, 1962," U.S. Geological Survey, Water Supply Paper No. 1812, 1964.

2. The latest critical review of coal resources was published by Resources for the Future, Inc.: Joel Darmstadter, Perry Teitelbaum and Jaroslav G. Polach, *Energy in the World Economy* (Baltimore: Johns Hopkins University Press, 1971) p. 46. They estimate 37% of the total world resource in North America, 57% in the USSR, and 9% in the remainder of Asia.

3. Controversies concerning the lag in coal technology for meeting the "energy crisis" became increasingly intense during 1972-73. Meanwhile, research and development studies retrieved abandoned programs of the 1960s and redirected them to contributions that individual firms and agencies could make to the mass production technology of the 1980s. Private firms sought to develop a strong patent position starting from a position of strength, while public agencies vied for designation of key responsibilities for filling the large gaps that existed between the initiatives taken by the firms. The engineering journal editors have been assigning top priority to reports that point the way to a future where coal, tar sand, and shale make up for the lack of petroleum. Therefore, some strong clues already exist concerning the specific processes and the approximate costs of these capital-intensive facilities for the extraction of energy from mined deposits. For example, the economics of the revised Kellogg gasification process appears to be sufficiently promising (in part because of a reduced potential for pollution) to suggest that it will be incorporated in many of the complexes of the 1980s: A. E. Cover, W. C. Schreiner, and G. T. Skaperdas, "Kellogg's Coal Gasification Process," *Chemical Engineering Progress,* 69 (March 1973), 31-36; H. A. Shearer, "The COED Process plus Char Gasification," *ibid.,* 43-49. The costs are naturally interdependent, but they seem likely to be able to deliver gas, automotive fuels, power plant fuels, and jet fuel at prices competitive with the long-term contracts signed for the delivery of liquid natural gas in the 1975-77 period. It seems quite possible that the world may reach a new energy price plateau for a decade or two, similar to the one that lasted from about 1953 to 1972, but this plateau would exhibit real prices approximately three times as high. M. E. Franks and B. K. Schmid, "Design of a Coal-Oil-Gas Refinery," *ibid.,* 62-64. Harry Perry, "The Gasification of Coal," *Scientific American,* 230 (March 1974), 19-25. A brief technology-cum-policy discussion of most of the alternatives for the United States is provided by the public affairs reporters for *Science.* Allen L. Hammond, William D. Metz, and Thomas H. Maugh II, *Energy and the Future* (Washington, D.C.: AAAS, 1973). The follow-up issue of *Science* (April 19, 1974) is in many ways even more informative.

4. A curious mixture of extremely speculative proposals and established technology goes into the concept of "the hydrogen economy." Hydrogen reduction of magnetite iron ore is becoming economical on a number of sites in conjunction with electric furnace operation. The principal use of hydrogen is in the production of ammonia for fertilizer and of methyl alcohol for solvents. There are, of course, large-scale demands for propellants from the aerospace industry. The present bulk price is quoted at 30 cents per pound, and many carloads of liquid hydrogen are shipped at that price, but it becomes competitive with electric power only in the neighborhood of 10 cents per pound. J. Bockris, "A Hydrogen Economy," *Science,* 176(June 23, 1972), 1323; J. Bockris, ed., *The Electro Chemistry of Cleaner Environments* (New York: Plenum Press, 1972); also *Chemical and Engineering News,* June 26, July 3, and July 10, 1972. A global appraisal is provided by C. Marchetti, "Hydrogen and Energy," *Chemical Economy and Engineering Review* (Japan) 5 (January 1973), 7-25. Methane from solar energy is in many ways competitive with hydrogen. See D. L. Klass, "A Perpetual Methane Economy—Is It Possible?" *Chem Tech,* March 1974, pp. 161-168. Much of the interest is centered in the Institute of Gas Technology in Chicago and the Oak Ridge National Laboratory.

5. Such industries might, for example, be based also upon salt mines, so that a variety of chlorinated chemicals would be produced. Raw materials for synthetic rubber, plastics and synthetic fibers constitute another natural set of coalplex products.

6. The research on fuel cells has been greatly reduced and the basic needs of the American space exploration program were met in the late 1960s. A fair review of the situation was provided by Thomas Maugh in *Science,* 178 (December 22, 1972), 1973, which was extended by correspondence in *Science,* 180 (May 11, 1973), 542. Exxon, in cooperation with Alsthom from France, is still engaged in development besides Pratt and Whitney. If this work on the improvement of the fuel cell does not fulfill the promise of the basic science the prospects of the "hydrogen economy" is greatly reduced.

7. K. R. Williams and N. L. Campagne of the Shell International Petroleum Company (London) have considered the conversion of electrical energy into hydrocarbon fuel using carbon dioxide directly as a source. They estimate that a $650 million plant would yearly produce 3.1 million tons at a manufacturing cost of 45 cents per U.S. gallon of a Fischer-Tropsch process gasoline. This process puts a top limit on the cost of liquid fuels as long as nuclear power is readily available. *Chemical and Engineering News,* 50 (July 10, 1972), 30. The carbon dioxide can also be fixed in a more classical manner by an "energy forest" or "fuel plantation" wherever land is cheap. Georgia sycamore trees are competitive with coal starting around $25 per ton. If maize were to be grown instead and processed into fuels, it could start competing with coal around $40 per

ton. George C. Szego, *Chemical Technology,* May 1973, pp. 275-84. These prices should be scaled upward according to indexes for chemical construction and interest rate changes.

8. John E. Bardach reports from the Hawaii Institute of Marine Biology on Coconut Island that most of the nutrients in the sludge can be converted into worms, which, when shaken free, make excellent food for fish. Personal communication, February 1973.

9. This alternative was generated while I was working with C. A. Doxiadis's "City of the Future" project as a consultant, and it was incorporated in an unpublished paper, "The Settlement of the Seas I: The Prospective Demands for Aquatic Surface," Ann Arbor, January 1964.

10. These ideas were first elaborated in R. L. Meier, *Science and Economic Development* (Cambridge, Mass.: MIT Press, 1956), and updated in the 1966 edition. Because the relative price of energy was dropping in the interim, there has been little interest in these novel but more expensive approaches to expanding the supply of energy. The need for a workable technology for producing the liquid fuels needed by mobile machines will be felt in the 1980s.

11. Alvin M. Weinberg, "Social Institutions and Nuclear Energy," *Science,* 177 (July 7, 1972), 27-34. A comparison is provided for the competition between coal and pressurized water reactors to come on stream in 1978. Nuclear plants for large metropolitan areas would produce electric power at a cost of 1.03 to 1.07 cents per kwh as compared to coal in a range of 1.08 to 1.24 cents. The higher cost from coal-burning facilities is due to sulfur dioxide removal and to water conservation with cooling towers.

12. Some of the most elegant decision analysis techniques have now been applied to a very different kind of seeding, that of a hurricane, but still relevant here. The authors go through an exercise in the estimation of the economic consequences of intervention in a large ongoing physical system, judging how much is government responsibility in the legal sense, and especially methods of assessing the value of information to be obtained from further experiments. R. A. Howard, J. E. Matheson, D. W. North, "The Decision to Seed Hurricanes," *Science,* 176 (1972), 1191-1202.

13. The Atomic Energy Commission is preparing a thorough analysis of the current uranium supply situation. Meanwhile, a long-term global review is provided by K. E. Zimen, "Nuclear Energy Reserves and Long Term Energy Requirements," *Angewandts Chemie* (Int'l. Ed.), 10, 1 (1971), 1-11. Zimen argues that the world would be forced to utilize magmatic rock (mainly light granite) for its uranium and thorium within a century.

14. I took up this discussion in an earlier book, *Science and Economic Development: New Patterns of Living* (Cambridge, Mass.: MIT Press, 1966), 2nd ed., pp. 101-119. In brief, space heating is desirable at least up to 10°C and in many circumstances somewhat higher.

15. During the Ekistics Symposium and the preceding seminars of 1966, a large amount of information from many sources was reported, with a rather remarkable conclusion arrived at from archaeological, cross-cultural, and design-based analysis which suggested that 6-7m^2 per capita covered living space is typically constructed in pedestrian-oriented societies under nonstressful conditions and a minimum of 8-10m^3 of enclosure seems tolerable for the bulk of an urban population over the long run. The conclusions appeared to be controversial according to the conventions of that period, so they were watered down to innocuous statements for publication.

16. I am indebted to Joseph I. Robinson for producing two such visions of the future (one in which he had lived for several years) and alerting me to the proposals made by other designers.

17. This economizing attitude toward design, combined with a few examples indicating how little a designer should propose, allowing the ultimate consumer to elaborate the final form for his ideosyncratic purposes, is given in Victor Papanek, *Design for a Real World* (New York: Pantheon Books, 1971).

18. F. Stuart Chapin, Jr., has conducted time-budget studies for subpopulations in American cities. He has found it possible to get all levels of the population to describe their activities in terms of whether they "must" act at that time or whether a range of options, including doing nothing at all, was open to them. F. S. Chapin, Jr., "Activity Systems and Urban Structure: A Working Schema," *AIP Journal,* 34 (January 1968); P. G. Hammer, Jr. and F. S. Chapin, Jr., *Human Time Allocation: A Case of Washington, D.C.* (Center for Urban and Regional Studies, University of North Carolina, Chapel Hill, April 1972), 242 pp.; Richard K. Brail and F. S. Chapin, Jr., "Activity Patterns of Urban Residents," *Environment and Behavior,* 5 (June 1973), 163-190.

19. H. W. Case and H. W. Hulbert, *Bikeway Planning Criteria and Guidelines* (Institute of Transportation and Traffic Engineering, University of California, Los Angeles, April 1972). This report condenses a very large share of the miscellaneous accumulated experience in the Western societies' planning for the bicycle, but not for the pedicab, cart, and other vehicles likely to use such facilities in the Orient. See also S. S. Wilson, "Bicycle Technology," *Scientific American,* 228 (March 1973), 81-91.

Energy and Water Supply   267

20. J. W. Scheel, J. E. Foote, "Bus Operation in Single Lane Platoons . . . ," Research Publication GM R-808, Research Laboratories, General Motors, Warren, Michigan. Passenger capacities of up to 28,000 passengers per hour per lane (about three times that of Chicago's Michigan Avenue peak) can be achieved with platoons of up to ten buses and passenger loading bays.

21. Typical sources for water treatment technology are T. R. Camp, *Water and Its Impurities* (New York: Reinhold Publishing, 1966); G. M. Fair, J. C. Geyer and D. A. Okun *Water and Wastewater Engineering,* vols. I and II (New York: John Wiley & Sons, 1966).

22. I have not been able to find an adequate review of the prospective potentials for using reject heat that is carried off by cooling water—the by-product of electric power generation and other high-temperature processes that until recently was known as thermal pollution, because when unutilized it often disturbed aquatic ecosystems. Each contribution to the literature is dedicated to a specific product or a kind of process in the context of a much lower energy price and therefore provides too limited a basis for describing the structure of the complex that is expected to result when energy prices advance further.

The warm effluent from cooling an energy-transforming unit is often best used to speed up biological growth. Thus it can accelerate the maturation of salmon, trout, shrimp, or shellfish, and economizes on the conversion of feed into flesh. What is important is the dependability of the flow, because if urban populations demand 99.9% reliability for their electric power, the livestock populations dependent upon waste heat are unlikely to be shocked and have their growth stunted. When sea water is used as a coolant, most of this low grade heat can be used to produce distilled water; in those cities that experience variable quality in the public water supply, this stream of highly purified water will be used for the manufacture of bottled drinks, beer, and ice.

23. These descriptions are based upon personal observations and deductions reinforced by communications from Douglas Campbell, who has been adapting the Hydroculture design to conditions outside Beirut. As with most irrigation schemes, these techniques apply to carefully leveled areas. J. Sholto Douglas, one of the original innovators in hydroponics, has now developed a technique suited to sloping surfaces. He unrolls flexible layflat plastic tubing on a smoothed area, trickles nutrient solution through it, and plants seedlings into precut slits. The nutrient solution is recirculated through plastic pipe. The tubing acts as sufficient support for the plants; *Women's Journal* (Manila), January 5, 1974, pp. 14-16.

The future urban system has thus far been considered as a whole, inasmuch as this is possible. Its toughness, vulnerabilities, and evolutionary path, the composition of its population, the anticipated stresses due to scarcity of inputs (food, fuel, and water), and its component entities have all been taken up, and projections made on responses suggested by the current state of knowledge. The principal purpose has been to identify a feasible path for urban growth that surmounts the obstacles posed. In the course of the discussion it has become evident that resource-conserving cities must have quite a different internal structure from cities that exist today or have grown to maturity in the past.

Structure is normally a function of the x,y,z,t coordinates of space and time, but for an ecosystem the positions of members of the populations relative to each other and the topographic features of the inanimate, constructed environment must be added. Structure can also be mapped in other dimensions, such as membership and social status, so that positions and relations can be established for a social system. Strategically, however, a discussion of structure must locate crucial subassemblies, infer how they come to be placed as they are and how they relate to each other. It is then possible to engage in the design process. A mental image, or concept, can be constructed for a new artifact that falls far short of an engineer's or an architect's proposal but is sufficient to guide him to a desired outcome.

It is useful to start from first principles and gain insights from nature itself. When a natural community is subjected to stresses, so that it must economize strictly on food, energy, and water, the most extensive space-using activities are cut back first, the effective boundaries of the community shrink, and normal periods of dormancy lengthen. When the living system experiences recurring shortages, however, and has adjusted to them as it would, for example, to a seasonal cycle or to repeated droughts, specific coordinated behaviors that assure the maintenance of the community become evident. Some populations accumulate internal reserves and external stockpiles before the shortages occur, others switch to substitutes; some go underground or form spores, so that essential instructions are preserved even though the organisms themselves have disappeared, and some build insulating layers to protect themselves from the most severe stresses. All of these primitive strategies for building and maintaining a community will need to be employed in the subsystems of cities, along with some that are more sophisticated—the kind that only humans, with the aid of machines, could invent and apply. Therefore, the following design proposals, using the simplest means of providing for day-to-day needs, incorporate economical responses to adversities caused by specific, anticipated resource scarcities.

Consider first the atom of a city—a household with an address, a small group of members, their pets, their plants, their stationary machines, their private vehicles, and a shell that provides protection from the elements. A boundary has been delineated for it that encompasses most strong interactions. This is normally a highly conservative unit of society, being the last to abandon folk traditions in child rearing and food preparation.

Whenever a household is separated from its original site and must settle into a new one, it quickly assembles a new shell, built out of whatever materials are at hand with whatever experience had previously been acquired. Thus the ubiquitous squatter settlement in poorer cities, regarded as undesirable slum by bureaucrat and tourist, becomes a marvelous demonstration for the human ecologist and the sensitive architect of the adaptation of households to a difficult environment. Step by step one can perceive the creation of order inside the shell and then, much later, the impress of this sense of order upon the immediate external environment—the threshold, the window box of flowers, a painted exterior, a tree, a balcony, perhaps even a front yard—whatever is encouraged by middle-class culture. With increasing security and investment of effort, one notes added furnishings, potted plants, children, pets, and simple machines. Gradually, reed mats and scrap wood are replaced by concrete blocks or bricks and the scrap tin roof by tile or slab. Artisan-built doors and window frames are installed, and if the natural shell-creating processes are not disrupted, a standard working-class, sometimes even lower-middle-class, house is evolved over the course of eight to twenty years. Most of these households, however, live close to the poverty line, so that the frequency of interruption is likely to be high. For a casual visitor or prospective tenant, the overall appearance of such a settlement during its first decades of existence is that of an uneven, disorderly development; some home sites appear to be no more than a collection of junk, but a few are almost gemlike in the precision of their construction and the elaboration of their immediate setting. The area closely resembles a community that has grown up under wilderness conditions where stresses stunt or cripple a noticeable share of the members but a few mature into noble specimens.

After World War II it occurred to a number of architects, planners, and community development specialists that the most economical solution to the housing problem would be to expedite this natural process. As Ian McHarg would put it, the impulse was to design with nature rather than re-place it. This means identifying sources for the failures, the delays, and the frustrations encountered by poor house-holds as they create places to live in the city. This is much more difficult than it sounds because observers and inter-viewers bring preconceptions born of urban upbringing and middle-class standards with them, while the households generally have rural origins, very often landless, and aspire to the working class but frequently must settle for less. Communication fails on many points. Once the dwelling creation process has been understood, however, a program can be prepared to expedite it. In the international agencies designated to improve housing and welfare, this activity is called "provision of site and services in self-help situations."

Household units are assigned a small plot of land in a surveyed tract with enough security of tenure to make in-vesting their own effort and capital worthwhile. The minimum services provided, often in a very crude form, are water supply, sanitation, and transport. The householder must do the rest. Usually this means collaboration with others in order to get a house built. If the "others" are kin-folk, he must put on parties, buy gifts, or provide mutual support. If they are friends from elsewhere in the city, information about opportunities may be a sufficient trade for the help that is obtained. If they are neighbors similarly engaged in construction, it is relatively easy to organize teams that rotate from house to house as materials are ob-tained. Thus, the completed structure is an outgrowth of the social network of the new homebuilder—a large and varied social network results in a rapidly completed and fully equipped dwelling, while a small set of human relationships leads to a slowly rising, inadequate shack for shelter. If a complete neighborhood or precinct is to be created, the sponsoring agency must find, in effect, a crutch for a crippled social network in each instance of failure to build a decent house. Or it could find customers that would buy out the assets of the unsuccessful households and quickly fill the breech. The agency must also be able to deliver, in one way or another, improvements in the supply of basic urban services in response to mounting demand from community group and the friends each householder had made in the process of housebuilding. John F. C. Turner and his collaborators in the book *Freedom to Build* have eloquently contrasted the usual methods with improvements in them for the housing of new urban inmigrants in almost any part of the world.[1]

The proper conditions for stimulating an urban self-help settlement are known in theory but are difficult to undertake and bring to completion in practice. The site, for example, should have access to more than one source of employment, but this implies that the land has value for other urban purposes and may be relatively expensive. The size should be sufficient to support a natural community (several hundred households) or at least a specialized quarter added to such a community. The dimensions of the individual plot should be no greater than would normally be occupied in a village (60-100 square meters), but this spacing often prevents the settlement from evolving into a middle-class community. The allocation of land to streets and public areas must by made in advance, and afterward they must be defended against encroachment. The assignment of plots must reflect whatever concepts of social structure and social justice exist in the community; otherwise the settlement will be riven by conflict, and households would move away rather than suffer continued insult or perceived deprivation. This means that a merchant household should be settled near the center of the area, but a household that tends a flock of animals or maintains a garden is best located on the periphery. At the same time, those households that are most senior or earliest to join should be given the greatest range of choice. The kind of title to the land that is offered and the rights of sale or transfer must be well understood, because the head of a household must make many kinds of deals with relatives, fellow-workers, and neighbors in order to put up a house that reflects his place in the community. If the title appears to be at least as clear and dependable as for village land, the household may sell its village property in order to invest in the city where the hope of profit from resale is obviously much greater.

Let us assume that these preliminaries have been successfully handled. The household obtains a site, puts up a flimsy shelter, and proceeds to look for building materials for a more permanent dwelling. Then a major conflict is encountered—if the adults are relatively fully employed, there is little time to build; if they are not adequately employed, there is little income left over for building materials. It is noted also that the efficiency of self-help construction labor is low (generally it creates value on the market at about half the wages given to ordinary labor) so that any opportunity for work at regular wages requires a deferral of construction. Thus most simple one-room houses take one to three years to complete, if they are completed at all. During this time, cooking, child care, washing, and other household activities are all conducted in what is agreed by all to be a highly inconvenient and inefficient manner.

Why does it take so long? Close observation reveals that most cheap building materials are heavy: 100-1,000 tons is typical for a complete house. They require strong men working together. Wood or bamboo, where it is available, require skill in the use of tools as a trade-off from heavy labor. The ideal material for self-help housing would be lighter than wood, so that women and children could participate in building, but requisite skill levels should remain as simple as those for the preparation of concrete blocks or slabs, so that the house can go up in weeks. At the same time the material should be modifiable, so as to accommodate unplanned members of the household. At a later date it should be possible to construct a second floor.

Materials that fill these requirements are appearing on the scene for the first time. Although not yet sufficiently economical everywhere, they promise to become competitive in cost throughout the world over the next decade. The principal candidate is a top-ranked insulating material— rigid polyurethane foam—but there are a number of competitors for special-purpose building ranging from plastic sheeting to ferroconcrete shells. The foam can be supplied as a sandwich-type board with jute, bagasse, particle board, aluminum, wood, or even polyurethane facing—also as a spray-on over a contained balloon, as a building block laid down with glue or mortar, or as a form-filling material.[2] Nonrigid foam made of the same material could serve as a substitute for rugs, mattresses, cushions, and wall covering. The weight of a house, including built-in furniture, could be reduced to as little as a ton and the time of basic construction to a month, or even a weekend. Any shape could be prepared, from an igloo or dome to a partitioned box or a substitute for a cave.

Although these possibilities existed in the minds of plastics chemists in the 1950s they did not start taking form until the 1960s. Paraskevopoulos and his co-workers in Ann Arbor worked out the steps that would convert a promising material into a dependable enclosure, with the needs of the rest of the world kept in the foreground from the very beginning.[3] In the 1970s the material began to be used on a large scale in the United States for the furnishing of automobiles and buses, for the lowest-cost houses, and for experimental structures of unusual design.[4] Experience will develop many alternative routes to what now seems to be a revolutionary approach in lightweight construction of dwelling units and local facilities, and by the 1980s these routes will appear to be straightforward. The new capability will have been fused with traditional approaches to construction, as Portland cement was earlier in the century. We must anticipate here the principal implications of the new technology for the enclosure of living space and the modifications of spatiotemporal structures in cities of the future.

One feature of polyurethane, and of other foamed plastics to nearly the same degree, is the difficulty of disposal, since it is not biodegradable like paper or wood. A few secondary uses could be found, particularly as soil conditioners, but it would be expensive to deliver to rural areas. Combustion is inefficient and fume-producing, with a dangerous tendency to flash when foam surfaces are exposed. The materials polyurethane would displace, such as brick and concrete, normally go into filling up the low places in a city in the form of rubble, but foam makes fills unstable. In 1972, however, two approaches to recycling polyurethane were announced.[5] In these the bulk of the products would go back into the production of polyurethane; the remainder is a kind of pitch that can go into road surfacing. Then a virtually metabolic solution to the city building process would be available, because in this approach plastic can be reused like metals and glass, generation after generation. Concrete is rarely worth salvaging for new construction. (See figure 8.1.)

A view of the future is best obtained by considering a supply station of building materials for a self-help community. It would contain fewer materials such as brick, cinderblock, tile, bagged cement, sand, lime, reinforcing rods, wire, and iron pipe, but would have drums of chemicals and hand-carts carrying steel cylinders with mixing valved for foam generation. Aluminum sheet is likely to be popular for roofing in tropical and semitropical environments, and plastic pipe is superseding metal for domestic purposes. One corner of the supply station would contain stacks of sandwich panel boards, many with distinctive surfaces and with inset electric plugs from which wires dangle ready to connect to a power source. The most distinctive feature would be that three square meters (thirty-two square feet) of five centimeter (two inch) board would be so light that it could be lifted into place by a woman or child, yet would be stiff enough to serve as a load-bearing wall. Many stations would stock stacks of shells, big enough for a roof, an extra room, or an outside toilet, but light enough for two people to walk away with. These could be tied down to previously prepared foundations anywhere in the vicinity. Windows and doors would be cut with a saw and appropriate frames and fixtures added when they could be afforded. The overall cost of enclosed space before wiring, plumbing, painting, etc., seems likely to run in the $20-40 per square meter range, which is what it costs now with more traditionally retailed materials.

Modifications of the site-and-service formula can be applied to denser settlements in the city. Usually areas that have been cleared of previous uneconomic settlement or have been reclaimed at the waterfront of a metropolis are ready for mixed residential, commercial, and, often, light manufacturing uses. The one possibility for low-cost development is the provision of space frames for *ad hoc* construction. Conduits make available the electric power, water, telephone, gas, and sewer lines, which are used as needed. These districts could adapt the new construction materials to their needs or resort to orthodox methods of

Light weight foam plastics can assume many more shapes than traditional materials. Where wood is scarce, and alternative materials ponderous, fire retardant foam structures can speed urbanization.

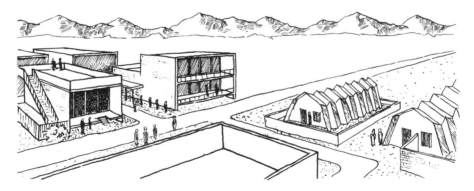

Figure 8.1 Quickly Fabricated Self-Help Housing
The primary value lies in ease of fabrication with unskilled labor—after the techniques have been standardized—and in the high-quality insulation afforded. Sandwich panel structures can also be designed so that few beams or very little framing would be required.

building. When assigned some cubage in a space frame holding a number of families the household is quite a bit more constrained in the structures it erects, so that more detailed planning and continuing coordination would be needed. (See figure 8.2.)

The new options require advice and assistance. Short courses would be instituted on how to paint, how to seal, and how to wire, and on procedures for applying for electrical and other utility connections. The means for obtaining credit are equally important; so some institutional means would have to be provided to supply households with the necessary capital to build. This review of the site-and-services approach to self-help housing for the bulk of the urban inmigrants suggests that the aim of programs will shift away from the actual production of dwelling units to the expedition of acculturation. Building one's own house becomes a readily understood and highly motivating lesson in procedures for successful urban living—getting land, gaining membership in a community, learning building techniques, approaching lending institutions, dealing with public utilities, and forming neighborhood organizations. In other words, the house is an introduction into the big city, and its completion indicates that an individual or a household has learned how to manipulate the levers of a bureaucratic society. Acquiring a higher skill, obtaining a better job, getting proper education for children, and gaining better health service all require still more sophisticated personal control of the situation in an urban society, and these are the next steps to successful urbanization. Most new urban communities must be made up of households that are relatively independent, autonomous, capable of taking care of themselves under all conditions except the most catastrophic, and—perhaps most important of all—able to accomplish this transformation without significant subsidy.

The next-largest discrete unit of structure in a city is the face-to-face community. In most countries an appropriate space is assigned boundaries, named, and given a core staff made up of an administrator, a policeman, and perhaps a maintainer of public roads and ways. It is large enough to contain from several hundred to several thousand households at the expected urban density. It can also be expected to

THE URBAN VILLAGE

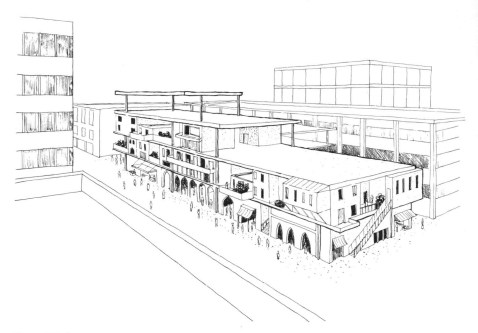

Figure 8.2 Self-Help Housing at High Density
It is possible to transfer rights to occupy space in a skeletal structure in such a way that families are encouraged to put up housing that fits their traditions and life-styles.

nurture up to a hundred or so private and public organizations, each of them with an address and a name, that enable
members of households to obtain or provide specialized
services; the space requirements of these organizations are
more various than households. A surprising number of
organizations will ignore the designated boundary, maintaining memberships that are scattered more widely in the city—
an index of the urban integration achieved by the community.

Attention here is focused upon the "urban village"; for a
household this is the kind of community that serves as a
halfway station between the social patterns of rural life and
a securely established, fully adapted place within the matrix
of the metropolis. A typical progression involves recognition of the hard life ahead when one is a surplus member
of a rural settlement; thus, unattached individuals spill out
of rail and bus terminals into reception areas near the
center of the city, later moving to urban neighborhoods
opening up for more permanent settlement. The normal
process is objectionable because it leads to dense packing
and congestion when population pressures are high, and
the social characteristics of a village are lost. They are more
likely retained when the minority who drift to the periphery
of a metropolis are received by nuclei of communities that
help migrants find work and transmit essential information.
Very often the name of a community in the metropolis reveals the ethnic or regional connection to the place of origin,
but even if it does not, the principal public institutions—
coffee houses, churches, trading companies, and the like—
take on names that will do so. Each ethnic group works out
procedures that ease the adjustment of inmigrants to city
life, but the same group often attempts to bind them to
some institution as well, such as a church or fraternal
association. These institutions maintain distinctive rituals
or norms of behavior that prevent complete integration into
the mainstream. The techniques for maintaining these
features of the settler's cultural identity and reminders of
his origins are extremely elaborate and ingenious; frequently
they produce and reinforce dramatically conflicting loyalties. Novelists dwell upon such phenomena when choosing
urban themes.

Elaboration of the techniques for providing "site and
services" for self-help on the part of new inmigrants must
face up to this prior body of experience with organization.

The Uses of Space and Time   279

Government has the option of constructing schemes that are equitable, distributing its assistance fairly to all needy inmigrants and creating integrated communities. On the other hand, it may take a much more ad hoc stance and assist the various ethnic communities, usually responding to the amount of publicity or political pressure that each such community is able to generate. The first approach results in a city like Singapore, with its diverse Asian populations distributed throughout public housing in a fine-grained pepper-and-salt kind of mixture; the second results in cities such as those of the Near East with their "quarters" containing the various tribal, religious, and regional groups. Experience suggests that, although nationalist ideology almost always favors rapid integration, the problems of coping with periodic floods of poor villagers anxious to resettle make the segregated approach more convenient to governments in the short run. Therefore, many urban villages will be made up of people who speak a minority language, have a distinctive religious practice, maintain a recognizably different diet, and contribute aptitudes and skills to urban services that often become quite specialized. These characteristics, when held by a whole community, will strongly modify a site-and-services formula.

The energy- and water-conserving features already discussed will interact with both the ethnic and the administrative aspects of a new urban community. Saving water and recycling organic waste lead to proposals for intensive gardening and stock raising, but Chinese settlers will choose quite a different set of plants and animals to cultivate from those selected by a Moslem population or any of the Buddhist or tribal groups. Efficiency in land use should in most instances reach the same high levels because ultimately the limits are set by the availability of sunlight and the metabolic efficiences of plants and animals, though some cultures seem to possess more of the techniques that accelerate achievement of optimal output levels. The Chinese, for instance, seem able to draw upon Japanese experience in addition to indigenous accomplishments very readily, as illustrated in Formosa, Singapore, and parts of Malaysia.

The basic formula for creating the urban villages best suited for cities in Asia and Africa can be spelled out; the strong forces for variation are recognized, and implicit allowances can be made for them. The metropolis should

grow at the periphery by adding designated units of 100-
1,000 hectares each for urban villages, some of them homogeneous and others quite specialized. Growth sequences
and the evolution of transport connections with the metropolis coincide with those already described in Chapter 7, but
other features are equally important.

The inmigrant population in the community is likely to
accumulate in stages. An initial organizing and preparing
group is needed to convert land from rural purposes with a
surplus product that is channeled into a central urban
market to intensive use, often with added water, where
much of the consumption is expected to be local. Leveling,
draining, ponding, piping, road-making, and other land de
development work must be undertaken before massive
settlement occurs. The legal and administrative work involved in transferring the land from, say, a hundred peasant
owners to perhaps a thousand households, cooperatives,
small enterprises, and municipal agencies is a major undertaking; its complexity is increased by the need for honesty,
speed, justice, and openness to inquiry by potential residents
and other interested parties. The reason so few planned
urban villages have evolved to date, even though they fill
a desperate need felt by every growing metropolis, is that a
high degree of organization is required. Top organizers in
the society are usually available only for prestige projects
such as electric power systems, airports, and export industries. A good basic plan, however, should make it possible
to build urban villages with ordinary organizing competence.
(See figure 8.3.)

Three kinds of capabilities seem to be required. One of
them is immensely practical, requiring resourcefulness in
overcoming small-scale crises during construction. These
could be caused by mistakes, nondelivery of supplies, or
abnormal weather. A person with such capability could
be a small general contractor if he possessed the capital.
Another is the ability to conceptualize groupings of plots,
proposing ways in which public facilities could take advantage of terrain or existing structures, and obtaining information about new products or techniques. A person with
this ability often has architectural or engineering training
but is rarely a graduate of a professional school. The third
capability is that of understanding how the various bureaucracies work, maintaining a number of friendships and

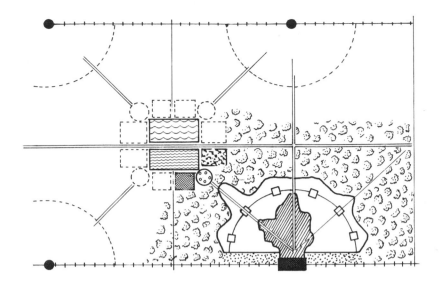

Station	■	Fish Ponds		Electric Rail	+++++
Light Industry		Oxidation Ponds		Main Roads	=
Commercial		Packing Sheds		Secondary Roads	—
Residential	○	Cow Colony		Cycle Tracks	—
Gardening		Poultry	⊙	Adjacent Centers	●

Figure 8.3 Urban Village

A self-help community must be allocated resources sufficient to allow it to work its way up to a minimum adequate standard of living. This is one of the shapes that it could take in a sub-tropical or tropical climatic zone. The population might peak at 20,000-30,000 members living off 300-400 hectares. Recycle facilities are shared in part with other urban villages in order to reap benefits from economies of scale. One can find approximations of the urban village that have evolved without special planning in Japan, Taiwan, Korea, Hong Kong New Territories, and Java, but all these present versions are vulnerable to land speculation. Modern prototypes need to be designed which can withstand all but the most intense pressure for densification. Suffi-cient security of tenure must be offered to encourage continuing investment of savings in land and human resources. The size and layout suggested here are intended to economize upon water, fuel, fertilizer, and labor in that order. Communities like this are needed to prevent squatters from occupying the circulation space in the central parts of the metropolis.

acquaintances in key agencies, so that informal means of expediting can be used to reinforce the formal. The person with this ability accompanies the self-help homebuilder in his visits to the offices of the utilities and the licensing bureaus, serving as a knowledgeable advocate. It is possible that all of these abilities might have been acquired by a single person, but more likely it would take a group working with an acknowledged headman or elected boss to carry out these functions. If any element is missing, a central urban development authority of some kind must take responsibility for its provision or else risk a defective, or even a failed, community.

Once the organizational preliminaries are out of the way, a period of rapid building by pioneer households ensues. Mostly it is only their own shelter that is constructed, but the essential services such as the school, production facilities, and, for some ethnic groups, a place of worship must eventually be provided. The organizing force is transferred from the external metropolis-oriented launching agency to responsible leaders within the community. Some of these people stay with the community the remainder of their lives, roughly thirty to forty years, becoming patriarchal leaders. Others graduate to become leaders in unions, cultural groups, firms, bureaucracies, and political parties that serve a larger segment of the metropolis.

The most satisfactory urban villages will devote larger amounts of land to intensive food production than they use for settlement purposes with a site-and-services formula. Some land allocations in the past have assigned 150-250 square meters of land to a household, thus assuring small private gardens, but this policy has led to inefficient use of land. The gardening enterprise needs to be some kind of community corporation, using whatever form of cooperative operation that is most familiar to villagers. Technical assistance must be available from an experiment station. Often a loan has to be obtained before sufficient water can be introduced, and high-yielding crops take over. The collective gardening activities will create a solidarity among the least modern component of the community and a source of support in very hard times. The marketing of periodic surpluses brings the community into contact with consumers who are better established in the metropolis. As the community matures, the gardening is routinized and may be regarded as only one of several specialized enterprises operated by members of the community.

The third stage for an urban village will be that of adding a new stratum of inmigrants, generally more educated than their predecessors, who use the community as a base for seeking out productive jobs elsewhere in the metropolis, either in the service sector or in industry. Often they will have to compromise, because of low seniority, and accept work and opportunities for study on shifts with odd hours. Filling their needs for services within the urban village would extend the range and the flexibility of the internal agencies and enterprises. The settlement characteristics would be pushed much closer toward those of the main body of the metropolis, and density would substantially increase. Many houses would be remodeled into flats, and a few would evolve into boardinghouses. The kinds of instruction available would multiply many times but at the same time move away from the simple skills taught initially. Many more people would belong to organizations—clubs, unions, cooperatives, and partnerships—outside the urban village.

A decade or more later we can expect the processes of urban redevelopment to get under way. Many households mature and disperse. If the expanded community is centrally located with respect to the new dimensions of an enlarged metropolis, its garden and pond surface may be allocated to more valuable metropolitan activities. The whole area might eventually be devoted to multistory buildings with many interpenetrating, shifting uses. Bypassed communities, on the other hand, may be preserved and provide for the future modern metropolis some contact with the values and handiwork of its original settlers.

Fonseca started from the requirements presented by the Indo-Gangetic plain, where hundreds of thousands of such urban communities need to be formed over the next three to five generations, and he produced a plan for urban village development. He was able to infer the intermediate tasks that need to be completed adequately, and more or less in sequence, in order to create a healthy, productive urban community.[6] Self-help, assisted from the outside so as to direct the growth into a locale and structure compatible with plans for the growth of an urban region, seemed to be the only possibility for the urbanization required in that part of South Asia. He was able to illustrate the

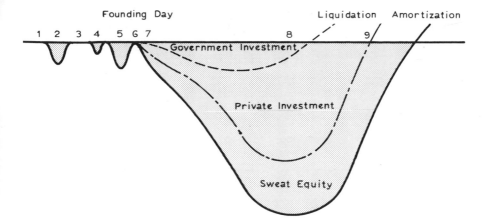

Figure 8.4 Investments in Site-and-Services Urbanization
Expected capital outlays for communities built by self-help techniques vary over time: (1) earliest attempt; (2) recognition of failure; (3) new formula; (4) second failure; (5) nearly successful attempt; (6) systematic approach using experienced organizers; (7) education and organization efforts accelerate; (8) returns from effort begin to appear; (9) rate of financial returns begins to exceed the investment rate. Time elapsed after founding day is expected to be five to twelve years.

spatial implications of balanced growth for an urban village. (See figure 8.4.) A half-dozen different attempts by myself and others to design prototype spatial structures for the urban village, each starting with somewhat different assumptions and working in different contexts, arrive at very similar solutions for the urban village. Unfortunately, no modern prototypes can be pointed out—only partial examples.

Other kinds of urban communities will be required by the growing metropolis. They will be created primarily to house the labor force of large industrial complexes; here the growth of the supporting urbanization must be coordinated with the capital investment in industry rather than intensive gardening. Because Western new town standards are accepted by leading professionals in government and industry in developing countries, they have been installed in these communities. Contractor-built housing is provided on prepared sites. The results are usually very bad; costs are several times greater per household settled than the average experienced in that metropolis, and morale is depressed to the point where strikes and political strife become endemic. The sources of the most costly mistakes are regulations, bureaucratic procedures, and institutional limitations that change from one locale to another even within the same country, so it does not seem worthwhile to attempt generalizations. It may suffice to remark that in 1966 the All-India meeting of the Institute of Town Planners resolved that the government should not accept any more new towns as part of foreign aid and technical assistance because they did not work in India. Townships designed by Indians have not worked well either, but they were at least built more cheaply and were less wasteful of land. Moreover, there is evidence of institutional learning in the design of industrial townships that may someday lead to adequate planning and development if the effort stays close to India. The technique for building industrial townships may differ greatly from the self-help urban village formula.

It should be pointed out that a mass transport network supporting one to two distinct urban villages per kilometer of line (preferably two to a single station) should deliver sufficient labor to operate the largest industrial facilities and accomplish it at less than half the cost of present networks. Aided self-help communities are therefore likely to constitute a rising fraction of the total effort of urbanization, even in areas dominated by high-priority industry.

Central districts are what distinguish a city from a town. The variety, complexity, and pace of public transactions there go so far beyond human scale or comprehension that special kinds of reporting devices are needed for mapping structure. The idea of a town itself requires a major leap in the imagination from the village-level experience, because it is a stage of aggregation where familiar face-to-face interactions are, to a large degree, conducted anonymously in markets, offices, schools, and other public places. The roles of storekeeper, salesman, policeman, civil servant, student, and at least a hundred others are collectively defined; their functions and behaviors are learned by citizens as part of the town culture. The properties of town centers have been captured by the city and fitted to serve its subcenters. These urban subcenters provide foci for 3,000 to 30,000 households and are in turn managed, guided, informed, financed, reorganized, and even entertained from central districts of higher order.

THE CENTRAL DISTRICTS

Ecologically the central district is a crossroads for mobile species and a concentration point for immobile objects. Highly specialized populations assemble there and collaborate so as to maintain the pace of interactions. Stationary machines, ranging from cash registers to typewriters and printing presses, are found in large numbers. Mobile machines move through, picking up and dropping passengers and packages, but are otherwise segregated to parking structures or stationed on the periphery in parking areas. Habitats for human populations are present, but almost all occupants are temporary residents of the central hotels. Plants and animals are virtually squeezed out of the central districts altogether (birds have often invaded but are regarded as a nuisance, and nesting places are consciously eliminated). The transaction-producing activity carried on by humans with the direct aid of their machines is cyclical, operating at quite low levels 60-75% of the time.[7] Very strong daily, weekly, and seasonal cycles remain, even though no essential element in the urban ecosystem requires such periodicity any more.

According to the classical theory of cities, the central districts are hierarchically ordered. A metropolis contains several centers with approximately the same functions and activities as independent cities, and one center that serves the whole metropolis but may still be outranked by a center that dominates a constellation of metropolises or megalopolis. Such organization of central districts was strongly confirmed for the Athens of 1963 by the group at the Athens Center for Ekistics.[8] The static hierarchic model was applicable before the population explosion in automobiles and independent of the decisions of multinational corporations or their counterpart governmental organizations. Some deviations from that simple hierarchy, however, are now detectable on a qualitative basis, which must be discussed because the forces behind their appearance are so vigorous that they will be important in the long run. It is relatively easy to design the shells of large cities in a strict hierarchical basis adjusted to the influences of topography, sacred sites, and sources of physical inputs. It is much more difficult to deduce a means of designing a better fit to new technology and the rapidly accumulating stock of knowledge, together with the social forces that respond to them. It is these technosocial features that generate the most surprises and provide us with the freedom to choose between significantly different alternative structures.

The central business district produces services for organizations through a life cycle—from the time they are promoted (gestation and birth) to their demise through being swallowed in a takeover or by dissolution through bankruptcy, both usually with the subsequent salvage of assets. As in any community where cooperation is the dominant pattern in conducting affairs, great emphasis is put upon the rule of law in the settlement of conflicts, yet the principle of the survival of the fittest still applies. The struggle to survive as an organized entity is becoming important even to the offices and bureaus of "big government," because budget makers now question the reasons for the existence of each unit, often requiring dismemberment and reconstitution. The mortality rates for private and public organizations, considered as a population, are greater than those for humans, even though the lifetime of an organization can be much longer than that of an individual.[9] In societies with mixed economies, whether predominantly capitalist or socialist, the floor space in the central business district is increasingly used to manage financial controls over flows between and within units of organization.

A central cultural district that is physically separate from the central business district seems to be emerging in leading metropolises. Images and symbols, instead of prices and budgetary allocations, are manipulated in a cultural district. Some techniques of communication, such as newspaper, magazine, and book publication, are still embedded in the central business district, but the supports for creative and critical work on film, tape, drama, design, and for writing of all kinds seem to be moving to the fringe of a large university campus. New styles in the presentation of popular art, music, and literature start in the emerging district and are often subsequently managed from there. The facilities of large metropolitan universities, especially the studios, laboratories, experimental groups, libraries, and seminar rooms, generate a large share of the momentum. It is stimulated simultaneously by rapidly declining costs in the recording and multiplication of cultural symbols and audiovisual messages. In the cultural districts of metropolises ideas from the past are continually resurrected, and novel symbols from other cities are picked up if they interest local clienteles. The pace of the exchange in this emerging central cultural district is too great to allow major creative work to be done on the site; it is a place for brokers to find appreciators who will back up the creators and provide innovators with enough funds to keep them working at least part time at their art. The central cultural district, as much as it exists at present, is a spinoff from the central business district; it has not yet fully arrived, but it is coming fast, and cities badly need some planning that recognizes the special requirements of this metropolitan function.

Another kind of central district is forming to expedite intermetropolitan exchange around the airport. Previously harbor facilities filled this function, and markets with offices grew up behind them. Now, however, the space requirements for movement by air, together with the effects of the noise, have forced the terminal for passengers, mail, and high-valued express shipments to a peripheral site. Hotels, conference rooms, communications facilities, computation capabilities, and recreational services are accumulating to handle the interfaces between producers and suppliers, parent organizations and their subsidiaries, marketers and their distributors, consulting groups and their clients. Meanwhile, the many tourists that are processed build up the volume of flow in and out of this specialized district and make it possible to exploit economies of scale when installing stationary mechanical equipment. As with culture, it is the annual 10-25% annual growth rates, not the achieved volume of activity, that make it necessary to plan the airport as a center for specialized activity that is at the same time intimately and directly connected with other centers in the metropolis.

Another kind of central district could very well emerge in the future, based upon the ultramodern information technology. Forerunners are already evident on Boston's Route 128, in New York's Upper Hudson and Princeton sites, and around San Francisco's Stanford Campus development. These are the principal birthplaces of the automata; the new kinds of central districts will be the locales where new species are planned and come into being. The probable characteristics of such an area will be better understood once the system properties of the automata have been discussed in Chapter 9.

The most critical resource for a central district is not the very significant amounts of energy needed to move the commuters in and out of it, as one would suppose from first inspection, but is *land*—buildable surface with high accessibility. Each working commuter requires, on the average, ten to twenty square meters of roofed-over working space; the equipment he works with takes up an increasing amount of floor space over time and may reach equivalent dimensions. This land needs intensive capital investment to make it useful. The designer of the buildings, equipment, and service facilities must know much more than the number of employees and their assigned tasks. Some addresses have acquired status, for example, as with the "City" in London, Fifth Avenue in New York, and the Ginza in Tokyo, and the buildings are expected to conform to what clients believe is proper for such elevated status. Also, many of the corporate entities and public agencies need to give evidence of the public-spirited basis for their efforts, and the designer is expected to reflect this relationship in the way the space is shared with the general public. The highest priority, however, is to use the three-dimensional central space to save time.

The best test of the health of a central business district is "response time." Given a fleeting opportunity anywhere in the world, how quickly will the intelligence sources maintained by organizations in the district pick up the information? How speedily can the corresponding internal information be assembled so that the dimensions of profit or "value added" inherent in the opportunity can be appraised? How soon can a decision be reached and a commitment made? How readily can money be mobilized, people redirected, and an ad hoc organization formed that truly takes advantage of the opportunity?

The opportunity might be a prospective shortage of a commodity in a far corner of the world. Within hours a central business district should respond by acquiring supplies wherever else in the world a surplus exists, and arranging for delivery through shipping contracts. Itineraries of its traveling representatives are then shifted so as to pay closer attention to subsequent changes, since new opportunities may arise. The central district able to communicate the easiest, and decide the fastest, is likely to gain from brokerage charges, and one or more of the operating organizations with offices in it may pocket a good share of the difference in value between the surplus and the deficit areas.

A central cultural district must operate in a similar manner. The opportunity may be the need for a series of video-tapes for cable television or a dynamic sculpture for under-water presentation. Those centers that respond quickly and perform competently will get the commissions. In all instances it is presumed that the error rate has been kept at a minimal level, since organizations that make more than their share of mistakes use up their resources and die. A new central district with less experience (so that a greater error frequency may be expected) will usually emphasize a short response time in order to compete, but it may also specialize by maintaining close ties with parts of the world which have language or political barriers, so it has the role of designated agent (Beirut, for example, acts for a number of Arab countries).

In the early 1970s, therefore, a number of new forces can be identified that will markedly change the ways in which the central districts of large cities work. New entries into the competition may well construct themselves differently from New York, Tokyo, Frankfurt, or Bombay. Indeed, because leading central districts are frozen into concrete, steel, and glass, and cannot modify their physical dimensions by more than 5% a year, it is worth considering in detail what a challenger might do to reduce its response time and take more than its acknowledged share of the opportunities away from existing metropolitan centers.

NEW CENTRAL PLACES OF HIGHEST RANK

Three revolutions are sweeping the civilized world today, though they have yet to make a signifiant impact upon the spatiotemporal structure of the large metropolis. The interaction among them is largely reinforcing, thus accelerating change. The most significant transitions appear likely to be made in the 1970s and 1980s. In their wake will come others that can only be dimly perceived.

One of these revolutions is based upon technology. Enhanced capability in worldwide telecommunications and computation affects first the military organizations of leading nations (in largely empty camps, not cities) and then the headquarters operations of public and private agencies. By 1980 communications satellites will allow telephone and private wire service to points anywhere in the world equal in cost and quality to what was available in 1970 to connect with suburbs and nearby operations in the hinterland. Meanwhile, the amount of computation of a routinized form that can be accomplished with a given capital investment will have increased by at least a factor of ten.[10] Equally striking will be the high capacity for portable computers, so that a rapidly increasing fraction of the automata in the city will more closely approximate humans, making simple decision while locomoting in the urban environment. Environments will need to be designed to help mobile automata as well as humans, even if the functions of the automata are largely limited to low-level tasks.[11]

The second revolution is in organization. Many hundreds of large- or middle-size corporations have penetrated the boundaries of three or more politico-economic systems and fall within the definition of multinational corporations. About 70-80% of the manpower in multinational corporations is organized around a technology or a formula for coordinating human activity that originated in North America, the remainder being from Western Europe, Japan, the USSR, and India (in order of importance). The recruitment of managerial talent for these rapidly expanding multinational firms has depended heavily upon the output of the better-quality engineering and business schools in America, which have become models for new educational programs overseas. At the same time the American schools opened their doors to the most promising students available, and this meant during the 1960s and early 1970s that a high proportion were students who obtained their first university degree in Asia (predominantly) or other parts of the world. Since the American students in American engineering and management schools are siphoned off into government, military, family enterprise, and local opportunities, this has left a clear path for students from elsewhere in the world to take up positions in multinational corporations. Thus the Space Age technology and organizational know-how created in America has been cosmopolitanized at the working level in the management of the major multinational organizations. Twenty years later the executive strata will have been similarly transformed.

Meanwhile, any formula for doing business that yields a better than average return on investment usually turns out to be even more successful in at least some countries elsewhere in the world. With improved telecommunications and convertible currencies, it is now possible to start up in a new country in a matter of one to three years, sometimes less. Thus many firms that are now purely national, or even regional, in character will be tempted to cross national boundaries. Their entry adds to the diversity of multinational organization and contributes to the astonishing growth rates experienced by multinational corporations as a group. Such growth is likely to continue for a long time to come because devices for bringing Eastern Europe and the Soviet Union into the network were being worked out in the early 1970s.[12] Nonprofit multinational organizations ranging from the World Bank to eleemosynary foundations, professional societies, and religious associations are smaller in scale but equally significant, because their work most often produces a consensus on matters where value conflict is known to exist. A multinational organization will normally have a world headquarters and several regional offices in central districts of major metropolises. These offices acquire capital and essential services for a number of decentralized operating units and manage the marketing of their outputs.

The third striking transition is a product of the struggle to find easy ways of converting one national currency into others despite varying success in economic development and the achievement of political stability. If relationships are relatively dependable, it becomes possible to move credit, in the form of various Eurocurrencies, from place to place in large amounts with extraordinary rapidity. Increasing assurance of monetary convertibility enables multinational firms to respond more quickly to the appearance of markets for their output. Indeed, it is the rapidity of these transfers that has been most upsetting for monetary stability. Nations must relinquish some sovereignty in the control of their financial affairs before an adequate system can evolve. Hope for success is greater now because defection from the international system no longer pays off heavily in the short run and can result in very large losses in the long run.

Thus a new situation is arising where nations have lost much of their control over (1) the applied science and technological knowledge developed within their borders; (2) many of their secrets regarding new developments and massive movements of men or equipment (because of surveillance by automata in earth satellites); (3) the private sector corporations that have reached a large size inside their own society; (4) the flow of personnel trained for professional and managerial posts across national boundaries; (5) the flow of funds across the same boundaries; and (6) the price structure within their own economy. Ownership of assets will be transferred to the highest bidder, and much more often it will be the efficiency of a metropolitan area rather than specific national policy that determines where management settles down to operate. Contests for power among nations, hitherto the central focus of international affairs, are being displaced by competition for influence in world markets on the part of multinational organizations and by competition among metropolitan areas for the provision of services to multinationals and their successors in the cultural sector.

With such trends under way, a major change should come about in the design of the central business district of the megalopolis and the metropolis. The best strategy will be to operate commodities and securities exchanges around the clock, along with many corporate headquarters and regional offices. Many services, from banking to restaurants, must follow suit. Some government offices will have to stay open to be synchronized with these activities and so will training centers. Thus the lights would remain on all night.[13] Airports are already operating around the clock, and retailing could easily expand its hours.

If organizations and services can program their activities so as to operate on a multishift basis, marked economies should result in the use of transport, power, water, sanitary, medical services, education, retailing, and other services. Instead of operating at capacity only 15-20% of the time over a year and being underutilized the remainder, a much reduced capacity could be installed so that the facilities are fully used 40-70% of the time. The actual amount of space required for a central district might be reduced by half or thereabouts and still be able to expedite the same volume of transactions. The increased compactness makes it easier to integrate activities when ad hoc procedures must be employed under stress.

Round-the-clock operation of central districts may solve many problems for metropolises in resource-poor developing countries. It would reduce investment in downtown elevator office buildings, schools, and high-capacity streets, and postpone very heavy investment in electric power supply, subways, bridges, and the like. It would very significantly improve the response time of organizations in the city for meeting local needs.

When multiple-shift operations have been tried in the past, they turned out to be impossible to implement economically. The extra shifts have yielded both low productivity and a higher frequency of rejects or errors, thus introducing a quality-control problem. Despite pay bonuses night shifts are rarely liked; the principal complaints revolve around the inconveniences of living out of phase with the rest of the urban society. The industries that already work around the clock, such as chemical plants, oil refineries, and power plants, normally are highly instrumented, continuous-flow processes that make few demands upon workers, except for emergencies.

Given these objections, it is apparent that success will require very careful planning. It must take into account psychological and social aspects as well as economic incentives. One would need to know, for example, the distribution of mood cycles ("early birds," "evening persons," and "night owls") in a population, options for shifts available to other persons in the household, time-budget profiles, degrees of insulation against disturbances and noise in workers' homes, and, especially, the range of possibilities for reorganizing methods for getting work done.

New telecommunications potentials make very different modes of round-the-clock operation feasible and perhaps desirable. Each type of position in the central districts, whether low status (e.g., building maintenance) or at the highest professional and executive levels, may be held by a relatively autonomous team ranging from five to nine persons. This team would organize its own schedule and guarantee that at least one knowledgeable, responsible person would be on site every hour of the year. They could exchange information through logs, tape recordings, files, telephones, and make arrangements within the group for on-the-job training, vacations, holidays, or illness. Even the allocation of pay could remain a group decision. In that case, a continuously functioning organization would be made up of a number of well-defined "positions" with outlined responsibilities, but each position would be filled by a group. Many precedents for group-organized work are known, and experiments are now under way in Sweden, Great Britain, and the United States to reconstruct even assembly lines, reducing them to coordinated group endeavors.[14]

It is simple enough to put Harlan Cleveland's image of *The Future Executive,* a "manager of creative tensions," into this picture.[15] He is either a solitary troubleshooter, thoroughly in control of his biorhythms and impervious to jet lag, or a member of a group of equals that, like an athletic team, know each other's moves, even those of the substitute players who may have less experience. Every standard profession could fit this structuring easily, especially since group practice in various forms has already invaded subcenters and centers of modern metropolises. It appears that the efficient solution for the future officeholder is to spend a third to a half of his time at programmed activities, usually "at the office," and the remainder in maintenance of skills or in political and promotional activities of various kinds. Thus the mode of organization already adopted at the university becomes an introduction to life in the "big organization," or in the small service groups that fill out the activities of central districts. Indeed, one of the best predictors of change in human organization in the metropolis of a generation hence is the informal organization invented by students and faculty in and around the largest

universities. The new knowledge and behavior is standardized, replicated, formalized, multiplied, and diffused
throughout the changing metropolitan environments by the
same people who learned it on the big campus.

It is easiest to imagine the districts that incorporate international airports operating weekends, holidays, and around
the clock, because most of them already do. Some special
services, such as florists and cocktail bars, still pick off the
various peaks, while others, such as hotels, coffee shops,
newsstands, transport, cinema, gymnasia, and conference
rooms, never close. Similarly, it is easy to imagine central
cultural districts emphasizing night activity that counters
the bias toward day life in the less dense and greener areas
of the metropolis. European and American cities can
change only slowly in this direction, and the Japanese are
almost as inflexible; but ambitious metropolises in Asia and
Africa can boost productivity in the service sector, especially the export of services, very rapidly by using this simple
strategy. Their modern sector is less constrained by privileged arrangements and archaic work rules; they can define
the jobs and shift arrangements and get a fit with the private
lives of the workers at the time operations begin without
extensive bargaining. The accumulation of services in out-
of-the-way Las Vegas was largely due to a capacity to
smooth out cycles. This could not be implemented as well
in Los Angeles or elsewhere but fitted the absence of clock-
watching among gamblers.

Urban designers can take the standard functions of the
central districts of today, state them as ratios to the total
value added created by the metropolis or to some other
relevant aggregate statistic, add the resource-conserving
requirements described here, and arrive at proposed solutions. The outcomes are mapped in space (see figures 8.5
and 8.6) and time. The specific solutions arrived at are
unimportant, because real metropolises are eventually
forced to abandon master plans and must rely upon continued replanning as they evolve and overcome exigencies.
The experience of thinking things through, however, leads
to a significant conclusion: with the technologies now at
hand, and institutions such as markets for land and air
rights that are known but not practiced everywhere as yet,
the worries about the size of the metropolis causing uneconomic levels of congestion at the center arise from frustrations that deviate from long-term trends and are therefore

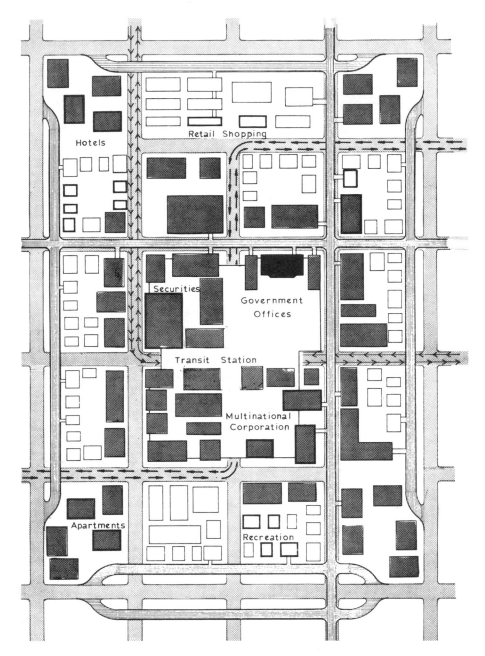

Figure 8.5 Energy-Conserving Ecosystem for a Central Business District
In this superblock high-salaried people move about by means of minibus with dial-a-ride features that also can connect with bus, ferry, or rail mass transit. Small vans are served by the same routes (light arrows). Superior access is provided to the bicycle mode of transport. Passengers and express from intermediate distances come by separate routes (heavy arrows). This layout was designed to evolve from a simple urban grid by redevelopment.

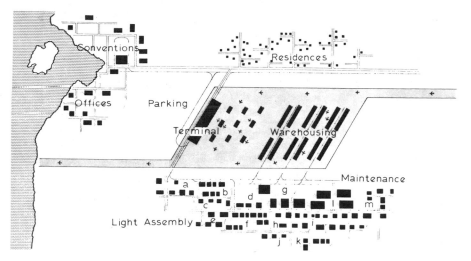

Figure 8.6 Core of an Airport-Based Metropolitan Central District
Because airports are established on open land at a considerable distance from the existing central business district, a relatively rational distribution of activities can result. Land is relatively cheap, given its superior accessibility, because of the presence of aircraft noise in the open spaces. Residences and public areas can be specially designed to exclude noise, while the warehouse, maintenance, and manufacturing district will generate noise of its own. Typical of the activities attracted to that district are express transshipment, catering, flowers, toys, medical equipment, electronics, machine shops, fine chemicals, biologicals, garments, fine fabrics, plastic molding, and luggage.

totally misplaced. There appears to be no difficult step in growing central districts, if they are started on flat sites. Each constraint that threatens to halt growth, whether due to congestion or to time lags in replacement, can be economically evaded. The required set of legal controls appears to be much simpler than those in force at present. Neither a new breakthrough nor the appearance of genius is needed.

RECREATIONAL ACTIVITIES

Cities are attractive to many people in the countryside for reasons that go far beyond the added support for human organization and the provision of jobs. Cities are also exciting places. Reports on the existence of fascinating forms and wonderful experiences filter out to the hinterland and set up expectations and challenges to the imagination that go beyond anything available near home. Many engrossing opportunities exist for spectators in particular, because those who merely watch on the sidelines need not undertake the responsibilities of full participation.

Villages are exceedingly dull places, particularly after dark, and towns usually liven up only one night a week, with another week or two of annual festivals; but the city bustles all day and offers night life in addition. As people become literate and better informed, the challenges of the city override fears of its mysteries; adventurous youth go to visit and many arrange to stay. As economic development proceeds, those who are attracted by the fun of living in cities, satisfying their curiosity about various life-styles with leisure-time activities, will make up an increasing proportion of the flow to cities. Recreation is the attraction; a job is the necessary evil. The consequences of this interest in fun and games—the design and provision of recreational facilities for public use—often cause great embarrassment for serious urban engineers and planners to whom the task is usually assigned; the solutions offered markedly distinguish cities from each other in their physical layout.

Some metropolises, mostly in Western Europe and Latin America, have wildly enthusiastic football (soccer) fans and must construct huge stadia (preferably in hilly conformations at the edge of a plain) to accommodate the spectators. Many cities in the Orient find that the cinema has great appeal, so that space must be found for air-conditioned moviehouses near the mass-transit stations or

the intersections of bus lines. Rituals surrounding the consumption of alcohol, coffee, and tea often become a form
of recreation, so a large number of private establishments
have opened to cater to varying tastes. Gambling sports,
like the sale of liquor, are often banned or controlled
because of the addiction problem; but, whether horse
racing tracks or casinos, they need to be fitted into the
metropolis. Central business districts nowadays provide an
enclosed arena for a number of sports and exhibitions. The
"fun city" concept of a metropolis almost always provides
entertainment in public places to populations made up
heavily of visitors but with guarantees provided by interested
residents.

Wherever the outcomes of contests are followed closely,
a demand for participant sports arises, providing a number
of alternatives for the "big game" category. The metropolis
of Tokyo provides us with an excellent example of the
adaptations made after the city had been built up and faced
demands that were very different from those of traditional
gymnastics conducted in a courtyard or entertainment
districts designed for revelry. In Tokyo, baseball invaded
scarce park space, while truncated games were played in
school yards, temple compounds, wide streets, and similar
sites. Swimmers concentrated in large central pools, or
they congregated at beaches. Sailboats displaced fishing
boats from the harbors that were most accessible from land;
oarsmen competed with motorboaters for the rivers and
canals. Golf links took over the flood plains of creeks and
small rivers, while driving ranges and putting greens were
set up in empty lots or on warehouse roof tops for night
and day practice. These lights and nets were equally suited
for tennis. At the same time hundreds of thousands of
residents with handbags or rucksacks converged upon railroad stations on holidays and weekends to go to resorts at
beaches and spas or to the mountains and forests.

In Tokyo, recreational movements out of the city normally evolve from group pilgramages to traditional shrines, to
visits to expositions, fairs, market festivals, carnivals,
amusement parks, and modern resort areas. The pattern is
set by classes of schoolchildren transported by bus for
special occasions and is maintained by public and private
bureaucracies, religious groups, and ethnic associations that
establish their own camps and hostels. Often the city
itself creates resorts for those of its citizens who might

otherwise be left out. Each of the twenty-three wards of Tokyo maintains several such sites outside the metropolis.

Cities that have been endowed with an English educational structure (most in developing countries had colonial backgrounds, but some were heavily influenced by British commerce) have extraordinary problems. They are under great pressure to maintain the original spatial standards for school grounds and playing fields. This requirement can become exceedingly expensive when elementary education has become universal and a much greater fraction of the age group seeks entry into secondary schools. Since schools without adjoining playing fields are judged to be inferior, the growing fringe areas are likely to get more than their fair share of new school sites and, in turn, urban families oriented to education and participation in outdoor recreation. Educational systems founded by Latin and Arab cultures are less likely to cause people to move from central areas, but the pressure on facilities and space can still be difficult to meet. The suburban phenomenon, where residences have more private space than the average but need even more public space for their preferred forms of play, is likely to arise in every urbanizing culture, though only in Asia does the sheer accumulation of urban population threaten opportunities for outdoor recreation.

An inkling of the potential complications can be obtained by observing Asia's most densely populated metropolis, Hong Kong. In 1969 the traditional seven-day work week was abolished, and roughly half of the labor force was handed a day a week to spend as it chose. Although weekend behavior seemed aimless at first—at best the time was spent at *mah jong* or revisiting relatives—a variety of recreational interests soon evolved. Groups hired minibuses for excursions, and traffic exceeded the capacity of the road system leading out of the city, so that Sunday congestion became a nightmare. Thousands instead of scores began to hike in the mountains, and ferries to other islands ran full. Even now the weekly outflow has barely made itself felt, although all the facilities are strained.

Hong Kong's main undeveloped asset is its indented coastline, with a variety of protected bays. First the islands and then the water surface seem likely to be developed to fit a variety of recreations. Although the life of the picturesque "water people" who have lived in *sampan* communities for many generations is vehemently rejected by the land-based population, and a majority of these aquatic households have recently moved to apartment blocks, the lore of living upon these waters remains available. It makes possible a quick, safe, cosmopolitan approach to water sports, even houseboat living, that might soon be acceptable to modern Chinese residents seeking extra living space and contact with nature. In the long run, Hong Kong's densities can be made quite tolerable despite a pent-up feeling that increases with income and education at the moment, but it will take many wide-ranging cultural adjustments, most of them borrowing concepts from the rest of the world.

On the assumption that Asia continues its rapid economic and educational development, gross estimates can be made of the expected urban demand for recreation out of the city. They indicate that access to the mountains, forests, and beaches must become highly organized, as in Japan. Even then planners will encounter extraordinary problems of congestion during arrival and departure, and, because of concentrated use, destruction of the natural environment will be severe. The sheer scale of the anticipated urbanization introduces the complications. If the new cities are restricted to existing technologies for the provision of outdoor recreation—the occasional escape from the urban surrounding—these large masses of urbanization would lack, in some cases by more than a factor of ten, sufficient accessible open land. Round-the-clock programming of transport and employment in central districts and capital-intensive industries help somewhat in improving access to open space but increases the rate of destruction of the wilderness because of overintensive use. Irreversible changes must be anticipated; after the more robust soils have been converted to the production of food and fiber, only the most fragile soil and plant communities will remain for recreational use. Cities can create virtual deserts in their nearby open spaces by exploiting their plant and animal populations beyond their capacity to recover.

Fortunately, the opportunities for improving the technology of recreation are greater in magnitude than those associated with water and energy. Again, the pioneering is being done in the most affluent countries, but it points the way to uniquely Asian, and later African, solutions. Producing fun along with exercise is a cultural invention;

it requires only imagination and a supply of fresh air. The windward side of a city will be preferred by physical fitness enthusiasts, even if atmospheric pollutants are not as concentrated as in the industrialized countries of the present. Since population tends to accumulate in coastal metropolises, the seaside is likely to be regarded as the most pleasant place for a visit.

It has already been argued that existing shorelines can be made much more varied and interesting. Reefs can be built from the most inconvenient urban wastes—in North America used tires are now roped together and dropped off barges into undifferentiated estuarine waters so that within a year a rich and varied reef community of fish is established in the artificial caves and recesses, which then attracts divers and fishermen alike. Protected inlets and bays can be populated with houseboats. Small harbors can be constructed. The necessary offshore industrial installations (nuclear power plants, mariculture operations, bulk-handling harbors, steel mills, jetports, and some offshore oil fields) can be combined with compatible recreational activities. Overall capacity for one-day excursions and vacations of a week or more could be built up to a larger scale than is found anywhere in the West, with economical designs that promise to make the experience less hectic and at least as rich. Estimates of the demand building up in a number of areas—next to the Bay of Bengal, the China Sea, the coast of Java, the Inland Sea of Japan, perhaps also the eastern Mediterranean and small portions of the Caribbean—suggest that there will be places where reconstruction and protection of the shoreline will not provide enough outlets. An early result would be a rise in the price of shoreline property and land or sea access to it.

A whole new ecosystem needs to be synthesized as environmental support for the occupation of deep ocean surfaces; a successful one could provide quick access to a full range of marine interests, from fishing and photography to the aquatic sports. Because the sea can at times become dangerous, even deadly, the early emphasis will be upon mechanical supports that are able to stand up against the onslaught of storms as least as well as natural islands and peninsulas. What would a stable seagoing platform cost? The quick, reassuring answer is that floating real estate can be produced in water that is a hundred meters deep or more for less than the value of land in central districts of such cities as Singapore, Bombay, or Lagos, and equal to land values in the major residential areas of Tokyo. A basic structure made of reinforced concrete appears to be more economical to fit out with essential services than some parts of the metropolis today.[16]

More or less simultaneously a number of laboratories have begun to explore the subsurface life of the deep sea. Developmental stages for each organism are being traced so that distinctions between species are possible. The food web of a few of the most highly valued species is being explored. The ethology and community structure of subsurface life are fields that have barely been touched, but the challenge is strong. Some of the knowledge gained will be used for animal husbandry in various approaches to mariculture, while the remainder is necessary for assuring a stable interface with the open sea.

Wherever land prices mount the highest at the water's edge, we must expect proposals for synthetic islands, such as are now being designed for mooring off Honolulu and Los Angeles. Plate-shaped platforms greater than 300 meters in diameter can be made stable in the worst storms and swells, and superstructures made of light materials can be built on them at no greater cost than on land. In deep water silolike spar buoys reaching 100 meters below the surface have proved equally stable; they could become apartment dwellings with elevators connecting rooms above and below the surface. Although the makers of oil-drilling rigs quote much more for moored seagoing platforms, it seems likely that costs can be reduced to $500 per square meter of usable platform or enclosed living space. The edges can be designed for swimming, surfing, fishing or beaches, in whatever configuration is suited to the most popular recreations.

Wherever new habitats for man are prepared, even in the wilderness, some urbanites find a permanent niche. Thus even if most of the facilities are designed for the short-term sojourner—a kind of water-borne Disneyland or Sea World complex perhaps—many city people will move in and create appropriate life-styles. Water-based settlers, wherever they exist today, have unusual sources of livelihood. For example, the large picturesque houseboat community afloat next to Sausalito in San Francisco Bay contains boatbuilders, musicians, sculptors, poets, songwriters, filmmakers, fishermen, and sea captains. In it also live a concertina expert, a puppeteer, an airline stewardess, an executive, a laser theorist, a bike rider, and a cartoonist. Virtually all the members of such neighborhoods are adults, most of them working irregular hours, with very few dependent children. Food supplies are brought in primarily when returning from places of employment, and eating tends to be simple, since the fare is prepared in compact galleys with limited refrigeration.

Energy for cooking, lighting, and space-heating in these forerunner aquatic settlements usually comes in by cable connection to a metropolitan electric utility. If that is not available, liquid hydrocarbon fuels serve handily, even if they are increasingly expensive. Battery-driven equipment is very convenient, and more such devices are now becoming available. Hydrocarbon fuels are used in small outboard motorcraft for local transport. In general, much less energy is used per active adult than in competing land-based settlements.

Current solutions for the handling of water supply and sanitation usually involve use of flexible connectors to land-based grids. Larger communities further offshore will no doubt develop a community service with a tender delivering fresh water, collecting sewage from a holding tank, retailing perishable foods, and perhaps delivering newspapers and the mail. Solid windblown waste may collect on the surface of nearby water; it could be skimmed by the same tender.

The design of a houseboat need not result in a box-on-a-raft, as 99% do today. Indeed, standard optimizing procedures, using economical materials with low maintenance costs and prefabrication techniques and seeking stability, safety, privacy, and a trim appearance, suggest a bowl shape for the hull, with a cylinder or inverted bowl for the superstructure, and narrow decks around the edge. Such forms have interesting consequences for communities separated from piers—the efficient allocation of surface area to households and neighborhoods tends toward the hexagonal, mainly because basic utilities could then be supplied by an underwater lattice of parallel lines. Density of such single household units would be quite high, perhaps 30 to the acre (75 per hectare). They will be most suited to shallow water in protected bays and estuaries, or the harbor of a floating atoll-like complex offshore.

Perhaps too much attention has been given to one of the exotic, minor directions that seems possible for future urbanism. It is offered primarily as an indicator of the safety valves that the present stock of scientific and technological knowledge provides for world urbanization. As we have shown, if much more space is needed, the urban regions have the option of using the surface of nearby seas. The resources needed to maintain such an urban population are no greater than for a land-based settlement engaged in the same activities. Since outdoor recreation—the physical search for fun—is in most cultures the greatest consumer of space, those activities seem most likely to sustain the pioneers. Although evolution of prototypes leading in this direction is currently most rapid along the subtropical shorelines of the United States, the synthesis of varieties of coherent communities seems likely to be left to Asians. They must create forms of social technology and supporting organizations free to make a selection from catalogs full of mechanical and electronic devices already invented and marketed by Americans to cope with the dangers posed by maritime environments. The Asians, together with perhaps the Egyptians and the Nigerians, must, in effect, invent and implement the utterly new approaches to full-scale urbanization.

The space-intensive demands for recreation of urbanites were taken up first because they are easier to project into the future than other recreational activities. The time-intensive features are more difficult to forecast because current rates of change in their technology are several times greater. Urbanites somehow find increasing amounts of time to absorb images presented by mass media so that viewing time now sometimes reaches an average of four hours per person per day, primarily through television. In modern cities television has, without planning or organization for the purpose, displaced the school as the dominant medium for the transmission of culture to the next generation. Children choose to spend time in front of a set without urging, whereas many of them, especially children of immigrants, must be coerced into going to school. Yet any simple scanning of television content suggests that contemporary television is extremely wasteful of human time.

Cities of the future need substitutes for popular television as much as they need substitutes for the automobile, the American bathroom, and a meat-based diet, but it is much

**CULTURAL
PARTICIPATION**

more difficult to demonstrate the need with quantitative measures. From the start, however, it should be admitted that television has brought with it a marked increase in awareness of the cultural milieu beyond the immediate social context; it can represent as much an advance in human liberation and welfare over previous uses of human time as the auto was an improvement over the horse and the streetcar. Criticism of television does not warrant turning back the clock.

Given these circumstances, it is perhaps most useful to judge alternatives for leisure-time expenditure in terms of the numbers of people that can be consistently attracted away from their television sets. Such activities must have greater than average value. We know that telephone calls, participation games, parties, religious services, classes that improve occupational skill, and sometimes public spectacles and community affairs will do this. A private hobby will also take time away from television viewing, but often a new phenomenon enters—the use of the same time for two or more different activities—because some hobbies can be maintained while viewing and listening. If human attention is to be allocated at such a high level of efficiency that overlapping uses of time become common, people must gain greater personal control over the content that comes over the channel of communication. They must also be connectable with each other as small specialized groups rather than as a mass, in the case of radio and television, or as individuals, in the case of the telephone.

The necessary technology already exists and is now being installed on a large scale—networks of two-way cable television.[17] If cities are planned in advance to absorb this new public utility, especially if it is combined with an overhead earth satellite relay, the installation cost and maintenance could probably be met by a $1-2 charge per month per household. But there will be additional costs, seldom recognized in present discussions among technologists, for the preparation and storage of videotapes containing useful information and interesting imagery. Individuals and households would be, in effect, purchasing their urban culture up to the limits of their income (or that of the public subsidies that they exploit), guided by the state of their knowledge and their curiosity. People have done this for a century already, acquiring printed material in the form of newspapers, magazines, and books, and it will be decades before the stock of knowledge on videotape catches up in quantity and range with the printed materials in bookshops and libraries. The most likely path of development for audiovisual materials will be to cover phenomena that are complementary to ideas in print.

This may sound like outrageous speculation, particularly to people in developing countries, but it should be pointed out that it is in these "software" kinds of industries that the poorest countries have an ultimate competitive advantage. Audiovisual production requires vast amounts of human time, imagination, and attention to detail, but minimal amounts of energy, water, scarce raw materials, and capital. Related industries, such as semiconductors, microcircuits, advanced instruments, computer programming, and technical film making, started from zero levels in 1965 in metropolises like Seoul, Hong Kong, and Taipei to become a leading body of urban employers and export industries by 1973. There is very little inertia in the communications sector of a metropolis, as compared to that of industries requiring mass, volume, and chemical constituents, and growth rates can be almost explosive. The past rates of change that people have been attuned to, particularly the members of the administrative and professional classes, are inadequate predictors of future enhancements of cultural communications. The potential offered by the technology coming into existence is much greater than the capacity of disciplined imagination.

But there is something still more fundamental in this argument that pertains to urbanization of all kinds: when resources become scarce, the urban ecosystem can survive through improved organization of activity in space and time. Enhanced organization involves larger stocks of knowledge and experience, increased flow in the transmission of messages and signals, and shortened reaction times. These concepts, and the processes of substitution that are implied, must be scrutinized more carefully. Thus far they have been considered only to the extent that they influence the spatiotemporal structure of the metropolis and create central cultural districts and headquarters areas for multinational corporations.

1. John F. C. Turner *et al.,* in *Freedom to Build* (New York: Mac-Millan Company, 1972), emphasize the wastefulness of standard professional and administrative approaches to the production of housing for the working poor. Urban communities that provide the necessary supports for lower-income groups are rarely built according to plan; they evolve from humble beginnings over the course of decades. Within such a community, the city and its administration provides a household the opportunity to build, and it is the members of the household who convert the obligations and contacts built up within a social network into a dwelling. A large kinship group, and an energetic householder who keeps up many acquaintanceships and is willing to approach agencies in the Establishment, will be able to assemble the credit, materials, licenses, artisan skills, and helpers needed to construct an impressive house within a few years. The availability of few kin and a restricted circle of friends combined with timidity in making contacts results in a hut that improves slowly over time. Neighborhood groups and cooperatives provide reinforcements to pre-existing social networks and greatly reduce the frequency of failure.

For me one of the most insightful treatments of the subject was provided by a consulting group that often worked with officials charged with initiating "site and services" projects. Alfred Van Huyck, the president of PADCO, Inc., identified three kinds: (1) temporary settlements receiving unskilled, unemployed, single men without accompanying families, impoverished refugees, etc., and are located close to centers of employment; (2) urban renewal townships, for permanent settlement that would evolve into blocks of flats, receiving "graduates" from temporary sites with jobs, literate inmigrants, refugees, with some resources, and newly formed urban households located within easy commuting distance; and (3) open-plot townships leading to single-family bungalow neighborhoods over the long run receiving a high proportion of skilled and clerical workers and located near the end of a bus line. In Karachi, where land is relatively cheap, the defensible plot size seems to be 50 m^2 with community water taps, 60 m^2 with potentially private connections, and 120 m^2, respectively. A series of incentives and tenant selection techniques must be used in combination with continuous community development support differentiated in type according to community. The urban village as proposed here would normally contain roughly a third of type two settlement and the remainder type three. Central districts would have the first and second types set up on their periphery. The proportion would be greatly disturbed by an influx triggered by a food crisis.

2. Because there is a continuing stream of inventions, adaptations, and new applications, the leading plastics journals report on polyurethane rather frequently. See B. D. Whitney, "Plastics to push out stone and concrete?" *Engineering,* 209 (February 1970), pp. 133-134; "Production of Thin Sheet Polyurethane Foam Structures," *SPE Journal,* 27 (June 1971), 54; "Free Flowing Foam," *Industrial Design,* 18 (April 1971), 45; Julian Kestler,

"It's a panel show for plastics in building," *Modern Plastics,* (May 1971), pp. 42-45. Most of the better developments will not be publicized in the journals at all but will become part of the expertise maintained by firms that bid on contracts demanding unusual performance.

3. S. C. A. Paraskevopoulos *et al., Structural Potential of Foam Plastics for Housing in Underdeveloped Areas* (Ann Arbor: Architectural Research Laboratory, University of Michigan, 1966), 2d ed.

4. Polyurethane foam was expected to grow more rapidly than any other category (*Modern Plastics,* October 1971, pp. 100-101.), reaching a level of a billion pounds per year in 1980, when it would reach 2-3% of the lumber production in the United States. Since then rigid polyvinylchloride (PVC) foam extrusions have fallen below the cost of wood moldings and received a major boost, while questions were being asked about the fire retardant grade of polyurethane (*ibid.,* March 1973). The isocyanurates offer an alternative raw material that is much more fire retardant and is only 15% more expensive than polyurethane ingredients. Building frames, commonly used for American construction in wood, can henceforth be produced from extruded vinyl foam that is naturally fire retardant.

5. Polyurethane recycling seems likely to follow the experience already acquired in the recycling of rubber, particularly from auto tires. Much of the building material may need less purity and meet less rigorous specifications than automotive, furniture, aircraft and other such uses. Therefore, the materials might enter the urban system as seating pads and shock-absorbing bumpers, which are common examples requiring precise formulation, with a half-life of five to fifteen years. In its second life that material might go into factory-made panels for structures designed to last for twenty to forty years, and then for third and succeeding lives into foam sprayed upon forms and surface coatings with shorter periods of use before scrapping. In each cycle a third or so of the material is lost and could be added to asphalt for road surfacing, thereby becoming a high-grade land fill.

6. Rory Fonseca, Professor of Architecture, University of Singapore, started with earlier versions of these ideas and evaluated their potentials in the course of a field trip in the Indo-Gangetic plain (unpublished, 1972). A slightly abbreviated and reworked version of his sequence of tasks is listed together with the locus of prime responsibility.

Task	For Whom?
1. Identification of potential sites	Metropolitan planning agency
2. Analysis of constraints affecting viability	Metropolitan planning agency

3. Assessment of soil resources, local opportunities	Metropolitan planning agency
4. Well drilling, leveling, experimental plots	Operating agency
5. Water and power connections	On-site operating group
6. Legal structure for local government	Operating agency
7. Land transfers made, credit arrangements	Operating agency
8. Nearby employment and markets assessed	On-site operating group
9. Initial settlement site subdivided	On-site operating group
10. Ponds excavated	On-site operating group
11. Erosion and flood control provisions	On-site operating group
12. Pioneer groups enter: "model homes"	On-site operating group
13. Basic sanitary services activated	On-site operating group
14. Algae pond complex activated	Joint with local public unit
15. Drainage completed, algae consumption begins	Joint with local public unit
16. Private production enterprises launched	Pioneer community membership
17. Irrigation system, first stage	Local government
18. Garden and animal raising coordinated	Local government
19. By-products and compost activated	Local government
20. Extension of utilities, street improvemnts	Local government
21. Construction materials, training center	On-site operating group
22. Massive influx of settlers	Joint with local government
23. Production expansion and organization	Local enterprises
24. Cooperatives formed, new directions sought	Operating agency and local government
25. Plan for completing development	Operating agency and local government
26. Community fills in remaining openings	Local government
27. Coordination with neighboring communities	Joint with metro-planning agency

Ultimately this list will take the form of a diagram which illustrates the development of responsibility over time and the feedback of information that allows the metropolitan agencies to learn as they launch an increasing number of urban villages.

7. The theory behind the emphasis upon transaction rate as a cultural and economic growth indicator is presented in R. L. Meier, *A Communications Theory of Urban Growth* (Cambridge, Mass.: MIT Press, 1962). These ideas are amplified in "The Metropolis as a Transactions-Maximizing System," *Daedalus,* 97 (Fall 1968), 1292-1314.

8. This Study of the "Human Community" is summarized and indexed by C. A. Doxiadis, D. Iatridis, and others in *Ekistics,* 33 (June 1972), 423-424, and 489 ff. Reports have been appearing over a period of ten years. I was privileged to participate in the very early stages. See also Brian J. L. Berry and Frank E. Horton, *Geographic Perspectives on Urban Systems* (Englewood Cliffs, N.J.: Prentice-Hall, 1971).

9. The mortality of firms in the United States appears to be in the neighborhood of 50% in the first two years. B. Mayer and S. Goldstein, *The First Two Years: Problems of Small Firms Growth and Survival* (Washington, D. C.: Small Business Administration, 1961). A much simpler survey of industries in the Calcutta metropolitan district suggests that "infant industry mortality" was at about the same level in the 1960s: R. L. Meier, "Industrial Development in the Calcutta Region," in *Observations upon the Developmental Character of Great Cities,* Working Paper No. 94, Institute of Urban and Regional Development, University of California, Berkeley, March 1969, pp. 56-112. As far as I can discover, life tables have not been prepared for social organizations. The nearest is Freustein Wedervang, *Development of a Population of Industrial Firms* (Oslo: Universitetsverlaget, 1965).

10. The explosion in channel capacity and computing ability is brilliantly treated by James T. Martin, *Future Developments in Telecommunications* (Englewood Cliffs, N.J.: Prentice—Hall, 1971); Richard S. Bower, "Market Changes in the Computer services Industry," *Bell Journal of Economics and Management Science,* 4 (Autumn 1973) 539-555.

11. Computing capacity not only will be drawn upon to regulate the operation of the machinery, by preventing undue strain and saving energy, but also will be installed in the designed environment at points of interactions. It will allow close control and add to precision. A fair example is a device that will fill a series of containers of different shapes and sizes with different ingredients, as they are introduced or ordered; another is a system that will read checks written out to department stores and banks and then endorse them. The size of a "single chip" microcomputer is about that of a ladies wristwatch, while the same technology applied to a much faster mini-computer in a tray of "computer-on-a-card" form is the size of a small atlas. Between 1972, when experimental introduction began, and 1975 the manufacturers predict a market roughly equaling all other computers; *Business Week,* May 12, 1973, pp. 180-182.

12. In order to work within their constitutions, which forbid private ownership of industrial facilities, a variety of socialist enterprises are being formed as corporations in the capitalist world. They may set up their accounts and enter into contractual arrangements like a multinational firm but formally hold title to factories and inventory in their own country in the name of the people. Thus surplus capacity in Poland can be producing parts for West German vehicles, and a manufacturer of fashionable cotton clothing can extract a profit greater than is obtainable from licensing procedures.

13. The newest office buildings in the central business district of San Francisco in 1973 were already refusing to sign leases with tenants who were not prepared to engage in round-the-clock operation within four years. Thus, in a metropolis with many branch offices but few headquarters, the longer-lasting facilities are already being designed to handle a very high rate of transactions between large centers.

14. Originally suggested by Frederick Herzberg in Herzberg, Mausner, and Szyderman, *The Motivation to Work* (New York: John Wiley & Sons, 1967), in response to the rationalization of mass production based upon the division of labor and economies of scale, we now see a number of proposals for reform and hear about experiments leading in those directions. Perhaps the most elaborate are those at American Telephone and Telegraph, with Robert Ford as personnel director for manpower utilization, if only because of the size of the organization and the routine nature of many of the jobs. Thinking has been brought to a head by such people as Neal Herrick, one of the principal authors of *Work in America* (Washington, D.C.: U.S. Department of Health, Education, and Welfare, 1972). In the long run (meaning more than ten years) I expect that new modes of production based upon groups or teams as well as individual initiative. The freedom to begin work at one's preferred starting time can be accommodated within a margin of several hours by an organization if members of a unit can be decoupled. Higher levels of education in the working population allow it to learn new tasks quickly and gain satisfaction from the newly acquired competence. Efficiency for an organization in the future will depend less upon the physical output and more upon the elimination of errors in the product or service. We know from experience and experiment that errors are greatly diminished when morale is high, and also that groups make many fewer mistakes than individuals engaged in the same task; therefore, the kinds of organizations that the city of the future must support are more like the Volvos, Xerox's, and the small high-technology firms clustered around major research centers.

15. Harlan S. Cleveland, *The Future Executive* (New York: Harper and Row, 1972). He introduces a nonacademic, future-oriented organization theory that depends upon a collegial, consensual style.

16. The discussions regarding ocean complexes among technologists in Japan are now focused on floating cities of truly gigantic dimensions. Their thinking extends to the export of the polluting-type industries—electric-power production, steel, oil refining, petrochemicals, some plastics, single-cell protein, and similar products— and to the high seas, where there are no neighbors to object. Japanese industry expects to provide housing for its workers near the factory. A speculation by the Mitsui design group required a platform area of 95 km^2, a 40 megawatt power plant, a 20,000,000 ton steel mill, a desalination plant, and chemicals production to match. Anticipated construction time would be about a decade. *Chemical Economy and Engineering Review* (Japan), 4 (November 1972), 58-59. In comparison the studies in ocean technology at the University of Hawaii in Honolulu deal with immediate design problems in hope of obtaining economical floating modules from which larger synthetic islands can be fabricated at sea. Their target date is 1976 for exhibition and entertainment complexes off Honolulu and Okinawa. John D. Craven is the group leader, with John Bardach directing research in the related marine biology.

17. The feedback provisions in cable television are limited to two to six keys, but more elaborate transmission is possible through a telephone linkup. Further implications are discussed in the next chapter. A policy evaluation that seems to age very well is that of the Sloan Commission on Cable Communications, *On the Cable: The Television of Abundance* (New York: McGraw-Hill, 1971).

Meeting urban needs in the face of increasing scarcity of energy, basic materials, accessible space, and human time has prompted designers to turn to telecommunications. The economical design that is chosen after reviewing a wide range of alternatives almost always employs directly and indirectly several times as much telecommunications capacity as its predecessor. There appears to be a fundamental reason for such substitutions in consumption—the means of shifting mass consumption into more economical modes depend upon dialogue, the transmission of factual information, persuasion, and feedback from efforts to change. All of them require copious use of communications channels wherever the consumer habits are thoroughly ingrained. Cities have from their beginning incorporated the communications capabilities that give them a chance of surviving extreme scarcities because the authorities, the holders of the reins of power, sensed that the channels were needed for control of the political situation. Avoiding the consequences of resource scarcity was not the principal purpose.

Nevertheless, since cities came into existence more than 7000 years ago, their institutions have been used by man to evade the consequences of the law of diminishing returns. In its simplest and most fundamental form that law states that continually increasing effort applied to extracting a resource from the natural environment quickly reaches a point where the returns per unit of effort get smaller. Man's use of the city in this manner shows no evidence of premeditation or planning but only of evolutionary growth in competence and incremental understanding. When humans were restricted to food gathering, hunting, and primitive agriculture, the increasing effort was applied by a growing population within a limited territory, and that extra pressure on resources brought about lower average returns within a few years. However, the apparently unconscious invention of cities expedited trade and encouraged specialization, thereby extending the domain to be exploited and adding to the possible combinations of what was found in the environment. The law still held, but often the effects could be postponed by engaging in more trade and acquiring a greater range of skills.

Substitution and *innovation* were equally significant processes in evading the law.[1] When the supply of one material was scarce, the city had more opportunities to find substitutes, and its artisans were more likely to take up better ways of using materials (often improving upon them) than their competitors in the camps, mines, fairs, and other sites. Then, most significant of all, the process of manufacture was organized into industries. Manufacturing firms made many products simultaneously, systematizing even the innovation process, and found uses for materials that had previously been discarded. The contribution of cities has been to accumulate *knowledge*, which up to this point has uncovered more resources than have been expended. Now it has also generated a realization that the capacity of the earth has some well-defined limits.

Pressed by a still growing population, these processes of substitution, innovation, and organization must be accelerated in cities so as to extend the period of usefulness of a dwindling stock of natural resources. It is significant that all of these processes now converge upon a single kind of resource that will have to be drawn upon much more intensively than any other—the communications channels made available by the electromagnetic spectrum (see figure 9.1). A communications channel is, like the soil, a renewable resource, but both are nevertheless subject to the law of diminishing returns. If a channel is overexploited by sending through too many messages within a given period of time the signals are received in a garbled form, information beyond the capacity rate being lost more or less at random. With some codes it may be entirely lost. These channels can be polluted, most easily by electric sparks, coronas, and other sources of stray electromagnetic radiation, so that care must be taken in a congested settlement to preserve their integrity.

The reason communications are a favorite substitute is that innovations for the development of new capacity— those in hand but not yet extensively used, and those made possible by recent scientific developments—offer the prospect of declining costs, even if the intensity of use were to be multiplied a thousand times.[2] There are limits for specific installations, but for at least the next generation replacements or substitutes will handle more signals for a lower average cost. The outlook for virtually all

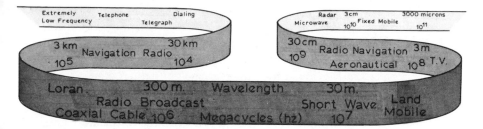

Figure 9.1 Allocations of the Spectrum Resource

The portions of the spectrum in greatest demand are shown in the foreground, When local shortages are felt, leading to channel interference, those on the left are likely to be transmitted by cable, while those on the right may be enclosed in wave guides. The city of the future will very likely require networks of both, with some equipment translating from low frequency (e.g., telephone) to high frequency (e.g., microwave, laser). This strategy gains channel capacity. For at least three decades to come the unit cost of using the spectrum resource is expected to decline, even though all other natural resources become scarcer and more expensive. Because of the substitution of this resource for others, spectrum use is growing several times more rapidly than domestic product. The rapid expansion of the population of automata draws upon these unusual features. Telecommunications channels create interdependencies that reduce the likelihood of catastrophe but increase the frequency of alerts, so that people are more conscious than before of impending dooms.

Spectrum: The Ultimate Resource 319

commodities supplied by other natural resources is strikingly different—rising costs with increasing demand even with anticipated improvements in technology. The exceptions other than communications, including such commodities as salt from the sea and "rare earths" minerals, are trivial.

The way in which a channel in the electromagnetic spectrum is introduced as a substitute for the use of water, energy, or a raw material in a productive activity is not briefly or simply explainable, because the substitution process is carried out within complex urban institutions. Neither is the move to communication in recent decades widely understood. Economists have simplified their accounts by not introducing information measures as specific inputs for production functions. Marshak and his co-workers have tried to rectify this oversight, but applications of their approach are not yet evident.[3] Lacking adequate theory, therefore, we are forced to illustrate this process of substituting communications, or message, inputs with examples drawn from technology.

COMMUNICATIONS THAT SAVE WATER

Recommendations in Chapter 7 for drastic conservation of water during periods of short supply were directed at (1) new sources, (2) recycling and prevention of waste, and (3) a lessened demand made possible by shifts in behavior and the design of habitats. Projects with these aims were to be rationalized with the aid of a water market. In what ways do these specific recommendations draw upon the telecommunications channels and require growth in exploitation?

The concept of a market for water is a good place to begin. A modern commodity market is wholly dependent upon telecommunications and computing. The transactions themselves, the transfer of rights of use, are handled by telephone calls to the exchange and completed when funds are transferred from the banks of the buyers to those of the sellers. However, the score or more messages associated with a single transaction amount to only a tiny fraction of the number required to gain information leading to presentation of the bids and offers that set the prices. Estimates of a change in the water supply depend upon world meteorological surveys, which have become a continuous synoptic system for interpreting data obtained from thousands of manned and automatic reporting stations, giving special emphasis to the forecasts made for local and proximate watersheds. Supply estimates also depend upon progress in the construction of reservoirs and aqueducts. Estimates of change in the demand for water are strongly determined by the amount of sunshine (which causes transpiration and evaporation) forecast, new industrial and domestic requirements, the effectiveness of the management of recycling systems, and shortages appearing in nearby watersheds.

Each major water user—the electric power generating facilities, the fossil fuel processing industry, the producers of vegetables and fruits, the distributors to residential grids—must judge the supply, compare it with their own projected needs, and enter the futures market to the extent that minimum needs are guaranteed. We have some understanding of relative amounts of communication likely to be employed in a water market by comparing it with commodity markets where transactions of equivalent value (a few million dollars' worth per day in normal times for a metropolitan area of ten million population) are handled by brokers or by newly designed electronic markets. The site of the commodities and securities markets is now in that place in the central business district which sends and receives the most messages per unit of land. Water would join the other commodities because no other place in the metropolis can be found where this volume of transactions can be readily managed.

New sources of water, such as imports from other watersheds or desalination projects using reject heat and off-peak power from generating stations, will be dependent upon the bids made for water supply contracts. For example, a plant for the preservation of perishable foods must go to the market to get a guaranteed supply of highest-quality water; its bid could be high enough to justify the costs of distillation if those costs are not raised by the same phenomena pushing up the demand for water (interdependence is common in developing societies). Holding down water costs in such a plant will require a sensitive hour-by-hour interplay between signals coming from the manufacturing or delivery processes and the settings of valves. Within a few years after the initiation of a market, the automatic instruments reporting temperature, salinity, acidity, and other relevant properties can be linked directly to the process controls designed to maximize value added in manufacture, thus closing the cybernetic loop. Relatively modest amounts of computing capacity are required along with an allocation of spectrum sufficient for tens or hundreds of standard telephone channels. These estimates of communications use remain equally true if water is to be moved by pipeline or tanker from one watershed to another.

The nearest approach to the idealized water market where this instrumentation and data processing is already being put to work in a rudimentary form is found in Israel. The whole settled portion of that country is no larger than the San Francisco metropolitan area (containing a population of about five million). A National Water Carrier was set up to connect all significant sources of supply. Action has been taken to recover 90% of the available rainfall, and sewage water is recycled. Even the flash floods, where quick drainage to prevent property damage is a matter of concern, are caught and spread out on porous land to recharge underground storage. Weather data are watched very carefully, and planes are sent up to seed likely clouds, a process that the Israelis hope will eventually add 20% to their supply. Nevertheless, projected demand, if uncontrolled, is expected to exceed supply by at least 50%.

A system of water accounting is used for long-range planning. It reveals that dispensing water to the highest bidder would result in serious inequities. The Israeli farmers, for example, have mature orchards that require water to survive, but the citrus markets in Western Europe could register prices that prevent farmers from bidding high enough for water. Equally important is the sentimental attachment to trees and greenery so often encountered in arid areas. Thus, as a matter of national survival tempered with social justice, both of which are held above price, water is administratively allocated to various uses. Agriculture will be limited to a few small projects beyond present operations, and added supplies will be assigned about equally to industry and domestic uses.[4]

Under the pressure of these quotas, great effort is being made in some sectors to extend water use efficiency. Fundamental investigations on the use of water by plants have been stimulated, and the technology of trickle irrigation is being perfected. Also, careful attention has been given to techniques of growing plants with brackish substandard water supplies. Because politically powerful agricultural interests have guarantees of water for the not-too-distant future, the urban users may become so desperate that they will be willing to accept the necessity that some trees must die. Israelis refuse to discuss this eventuality publicly. In the most reasonable projection the National Water Carrier would buy up the irrigated land coming onto the market, retire it, sell its water rights, and redistribute them to the highest bidder. Thus Israel provides us with a fascinating example of the political processes leading to the institution of a water market.

When water demand in and around metropolises elsewhere in the world is scrutinized in the light of the Israeli experience, it appears that the American bathroom could acquire the same kind of established, or "grandfather," rights as irrigation agriculture. The bathroom represents a major investment and a way of life that can be bought out once it has become established only at great expense and after considerable delay. Substitutes for flush toilets that use only a tiny fraction of the water should be sold to newly urbanizing people. Similarly, community baths of various kinds, each of them suited to subsequent introduction of local recycle systems, need to be promoted in the media. The needs for water in food preparation as well as the water used for cleaning surfaces, can be simultaneously rationalized. All of this preventive action will require persuasion, calling for audio-visual demonstrations of alternative solutions and a dramatic display of water-conserving behaviors. Audiovisual channels require many times more band width (i.e., channels) than is needed for data transmission; thus a temporary shortage in standard broadcast channels of higher quality could postpone rationalization of a water market. Fortunately, channels are available on a cable network at a very low cost, and, for other reasons, cables are likely to be installed at the outset of urban community construction from the 1980s onward.

As this transition to high levels of efficiency in water use is mapped out, it becomes apparent that the spectrum requirements of the instruments (such as the radar that analyzes clouds, messages from the radio sound balloons) and networks connecting them with automata in the weather-forecasting offices or the commodity exchanges are quite small compared with those required to induce shifts in life-style and the acquisition of more appropriate habits of cleanliness. Education, in this instance the transmission of simple rules for living that add to one's own convenience and minimize damage to other people's opportunities, is the large consumer of channel capacity.

ESTIMATING POTENTIAL ECONOMIES

The only way one can be persuaded about the economies of a substitute process, especially about an alternative that introduces extra communications channels, is to engage in the actual design of alternative processes. To do this, one finds an archetype of the original process, specifies its location and organizational context, sets up a measure to judge the efficiency of the designed solution (in the case of water it was liters required per capita per day), and then generates solutions. The promising alternatives, meaning those that significantly reduce consumption of the scarce commodity, are then subjected to economic analysis. If the economics look good, a number of other feasibility tests are applied. Are there external diseconomies, similar to pollution, to be taken into account which therefore limit applicability? To what extent will the best solutions fit other sites and contexts? This is not the occasion for a digression on the practice of the design process but for a summary of the outcomes (the most highly respected designers have worked out short cuts that allow them to assess a wide variety of alternatives rapidly, and the paths their private analysis takes are difficult to describe). The level of consumption to be achieved through organized, built-in responses to scarcity—one that will not cause lasting damage to, or serious interruption of, development programs—can be presented. The key assumptions and conditions implied by that level will follow.

In subtropical and tropical regions (which contain most of the population to be urbanized), the minimum steady-state consumption of water seems to be about fifty liters per capita per day. This minimun level might be reached if the urban price for potable water went up to several dollars per ton. At this price water is no longer available for gardening, and the algae-free effluent from the sewage treatment ponds is chlorinated or ozonized, filtered, and introduced directly into drinking water. Bath water is filtered and reused for baths. Industrial production in water-intensive industries would be curtailed wherever added cost restricts demand, but few jobs would be lost, because these industries employ a small share of the labor force. Some labor would be switched to quick water conservation projects such as well drilling or the covering of reservoirs to reduce evaporation. Cultural activity could proceed undistrubed except that lessons in watersaving might displace other lessons in economizing presented in the mass media (such as those on nutrition). Perhaps the greatest actual suffering from a water shortage of that severity would be attributable to dust, but in that respect the metropolis would be no worse off than the countryside and may actually be better off because of the prevalence of trees, asphalt, and windbreaks.

The same design-based exercises show that minimizing water use for *food*—the industry that requires the largest allocation of this potentially scarce resource—will bring about a major transformation in the structure of the urban ecosystem. The sizes of the interdependent livestock populations will markedly change, with fish and fowl displacing other livestock, and there will be greater emphasis upon vegetables (grown with recycled water and plant nutrients) that are fed directly to humans. Thus, the American hamburger and frankfurter, just now being enthusiastically accepted in Japan and metropolitan Asia, is as inappropriate as the bathroom if water becomes subject to periodic scarcity. Dairy products—milk, yogurt, and cheese—are only a little less wasteful. Since these prospects hold for most of the growing metropolitan areas of Asia and Africa, and some of Latin America, a program for shifting consumption styles becomes very much a part of the transition to a new urban ecosystem. Consumers must be induced to buy and appreciate a variety of carefully formulated and balanced proteinaceous foodstuffs produced from vegetable sources. The intermediate foodstuffs (soy flour, peanut meal, algae paste, yeast powder, flavorants) would be produced by highly instrumented continuous-flow processes, operated largely by automata that control the various steps via telecommuncations in order to maintain the quality and prevent waste. The conservation of mechanical energy for refrigeration is also substantial. Thus the planned response to water shortages could be launched by preparing consumers for the eventuality and later, when the shortage is actually present, through manufacturing processes monitored by automata with the aid of telecommunications channels.

The key feature of any design for resource-conserving urbanism is a set of cycles that supports the human populations and allows internal reuse of scarce ingredients. A tighter recirculation scheme, which permits as little as possible to slip away as effluent, must economize on essential plant nutrients as well—especially on fixed nitrogen and phosphate. Losses occur because of nitrification—bacterial transformation of valuable fixed nitrogen returning it to the original free nitrogen of the air—and to the locking up of phosphate into highly insoluble salts that are thinly dispersed. Careful monitoring by the communications system, followed by redirection of local flows or rebuilding of component facilities, should bring about a reuse of the original fixed nitrogen and phosphorus that provides three times its present effectiveness. Eventually, however, the total cost from salvage will approximate the cost of producing and delivering virgin materials; recycling should not go beyond that stage. With such a communications backup for the management of food and water cycles in the urban ecosystem, it seems reasonable that inputs from regions outside the metropolis might amount to 4,000-6,000 "original calories" (i.e., dry weight organic material produced via photosynthesis) per urban resident instead of the 20,000-30,000 original calories consumed by North American and European city dwellers at present. (Water requirements in intensive irrigation agriculture are proportional to original calories produced in vegetation.) This economizing upon nutritional sources of energy appears to be possible without increased injuries or loss of physiological function in humans.

Because of foreseeable scarcities in supply, urban designs for the future must concentrate first upon economizing on those premium forms of energy—*the hydrocarbon fuels*—which are most advantageous in transport. The solutions arrived at earlier depend upon substitutes for the private automobile, particularly bicycles, but also buses, boats, electric mass transit, and airlines. An obvious substitute for transport of any kind is to transmit information instead of people or goods, since messages are virtually weightless and frictionless, but how should one proceed with the design of such a communications system? The social processes by which communications substitute for trips remain largely hidden from view. This is one of those stubborn problems that so far resists reduction to a

simple ratio or conversion rate, even with the aid of standardized conditions. Harkness's review of the accumulated
experience reveals many expressions of confidence that
messages will displace trips, but notes very few concrete
advances.[5] Passenger transportation in a city reveals a basic
need for establishing trust between two human beings who
are normally separated and then a maintenance of that
bond between them despite the presence of competing
contacts. It is obvious that messages will help these processes, but we cannot yet assign numbers to the degree of
substitution achievable.

An interesting feature of transportation is that the poor
spend a greater part of their income and time upon it than
do middle-income people or the rich. Obviously they are
more dependent upon human bonds for security than
those who have accumulated property and have money in
the bank. The poor also have less education and therefore
less ability to draw upon communications systems for
alternatives. Cities with rising incomes that approach
adequate levels are investing heavily in education (which
is itself almost pure communication), and the share of
income devoted to transport is gradually declining. Judged
by expenditures on telephones, mail, printed materials, and
specialized channels, the proportion of personal income
devoted to communications tends to rise as personal income rises. Thus an energy-using service (10-30% of the
expenditure on transport goes to fuel and power) is already
being displaced to some extent by communications services
(with 1-5% spent upon energy) as inmigrants make their way
up the social hierarchy within the city and become
urbanized in the process. Economists are satisfied with the
measurements of the elasticity of demand, which underlie
the foregoing generalizations, but they are insufficient for
constructing a plan.

Perhaps the best solution in transport, as with water, is
variable pricing. This means setting up minimarkets in the
buying and selling of trips. Anyone insisting upon moving
at peak periods, thereby increasing the strain on transport
capacity, should pay a premium; those traveling at off-peak
periods would get a substantial reduction in charges; those
preferring modes of movement using substantial amounts
of scarce hydrocarbon fuels would pay more, while bicycle
riders would move through the city at virtually no out-of-
pocket cost. The scheduling of movements in a transport

network is already communications-intensive, but adding variable-price trips and providing the public with information about options open to it, should multiply the flow of messages severalfold. As the interaction between the transport system and its public reveals more information about true costs and specific wants, both producer and consumer go through a learning process that leads to more efficient use. It has already been suggested that an energy-economizing system could save up to 90% of the hydrocarbon fuels—if that became necessary.

The conservation of electrical energy is somewhat less important than that of hydrocarbon fuels so long as breeder reactor technology seems likely to appear on schedule. The issue is much more a matter of saving capital investment per resident, thus allowing a more rapid rate of urbanization. We have proposed savings in domestic use of energy through (1) redesign of furnishings so as to eliminate bulk and the loss of activity space; (2) extensive use of insulation (which is one of the reasons why polyurethane foam looks promising as a new building material); (3) use of natural ventilation, aided by fans as necessary, instead of air conditioning; and (4) the introduction of more elaborate comfort controls than thermostats in order to save the expenditure of energy when a space is not in use. Only in this last instance is there any demand for spectrum, and then so highly localized that no conflicts are foreseen.[6] The need for energy when people live in apartments with five to eight square meters of floor space per capita is greatly reduced in a cool temperate climate, because body heat and normal lighting become a significant contribution to domestic heating. As for the tropics, where human comfort does not require added energy in the form of heat, the overall levels of energy use can be reduced to a tenth of the American urban consumption or less, with 50-70% of the savings attributable to reduction in floor space, 20-30% to communalizing bathing, some washing, and some food preservation, 10% to a drastic reduction in air conditioning and refrigeration, and 5-15% to controls that fit interior environmental conditions to the particular requirements for comfort of the occupants.

Occasionally scientists, especially geologists but sometimes ecologists as well, express fears for certain scarce raw materials. There was a time when the continuation of modern civilization depended upon certain apparently scarce

materials (e.g., phosphate, potash, copper, nickel, platinum), but over the last several decades adequate means of
substitution or of salvage have been developed to meet
every threat of shortage. What is expected to happen is that
some materials will become scarcer and their prices will
rise relative to others, thus encouraging the further use of
substitutes. But will these changes in price affect the
solutions already proposed, especially those based upon
telecommunications and automata? A quick review of the
prospects is warranted.

The nonferrous metallic elements—copper, zinc, lead,
tin, nickel, and silver—are actually very scarce in the
earth's crust as compared to iron, aluminum, and magnesium. They have been concentrated in a few locales, but
those deposits are almost exhausted, so the world is moving
toward exploitation of lower- and lower-grade ores. These
deposits require much larger amounts of transport, reduction of particle size, and chemical treatment per unit
extracted. The substitution process is already well begun.
Copper was once thought to be essential for electrical
power distribution, but aluminum systems have been used.
Aluminum power distribution networks have required
more maintenance, but it now appears possible to design a
system in which 90% of the copper is replaced by aluminum. The zinc used in casting metals and preventing the
corrosion of iron has a variety of substitutes in the form
of plastics and surface coatings. The lead in gasoline is
already on its way out and is slowly being displaced from
paint pigments by a set of formulations that are less toxic.
The tin that prevents corrosion in containers is rapidly
being replaced by cheap plastics and lacquers and by
improved methods of perservation; tin in alloys for printing
and bearings is being displaced by electronic and photographic methods of achieving the highest-quality repro-
ductions. Nickel in stainless steel is replaced by a variety of
approaches to corrosion prevention, so that ordinary steel
or trace alloys can be used without loss of performance.
For all of these substitutes the system design requirements
are simple, and the impact of a shortage on the growth of
communications is not significant. In the instance of silver,
which has been all important for some of the communications media, its uniqueness for the ever expanding field
of photography is now being challenged by a number of
photosensitive dyes used in increasingly popular color

photography; another alternative is to depend upon the phosphors in a color television tube for capturing an image.

In each instance it appears that a three- to fivefold increase in relative price should attract substitutes, diminish the per capita consumption in urban society to as little as a tenth of present levels, and greatly increase opportunities for salvage and reuse of scarce ingredients without leading to any breakdown in the urban ecosystem or even causing noticeable harm.[7] These substitutes, and more efficient uses of scarce minerals, will require notably greater investment per unit of production capacity, with greater employment of telecommunications equipment, but the measures for saving water, food, and energy should bring about major reductions in the need for nonferrous elements and their replacements, so that total investment requirements per capita may not increase at all.

In all the instances of technological substitution, standards of performance need to be defined much more precisely, and the whole system for delivering a service to humans needs to be analyzed, before determining the most suitable alternative to present practice. The process of fitting designs to life circumstances requires much more instrumentation and data accumulation and a much greater emphasis upon acquiring information about differentiated user needs. The increase in communication and computation that will be required to operate a body of materials-producing organizations that reflect a significantly wider range of competences than at present is perhaps a hundredfold greater. Not unexpectedly, the conservation of scarce materials pushes us to the same kind of solutions that were encountered in the previous discussion on conserving space and time—more ongoing data collection and better organization.

FERTILITY LIMITATION

A serious criticism can be made of the foregoing proposals for limiting the use of scarce natural resources. Although the plans provide for an adequate production and distribution of goods and services in future cities and assure that opportunities to achieve a minimum standard of living become equitable, that is, available to all households, in accomplishing these aims many of the stronger existing constraints upon population growth are removed. Stresses induced by overlarge families would be relieved by residence in places like urban villages, which are designed for self-help, and by enhanced flexibility in house construction. Greater control over water would assure its continuous purity, thereby reducing infant mortality and increasing the number of surviving children. It appears that the difficult population problem faced by every developing society will be made still more difficult by improved design of cities unless something extra can be done to reduce human fertility.

No more important resource-conserving measures exist than those that bring about a reduction in the size of the future population. They are even more important for socialist and democratic societies, which emphasize equalitarian distribution of services and goods, because in them the appearance of extra population automatically generates a formal demand for the resources needed to produce a level of services and consumer goods up to the established standard. Therefore each metropolis must exert influence not only over its own citizens but also over all those rural areas which are likely sources of inmigrants, so as to reduce fertility. The term *influence* implies not only the transmission of concepts and common values, but also the ability to induce changes in behavior. Despite their importance, so little is known about these influence processes that we cannot arrive at even a rough estimate of the volume of messages required, and we have no better idea of the content of the messages. The subject is still highly controversial, and a review of the current situation with the aim of discovering communications strategy will reflect some of its sensitivities.

Experience with family planning and fertility controls in less-developed societies is now recorded, and to some extent evaluated, by the United Nations and the Population Council.[8] What each review of this experience emphasizes more than anything is that there is a great variety of attitudes and cultural inhibitions related to this subject, and that no standard institutional approach to family planning will be generally applicable. Experts are rarely able to forecast responses to programs aimed at accelerating the acceptance of family limitation even in a single locale.

The economic returns from averting a birth in a poor society with high birth rates and dropping death rates are remarkably high. George Simmons carried out an estimate for India that was more careful than his predecessors'; he arrived at a contribution to the gross national product of

7,800 rupees per averted birth for the 1966-67 period. This was about ten times the GNP per capita.[9] As long as some hope exists for obtaining desired changes in behavior, that level or return (the investment then was less than 100 rupees per birth prevented) will justify many times more promotional effort than at present, since it far exceeds returns on investment in industrialization and transport. In 1972 the World Bank was persuaded to back up this investment process with soft loans to large projects in India and Indonesia. However, even if the best management is found for the job and the past levels of acceptance are maintained, no one can rightfully expect anything better than a gradual demographic transition requiring decades to complete.

Although about a third of the world is now approaching an equilibrium based upon low death rates and low birth rates, population changes do not respond readily to social policy. Neither the most affluent, nor the most educated, nor the most coercive societies have demonstrated any real control over human reproduction; those that have been relatively successful, such as the Western European and English-speaking nations, still experience major unexplained and unplanned shifts in fertility. If an urbanizing society were to establish provisions for bringing about reduced birth rates, there is still little assurance that the initial efforts would be effective enough to justify the cost. The best hope, therefore, seems to be openly experimental—to try a number of different policies simultaneously and learn what seems to be effective for each locale.

How should one start? Contraceptive materials and legal access to abortion and sterilization are obviously a prerequisite. Many of the urbanizing societies of intermediate size have not yet made this step. The information distributed about such opportunities encounters a number of taboos, but progress can still be made. Every society has informal or underground channels of communication for the transmission of news that cannot be discussed in polite circles; societies that still prohibit the use of birth control pills, and even a public discussion of its significance, are unable to prevent a black market from flourishing. Opportunities for illegal abortion proliferate, and knowledgeable people find ways of obtaining intrauterine devices, condoms, and diaphragms. Yet birth statistics show that only a small part of the population is successful in getting the materials or service in time. Most of the top professionals and part of the upper class will restrict family size in order to enhance their own mobility and freedom to socialize. This is true even five to ten years after liberalization of the law and the launching of a strong program for fertility reduction. Exceedingly few poor people, who have the most to gain in the long run from having small familites, manage to protect themselves against excess fertility. What seems to be lacking in the bulk of the population is the stimulus that brings about a search for control, followed by adequate information.

Progress is accelerating, but still much too slowly. Only two countries in the 1950s and eighteen others before 1970 had set up national family-planning programs. Their efforts could be evaluated by a variety of criteria covering acceptance, degrees of political support, and evidence of fertility reduction.[10] The total population of these twenty countries was 1,116 millions or about 30% of the world population, but only in six of the countries (together containing 2% of world population) were there vigorous programs aimed at providing services to all married women of reproductive age. In two others, programs were tolerated without political support, while in the remaining dozen the backing was qualified or partial. At the time these data were being reported Berelson summarized the situation as "impressive, frustrating, uneven, inadequate and doubtful or unknown; the prospects are promising and dubious."[11]

The management of the family-planning program seems to be thorough in only a handful of countries. A program's duties should include seeking active support in national plans and political backing from leading parties, as well as making "contraception readily and easily available, publicly and commercially throughout the country," as the Population Council delineates in its evaluation efforts. An important achievement in a poor country is the justification of the use of scarce foreign exchange for importing contraceptive materials not made within the country.

The first efforts of a family-planning management must include the recruitment of respected members of the medical profession. If folk healers and herbalists are important to the common people, members of those crafts must be sought who will lend their wholehearted cooperation and be willing to learn the basics of this new health service. These trained practitioners will carry the message to their colleagues in the healing professions with the authority of specialists. The family-planning managers should try to get the subject of birth control and family-planning practices taught in medical schools, since little of that information is regularly transmitted as yet even in Western countries. The participation of doctors also puts an imprint of authority and trustworthiness upon ideas conveyed to the general public.

The managers need to lay out a program for getting family-planning advice to all married women in the reproductive age group, although in many societies prevailing customs require prior consultation with the husband. To create and maintain such an administrative structure, a huge training program must be mounted. A special feature of careful management in fertility limitation is contact with women immediately after childbirth, which involves close cooperation with maternal and child health clinics and with midwives. The standard practice of midwifery must be redefined so that pay is no longer proportional to the number of deliveries attended.

A good management will find ways of advertising its services in the mass media, so as to support the efforts of field-workers who visit homes of potential clients. Finally there is a record-keeping requirement, with files for each client, inventory controls, reconnaissance information, distribution of rewards and incentives, and the like. From these records it must be possible to evaluate past performance in each district and direct the efforts of the staff. From district-by-district assessments and from information based upon continuing research and development, it should be possible to lay out improved tactics. The complexity of such an operation, compared to the present state of both private and governmental organization in a poor, developing country, indicates why we see no fully adequate program. The best among the existing organizations in developing countries are found in South Korea, Singapore, and Taiwan, while Indonesia, among the poorest countries, appears to be trying the hardest.

In the twenty reporting countries it is evident that urbanization is strongly associated with success in reaching married women. Female school enrollment and the availability of radios—two statistics involving social communications that are available or can be estimated for all these countries—are, of course, strongly related to contraceptive practice. One other indicator of program participation is the age at marriage; those societies that provide social roles and work outside the household for single women up to or over the age of twenty demonstrate a rather rapid rate of acceptance of family planning after marriage. (See figure 9.2.)

A program of family-planning promotion can define its task too narrowly. All the evidence suggests that fertility control is merely one aspect of competence in modern living, and that many pieces of knowledge and elements of skill which tend to reinforce each other are simultaneously required. In other words, most of the antecedents and the concomitants of family planning are not normally associated with birth control either in the public conception or in the minds of civil servants preparing government budgets. Communications in the schools and, perhaps even more outside and beyond them, are needed to acquaint people with opportunities in the modern sector of the city; these messages can be conveyed by mass media and reinforced by discussion in many community-level associations.

The largest part of any program affecting fertility control must be directed at young adults and more to women than men. Almost universally, traditional societies invest far less in women than men. And this relationship is maintained or accentuated when first building up the human capital required for a modern society. Illiteracy among women, for example, is far more common than among men not only in the twenty societies reporting but among all others that have yet to put together a national program. Women are also less traveled, less politicized, and much less frequently selected for leadership roles, so that they have little contact with a modern approach to family formation and with community participation. They are, however, accessible through mass media once basic schooling is provided. In the media, fertility control will be juxtaposed with many other behaviors that make up a young wife's role in the city: learning to use the new detergents; applying concepts of proteins and vitamins to cooking; understanding the operations of the local health facilities; discovering the potentials of new sewing machines; fitting into the coordinated effort of labor brigades or factory-type production; using powered tools and implements; calling strangers on the telephone to obtain advertised services; and imparting precise, objective reports of situations. To

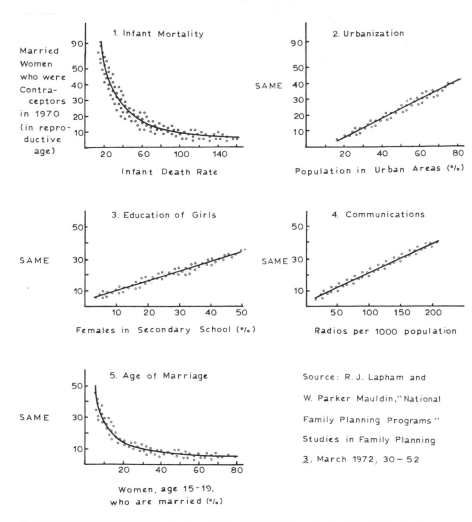

Figure 9.2 Factors Influencing the Acceptance of Family Planning in Developing Nations
Analysis of all modern data available up to 1970 suggests that communications activity is a
somewhat stronger influence than the degree of urbanization, but that the education of girls
is highly significant. The quality of health services, as indicated by the infant mortality rate,
and the age of marriage accepted as normal by the society are also powerful determinants
of acceptance. Very likely, rapid success in achieving acceptance will depend upon the identification of local incentives that affect willingness to undertake the reduction of family size
and go beyond these five common significant factors. (Regression lines are reasonably accurate,
but the data points were supplied by the draftsman to illustrate the approach.)

anyone brought up in a traditional society, which had necessarily evolved customs that countered high death rates by promoting even higher birth rates, the concept of family planning appears extraordinarily radical, though it seems quite ordinary to the urbanite. The urban behaviors lead outward from the family and connect it with a variety of modern institutions; the well-managed contraceptive service should become such an institution. The new service should draw upon relationships with other modern institutions as a reinforcement or stimulator of contacts with its clients. (See figure 9.3.)

The number of acceptors among married women in the reproductive age must expand from a level of 5-20% in the cities, which can be rather quickly accomplished with well-organized effort, to something like the 50-80% that is needed to produce demographic equilibrium. Observations and local reports in Asian and Latin cities suggest that three different features of mass media may offer promising possibilities if allowed to do so by the authorities. They can motivate and reinforce innovative action leading to modern formulas for organizing behavior, several of which are necessary for the control of fertility.

The first of these features is continuity drama, equivalent to the American "soap opera." The tragedies, struggles, and small-scale successes of ordinary people and popular heros are recapitulated and elaborated in new settings. In Japan during the 1960s, several of these serial dramas were so moving that work in the small shops ceased, with both clerks and customers paying attention to the day's episode before business was resumed. Older women exclaimed that this was indeed the living truth, while female apprentices merely gaped. In Puerto Rico girls lived many lives working out the human dilemmas raised by employment in factories before they were old enough to apply at the personnel office. Where these programs exist, housekeeping schedules revolve around the times the most popular serials are broadcast. The result seems to be the evolution of a new consensus regarding the responsibilities of the individual in society; it replaces the eternal verities and rural myths previously propagated by aphorisms and illustrated by folk opera or occasional puppet shows. Very often traditional actors and puppeteers volunteer for work in the telecommunications media; they are quite willing to trade in old

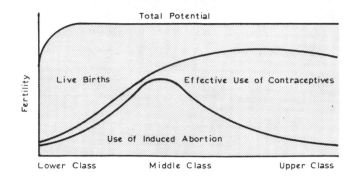

Socio-Cultural Status

Figure 9.3 Fertility Control and Sociocultural Status during
Modernization and Development
The reason for the dip in fertility in the bottom strata of the lower
classes, especially the illiterates, is attributed to enforced spearation
of the sexes by labor camps, prisons, military service, domestic
service, etc. A small upper class may again have larger families
because of the availability of servants. Abortion appears to be
extraordinarily prevalent in most societies.

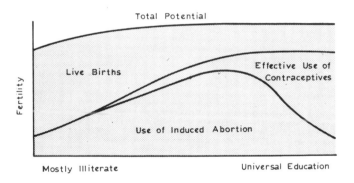

Indications of Modernization

The widespread use of abortion as a means of birth control will
be an issue in virtually all developing countries, even those under
communist regimes where abortions are most prevalent. With
greatly limited, or solely illegal, abortions most of the fertility in
the charts is transformed to live births in households that can
least afford them.

themes for new ones. In Korea they provided some of the most effective propaganda for contraception.

The second feature of media presentation is the "commercial" or action-based advertisement. It is carefully produced so as to get the clearest, most unambiguous message across to new customers, who are numbered mostly among the young, the upwardly mobile strugglers, and the stay-at-homes. Since the job of persuasion must be completed in a minute or less, mnemonics are supplied for remembering the context, sequence, and justification for recommended behavior. These are very much appreciated by the confused amateur in the marketplace and the new consumer. "Singing commercials" become refrains that serve as an urban substitute for folk sayings devised to meet traditional situations. Breakfast cereal and soft drink jingles are more significant in cities than the aphorisms of wise owls or badgers, although folk characters and animals may be recruited by television cartoons for new roles. Often too great a dependence is placed upon this approach, but its directness appeals to top executives.

A major test of the direct use of advertisements for family planning was conducted in the United States in 1970-71.[12] Professionally prepared spot advertisements for television, radio, newspapers, and magazines were run for six months in separate metropolitan areas at different degrees of exposure. "Stop the stork," it proclaimed. "Unless you really want to have a baby—don't get pregnant." Another theme directed at married couples was "Family planning—for couples who want children . . . later." A typical illustration on television: a chicken mistakenly hatches the egg of a huge stork and exhausts herself carrying buckets of worms to keep it alive. Special telephone numbers were provided to obtain more specific information. Virtually all members of the fertile age group understood the message, and television proved far more efficient in transmission than the other media. Response in the form of letters to the editor and telephone calls was predominantly favorable in three cities, and mixed in the fourth, yet no net increase in contraception was recorded then or shortly thereafter, despite a finding at the time that about 40% of the pregnancies were unwanted. It is possible that preventive action can be stimulated by the right kind of advertising, especially specific information about the location of clinics, but it cannot be expected to achieve large and rapid results. Fundamental changes in outlook on life, followed by careful and consistent attention to details, are together prerequisite to effective fertility control. These findings for American cities correspond closely to the less systematic observations made regarding effectiveness of the media elsewhere in the world; they all show that the approach to successful recruitment of 60-80% of the couples must be broad-based and largely indirect in its appeals.

The third promising use for the expanded channel capacity is based upon the concept of a "good game." It must combine the proper mixes of risk and security, of skill and luck, of cooperation and competition, and or organization and sanctioned bedlam. Soccer and other versions of football are favorite transmissions of the mass media in growing metropolises. When growth slows down, the football leagues may remain, but interest switches to the pools that organize routine gambling on outcomes. Sweepstakes and state lotteries are simple games, important to people who have not been successful in establishing themselves and who desperately need a stake to survive at the status they believe themselves to hold. Many of the popular games, ranging from *mah jong* to Monopoly, are not played through, or transmitted by, the mass media but are supported psychologically through commentary supplied within programs. The casting of horoscopes, which in many parts of the world is a pseudoscientific urban function, may be regarded also as a game, but one that is played against the future instead of a single opponent or a team.

Fitting appropriate participation games to the news media, taking advantage of the low-capacity feedback channels available in modern cable television, is a special challenge that could have significant social effects. One could imagine quite large populations becoming involved in a game of "Life" or "Careers," in which each participant made key choices for the principal characters, Subject to the statistics of contemporary society, they would discover how well they chose in advancing the careers of the principal characters by following the appropriate continuation of the scenario. The effects of unwanted pregnancies become extraordinarily dramatic when attempts are made to maximize upward mobility.

Objections may be raised to the rather pragmatic Western overview taken regarding this linkup between mass media

based upon telecommunications and family planning.
Many members of leading groups in the countries concerned
believe that a "socialist" or a religious approach to the
necessary fertility reduction, employing more controlled
and orderly program content, offers a much more "decent"
path to moderization. No doubt, a number of variants
based upon Asian and African ideals (i.e., a new socialist
version of modern urban living, a Muslim formulat, a
Nichi-ren Buddhist way, and so on) will be attempted, but
by definition they intend to monopolize channels and
thereby exclude a wide range of possibilities opened up in
the world as a whole. The risk of a major Malthusian disaster is increased by narrowing, for reasons other than
effectiveness, the choice of images, methods of communication, or allowable behaviors. If the risk is knowingly taken,
however, in order to achieve other human ends, it is
difficult to object. A social communications policy must
have many more goals than just fertility reduction and
speedy modernization of urban immigrants.

Recasting fertility reduction as an attitude change problem, susceptible only to communications on a broad front
that accelerates the modernization process, has just begun
to occur.[13] Although a dozen different techniques of
contraception, sterilization, and spacing are known by the
medical and social welfare professions in all major cities,
government agencies have not been reorganized as yet
so as to respond to the challenge. Claims for spectrum,
viewing time, facilities for producing programs for the
mass media, and top talent for designing the programs
have not yet been made. Many partial precedents can be
found in the broadcasting experience of Japan, elegant
approaches to evaluation in Taiwan, quick pragmatic
opportunism in South Korea, high political priorities in
Java, and penalties for an overlarge family in Singapore, but
nowhere yet has a fully elaborated program been put
together that was given sufficient priority to obtain top
managers and work out middle- to long-run strategies of
social intervention through the mass media with backup
from the community.

Even then, very likely, the response to communications
through the mass media unreinforced by other methods will
be too slow. Reward systems in the society must be changing simultaneously. A form of social security in old age
must be provided that is independent of bearing sons. This

could, for example, be free life insurance for families with a single son and an equivalent grant for those that have no son at all. There need to be community service roles for women who presently are allowed no other function than that of rearing children, even if the roles are places in work brigades organized in the Chinese mode. Often a society has such reward systems operating in its cities, but they are accessible only to a tiny minority. The city of the future must invent popular institutions, open to anyone, that provide added comfort, income, social status, and excitement to couples of low fertility. Then the communications systems can be employed to speed up the process of adjustment. Attitude changes influence votes, votes change governments, governments modify reward systems, and the significance of reforms in rewards must be communicated to citizens for personal decisions. These transitions take time, and that is why population equilibrium will not arrive soon.

PUBLIC ORDER FROM COMMUNICATIONS

The recent discovery that social communications are by far the most potent internal force for political stability has yet to have a major effect. The original findings were based upon 88 reporting countries in the post-World War II period. Cutright found that variations in a simple index of representative, responsive government could not be explained to any significant degree by the well-known transformations, rural-to-urban migration, industrialization, or increase in per capita income, that had been linked to the growth of democracy by historically oriented scholars working from case studies. He found instead that use of telecommunications media, newspapers, and the postal system were powerfully associated with "political development."[14] (See figure 9.4.)

Political scientists had sensed some of the significance of social communications for the performance of the polity, particularly as they probed conditions underlying concepts of governmental legitimacy, but this strong relationship came as a surprise. McCrone and Cnudde recomputed the Cutright data using new path-analysis techniques that are better suited to the identification of causal relationships. The necessary antecedent conditions for communications to have an effect were isolated.[15] Moreover, the index was related to Lipset's earlier quantitative representation of democracy.[16] An outspoken minority refused to accept

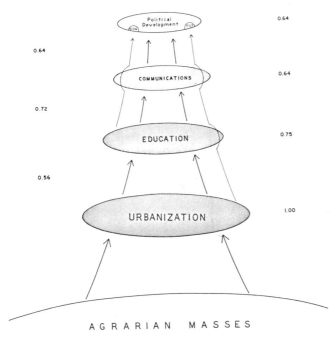

Figure 9.4 Development of Political Order, 1950-1960
In a predominant share of the instances, political development
follows upon extensive internal communications activity—which
can be built up economically once people have been educated. Education is more readily provided, however, after people have been
urbanized. Shortcuts are sometimes possible for former colonies,
while military invasion in the previous generation seems to have
an inhibiting influence. Data are taken from eighty-eight reporting
countries; the indexes were prepared by Cutright (1963), the path
analysis by McCrone and Cnudde (1967). Not shown here are the
influences of tribal and caste dividions among the original rural
population, since the data are severely limited.

the findings,[17] but counterexplanations did not appear.[18]

The newest body of theory, applicable to stabilization of the political order, took over from others that had been qualitative and conjectural. Over the course of a few years, however, it assumed characteristics not dissimilar to those of general evolutionary theory, backed up by population genetics in the area of biology. Just as evolutionary and related theory could be used to guide selections in plant and animal breeding, leading to astonishing improvements in performance (though not to forecasts of direction in evolution), decision makers might similarly use this distillation of recent world experience. A national planner would infer from this early work that increasingly democratic governmental structures were achievable as a poor tradition-oriented society invested first in *urbanization* and the associated industrialization, then in *education,* which is made much more effective and economical by the agglomeration of population, and later in *communications* facilities, the impact of which depends heavily upon educated users. The active use of communications media serves as a strong indicator of self-organization, which is synonymous with democracy as it permeates all aspects of public life. There have been exceedingly few exceptions to this sequence of internal transformations, although in America the emphasis upon communications came very early in its history as compared to urbanization. The demands for self-organization in America seem to have stimulated technological innovation in communications to an extraordinary degree, since development of private and public service for telegraph, incandescent light, telephone, and phonograph came along very fast. Because of this, the apparent commitment to democratic processes ahead of urbanization in America is not embarrassing to the theory.

Is it possible to uncover more explicit directions for the new urban institutions that set the pace for change within the nations? Again, we must depend upon data generated in recent years by all the reporting countries. Attention has recently been concentrated upon special prerequisites for a stable public order, such as the right of any member to hold public office or vote for someone he prefers to see in such offices. Such rights imply contests, and virtually all true contests involve the "outs" running against the "ins." Thus we see cities in particular becoming an arena in which opposition to the existing circle of power holders

is tolerated and even, to some, extent, supported by the
institutional structure. Dahl has found a descriptive term
for the political structures that are most advanced in levels
of participation, openness of entry into the office-holding
leadership, and liberalization of communications channels.
He calls it "polyarchy," often preceded by the adjective
"inclusive," referring to the lack of official constraints
upon the emergence of leaders. He labeled a restrictive
government, which in moments of stress is overturned
by revolution because it has no loyal opposition (and is
usually replaced by others of similar ilk), a "closed hegemony" (See figure 9.5).[19]

Of the 140 nominally independent governments in 1970,
only about 25 had become functioning polyarchies, while
a dozen more seemed to be within reasonable reach of
that formula for a democratic public order. Since some
of the latter group were very small and others published
inadequate statistics, the number of successes to be reviewed was reduced to 31. They registered considerably more
urbanization, education, and income per capita than the
remaining 109 nations. Significantly, these statistics of
socioeconomic advancement and the concomitant liberalization of the political system are produced by countries
dominated by metropolises (the possible borderline
exception is Costa Rica, with only 30% urbanization, and a
single metropolis, with 22% of the population), while a
majority of those classified as closed hegemonies have
little metropolitan life. A conclusion to be derived from
inspection of the world data collected by Dahl is that
urbanization is associated with conditions suited to polyarchy, though by itself it appears to be insufficient to
assure such forms of government.

Progress toward polyarchy is helped if a country has had
a strong infusion of political culture from some polyarchy
established at an earlier date. Australia, Canada, and India
obtained their structures from the United Kingdom, and
Japan from the United States. Progress is also helped by
a minimization of cleavages between religious or ethnic
groups within the society. Land reform leading to a
society of free farmers from which the bulk of the emigration to the cities is drawn also seems to contribute to the
capacity to form a polyarchy. From the full collection of
such observations one may infer that low levels of censorship in the media, combined with measures promoting

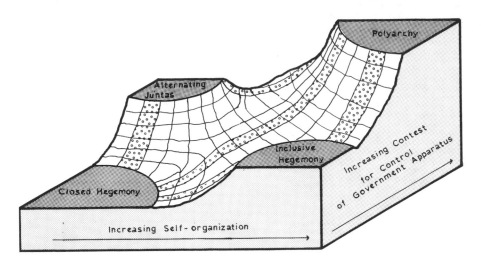

Figure 9.5 The Transition to Polyarchy

The path to a stable, self-organizing public order has already been negotiated by about twenty political units, according to Dahl (1971). Those that fail to find a form that allows an opposition to organize itself sufficiently to take over the government peaceably, if the population so elects, continue to experience political disorders. Some may dissolve and allow more modern institutions to form in the cities. The metastable conditions are visualized as plateaus or false peaks. Achieving them appears to represent progress to people inside the society until they discover that further progress in moving toward a stable political order is imposingly difficult. This model is based primarily upon post-World War II experience, combining data from all reporting nations; it emphasizes polar types in order to make clear distinctions. Better data are expected to show that the maintenance of public order in those states that have reached polyarchy is not easy or complete. An enhancement of public commumications is believed to make the difficult steps more negotiable.

Polyarchy
1. Freedom to communicate
2. Freedom to form and join organizations
3. Right to vote in equitable elections
4. Government sponsors fair competition

Closed Hegemony
1. Monopoly control of public expression
2. Official constraint of voluntary organization
3. One-candidate elections, if any
4. Ideological determination of new entries

equality of access to sending as well as receiving of messages over the media, make up an important part of the requirements for creating a stable, noncoercive political order.

Polyarchy is an economical way of operating an urban society because the cost of convulsive redirection and the waste of resources in internal conflict, including the effort spent in propping up an obsolete government, are all reduced to a low level. It is a system that produces a great deal of open discourse about conditions of life, opinions, and injustices, while awareness of these personal reports makes it possible for governments to respond to felt needs in the population. If it seems that the party in power will fail to satisfy public expectations, its opposition stands ready to persuade a majority of the electorate that it can run the state. The opportunities for a democratic public order at the metropolitan level are improving markedly, since there is an increase in the levels of education preparing the way to competence in communications and the unit costs per transaction provided by the new telecommunications systems are markedly reduced. It can be claimed, without contradiction from the available comparative data, the communications capacity substitutes in part for the military and police allocations that until now have been needed to maintain order, such as existed, in growing urban regions. When communication networks are functioning, people are no longer ordered or told how to behave but are shown examples in a variety of contexts which avoid conflicts with the aims of the society; most of the time they take the hint and choose to direct their overt actions so that they fit within the suggested set of behaviors. [20]

When conforming is not rewarding enough, people can organize so as to intervene locally in the social and physical environment and produce what are believed to be better conditions. This action may have many interesting outcomes. The result could be a church, temple, mosque, or synagogue with lively institutional activity directed toward maintaining a very different set of value premises, a distinctive street scene evolving from intensive neighboring, a commitment to music and classical dancing as a way of life, together with the halls and outdoor stages necessary to demonstrate it, or a context within which homosexuals might openly congregate. A metropolis can make room for a large number of such self-sufficient cells, each of them propagating its own behavioral norms, although only a few attract first-generation immigrants as an alternative to assimilation into popular culture.

One exceedingly important self-defeating property of rapidly improving communications capabilities in cities must be noted here. Transgressions of the norms of a democratic order are, as a consequence of the increase in flow, credibly reported to the most competent citizens in rapidly increasing numbers. They represent salacious news and the most easily recalled events. The more rapid the actual improvement in communications flow, enabling the system to become more comprehensive in coverage, the greater will be the number of errors, faults, local disorders, and moral lapses that will be detected. At the same time, a knowledgeable individual is commonly working at a node for communications and so is able to expand his network of contacts and the number of lines he can keep open. Thus the frequency of failure to meet norms is doubly amplified—once for the system itself and again for the interface between a competent person and the system.

Under these circumstances the educated communicator subjectively senses an alarming increase in the number of lapses. He is aware of twice as many faults as compared to a few years earlier. Since messages directed personally by an individual are more readily believed than published data, the elite communicator, regardless of training in objective analysis, is likely to be convinced that public order in the city is disintegrating. Elite communicators associate with each other and share their alarms. Therefore a high level of consensus evolves among a body of experts who become uniformly pessimistic about the maintenance of public order. As the general public tunes in and becomes better informed, it is alerted to the feelings of the experts, and a disturbing malaise could result.

The opposite trend, a sharp *decrease* in the reports of lapses reaching the best-informed people, is not necessarily a good sign. Indeed, the most likely interpretation is that covert censorship must have been applied somewhere in the social communications system, and the capacity to respond to some kinds of emergencies is accordingly reduced; the city has thereby become somewhat more

vulnerable to disaster. Urban communications systems
have very peculiar and unexpected properties!

The messages relating to public order employ spoken
and written language along with increasing proportions
of videoscope and photographic transmissions. They flow
through the telephone, radio, and television channels in
the spectrum. The amount of communication capacity
that is used is small as compared to what is available altogether. However, very large chunks of it have been
claimed by the military, so that plans for the political
development of cities may encounter temporary problems
of resource scarcity in the foreseeable future. The military
may be asked to share the most convenient band widths
for mobile transmitters, for example. However, the human
populations in a city are not the only consumers of the
spectrum.

With regard to the ecology of the city, it quickly becomes
evident that the electromagnetic spectrum is the medium
or "space" within which automata normally act. Incon-
spicuous to the human eye, because the circuits are inscribed
microscopically on crystalline surfaces and racked up
behind the walls or packaged unobtrusively, the population
of independent automata is expanding very rapidly. Other
automata cluster in core storage in computing centers as
programs that are galvanized into action inside time-shared
equipment whenever a query is submitted to their account
number or name; they are retired into the limbo of a tape
bank when the demand for the services they provide has
slackened. Most automata are scrapped as soon as they
become obsolete; they are rarely repaired and kept going
like vehicles. The replacements are almost always smaller
(in cubic dimensions, not the list of instructions), more
stable, and capable of more complex decisions.

These automata take on the routine, monotonous,
numbing work of the city without demanding much
floor space or land. Many use delicate sensors that are
affected by changes in environment, so it is not uncommon
that the most carefully controlled micro-environments
are designed to suit automata rather than humans. The
inputs to automata are either data acquired from their
surroundings, including other automata, or items edited
by humans. Simple decisions are the most frequent outputs;

they are generally relayed by the communications channels to administrative centers. They are designed to transmit much more information per unit of time than is typically communicated by humans, so that the message on a telephone line from an automaton is a high-pitched burst of modulated sound.

On the channels that link up cities everywhere in the world, transmissions between automata, including the sensing instruments reporting to them, will probably exceed those between humans sometime during the 1970s or the 1980s. A decade or so later we must expect that the process of substitution of communications for other scarce resources within the cities will have doubled or trebled the flow of messages between people but that the increases in the flow between the automata will be much greater; the volume is expected to catch up with and surpass the total human use of the channels.

Future populations of automata will continue to be primarily engaged in regulating the environment for man. Their duties will include equilibration of the supplies of water, gas, oil, shipping containers, railroad cars, aircraft, and electric power *between* cities first. Later the human organizations handling distribution *within* the metropolis will delegate much of their operations to automata. Another huge task performed by automata will be the processing of monetized transactions, mostly in the form of taking credits out of one account and placing them in another. Also after completing economizing calculations, automata will be expected to transmit instructions of many kinds to the numberically controlled machine tools as well as to human operators of vehicles. They will be printing books, manipulating visual displays, and otherwise distributing information that enriches the urban environment for humans. The trend suggests that the claims of the automata upon the spectrum in the future will be more extensive than those for the humans.

In the 1960s, Japan, as a pacemaker for postwar development, discovered that its future progress as a society endowed with inadequate reserves of natural resources lay in the process of "informationalization" through the use of telecommunications and computation. The perspective plan drawn up in the prime minister's office in 1968-69 worked through a number of well-informed

technical projections that lay behind the economic projections. For the 1965 to 1985 period the following rates
of growth were anticipated: [21]

Telegraph	0.5% per year
Magazines	4%
Newspapers	4.5%
Telephone	10% to 1975; 5% thereafter
Television	12% to 1975; 17% thereafter
Data transmission	45% to 1975; 38% thereafter
Computation	93% to 1975; 58% thereafter
Total for the society	11.5% to 1975; 17% to 1985

In Japan all these various forms of information transmission
are readily convertible into characters per second, so that
it is possible to compare flows of numbers with language.
Measuring the total transmission for society has much more
meaning than it would in a Western society. The growth
in informationalization is to be compared with a projected
growth rate of 8% in the GNP at this time. Thus information-based transactions, particularly services rendered by
automata, are due to become a significant component in
national product.

Japanese society has demonstrated that a path exists
from a poor, densely populated Asian economy to a relatively affluent (i.e., capable of providing everyone with a
minimum adequate standard of living from less than a
forty-hour week of organized work) economic system
based upon international specialization. It has almost
completed its urban transition; indeed, there is a strong
belief that the tide will change somewhat and that some
people will resettle the countryside, although they will
still be engaged in modern urban types of economic
activity. The demographic transition is almost complete
as well, so that the continuing rapid growth in production
results in equivalent increases in goods and services per
capita. Most expansion now is planned to be in services
associated with computation and carried out by automata.
Japan's experiences and anticipations offer one of the
most hopeful models for Asian development as well as a
promising strategy for averting castrophe, even though the
Japanese demand for scarce resources remains far too
large. If the Japanese case is any indicator of things to
come, the institution of adequate fertility control and

completion of urbanization should be followed by a population explosion in the automata. Japanese urban society has many unfilled jobs for humans (estimated at 3-4% of the total employment in 1973); thus it must either depend increasingly upon automata or contract the work out to urban regions overseas.

The presence of modern automata in the urban ecosystem is so new that we have little experience to draw upon when appraising future potentials. It is like judging the impact of electricity in 1890 or of the automobile in 1910 when changes in the offing were recognized as being revolutionary, and many of the directions could be foreseen, but the actual dimensions of the transformation could not be believed. The use of ecological considerations help us to comprehend at the community scale what some of these implications are; they are indicators to planners regarding what institutional changes are needed soon if these opportunities for preventing disaster are to be exploited. Governments do not have direct control over automata, and automata are not recognized legally in any way except as creatures of copyright and patent law. Therefore they qualify sometimes as property (public, corporate, or private) until set free in the public domain after a specified period of time. Those controls are clumsy and archaic and are not to be considered even in the same sense that the government maintains import quota and production limits over plant populations used in crops or over the stocks of animals used for food and household pets. The one area where controls have been relatively effective is that of migration across national boundaries; whenever the software associated with automata was felt to be sensitive to national defense, administrative measures have been taken to restrict their movement until equally elaborate automata have evolved elsewhere which counterbalance the military advantages that result from a monopoly.

In the 1950s and 1960s it was widely believed that robots backed by automata would displace many human workers from the labor force. The phenomenon was given a special name, "automation," and this term quickly assumed the meaning of a threat. Many industrial workers felt that a conspiracy was forming that would deprive them of their jobs. Careful analysis showed that even then (and more so later) the firms engaging in advanced mechanization, which at some points drew upon computer capabilities, were

increasing the number of employees. This was true of the
industries involved deeply in "automation," and even more
the case for the industries engaging in the more sophisticated "cybernation." The alarm expressed about the takeover
by robots was misplaced because only small-scale, highly
localized shifts occurred at a modest rate of change.[22]
The industries most affected were those which were *unable*
to adopt information-intensive, error-controlling methods
of production, because in them the pay scales lagged, and
bankruptcies or reorganizations caused localized unemployment.

Ecological inferences are usually made within the context
of a fair description of the living, behaving system. Boundaries must be specified and subsystems identified. Some
quantitative estimates of population sizes and dynamics
are in order. Only then is it possible to discuss interdependencies of the prominent species, which are what interest
most of us. Much of this material was covered in Chapter 1,
but the future dimensions of the population of the human
species had to be assessed before those of the automata
were open to analysis.

The original concept of a robot was that of an automaton
capable of manipulating its physical environment in a way
approximating that of man, but in an era of assembly lines
the manipulation became so simplistic that the cybernation
required did not always deserve the rating of automaton.
The world population of robots in 1973 is estimated at
3,500, the majority of which are installed in Japan.[23] At
the present time, however, the growth rate is reported to
have reached 30-50% per year. The work robots do is most
nearly that of the cat's paws in Aesop's fable, which were
needed to get the hot chestnuts out of the glowing coals in
the fireplace. They are introduced also in places where
fatigue and interruptions could cause expensive mistakes in
manipulation if humans were at work with standard tools.
Error prevention will probably be the most common justification for the use of robots at critical points in an industrial production in the long run.

The population of automata is still uncertain because of
the lack of adequate definition. We are fairly sure that most
of the 80,000 or so minicomputers are devoted to a single
purpose, such as operating a nuclear reactor, and that
there lurks within their recesses at least one functioning
program complex enough to be labeled an automaton. In

a time-sharing service facility the accounts at the same scale (i.e., $20,000 a year or more) are presumed to provide niches that are almost as promising. The far more numerous accounts that are smaller than this provide the gravest difficulties in definition and enumeration. The civilian center with the most computing capacity is operated by the U.S. Social Security Administration, which addresses itself to the maintenance of 100,000,000 or so individual accounts. Insurance, banking and credit, transport movements, spare parts inventory, and marketing services are already large users of computing centers and are still rapidly expanding. If we accept a rather low standard of decisionmaking in the judgment of practitioners in the design of artificial intelligence, we might assert that the population of nonmilitary automata in the world in 1973 approximates a half-million. The rate of growth is somewhat less arbitrary—it should be even more rapid than the accumulation of computing capacity since many firms and agencies have now proceeded beyond the experimental, exploratory, and pioneer demonstration uses of such facilities. Worldwide, this rate of growth in the numbers of automata should be 20-30% per year, which means that if the rate is sustained it would be seven to twenty times larger a decade hence and perhaps a hundred times larger by the turn of the century after allowing for maturation of the industry and the commitment of some of the capacity to some truly gigantic schemes.

The greatest single deterrent to the projected growth of automata in cities is the paucity of mutual affect between the human user and the computer. The friendly automaton, such as the computer named HAL in the cinematic version of *2001: A Space Odyssey*, does not seem likely to come into existence. What is needed actually is a system that will take in and interpret (or translate) information equal to or a little greater than the telephone at a cost no greater than the telephone in that city at that time. People did learn rather quickly how to take a mechanical object like the telephone and fit it into the urban social system to the point that the handset became virtually no barrier at all. Chapanis has shown that two persons cooperatively involved in half-hour problems yielding joint payoff will take only 10% longer to solution using voice mode (i.e., telephone) than using omnimode.[24] Despite the extra time, 15% fewer words were used. The typical mode of entering the computer—typing—took 120-130% longer for the problem solving than for omni-modes, and it was accomplished with a fifth to a sixth of the words. Handwriting used even fewer words (a seventh), but the problem was solved much more quickly than for typing. This means that the respondents (all of them young city dwellers) found their natural pace with all channels open—they could handle interruptions without significant loss—but that typing, which was the most precise means of communication, was very much less effective; voice alone is the best compromise if it can be implemented at the interface of a computer. At this stage major break-throughs in several features of linguistics and complex learning theory are required before an adequate interface capacity can be achieved.

Scientists appear confident that these problems can be solved despite a record of two decades of unwarranted optimism during which it was believed that an adequate solution was only a matter of months away.[25] If they should eventually succeed, there appears to be no resource limitation that would prevent a population explosion in automata. The raw materials required are in more than adequate supply; the energy cost for producing an autom-aton is mostly indirect and is not insignificant, but it remains small as compared to bringing a human infant into the world. The potential lifetimes for humans and automata are comparable (fully automatic telephone exchanges are designed for a forty-year life), but hitherto most automata have had a high "infant mortality" rate and low "life expectancy" because of intense competition. The colonies of automata in a computing center, some with populations up to several hundred different types, most of them functioning only a few minutes at a time, will have a high population turnover and accelerated rate of evolution. Death amounts to erasure from the memory store. The physical equipment that maintains the colony would be stripped for salvage and then cremated (pyrolysis) for recovery of the platinum, silver, gallium, germanium, arsenic, and other scarcer elements. Those automata that were valued would have been transferred to new equipment.

By the time the urban transition is complete, the number of discrete automata should rival that of the human occu-pants of cities if suitable "symbiotic" relationships can be devised. The prospects here are different than for those of vehicles because the fundamental science has yet to be introduced. Once the needed breakthroughs have been achieved, the technological response using economical mass-produced devices can be accomplished in a shorter period of time than for electrical or mechanical technologies.

It is worth observing that long-term extrapolations of employment in society, such as those discussed recently by Daniel Bell, lead to a forecast that most workers will be engaged in the production of services—a category that has come to be so all embracing for metropolitan societies it conveys little meaning.[26] Bell has gone further, arguing that it will be in the newly labeled quaternary (information processing) and quintenary (knowledge production) categories that the impressive growth will occur. The significance of improvements of the interface between humans and automata is that more human roles can be productively added in the quaternary and quinternary categories. Moreover, reduction of the barrier between the human and automaton will make possible a wide range of interactive games that generate more rewarding recreation (an activity that may be rarely separable from education and work in the long run).

The structure of the mission-oriented human group seems likely to change in the future. Not only is it expected to accommodate itself to fulfilling its responsibilities to others around the clock, but it admits one or more automata to the group. A portion of the group will specialize in editing information to be transmitted to the automaton and in querying its memory for information needed. However, most of the stored information would be either acquired automatically from the physical environment with the aid of arrays of instruments with transducers or selected from subscription services that make up the specialized mass media. Thus the bulk of the communication within urban surroundings will be carried out by the automata whose interfaces on each other are simple, smooth, and relatively free of error. The sensitive communications that add new responsibilities may be expected to remain between the humans on the team.

The electromagnetic spectrum seems likely to be the primary resource for the quaternary, or data-processing, category of productive activity. This is to be compared with the fossil-fuel energy resources that are predominant inputs to transport and electric power needed to expedite the basic tertiary activities, the mineral and forest resources that bulk so large in the secondary, or manufacturing, activities, and the water and soil that are basic to primary activities. That set of connections induces us to ask the question: What is the basic natural resource for knowledge-based activities? At the moment it appears to be human *attention*, free from distractions, yet supported by the four more fundamental resource streams. With communications channels carrying a thousandfold more signals, and the bulk of the gross domestic product dependent upon the activity of the automata, the opportunity to allocate intelligent attention to novel phenomena may become quite precious. Resource needs for further growth de-emphasize concerns for energy, water, and materials in the physical environment and begin to focus on the use of human potentials.

Notes

1. The principles for substitution where traditional natural resource supplies are extended by means of installing communications systems were succinctly stated in the *Encyclopedia of the Social Sciences,* under, "Social Planning," subentry, "Resources Planning."

2. In an era of solid-state components, the costs of telecommunications are almost completely capital costs since very tiny amounts of energy are required, the labor required for maintenance and repair is a minor factor, and the raw materials are plentiful. The economies of scale are striking; the costs per circuit-mile in newly installed systems decline from $200 apiece for a hundred to $5 apiece for 16,000 (1969 prices). The most complete study I have seen of the considerations involved in substitution by communications-intensive technology was carried out on the Picturephone, a development that was indefinitely postponed by American Telephone and Telegraph management in 1972. Edward M. Dickson and Raymond Bowers, "The Video Telephone: A Preliminary Technology Assessment," Cornell University, June 1973, litho. Here, as in most other instances, advances in the underlying science and the availability of pure substances encouraged engineers to design instruments and systems which added to our capability in an intuitively desireable way—combining visual information with voice over telephone circuits. Efficient cameras were designed that incidentally also made possible transmission of patterns originally present in the invisible infrared. A careful review of the alternatives in the social system showed that, if used, a videotelephone would substitute trips for (1) executives and consultants, (2) outpatients and medical personnel, (3) students in technical courses, with a ten- to hundredfold saving in energy and a considerable saving in time. The problem was that of finding enough uses to warrant the large introductory investment cost and to reach a scale at which economies would accrue. That may occur when satellite communications dominate the globe. Joint Technical Advisory Committee of Institute of Electrical and Electronic Engineers, *Spectrum Engineering: The Key to Progress,* Washington, D.C., March 1968; Peter C. Goldmark, Chmn. *Communications Technology for Urban Improvement* (Washington, D.C.; National Academy of Engineering, June 1971); also "Communication and the Community," *Scientific American,* 227 (September 1972), 142-151.

3. Jacob Marschak, "Economics of Information Systems," *Journal of the American Statistical Association,* 66 (march 1971), 192-219. The work of H. Theil, *Economics and Information Theory* (New York: Rand-McNally, 1967), is quite different; he is concerned with the relative amounts of information in the reports about the economic system, not as inputs to processing.

4. Israel Dostovsky, "Water for Israel," *Bulletin of the Atomic Scientists,* 28 (October 1972), 11-18; Joel R. Gat, "Water Resources in Israel," *ibid.,* 24-28.

5. Richard C. Harkness, "Communications Innovation, Urban Form, and Travel Demand," Research Report No. 71-2, Urban Transportaion Program, University of Washington, Seattle, January 1972. His model of the substitution process in "Communications substitutes for Intra-Urban Travel," *Transportation Engineering Journal TE3,* August 1972, pp. 585-598, relied heavily on Bell Telephone's Picturephone technology—a development that seems unlikely to be commercialized. No high payoff use has been found which allows convenience uses to be added on at marginal cost.

6. In the brief period of 1971-1973 a coordinated effort to reduce risk of fire loss and casualties in high-rise office buildings led to the design of alternate systems for communication and control throughout the structure. While the networks are automatically triggered by fire, short circuits, pipe rupture, earthquakes, and other foreseeable events, they also deliver a stream of data to a console in a control center. Information routinely available at the control center promises to allow a reduction of power and heating requirements by 20% before any attempts are made to educate the office workers. After having learned the best way to use their office environment, workers may add some extra energy economies. Special Report to *Business Week,* September 29, 1973.

7. I am indebted to John and Magda McHale for an opportunity to see their analyses of responses to the kinds of scarcities expected in the next five decades as part of their "Timetable Project"; see *Annals of the New York Academy of Sciences,* 184 (1971), 440. In technological journals one finds concurrence in the specialties in which the man is an expert, but often doubts are expressed about the supply of substitutes elsewhere.

8. As President of the Population Council, Bernard Berelson is responsible for the highly informative annual report of that organization. The 1971 *Report* (April 1972) recounts research being initiated in the areas of fertility trend analysis, role of management techniques in family planning programs, the impact of the Green Revolution, changes in statutory law, interactions with educational attainment, and the significance of studies on environmental quality and quality of life, all of which would have contributed to this analysis if they were available at the time of writing.

9. The accounting techniques by which one arrives at an estimate of the marginal cost and contribution of a person to an economy has been highly controversial. I used a hypothetical population with a $100 per capita income and "typical characteristics" and arrived at a pessimistically low figure, or about 25% of the per capita GNP. R. L. Meier, *Modern Science and the Human Fertility Problem* (New York: John Wiley & Sons, 1959), p. 83. Stephen Enke has devoted much more attention to the issues, including the invention of economic incentives for reducing fertility, and settled for relatively simple calculations in his "Birth Control for Economic Development," *Science,* 164 (May 16, 1969). The more classical

analysis which provided the figures cited in the text is provided by George B. Simmons, *The Indian Investment in Family Planning* (New York: Population Council and Key Book Service, 1971). Simmons and Enke are in rough concurrence in their estimates regarding India, but David Wolfers, in his review, *Family Planning Perspectives,* 5 (Summer 1973), 189, feels that their mode of estimation has greatly overstated the returns to society. The true value seems to lie somewhere in between their estimates and mine.

10. Roger J. Lapham and W. Parker Mauldin, "National Family Planning Programs: Review and Evaluation," *Studies in Family Planning,* 3 (March 1972), 29-52. The Chinese cannot be analyzed on a comparable basis, but recent reports indicate that a vigorous program is again underway; Anibal Faundes and Tapani Luukkainen, *Studies in Family Planning,* 3 (July 1972), 165-176. The consequences for education are assessed by Gavin W. Jones, "Effect of Population Change on the Attainment of Educational Goals in the Developing Countries," in Roger Revelle, ed., *Rapid Population Growth* (Baltimore: Johns Hopkins University Press, 1971), pp. 315-367.

11. Bernard Berelson, "National Family Planning Programs: Where We Stand," *Science,* 169 (September 4, 1970), 931.

12. J. Richard Udry, Lydia T. Clark, Charles L. Chase, and Marvin Levy, "Can Mass Media Advertising Increase Contraceptive Use?" *Family Planning Perspectives,* 4 (July 1972), 37-44.

13. Everett Rogers carried out a number of field experiments in social communication, especially in the Muslim countries, which will be crucial over the long run. He admits that family planning needs a clinic-based service as a foundation, but an underdeveloped society cannot wait for the client to drift in and ask for assistance— it needs to make direct contact. Arguing that current WHO policy is not enough either, he describes the role of mass media in the process of breaking taboos on speaking about sex. Very often missing is a program depending upon paraprofessionals who establish face-to-face contacts at home and at the place of work and use homegrown words and symbols rather than alien-sounding neologisms. Everett M. Rogers, *Communication Strategies for Family Planning* (New York: The Free Press, 1973).

14. Phillips Cutright, "National Political Development," in Nelson Polsby *et al.,* eds., *Politics and Social Life* (Boston: Houghton Mifflin, 1963), pp. 569-582.

15. Donald J. McCrone and Charles F. Cnudde, "Toward a Communications Theory of Political Development: A Causal Model," *American Political Science Review,* 61 (March 1967), 72-79.

16. Seymour Martin Lipset, "Some Social Requisites of Democracy: Economic Development and Political Legitimacy," *American Political Science Review,* 53 (1959), 69-105.

17. Hugh D. Forbes and Edward R. Tufte, "A Note of Caution in Causal Modeling," *American Political Science Review,* 62 (1968), 1258-1264.

18. Gilbert R. Winham, "Political Development and Lerner's Theory: Further Test of a Causal Model," *American Political Science Review,* 64 (September 1970), 810-818. He refers to Daniel Lerner, "Communications Systems and Social Systems: A Statistical Exploration in History and Policy," *Behavioral Science,* 2 (1957), 266-275, and *The Passing of the Traditional Society* (Glencoe: Free Press, 1958).

19. Robert A. Dahl, *Polyarchy: Participation and Opposition* (New Haven: Yale University Press, 1971).

20. Erving Goffman, *Relations in Public* (New York: Basic Books, 1971). See also his *Behavior in Public Places* (New York: Free Press, 1963).

21. Toshio Sanuki, "The City in Informational Society," *Area Development in Japan 1970,* 3, pp. 9-23. Brief references to the underlying studies appear in various places, mainly speeches of leading figures in Japan and articles in journals addressed to world audiences. See Kenzo Tange, "Japan in the 21st Century," *Japan Architect,* September 1971, pp. 81-98.

22. In 1955 I undertook an analysis of the impact of information theory and cybernetics upon the social system using a number of projection and forecasting devices. The findings were reassuring to me but not very persuasive among those who felt concern. They indicated that the employment displacement effect should be only of the order of a half percent of the labor force per year at most, which was small as compared to the impact of advances in ordinary mechanization. The latter were still affecting agriculture and forestry very seriously in the 1950s and the 1960s. The publicly stated opinion of many experts based upon much less analysis was contradictory, and it was the tendency of the educated public to expect the worst to happen. R. L. Meier, "Automatism in the American Economy," *Journal of Business,* 29 (1956), 14-27. Subsequent studies showed that the displacements were well within the projection, and that the unemployment among the youth was attributable to the rise in the birth rate that started in 1940. The President's Commission on Automation, *Technology and the American Economy* (Washington, D.C.: 1968). The early study also undertook to forecast on the basis of the scientific potentials alone, since the technology had not yet been disclosed or invented, the relative role of "machine-machine communication (automatism)." It suggested that volume would catch up with the growing rate of "person-to-person communication (machine-interposed)" about the year 2010-2020. R. L. Meier, "Communications and Social Change," *Behavioral Science,* 1 (January 1956), 43-58. Now that

a large share of the technology has been developed, and important populations of automata have come into being, that projection remains the most likely among the alternative futures.

23. I have brought the estimates up to date, based upon the review made by Alfred Rosenblatt, "Robots Handling More Jobs on Industrial Assembly," *Electronics,* July 19, 1973, pp. 93-95.

24. Alphonse Chapanis, "The Communication of Factual Information through Various Channels," *Information and Retrieval,* 9 (April 1973), 215-231; "Prelude to 2001: Explorations in Human Communication," *American Plychologist,* 26 (1971) 949-961. Also Edwin B. Parker and Donald A. Dunn, "Information Technology: Its Social Potential," *Science,* 176 (June 30, 1972), 1392-1396.

25. As this was being written a circular came to hand which illustrates the kind of pragmatic approach that quite often discovers a solution ahead of theory. It advertised a new service called Community Memory, which is produced by hiring Grace Cybernetics, a nonprofit collective operating out of Resource One, Inc. The latter organization was created to operate the San Francisco Switchboard, which has become a remarkably effective means of mobilizing assistance and information among the participants in the counterculture, but it is done on a voice-to-voice basis without access to any mechanical data bank. The collective had obtained an over-aged (six to twelve years) computer, repaired it, and asked whether it was possible to extend the switchboard with specific information about opportunities. Entry into the system is achieved through a terminal in the most popular discount record store; it employs an initial set of key words but a further elaboration depends upon the offers that are admitted to system. For example, if several members of a specialized commune take to the road, it can advertise for like-minded individuals just off the highway. Financing is achieved initially through contributions made whenever money changes hands, later they will improvise. If systems like this solve the interface problem (at least a tenth of the users learned computer programming in high school or college, so that it is now easy to get help), a huge amount of service can be produced at exceedingly low time and energy cost.

26. Daniel Bell, *The Coming of Post-Industrial Society* (New York: Basic Books, 1973). Chap. iii in particular deals with the "knowledge society," but that study does not take into account features of technological trends that became evident after about 1968, such as the decline in significance of the aerospace industry and of much of physics.

WHAT CITIES PRODUCE FROM NATURAL RESOURCES

A very important conclusion can be drawn from the preceding review of the technologies available for the production of food, water, transport, power, and communications. *If a different kind of city is built, the demands for resources could be eased without significantly detracting from quality of life potentials. Consumption could be held well within the carrying capacity of the earth. Moreover, the economical solution presumes a future world society that is predominantly metropolitan.* The prototypes and precedents for the technologies and programs already exist, and the economic feasibility of these approaches to conservation has been tested. But all these things remain unattainable, unrealized potential if one cannot discover a path from the present predicament to the more equitable outcome. There must be a procedure for overall optimization, so that, among the options available at a given time, the better ones can be chosen. There must be an institutionalized process of designing new systems for meeting human needs.

As far as it has advanced over the past few decades, urban economics is still not helpful. In practice even more than theory, it has operated on a limited set of propositions. Thus, until now, attention has dwelt almost exclusively upon cost minimization. A huge amount of effort has gone into the analysis of the various mixes of inputs into urban services, but a trivial amount has been focused upon the outputs. We know that cities transform natural resources into wastes and something else. How might they go about optimizing with regard to these other outputs— eliminating as many aspects of "ill-fare" as possible and increasing the amount of welfare? Gross domestic product is not a good indicator of what needs to be maximized because it represents only a part of the whole. Even that part is not readily obtainable from the accounting systems used by individuals, firms, and public services in the respective cities. Indexes of the total product require that we look outside economics and consider both the socio-cultural system of the human species and the encompassing ecosystem. The critical choices to be made are those of the policies of long-lived institutions that organize the collective effort. The alternatives need to be weighed according to measures of social returns obtained from the expenditure of resources.

The most primitive and demanding concern in a living system is that of survival. For food and related necessities of life the security of provisioning is enhanced by stockpiling (granaries, reservoirs, warehouses, tank farms) and by engaging in worldwide trade, so that the maximum number of sources is opened up and the channels for transshipment have been developed. Only in that way can the metropolis survive unscathed the massive failure that will occasionally occur in its immediate hinterland. Freedom from incidents involving dire want depends upon the accumulation of a full complement of stocks, but even more upon interdependence among cities. *The more open and interconnected a metropolis is, the more secure it is against extreme adversity.* Indexes of performance can be devised from this criterion. That is why this analysis began with dooms, Malthusian and otherwise, and the means for avoiding them.

After basic sustenance comes a concern for health, which may be thought of as organism-environment conditions (contexts) that allow individuals *freedom to act* and offer at the same time a measure of public safety, so that risks of such action are kept within a tolerable range. Populous metropolises increase the scale of the propagation of epidemics, the frequency of intersections of path (where collision must be avoided), and the explosiveness of public disorders. A variety of indicators are used, at present almost entirely of the kind that register costs (morbidity rates, vehicular accidents, delinquency and crime, addictions), but virtually none on the output side—the freedom to act without destructive interference.

The new indicators must be collected by the professionals who staff the organizations that provide urban services. Then they can much more easily learn how to improve performance. These professionals need schools for training new cohorts and associated systems for communication and information storage. Their institutions, too, must be fitted into the new metropolis; their presence in the city is an indication of commitment to extracting more from the resources consumed.

It is noted in passing, again, that the greatest absolute hazard for cities—the stockpiles of intercontinental ballistic missiles and the nuclear weapons they carry, together with the beginnings of antiballistic missile installations that would contaminate neutral, nontargeted metropolitan areas by fallout—require utterly different kinds of interventions. These life-and-death concerns are the agenda for nations with military establishments; the fate of cities rests in the hands of national executives, their diplomats, and military risktakers. Agents of the nation have a presence in the city, although the fighting equipment and manpower are positioned outside.

If the political system made up of nation-states disintegrates, not all metropolises would be totally destroyed. The cities that survive, it appears, would be swamped with refugees.[1] The attitudes and beliefs of all survivors would be shaken so completely, however, that the future of cities would move onto a different trajectory. The prospects, alternatives, and accessible resources would all change. (The Chinese once argued that the major remnants would be Chinese, but now they are less confident.) The bases for forecasting used here, even the economic evaluations, would be rendered obsolete. This is a nightmare that must be ended through disarmament and increased levels of international understanding. Whatever cities do to promote health and welfare should not conflict with this overriding obligation for preventing catastrophe. Fortunately, very few instances can be imagined where a conflict would occur; it is important, nevertheless, to distinguish the higher priority of the global system of nations, even if it is not discussed and analyzed.

The threat of internal disorders is more immediate than catastrophe visited from the outside. One way of preventing discontent from boiling over is to distribute the goods and services in a fair fashion. This does not mean perfectly equal shares for all or reward according to marginal contribution to product; rather, it is a compromise that also allows efficient organization of the production and consumption system. Thus it is proposed that each metropolis define a minimum adequate standard of living—a level of consumption that could maintain most people at the threshold of comfort and convenience, but not beyond. Just enough food to be healthy and active, enough space for living but not entertaining, enough

THE MINIMUM ADEQUATE STANDARD OF LIVING FOR ALL

warmth or coolness in home and workplace to be able to function well but not a temperature and humidity continuously maintained in the precise optimum range, and sufficient transport to participate fully in public life, but not necessarily ownership of a private vehicle. The concept of minimum adequate standard was implicit in all the proposals for substitution of resource-conserving technologies for present methods of production that were put forward in previous chapters.[2] In each instance it was shown that enough water could be conserved, or energy produced, or raw materials processed to accommodate the masses yet to be urbanized. Now it is necessary to describe plans and programs concerning how these potentials for supply can be distributed.

The metropolitan policy proposed here sounds quite reasonable: the society should endeavor to increase the number of people living at or above the minimum adequate standard for that climate and for the subcultures that have settled in it (See figure 10.1). This implies an index not dissimilar to the American poverty index (fraction of the population living below the poverty line) but based upon actual living conditions rather than expenditure rates.

A continuous sampling of the metropolitan population should be made, to point out not only who are the deprived and where they live but each aspect of human life that falls below the minimum adequate level, so that the effects can be gauged. Thus, insufficient food leaves one hungry and listless much of the time, but poor housing usually takes effect only in nonsleeping periods at home (say, six hours a day for adults and twelve for children). Similarly, inadequacies in health facilities show up in time lost for social participation due to preventable illness. Inadequate schooling would be defined by levels needed for keeping the urban society going at steady state (the ability to communicate in the words and numbers employed routinely in modern society and mastery of the skills needed to work with machines and automata require organized effort equivalent to about ten years of full-time schooling for the typical person). Availability of transport involves large and very different kinds of samples if traffic administrators are to minimize time lost in travel. Part of the minimum standard would undoubtedly be framed in terms of access to public transit networks

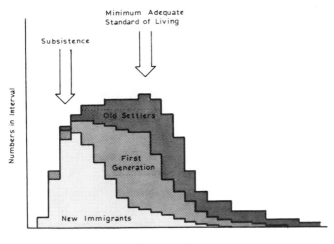

Figure 10.1 Household Expenditures for Accelerated Development in a Growing Metropolitan Area

Policies for income distribution and consumption should aim at the minimum adequate standard of living. Most of the recent inmigrants will be living in equilibrium with rural areas, i.e., close to subsistence. People living at levels less than subsistence manage to survive with the aid of gifts and relief provided in kind rather than cash. High-level consumers would most often work at jobs equivalent to those open in metropolitan areas with full employment. Subsistence levels can be most readily accommodated in urban villages designed to encourage steady improvement and living standards. The minimum standard of living would dominate the new housing that served the growing industrial and commercial districts. Those living somewhat above the minimum adequate standard would consist of officials and professionals required to compete with or mix with members of the affluent societies of the world.

so that trips necessary to health and family welfare are feasible.

Connection to electric current is on its way to becoming a necessary ingredient of the minimum standard, considering its function in lighting, economical and clean modes of cooking, television, ventilation, and similar fundamental conveniences. Living in cities without it may become a significant deprivation henceforward, and electric appliance censuses may yield a highly sensitive indicator of the achievement of adequacy. A monthly sample survey could reveal readily enough most of the deficiencies in the city according to section of the city, the category of service that most often fell short, the substrata of society that were most subject to deprivation, and the seasons during which most of it was experienced. It should be sufficient to allow adoption of a policy that justified taxing those consuming at levels above this minimum adequate standard and to suggest reallocation of funds so that they could be used to bring the most people up to the minimum. Whenever the gap is great and major programs must be mounted to overcome deficiencies, it is likely that much more information will be necessary, so that a large-scale benchmark type of study might be needed to concentrate on problematic subpopulations living in the city. The metropolis thereby learns enough about its deficiencies to set about improving them.

THE SELF-IMPROVING METROPOLITAN STRUCTURE

These elementary, equity-promoting policies cannot be carried out in an urban area independently. They must be superimposed upon the requirements for achieving rapid economic growth—the role of the metropolis as an economic engine for moving a society toward a developed condition—and upon the normal migratory shifts observed in urbanizing populations. When these extra forces are taken into account, a typical physical form or shape for the self-improving metropolis emerges. The growth process has the property of a simple theory because it generates some expectations about the dimensions, densities, appearance, and the spatial distribution of functions in a city that must be very stingy in its use of resources. Yet it is as able to accomplish the task of expediting the self-organization that produces welfare as the metropolises of São Paulo, Seoul, Singapore, and others in recent years. The process by which such structure comes into being is most revealing.

Cities tend to accrete populations in three ways: (1) self-sufficient households from other cities; (2) school graduates from the country and town in search of opportunity; and (3) the distress flows of population that cannot be supported in their original homes. The inmigrants from other cities usually expect to consume more than the minimum adequate level, yet they are regarded as desirable additions to the population because they bring with them industrial skills, organizing experience, and bank accounts. As a result major increases in productivity become possible within short periods of time. The residential areas they prefer are either high-density apartment districts close to the respective centers of a growing metropolis (primarily the recent school-leavers with added work experience, often married) or new suburban communities.

The second group of inmigrants consists of large numbers of school-leavers with less background, who infiltrate the existing precincts of the city with the aid of kinship and other connections. They come from villages, towns, and small cities and demonstrate capacities for learning and adapting very quickly. Many join the first group and move to another city within a few years. The shortfalls from "minimum adequate" they create are mainly attributable to overcrowding and shortage of infrastructure. The postwar flows into Japanese cities, for example, were primarily of this "pull" type of movement; they were facilitated by the very large-scale prior investments in the elementary and early secondary education of both sexes.

The third and final category—the people who were "pushed" or fled from the countryside because of Malthusian pressures or political disorders—at present set up the new squatter settlements, but in the future would be assigned the assisted "site and services" type of peripheral settlements. These people often drop back to subsistence levels during times of cirsis but may struggle successfully and achieve the minimum adequate standard before the end of two decades or so of residence in the urban region. Those that do not make it in that time are likely, as are the disabled, to become part of the permanent welfare load.

These three main flows (many lesser ones can also be identified) tend to create a city with central areas being rebuilt to meet minimum adequate standards, but the complexity tends to slow down the reconstruction, so that most needs other than housing will be adequate. Newly building peripheral areas must be rather patchy, with the high-amenity areas demanding and receiving superstandard facilities in order to attract and hold top professionals from elsewhere in the world where incomes are much higher, and most of the remainder starting well below the standard but programmed to reach it in two decades or less. The simplest possible spatial representation, one that assumes homogeneous space (no physical or political boundaries, no elevations, no soil capability differentiation, no defense needs, no sites to be preserved) is presented in figure 10.2.

Surveys of actual consumption levels carried out to discover conditions leading to underconsumption and overconsumption can also be used as a basis for the design of partially constructed subassemblies, housing "packages," and neighborhood projects that promote efficient consumption. Thus a number of different life-styles can be accommodated in the residential areas surrounding the respective central districts. Those that are not disturbed by noise (perhaps because their own preferred activities are noisy) may concentrate in the airport sector, while those that place a high value upon cultural pursuits and knowledge acquisition would cluster in the vicinity of the central cultural district. Since nuclear families will have different requirements at different stages in the life cycle, they may change their domicile two or three times; but traditional families will prefer more fixed locations. Each life-style must have an opportunity to contribute to the action within the city, directly or indirectly enhancing export capability. The minimum adequate standard of living is calculated to provide the opportunity to participate and make a contribution; other indices must be used to discover what public interaction is actually generated.

The composition of the minimum adequate standard of living itself has been slightly modified since it was first put forward in 1956. At that time it was framed as a recapitulation of the goals of the welfare state, put into dimensions and categories that allowed substitutes to be proposed that were based upon newly available knowledge from science and technology. Now it includes (1) more variety in diet, (2) more land rent for residence in cities, and (3) cable television to provide a practical substitute for formal

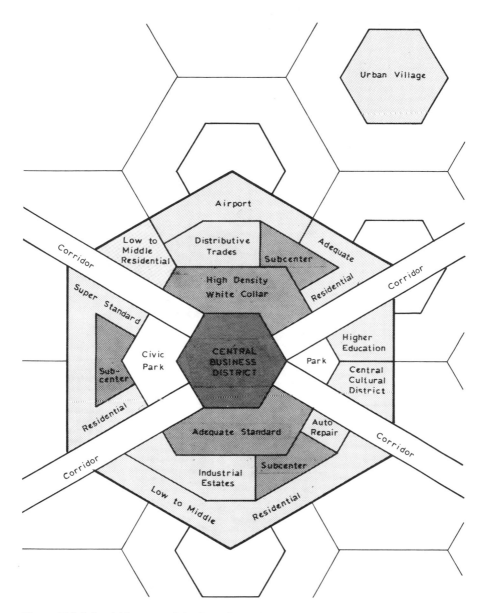

Figure 10.2 A Spatial Structure Suited to a Future Metropolis
This assembly of specialized urban functions on the land minimizes the expenditures of energy and human time. Areas and relative locations represent a rough balance of land use. Approximating such a structure could allow successful competition with other metropolises. Bodies of water will warp this idealized pattern.

education as well as a major medium for highly diverse cultural participation.

The concept underlying the choice of consumption levels represented in the minimum adequate standard of living is that each person should be given the opportunity to maintain a condition of physiological comfort, and the most economical technologies for providing food, shelter, and clothing should be applied to meeting those needs. In addition, people should have sufficient free (i.e., discretionary) time to engage in cultural activity that is roughly equal to levels achieved in Europe and North America, but again the transport and communications services supplied would be the least costly mix that would still yield the necessary convenience. Not only is conspicuous consumption ruled out, but also many technologies left over from the first three-quarters of the twentieth century that appear to be excessively wasteful are eliminated.

Disagreement will most likely be encountered in the programming of health, education, social security, and urban services. For a member of one of the affluent societies they seem to be understated, although for members of poor societies they appear to be unnecessarily luxurious. The levels of staffing chosen, and the standards to be met, depend very heavily upon preventive medicine and voluntary, cooperative approaches to education that assume the student to be highly motivated to learn, rather than be required to attend by force of law. It is also implied that the cultural activity, including recreation, would draw upon plentiful resources, such as the electromagnetic spectrum, marine surfaces, and nearby wastelands, rather than upon popular areas and scarce commodities, and that the demand for trips would be no greater than at present in developed societies. The trips and equipment have already been explicitly included in this budget. At this Spartan level of adequacy, for example, trips to snow country are allowed, but ski clothing, equipment, and instruction are extra, or superstandard.

It is interesting that, despite inflation, prices have not changed very much over two decades. Improvements in technological efficiency are responsible. Difficulties of comparing equivalent conditions in an affluent society are emphasized by parallel pricing for hypothetical urban communities in California and South Asia organized to maintain as economically as possible the same levels of comfort and convenience. The 250-280% differential in cost is shown to be mostly due to physical stature, population density, and cultural emphases.

In cities a strong economizing process is at work; it brings about fundamental internal structural change that becomes evident to residents and visitors only on rare occasions. Cities get reconstructed and reorganized so as to "save time." This sounds peculiar, because the actual time of living slips away regardless of any modification of the physical or institutional environment; if there is any lengthening of the life span, the outcome is an unanticipated consequence of the reorganization of facilities. What is actually achieved by "saving time" is that a set of activities necessary to the maintenance of human life requires less time to complete than before, allowing greater freedom of choice in the remainder of human activities. To state this another way, we can say that cities are expected to facilitate transactions so that time is left to engage in more transactions. Some cities are vastly more effective than others, when viewed this way.

A common-sense way of comparing cities is to consider how much time must be committed in order to assure subsistence or to reach the threshold of sufficiency in different metropolitan areas. This comparison can be carried out by proposing a way of life that draws upon the marketplace for the full set of human requirements at minimal cost. This is not the strict "standard marketbasket" approach to a cost of living index because it recognizes only the most economical means of filling needs, and not the typical existing demand. Then one can go to the labor market and ask how much time must be spent as an employee of a going concern in that city in order to meet the cost of the requirements.

All sorts of precautions must be kept in mind when making comparisons of this sort. The calculations are realistic for only a few people, who must choose between living in either city, and not the average. In addition, cities have differential taxes that apply to sojourners and immigrants at the same time that they provide a variety of free services. "Europe on $5 a day" describes a number of devices for exploiting such free services, but Amsterdam and Copenhagen have found that the idea became too popular. They then cut back the access to subsidized

TIME BUDGETS AND TRANSACTIONS

Table 5
A Minimum Adequate Standard of Living, 1973

	South Asia	California
Body size of typical mature adult	50 kg	75 kg
Dietary allowance (population average)	2,300 cal/day	3,000 cal/day
Food Cost		
Protein: 20 and 30 kg/yr of which 10 and 20% meat, fish, eggs[a]	Rs. 215/yr.	$66/yr
Carbohydrates: 300 and 360 g/day	110	22
Fats: 50 g/day	15	2
Fruits and vegetables: 0.5 and 1.0 kg/day	240	145
Total food cost	Rs. 580	$235
Rent		
Enclosed floorspace, 6 and 8 m^2 per capita	380	$80
Add 20 and 30% for furnishings	55	24
Total Housing	Rs. 435	$104
Utilities		
Electric: 12 and 25 kwh/cap/mo[b]	Rs. 85	$7
Water: 50 kg/day upward	25	2
Heat	none	10
Telephone (shared with 4 and 1.5 others)	125	30
Cable television: color (shared with 5 and 2 others)[c]	400	130
Total utilities	Rs. 635	$179
Household and personal		
Cleaning, utensils, paint, repair, etc.	Rs. 100	$15
Apparel: 4 and 6 kg cloth, sandals and shoes	300	75
Laundry (100 kg/yr)	50	10
Haircuts	20	30
Newspapers (400/yr, shared)	15	7
Postage (30 letters)	10	3
Total	Rs. 495	$140
Transport		
Local (200 and 300 rides/yr)[d]	Rs. 100	$75
Intercity	50	50
Total transport	Rs. 150	$125

Health		
1 prof., 2 subprof., 2 techn., and 5 ordinary per 1,000 persons	Rs. 70	$130
Medicinals and supplies	70	20
Total health (Life expectancy 65 and 73 yrs)	Rs. 140	$150
Education		
10 years and 12.5 years, 300 and 250 students/1,000	Rs. 300	$125
Urban services		
Police, fire, traffic control, waste removal, etc.	Rs. 50	$20
Social insurance		
Disability, old age (add 5%)	Rs. 150	$54
Minimum adequate standard of living[e]	Rs. 3235	$1134

[a]The added animal protein is in part complementary to the added input of vegetables, in part due to body size, but mostly attributable to cultural differences.

[b]This figure is highly variable. No allowance for water pumping is made here, but merely cooking, fluorescent lighting, fans, solid-state electronic equipment, and light motors.

[c]Assumes a modern system that can be linked to the telephone on some occasions. The most convenient arrangements for video taping are not defined as yet, so this charge may be a low estimate. The South Asian version is assumed to be much more labor intensive.

[d]Independent of pedestrian and bicycle trips. The American rate is higher because of necessarily lower urban density for economical solution, which in turn is attributable to larger body size and a cultural background that puts a high value upon spaciousness.

[e]Omits cultural activities beyond those included in education, television service, and travel. Cultural activities can be the least demanding upon scarce resources, so will be promoted heavily as sources of urban employment. Some of these may later be incorporated in the minimum adequate standard, but no estimate can be made now.

facilities. Incidents like this cause us to attribute "true costs" to service provided to added population, rather than the reported price. Usually the "fair share" of expense is a per capita calculation, but occasionally marginal price costing is applicable because it determines changes in budgetary allocations and sometimes market price. The basic idea is to find a figure for time needed for self-support that is neither parasitic upon the urban society nor an exploitation of the stranger by the city. Therefore one should also make an allowance for the nonparticipants in the labor force for whose support a worker is responsible, so that each is expected to work long enough to support his fair share of the dependents in the population, which normally ranges from 1.4 to 2.1 per registered employee.

In an Indian city, where the marginal worker makes 20-30 rupees for a 48-hour week, the wage is not really enough to support more than one other person even under the humblest conditions. More can survive only by squatting virtually rent-free on undefended land or by depending upon a partially subsidized food ration. Spare time must be spent scrounging for a little extra income, looking for salvageable building materials, or contributing time to some kind of communal organization in return for services. Thus, at a subsistence level of living an individual worker at the margin may support himself plus the two others that depend upon him on the average (often residing at a distance in a village where essential services are much cheaper than in a city, and his remittances supply the dependents with their cash requirements) with about 50-70 hours of time commitment per week. A minimum adequate level is achieved only by the minor fraction of the population who get well established in the urban economic system.

Compare this with California, where hundreds of thousands of people have opted to live modestly within the matrix of a highly organized and productive urban society. The subsistence level of living can be purchased in the market economy of California for about $400 per capita per year. The diet might consist of maize, beans, flour, vegetable oil, sugar, spice, and garden produce; the rent is for unproductive land at the periphery of the city in salvaged shelter without electrical connections; transport is by foot or on a truck that takes one to work or to the town center; health, educational, and nonmarket services are paid for at cost as provided. For illiterate or barely literate workers, who can legally claim the minimum wage, this subsistence level can be achieved for themselves and one and a half others dependent on them with ten to twelve hours of work per week, including time spent on the garden. Life at subsistence is deemed a public nuisance, however, and people living that way find themselves in violation of many ordinances having to do with sanitation, housing, safety, licensing, and the like.

The minimum adequate standard of living in California would not provide much in the way of convenience, because many instances of delay and nonresponse in the delivery of goods and services would be encountered. Nevertheless, it is possible to select such goods and services and to find suitable niches in the metropolitan areas. Typically, it would involve operating a small garden to back up a diet restricted to vegetable proteins with a bit of fish and chicken, starches based upon pastas, biscuits, rice, and bread, and fruit at the peak of the season. Housing would be shared with others and limited to low-rent districts. Transport would be by bicycle, bus, or mass transit. Health insurance would be charged at standard rates and education be bought at cost up to 12.5 years, which is the average. These costs of living appear to be in the neighborhood of $1,100 per capita per year, while labor with such levels of education should be able to claim an average urban wage, which in 1973 runs about $5.50 per hour plus fringe benefits that vary with the circumstances and may not have value to the marginal worker. The average worker in California should support about 1.3 extra persons as dependents. Thus about ten hours of work per week is necessary on the job. A few hours of work in the garden should be added to this, and an indefinite number of hours waiting for rides and public services. At this earning rate, however, many would find that buying fresh produce from a supermarket is more efficient than gardening for themselves.

Obviously, Americans work much longer than is necessary. Why do they do it? It appears that most are caught in a status game, whereby people must display symbols of success in order to establish or maintain their prestige. These symbols often require consumption at a high rate (autos, large houses, exotic foods, out-of-town travel, sporting equipment). Others wish to build up a surplus to be used for future security. A surprisingly large number of people, probably increasing over time, get more satisfaction out of their job than they would get out of alternative leisure, disregarding the pay. The fact that work has become fun does not diminish its economic productivity.

It is possible to put together a time budget for a society that distinguishes between things that people feel compelled to do, in order to maintain their property, their standard of living, the safety and welfare of dependents, and their place in society, from those things that they undertake voluntarily for personal gratification (sleeping, eating, relaxing), which are labeled as consumption. Thus James Morgan and his co-workers were able to take into account women's work in running a household and rearing children, men's work in maintaining property, time lost due to the journey to work and waiting in queues, and work done in helping others. They could attribute a money value to this effort, based upon the wage rate for the best alternative marketable work, so as to arrive at a new and corrected figure for the GNP. The findings from such a survey did not suggest any major hidden discrepancies or injustices but did show that many more of the poor were engaged in self-help outside the marketplace that were the remainder of the population.[3] Simultaneously, by means of follow-up studies, the amounts of nonexchange transactions—the "grants economy" within family relationships and among friends—were estimated at 40% of the GNP in the United States for 1970.[4]

Many of the poor are found among the aging, and many others among the disabled. A high proportion of these people have withdrawn from competition in the status game; they are content with extracting a minimum adequate level of living from the socioeconomic system. An increasing number of young people are adopting the same attitude. It is perfectly possible to live adequately on incomes that are well below the official poverty line in the United States, but it requires sophisticated consumership and residence in unpopular locales.

THE CITY AS A SYSTEM OF TRANSACTIONS

The time budget approach to social accounting is needed much more for identifying the "free time" activities that need to be expedited in cities. The most fundamental satisfactions and dissatisfactions with urban life seem to be based upon the range of opportunities provided by the city for the use of spare time. How does one gauge improvement in opportunities? People themselves must be the judges of what is rewarding. Note that when they choose to use their time a *transaction* results between two or more parties or between a party and the environment. People appear to be alert and happily participating in cultural affairs when a relatively high frequency of transactions is observed; they are apathetic and dour, possibly also fearful, when the frequency is low.

Before proceeding any further, the term *transaction* should be defined. It can be said that the metropolis produces *action*; in general, the more action it fosters, the more attractive the city. A transaction is a countable package of action with a beginning and an end, a purpose or meaning, and a transfer of information. It could be a trip, a telephone call, a lecture, a face-to-face exchange, or even the recognition of a cue in the environment that enabled one to reorient himself. For each observable transaction, reports could be made regarding *who, when, where, what* transpired, *how,* the quantities transferred between parties, the *linkages* with prior and succeeding transactions, and, occasionally, other pertinent information. The average employed person in the United States in the mid-1960s was estimated to be engaging in about 150 transactions per day in various public arenas including absorption of messages transmitted through the mass media, while people working as professionals would normally be operating at about twice the average level.[5]

Life at school is organized so as to produce a large number of public transactions. Life in the cities of developing countries is much lower than that. The telephone and the mass media are much less available, women and children are kept at home much more, and the social networks—the set of people and organizations with which one normally acts on a basis of mutual acquaintanceship—are smaller and less diverse. But healthy people, given free time and access to both transport and communications channels, will quickly find reasons for initiating transactions, and they gain great satisfaction from their completion.

If it is to promote human welfare, a city should become a transactions-maximizing system. Each social transaction is undertaken in the expectation that both parties would gain from its completion; therefore, the greater the transactions, the greater is the expected gain. A purchase, for example, is expected to be more valuable to the buyer than holding on to the cash. Each conversation entered into voluntarily adds to the information held by the participants; indeed, close analysis shows that most conversations may be regarded as positive sum games. Each contact with the environment, natural or artificial, produces knowledge about the real world. We may conclude from this argument that as long as the *quality* of the respective transactions is maintained, increases in the number per capita per unit time should result in richer lives for citizens and visitors.

What can be said about trends in the quality of a transaction? Normally, if the expectations of gain have not been fulfilled, for both parties, that kind of transaction is less likely to be tried again. Thus declining quality leads to reduced frequency and an exploration of alternatives when and if they appear. That is a good overall indicator. However, analysis shows that if the cost of entering into a transaction (measured in time or effort) is reduced, the prospects for gain are increased. Thus urban infrastructure is designed to interpose machinery, particularly telecommunications equipment, to speed up interaction between people when separated by space and time. Moreover, the noise level, frequency of error, and the likelihood of interruption—all of which contribute to the cost of transaction—are subject to control. If service is improved, the transaction rate should rise.

The city henceforth can make a major additional contribution. Many of the least valuable transactions—the necessary but routine, trivial, and boring demands upon attention—can be increasingly handed over to automata. This substitution releases time to search for more rewarding action and produces a net increase in the rate. Any metropolis that saves time creates the opportunity for greater satisfaction through cooperative behavior. The metropolis that provides such opportunity is an attractive place.

Transaction counts offer more direct indexes of performance for a metropolis than do measures of gross domestic product. They are easier to compile because the increasing use of equipment requires scheduling and programming—each subsystem makes continuous counts of its service, usually by automatic means—and the data must be compiled for managers and planners. The managers must be able to explain any reported slowdowns or shifts in activity, and the planners use the information for proposing additions to the infrastructure. From such data an "index of social product" could be prepared that aggregates social values more comprehensively than a gross domestic product revised with the aid of time budgets. Differences in social product, on a per capita basis, between city and country should be markedly greater than differences in income. Presumably differences between cities would also be highly significant.

If such an index based upon transactions were to be prepared, planners would be likely to use it for preparing better cost-benefit proposals for new projects. Agencies involved in settling conflicts would use similar arguments to justify their decisions. However, as the uses are probed, it becomes apparent that transactions build up long-term effects that must also be weighed.

Skeptics will hold certain reservations concerning a transactions-maximization policy for cities. For example, some transactions (such as gambling) tend to be addictive. Others may set up struggles and active feuds that polarize populations and destroy trustful relations, so that a current spurt of transactions results in a reduction over the long run. Still others are exploitive, in that one party captures virtually all the benefits from an exchange, and the resulting inequities start inhibiting further transactions. Many types of such transactions are defined as crimes. Another kind of transaction to be avoided is the accident, since losses due to human error are, by definition, significant. Finally, if the rate of transaction becomes so high for some people that the demands for transaction queue up and the queues get longer, additional errors are made, and stress builds up in both the responder and the initiator of transactions.[6]

One can gain a sense of some of the difficulties of using transaction rate as an index of city performance by observing the daily volumes on the stock exchanges that deal only in the ownership of capital. Short-run bursts of speculation on the part of small investors have the appearance of a fad or social epidemic, but the consequences do not seem to be cumulative or constructive. At certain turning points for the society, such as the projected upswing of the business cycle or a sweeping reduction of tariffs and quotas, the larger holders of securities tend to redistribute their portfolios, with strong acceleration of the volume of transactions. It is only the long-range trend independent of such fluctuations that signifies healthy growth. The presence of

more shares, bonds, and warrants of more firms with a
greater range in size inevitably results in a volume of transactions that is enlarged by less fluctuating.

CREATING
VIABLE
ORGANIZATIONS

A still more sensitive test for judging the performance of
the physical and institutional environment of a metropolis
is to consider the degree to which it provides the setting
for the synthesis of organizations, outside the marketplace
as well as within. Self-organization is a process whereby
people voluntarily associate themselves with each other in
order to achieve something worthwhile to the members,
but at the same time they create an entity with a life of
its own—a date of founding, a name, an address at which
it can be reached, and a basis for engaging in social transactions as a unit. In law, the organization is treated as a
person with special characteristics and responsibilities
depending upon its charter.

The social process of creating new organization follows
upon a history of prior transactions between principals;
they built up levels of trust in each other as well as a
common set of expectations regarding the behavior of
others, and that experience allowed them to discover a
common interest that would be served by a given form of
association. If the organization does not create added value,
it dissolves; therefore, its continued life indicates that
either extra values are being contributed to the participants
or they remain confident that such returns will be forthcoming. The organizations stimulate social transactions
among their members by providing settings that expedite
the flow of specialized kinds of such transactions. Organizations are countable things, once a practical definition
of viability is established; even those in the underworld
can be inferred, because they will be given a name.

Defining an organization with a minimum of ambiguity
is as difficult as defining the smallest biological units of
life. Since the typical organization is observed every day,
the way the biologist sees cells and organisms, the central
concept is readily comprehended. The difficulty appears
in deciding between an inert and nonorganized entity and
an organized one. We shall call an organization any collection of people—two or more in number—who transact as
a unit in public with others. In order to do this, they need
(1) a name, (2) an address, even if shifting, and (3) at least
one responsible officer. Thus a household is an organiza-

tion. Also branches, offices, bureaus, and divisions in a
bureaucracy can be regarded a separate organizations. A
school is an organization, but a class in that school may or
may not be one, depending upon the manner in which it
functions. An active urban resident may participate in ten
or more different organizations, being relieved of some
responsibilitles by the fact that some are dormant and
called back to life in the event of a threat (such as a volunteer fire brigade). Most people have difficulty recalling all
the organizations they belong to, unless the interviewer
carries with him a check list of all the various categories
known to exist in the culture. If organizations are regarded
as producers and distributors of values, then surveys like
this are needed to discover the extent of the distribution
of such values, particularly of the nonmarket type.

Modernization, industrialization, fertility control, and
polyarchy all imply shifts away from household operations
typical of the traditional society; functions that were
implicit, almost unspoken, and the ties that were as invisible as those that bind a species to a community within
an ecosystem are now made explicit and are sometimes
controlled through licensing. Urban society takes on the
appearance of a jumble of special-purpose organizations—
firms, cooperatives, corporations, clubs, societies, associations, unions, teams, units, offices, branches, parishes,
ensembles, syndicates, gangs, and so on.

Each society evolves a number of organizations where
the mutual obligations, rewards, and incentives are patterned differently than exist elsewhere in the world. The
way in which musicians come together, for example, is
very diverse. Nevertheless, their survival in the city in
competition with imported cosmopolitan organizations
causes their identity to be sharpened, redefined, and very
often introduces a core of specified relationships such as
keeping records, balancing books, preparing some kind of
charter or statement of purposes and formal rules for the
selection and replacement of officers.

Planners of urban development therefore have available
a welfare phenomenon that can be isolated—representable
by several different kinds of counts of organizations (e.g.,
business, social, cultural, and religious) that reflect human
responses to opportunities in infrastructure and institutions. Each of these organizations is a multiplier and
expeditor of transactions. As long as the size distribution

of organizations remains roughly constant, as it should during conditions of growth, the expansion in the number of viable organizations should be a more sensitive indicator of welfare than existing measures, a better predictor of future conditions than investment rates, and, at the same time, simpler to assemble. Planning implies intervention into the affairs of the city in order to prevent bad things from recurring, pointing the way to better harmony in human activity. Since passing a law is seldom effective by itself, officials need other levers for implementation of plans, and the identification of organizations can serve this purpose. Planners may seek the cooperation of existing organizations, or they may serve as midwives at the birth of new ones that are designed to be more effective.

Whenever extraordinary growth and development has occurred in the postwar period on a regional scale, one can find an unusual kind of organization at the center of things. This kind of organization has undertaken to sponsor the creation of other organizations. To do this, it will search for new niches for enterprise, find groups willing to undertake that specialized activity, work informally as an advocate to remove obstructions imposed by the bureaucracy, become well informed on recruitment (particularly of the labor force) and locational risks, arrange for credit if it is needed, and act as troubleshooter in times of distress.

Perhaps the most studied instance is that of Puerto Rico, a quasi-independent territory with 2,500,000 people in the Caribbean. Puerto Rico emerged from World War II with population density and slums equal to the worst found in Asia and with virtually no resources upon which to base industrial development. Because of the efforts of its Planning Board and its "Fomento," Operation Bootstrap was launched—a campaign in which they diligently sought out initiators of organizations. Its publicity indicated that it sponsored new industries that would better organize the work of Puerto Ricans and make them more productive, but closer study revealed that it assisted in the birth of private schools, laboratories, design studios, hotels, gourmet kitchens, labor unions, community associations, yacht clubs, and many other strange nonindustrial organizations.[7] The success (Puerto Rico has since risen to the top tier of development in Latin America) is attributable to the num-

ber and range of organizations that survived as a result of
the incentives provided or the assistance given. As is common in many fields of science, I shall refer to the general
phenomenon by the popular name of the first instance
that has been fully described.

In Japan the equivalent agency has been the Ministry of
International Trade and Industry (MITI), but its style was
utterly different. MITI set up missions for investigating
markets overseas, for collecting statistics internally, for
supervising quality control of output, and for backing up
regular extensions of credit. It negotiations and many of
its operations remained private, almost secretive, but the
conditions for the appearance and growth of tightly knit
Japanese industries was managed, mostly by preventing
existing organizations from becoming their own worst
enemies, with superlative success.[8]

In South Korea, the Ministry of Construction was important in the beginning of their record-breaking development, but soon several other key agencies, especially
the Mayor's Office of Seoul, followed suit. In laissez faire
Hong Kong it was a group of merchants and bankers within
the Chamber of Commerce. In Singapore it was the Economic Development Board. In all instances a close look
reveals, not one organization-stimulating organization,
but several, with interlocking directorates and complementary responsibilities. The successful ones have a
sophisticated, information-rich, quick-acting approach to
the bottlenecks for organization inherent to that locale.

The promotion of organizations can be understood best
in terms of the life history of a typical success. Such an
organization is founded in the full knowledge that it was
preceded by attempts that failed and dissolved. This time
an improved formula for the commitment of time, effort,
and financial resources results in services that are more
widely appreciated, and more people are trained and coordinated for their production. The result is surplus value,
or social profit, sufficient to make up for the prior investment and the losses incurred in the previous unsuccessful
attempts.

A representation of the Fomento-like organization-promoting organization that is rewarded with prestige and
funds if it stimulates viable organizations is offered in
figure 10.3. It sifts data from the urban environment that

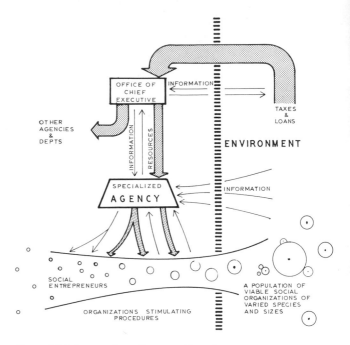

Figure 10.3 Context for a Fomento-Type Agency
Scarce resources and information can be directed to social entrepreneurs so as to enhance the viability of their organizations and
increase the likelihood of producing surplus value. The existence of
new organizations that promote the welfare of members also
enriches the socioeconomic environment. The increased activity
and wealth can be taxed so as to provide a basis for expanding
public services. If the agency appears successful, it will be able to
justify enlarged subventions for the promotion of more organizations, thus accelerating economic, social, and cultural growth until
the dissipative forces (not shown) become significant. Successfully
developing countries have created several very different versions
of the organizations-stimulating agency.

suggest where niches for new organizations probably exist, identifies people who are capable of becoming social entrepreneurs, makes sure that they have access to the latest technology, the right kind of workers and suppliers, the most advantageous location, sufficient credit, and often some kind of official incentive, such as a tax holiday. The aim is to maximize the overall social profit, making sure that the entrepreneur receives enough to keep him interested, but the remainder is distributed widely throughout the society.

Rather than drawing upon history, I shall try to describe how such an agency might work in the near future, using the opportunities open to a metropolis—if it badly wants to develop but is constrained by a scarcity of resources, a history of frustration, and intense social and political pressures. The relatively novel technique of gaming simulation has been employed to illuminate the potentials.

Bombay was chosen for carrying out more detailed tests of the model for developing high-output cities because it appears ready: it is a coastal metropolis that could undertake the same kind of developmental thrust that was registered over the last decade or two by Tokyo, Seoul, Singapore, Hong Kong, and a few lesser cities in the Far East. Moreover, if Bombay finds a formula for regional takeoff in social and economic development, other major metropolitan areas would try to follow it, particularly Ahmedabad-Cambay, Cochin-Ernakulam, Madras, Vishakhapatnam, and perhaps a part of the Punjab around Ludhiana. Even lethargic Calcutta could be stung into action. In neighboring and, to some extent, competing countries, Dacca, Karachi, Lahore, and perhaps Colombo would be stimulated to plan in self-defense, undertaking their own versions of accelerated development. Meanwhile, quite independently and almost totally out of contact, Djakarta, Saigon, and Manila are expected to be mobilizing for development; they are smaller, less well connected, and initially disadvantaged as compared to Bombay, but any of them could still become a pacesetter. Finally, just as significant as the above arguments for choosing Bombay is the fact that the metropolis has reached a turning point. It has been presented with some unique opportunities for physical expansion that give it an unusually good chance for leadership.

SCENARIO EIGHT

Building the
New Bombay

Bombay was founded on an archipelago that was converted into a peninsula as the city grew. Expanding northward toward the hills and tidal flats, Greater Bombay has already packed more than six million people into houses, apartments, and tenements, far beyond their planned capacity. It has now been handed a chance to expand across a shallow bay, called Thana Creek, to occupy its eastern shore and the valleys and hillsides beyond. The industrial development corporation of the state of Maharashtra created the City and Industrial Development Corporation (CIDCO) to take over and develop the land for urban purposes. CIDCO promptly began to assemble the largest urban and regional planning organization in South Asia. The task at hand is clearly the most complex encountered in that country, although it is still small as compared to what needs to be undertaken in the near future. The existing population on the land is rural, thinly distributed, and not highly productive; thus the resistance of the displaced populations seems to offer no serious impediment, even though it is headline-catching in the initial stages. Hundreds of modern industries banned from Bombay because of existing congestion and overcrowding are clamoring for a chance to locate in the trans-Creek area, if the regular urban services of water, power, telephone, transport, housing, education, sanitation, and police protection are provided at standards sufficient to allow them to produce goods of export quality.

Preparations for planning were carried out in a way that avoided earlier mistakes in Indian metropolitan planning. Civic groups, leading families, and top administrators were involved along with local politicians in an extended discussion of what was called the "Twin City proposal," because the scale was so large. Quite early, a small group of private architects and planners created and published a glamorous counterplan, which required discussion and led to a merging of several independent themes of imaginative effort. Because the leaders became involved in planning for their city, instead of struggling with a plan laid down by higher authorities, the principal sources of political opposition to change had been induced to consider compromise solutions rather than fight for perfection. Massive quantities of outside help, such as was given in the instances of Calcutta, Delhi, and the Green Revolution in the past, were no longer needed or desired, because Indian universities and institutes had begun producing graduates with the requisite basic training, and this meant fewer delays due to misunderstandings between the United Nations, AID, the Ford Foundation, and other technical assistance groups and the Indian staff who would eventually make the decisions, implement them, and be responsive to the critics. Thus the conditions as of 1971 were rather auspicious for bold action as compared to competing metropolitan areas.

How should CIDCO act if it used the land-development opportunity to advance human organization for all of Bombay and to aim the new growth so that it could support a minimum adequate standard of living for all residents? Obviously CIDCO cannot accept such goals and methods as yet because the principles are too new and untested. It is forced to plan according to principles promulgated twenty years ago and taught in leading schools starting ten years ago because such professionals can take responsible positions on its staff. Because of the inadequacy of past approaches CIDCO will often be forced to improvise, and learn by doing, if it is to succed at all; only when it is improvising is it allowed to borrow from contemporary thinking. It is possible to set forth a scenario portraying what might be expected if the resource-conserving proposals elaborated in the preceding pages were to be implemented and a strategy for the stimulation of self-organization adopted. Comparing the outcome with future planning documents would be fruitful for other planners.

In this case the scenario has been produced as the outgrowth of an experiment that aimed to incorporate as much political realism as possible in a projection. Two classes of twenty-five to thirty graduate students from many countries and many professions absorbed the available data concerning Bombay, including its relationships to India and the rest of the world (Bombay still prides itself on being the gateway to India). Their location in the University of California, Berkely, with a large and relatively complete library available because of publications obtained according to provisions of Public Law 480, enabled them to comprehend the large picture perhaps more clearly than was possible in Bombay. The local detail and the opportunity to see the places scheduled for change and contact the influential figures in public affairs, strongly influence the local agency, but the superiority of their understanding was reduced by setting the starting date ahead several years into the future. The student professionals studied factors affecting the survival of modern organizations in a Bombay environment and then proposed a population of new organizations to be initiated that seemed to have the best chances for growth and multiplication. They were aided in this exercise of imagination by the strong physical and industrial similarity of the San Francisco Bay region to Bombay, where Bombay in the 1970s produced about as many transactions as metropolitan San Francisco in the era of the ferries (early 1930s); so organizations added to the Bay area thereafter would be considered as nominees for the Bombay context. Would a new version be able to survive and grow in modern India? The gaming simulation was conducted at the end of these highly concentrated studies.

The procedure for gaming divided the students into teams representing the crucial political forces affecting metropolitan growth:
1. The national government (Centre).
2. The state government (State of Maharashtra).
3. The organization-promoting metropolitan agency (CIDCO).
4. The local private sector (Bombay Chamber of Commerce).
5. The world sector influentials (Multinational corporations).
Each team was given a set of stated objectives in line with the real situation as reported from India. They were to act upon authority granted in constitutions and charters within limits set by capital resources estimates drawn from the Five-Year Plan and the Perspective Plan, with certain additional discretionary quantities that could be directed to Bombay if the expected returns were clearly much larger than elsewhere in India or the world. Each team was expected to achieve its own ends at the same time that it recognized that the results depended in large part upon the maintenance of balanced development in Bombay. Thus the policies of the Centre and the State of Maharashtra were calculated so as to maintain the New Congress Party in power, and for both groups Bombay's development was only one claimant among many. The starting date was set at 1974.

While preparing a list of organizations that were "ripe" for founding at this stage in Bombay's history, the students quickly discovered an ecology of organizations and saw that they were faced with issues of what might be called "managed succession" in applied ecology. A number of new organizations could grow up as soon as a large facility had expanded to the point of stabilizing a locale or provided basic services (e.g., a new harbor results in a back-of-the-harbor complex of industries, services, neighborhoods, recreations, enterprises, and labor unions, but the variety of activities is expanded still further if a free trade zone is organized in part of the harbor district). Moreover, a sequential development, a series of differentiated "growth rings," could be indentified. An easily understood example is that of an oil refinery that makes possible fertilizer and petrochemicals, which in turn permit detergents, synthetic rubber, plastics, and paints, and these allow the production of tires, packaging, synthetic yarns, prefabricated panels for houses, and various pharmaceuticals. Therefore, CIDCO could economically generate new organizations by considering them as interdependent clusters and complexes and obtain a multiplication of benefits from its promotional effort by stimulating core activities. This is an old idea in industrialization, but too often before the associated non-market activities were not counted, and therefore virtually ignored, and ultimately this neglect led to a serious reduction in the potential benefits obtainable.

The better-known clusters included industrial estates, petrochemical complexes, business districts, and harbors (see figure 10.4). New clusters that depended upon the site and special opportunities had to be added for Bombay's future. Examples include (1) an end-of-the-ferry assemblage; (2) a telecommunications-computer development park; (3) a recreation-with-popular-education facility; (4) a multischool estate with playing fields; (5) a hilltop-hillside complex based upon the spinoff from electronic equipment now installed on metropolitan hilltops; (6) a fisheries-mariculture-oceanographic-studies-marina-recreational resort combination (see figure 10.5); (7) an urban village constellation of organizations; (8) a settlement house sponsoring organizations among newest inmigrants; (9) a community chest of voluntary service groups; and (10) a flock of audiovisual production groups producing for cable television. Each proposed organization could be assigned a likelihood of survival, with the infant mortality

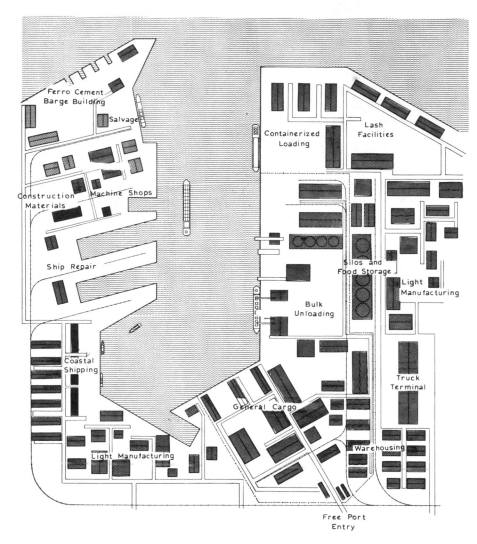

Figure 10.4 Complex with Heavy Industry at the Land-Sea Interface
This industrial community fitted together for New Bombay development resembles harbor
district solutions applicable elsewhere. Much of the industrial complex is forced to operate
multiple shifts in order to use the capital-intensive facilities efficiently. Wherever the tide
differential is great, as in Inchon (port of Seoul), the entrance to the harbor may be equipped
with canal-type locks.

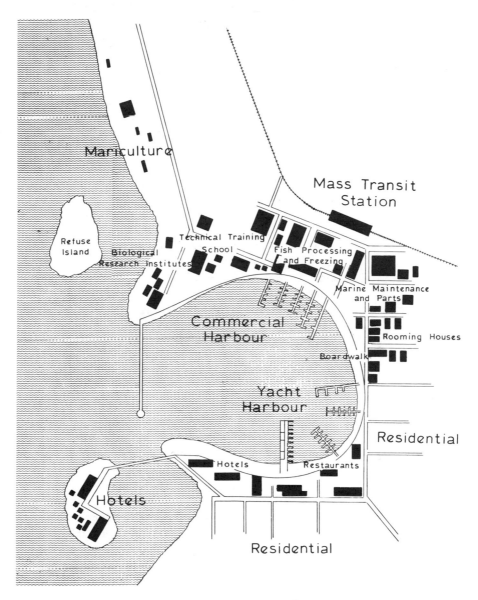

Figure 10.5 An Urban Complex Built around Fisheries and Mariculture
Example of a specialized urban community that can contribute significantly to food production within the metropolis. Warm water from a power plant on a nearby peninsula or island speeds up the growing of plankton, clams, oysters, shrimp, finfish, lobster, kelp, and abalone near the shoreline. Fish preservation facilities can be used jointly with deep sea fisheries, and the harbor development is supported by recreational uses.

What Cities Produce from Natural Resources   393

for firms in India maintained at the historic rate of 50% over the first two to three years after launching, though cooperatives and associations were known to be more vulnerable. Survival could then be determined by a table of random numbers.

Each proposed organization required the collection of information related to the activity in order to make estimates of effects upon the future metropolis. The following questions were considered: (1) What activity (or whom) does it organize? (2) Is it a firm, cooperative, community, agency, association, club, union, or something else? (3) Does it belong to the food-producing category, light manufacturing, heavy manufacturing, transport, educational, sociocultural, commercial, utility, or other? (4) To what cluster is it assigned? (5) What are the expected finance requirements and sources? (6) What are the land area and site requirements? (7) Is the employment mostly modern or mostly traditional, and how many in each category are likely to be involved? (8) What range of demand upon scarce resources is implied: large (where demand must be quantified), medium, small, or trivial? The scarce resources considered were water, access (in trips per day to congested centers), and risk capital. (9) Is this project dependent upon the success of some prior project? (10) What additions to urban potentials or export possibilities would result, if any? (11) What other critical features are inherent in the proposal that will affect success or failure—especially what kinds of political agreement are necessary?

Simultaneously a list of possible external events was prepared, each with a likelihood suggested by experts attached to it. For example, the reopening of the Suez Canal was judged to have a 0.7 likelihood of occurring in the first cycle (a two-to-three-year period) and 0.5 in each cycle thereafter. (It "happened" in both runs of the simulation.) Similarly, there were such events as a blight on the wheat, an assassination plot on political leaders, a pill guaranteeing birth of sons rather than daughters, and a Kashmir war similar to the war in Vietnam, each of which would have affected the viability of some of the proposed organizations in a predictable fashion.

After bargaining between the teams took place, a certain population of organizations was launched; some capital, access, and land were committed. Some of the assets were lost through bankruptcies and failures as decided by ex-

ternal events and random numbers. The resultant viable
population of new organizations would almost certainly
be imbalanced. "Newspapers" were prepared in advance to
transmit the headlines describing the protests of groups
in the population who felt ill-served as a consequence of
the imbalance. The one that came the closest to describing
responses to the imbalance obtained was immediately
distributed to the teams. On the basis of the apparent
efficiency with which investment capital was used, a new
allocation was assigned by a game director's group to each
team. With this capital they were expected to bargain for
a new cohort of organizations that would rectify the previous imbalance and cope with new external events. Those
proposed organizations could be either replacements for
previous failures, other projects from the previously prepared stockpile, or newly improvised proposals that filled
unexpected gaps. Again a table of random numbers determined which succeeded and which failed, and a new imbalance was produced.

On both occasions a significant part of the maximum
capital resources that could be released to Bombay from
Centre, State, Chambers of Commerce, and Multinationals
was not employed. The metropolis missed by a large
measure coming up to its true output potential. The
underlying reason in the first game was that the chief
minister of Maharashtra was disturbed by the political
effects of the promotional publicity needed by CIDCO
in order to develop its land to its highest value. The
majority of Maharashtra voters would feel that Bombay
with its new growth was too favored and was also
becoming too alien; so he held back much state participation in Bombay's development at the same time that their
prime minister in the CENTRE backed it. Simultaneously,
an active Bombay ad hoc public health group persuaded
the remainder of the CENTRE team that family planning
should be invested in much more heavily than the prime
minister had planned.

In the second instance of playing the game the student
stand-in for Indira Gandhi decided to implement as much
as possible the postelection statements of policy. A major
consequence was the de-emphasized interest in dealing with
Multinationals and a marked underuse of the expanding
potentials available from international trade. In the
last cycle the frustrated executives in the Multinationals

team decided to do their best to cause a change in government; thus they undertook (following a long Indian tradition started by the large landowners) to finance the publications and agitation of opposition parties, even if they were anarchist or Maoist and anti-business in ideology. Meanwhile CIDCO recognized somewhat belatedly that its land was a most remarkable asset that could produce much public profit for an overcrowded Bombay if it engaged in very active negotiation with other parties and in promotion of both employment-producing and housing organizations. One clique of students set out to reduce apathy and anomie among new inmigrants and low-income components of the population by creating special agencies to stimulate voluntary self-help groups. They were appalled to discover the effects of the high mortality rate among such organizations, recognizing that most of their efforts were wasted. They had encountered one of the fundamental problems of organizing the poor— those that fail to self-organize stay poor, while those that succeed move up and out as individuals. They graduate from the school of hard knocks in the slums and join the lower ranks of the establishment.

One simulation brought Bombay up to 1980 and the other to about 1982. In these instances the political difficulties reduced the capital investment level to 50-60% of the maximum available supply, including what could be brought in through the Multinationals (which we defined to include the World Bank and other official agencies, although the group is dominated by private corporations and banks). Nevertheless, the simulated Bombay grew, particularly in modern employment. Its income and population increased to a degree somewhat more rapid than in the past. Parts of its society remained badly off, and the frustration level was high. If, by some miracle, a favorable arrangement of political forces was found, within a few years the feedbacks should resemble the headlines about development that have occurred in some cities in the Far East. The "newsflash" prepared for that eventuality is of particular interest. It describes conditions to be expected when the takeoff is underway at full momentum. The code word DYN-URB refers to the dynamic urbanization outcome of the decision making, and is, of course, the most rewarding of the possible alternatives.

Game of FOMENTO
DYN-URB
NEWSFLASH
CIDCO reports that 52 major organizations (each greater
than a thousand members or a hundred fulltime employees
within the first year) settled in Greater Bombay last year,
as compared to 41 last year and 35 the year before that.
Organizations maintaining mailing addresses increased by
17% last year, while those added to the telephone directory
increased by 21%.
Surveys show that the number of trips made in Greater
Bombay actually increased by 10% last year as against an
estimated population increase of 8%. The Metropolitan
Transport Commission warns that more equipment must
be ordered immediately or breakdown due to congestion
will occur along D. N. Road and at Ferry Terminal.
Bombay's vigorous mayor receives strong backing from
the Chief Minister of Maharashtra in his program to eliminate encroachment upon public spaces by small shopkeepers, public markets, hawkers, and beggars. Circulation in the region is noticeably improved, and the city is
rated the cleanest metropolis in India.
The Maharashtra Industrial Development Corporation
(parent of CIDCO and a variety of other promotional
units) reports a consolidated accumulation of 550 crores
of assets, as against 810 crores of bonds still outstanding
and retains full title to 50,000 acres in the valuable Bombay metropolitan area. It has also granted its millionth
homestead privilege for self-help housing, having made
available more than 25,000 acres, and leased almost
200,000 more for intensive gardening.
The great burning issue of the period is what to do about
starting five new metropolises along the coast that begin
as satellites to Bombay. Can India build multimillion-size
cities from towns in only a decade?

What the simulation uncovered more than anything else
is the significance of *openness* for the development of a
metropolis. A large share of the useful production and
marketing knowledge exists elsewhere in the world, and
it can most quickly be put to work by collaborating with
a multinational corporation. Some of the most vital investments can be assured only by using the risk-reducing
techniques of the international banks, and they, in turn,
require continuous review in the early stages by visiting
experts, usually staff members or international consultants.
Reams of tabulated information must flow outward for
analysis prior to those visits. Unemployment, which is the
most fundamental kind of nonparticipation in urban organ-

ization, is now most readily treated by contracting out the services of surplus labor to the overemployed areas of the world—Japan and Western Europe. Branches, affiliates, and franchises of multinational firms can manufacture components, subassemblies, and even finished products if money, materials, people, and information can be moved easily across international boundaries. Simultaneously, the metropolis must be open to inmigrants from rural areas and to internal trade, especially remaining responsive to traditional institutions that direct public behavior in the countryside.

This same openness introduces grave risks to political leaders. It means that shocks are transmitted from the outside world into their constituencies, often without warning. The community appears to them to be rudderless, without control or direction. Openness results in both an erosion and a dilution of the constituency that backed them—because of a free flow of population. The political leaders are under great stress in any case because they must be modern men, capable of dealing with sophisticated outsiders, and yet must retain the trust of slightly educated people with traditional upbringing. Therefore, political leaders and bureaucrats respond very directly by seeking to reduce the risk somewhat by controlling through administrative restrictions the flow of money, goods, information, and people across political boundaries. With such actions they insulate themselves from external reality without recognizing that they are stifling the social and economic growth and diminishing the hopes for improving welfare.

Knowledgeable political leaders directing the affairs of developmental metropolises must learn to use the fruits of economic growth and improved social organization as a means for reducing vulnerability. This means that the planning agency, the stimulator of organizations, should be used as a source of information relevant to political decision making. Very likely its principal political role is that of identifying opportunities for retaining the loyalty of supporters and gaining new ones. The astute political leader recognizes that one of the functions of an organization is to exert pressure on behalf of its members where their interests are being frustrated. Thus the politician who learns to orchestrate a collection of pressure groups, making them an interdependent community, is the kind that is needed to lead during periods of maximum development. The surpluses produced through being open and opportunistic may be drawn upon to cope with the shocks transmitted from elsewhere in the world. Otherwise they are used to expedite internal growth and redistribution.

It is interesting to note that the automata do not seem to enter into this promotion-of-human-organization model of urban development in any significant way. Information transmission becomes exceedingly important, but it appears to be most valuable while it is timely but still crude and approximate. When information has been refined enough to be handled by computers, it seems to be supporting arrangements already settled upon within and among social organizations. The telephone system is exceedingly important, but automatic sensing, controlling, and processing equipment does not get high priority at interfaces between humans with real concerns. The automata seem to prosper in the back room, handling the routines or going organizations, while humans are busy at the organizational frontier synthesizing new arrangements for public order.

In conclusion then, we see that there are several answers to the query "What do cities produce from the natural resources they consume?" First, at the most fundamental level, it was shown that cities offer security for the survival of existing populations in the face of known sources of disaster. They are more robust than other communities in the ecosystem because they can mobilize resources from a great distance in times of peril.

At another level cities can, by careful distribution of scarce resources while assisted by advanced design, support increasing biomass per unit of resource. A proportionately larger yield in human numbers also results, and their appearance is paralleled by the emergence of new mechanical and cybernetic species. Census counts of all kinds will rise; only a few specialized, obsolete "species" will decline in number.

Efficient use of resources should result in even larger increases in interactions between individuals. The structure of the city fosters associations among the biota and between them and the machines. Thus we arrive at a more general unit of performance—transactions per unit time. Cities may wish to measure the action they promote either on a per capita basis or in terms of scarce resources.

At a still higher level of analysis most transactions are shown to result in interdependencies or bonds. These relationships may be mobilized to create and renew organizations. Therefore the propagation of adaptive, self-sustaining organizations with the potential of outliving their promoters and members is a more abstract output. Since they are an outgrowth of the savings from transactions, the population of viable organizations represents social capital. Organizations interact in a political system, a meta-eco-system, that must maintain a balance while gaining added competence. Measures of performance at this level are not yet readily available.

1. For a systematic analysis of big city government under conditions where large numbers of poor immigrants were being absorbed, but professionalization had not yet occurred, see Seymour Mandelbaum's *Boss Tweed's New York*. Cities like Bangkok have not progressed much further but others have already gone through several phases of urban reform.

2. Per capita averges tend to hide a wide distribution in household consumption levels. What had been repeatedly assumed was that the *range* of consumption would be narrowed (as in fig. 10.1). Also, the amounts to be made available would be sufficient to meet all the needs, but not enable very much consumption in excess of minimum adequate levels.

3. James N. Morgan, Ismael Sirageldin, and Nancy Baerwaldt, *Productive Americans* (Ann Arbor: Institute for Social Research, 1966).

4. Kenneth E. Boulding, Martin Pfaff, and Anita Pfaff, *Transfers in an Urbanized Economy: The Grants Economics of Income Distribution* (Belmont, Calif.: Wadsworth, 1973), p. 2. It offers some insights into Kenneth Boulding's forthcoming *The Economy of Love and Fear: A Preface to Grants Economics* and promises to cover the theory from private gifts to foreign aid.

5. R.L. Meier, "The Metropolis as a Transactions-Maximizing System," *Daedalus,* 97 (Fall 1968), 1292-1313; *A Communications Theory of Urban Growth* (Cambridge, Mass.: MIT Press, 1962); "Measuring Social and Cultural Change in Urban Regions," *Journal of the American Institute of Planners,* 25 (1959), 180-190.

6. R.L. Meier, "Communications Stress," *Annual Review of Ecology and Systematics,* 3 (1972), 289-314.

7. R.L. Meier, *Developmental Planning* (New York: McGraw-Hill, 1965), particularly the Introduction describing what Boulding called "the Fomentarian Revolution."

8. The Ministry of International Trade and Industry, referred to almost daily in the press of Japan as MITI, may be a partial exception in this list of crucial stimulators of industrial and economic growth. Although it played a vital role in the planning of strategic industrial growth and the identification of overseas markets, at the same time taking responsibility for quality control of exports, it often appeared to act as if it was a highly protectionist trade association that tended to delay international adjustments required of open economies. Perhaps one should give credit to the decision structure in Japan that integrated the government with industry, other agencies, labor unions, and banks. MITI often was the announced leader, but it did not always get along with decisions made by the international trade community of Japan, and sometimes was snubbed by enterprising *zaibatsu,* especially Mitsubishi,

the largest of them. Curiously, there seem to be no institutional histories of MITI, so there seems to be a clear preference for working behind the scenes. T. F. M. Adams and Iwao Hoshi, *A Financial History of the New Japan* (Tokyo: Kodansha, 1972).

GROWING THE GLOBAL METROPOLIS   Chapter 11

One of the most useful ways to test the feasibility of a
needed transition is that of tracing out a future somewhere
between the micro and the macro scales. In cities this would
be between the face-to-face community or the specialized
district and the national or continental levels, in much the
same way that a regional plan is interposed between the
national plan and the community plan. Tracing out an
expansion from existing nuclei of settlement into the total
life-space claimed to exist according to gross, averaged
calculations incorporated in the national plan draws much
local and highly relevant information into the planning
effort. The opportunities and hazards so revealed will
often deflect metropolitan regions from the courses of
development laid out for them by central planners.

A viable envelope for the growth of urbanism on the
Indian subcontinent was demonstrated to exist in principle
(if properly resource conserving), and its physical dimensions were illustrated in Chapter 4. Major shifts in behavior
were incorporated in the model, but when viewed in
aggregate they did not seem any more drastic than those
that have occurred in the past. On the other hand, if
the needed changes are discussed with observers of the
metropolitan region, one quickly gains the impression
that they are politically impossible to achieve. To those
who are acting in the arena of metropolitan politics, the
problems seem overwhelming. Their objections cause us
to look more closely at the political forces that seem to
stand in the way. What counterforces can be brought
into existence that might overcome or redirect the visible
opposition?

Persons absorbed in metropolitan affairs quite frequently
err in their judgments because they are unable to appraise
the effects of openness to world forces and the strengths
that it provides over the long run. Repeatedly in India,
Pakistan, Bangladesh, Indonesia, Egypt, and occasionally
in such places as Thailand, the Philippines, Ghana, and
Malaysia, the political impulse has been to simplify the
developmental milieu by excluding "undue" alien influences
in the hope of avoiding disturbing, uncontrolled social
change. What evidence is there that this reaction to potent
external forces is a miscalculation and diminishes future
prospects?

At least three different approaches can be taken to illuminate very different aspects of the growth of the metropolis as it progresses toward an interconnected world system. The first uses the gaming simulation as a working model of the internal situation and as a means of laying out plausible scenarios leading into one or more of the many possible futures. The second emphasizes the nature of the competition between metropolises and attempts to deduce market-type strategies that add to a city's control over its own destiny.[1] The third reviews the receptivity of the outs de physical or political world to overspills from the growing metropolises. If excessive crowding, overloads, new demands for recreation, or other needs for space are encountered in the course of growth, what are the opportunities presented by the external environment that allow cities to cope? Each of the above approaches draws upon existing models of systems analysis which have already been used in the discussions of technological feasibility and of global limits, but they allow some further generalization.

The structure of the future that affects cities embodies many of the characteristics of a self-fulfilling prediction. Thus if one or more metropolises find a successful path into a resource-conserving sequence of development, others will notice it. An outstanding success will breed an epidemic of imitation, some instances of which will improve upon the original. This policy-imitation process (with minor variations) transfers organizational innovations from one point to another on the globe with a normal lag of three to ten years. Therefore, out of a set of a hundred metropolises interested in social and economic development, we need at best a handful to make the essential moves in the beginning. Although Bombay is a leading nominee for setting the pace, it may happen that the politics of Ahmedabad, Lahore, or Djakarta will be more propitious. Gaming simulation, the first approach to charting development, will uncover choice-making behavior of people and firms when presented with innovations. A scenario of Bombay politics, plotted so as to progress in a strongly developmental direction, should have strong parallels in other cities.

Every growing metropolis is faced with some version of
the land shortage problem. As the gaming simulation of
Bombay continued into the 1980s, questions began to be
raised about the supply of land for new organizational
complexes. The land that had already been "notified"
was being used up. ("Notified" in India means that the
land is officially designated for public use with payments
for the value of land and building at that time remaining
to be negotiated; the occupant's status changes to that of
tenant subject to removal according to the needs of the
development authority, though in Bombay's case people
retained title to their homesteads in the villages and
towns.) At the 5-6% population growth rate that seemed
consonant with the installation of the infrastructure
allowed by the political conditions, the number of residents
in Greater Bombay would reach ten million by 1982-83.
Soon thereafter it would exceed that of Tokyo but would
still lack Tokyo's metropolitan services by a large measure.
Where was the new space to be found?

The next land that could be notified at Bombay's periphery was either tidal mud flat or quite hilly, even mountainous, forest. Both would be quite a bit more inconvenient to build upon and maintain. Access to the central
districts of Bombay could be fairly good for some of the
tidal flat surface, but for the more pleasant hilly areas it
would be much more expensive in terms of time and
energy consumption. Life on the flats would be alter-
natively windy and smoggy, probably noisy because of
expanded airport activity, and repeatedly subject to
flooding. If hilly areas were to be occupied, the most
likely locales would be two corridors, one to the north
along the rail line to Ahmedabad, the other eastward
along the line to Poona. Important concentrations of
medium-to-heavy industry had started settling along these
lines in the 1960s; by the 1980s population and industry
were expected to be several times larger, with most of
the terraces and valleys accessible to the stations already
claimed for urban activity. It would be truly expensive to
provide additional water in that terrain. A drastic alternative would be at least as expensive—blasting through the
hills to the south to reach the thinly populated Konkan
coast. Added population would have already collected
there around small harbors linked by LASH (Lighter-
aboard-ship) and SEABEE (Seagoing Barge) technology

and the installation of ferry service to Bombay. If the hills were to be tunneled, increased rail traffic from the south would probably stimulate the founding of a Bombay subway system, backing up an expanded electrified rail network at the surface or, occasionally, overhead. Of these costly alternatives, expanding south seems best.

Considerations such as these go into long-range regional planning for all metropolises. Bombay is fortunate that all of these directions lie within the state of Maharashtra; otherwise judgments and growth calculations would become matters dependent on very delicate interstate diplomacy. The regional planners need only to deal with the CENTRE, which can release large blocs of capital for investment in the urban infrastructure allocated in the context of national needs. Bombay's requests will be of unprecedented dimensions and often for services not found elsewhere in India (e.g., a modern superport for oil and bulk minerals). Because development economists remain convinced that capital expended upon urban infrastructure is generally unproductive, India has invested only in the national capital, a few state capitals, and a dozen or so industrial towns. Therefore, scrutiny of Bombay's proposals would be intensive, and Bombay's development would be carefully weighed against the needs of other cities, such as Calcutta, Madras, or Hyderabad.

Further, the comparison of alternatives may not be done well because Indian planning, like that of so many developing countries, has emphasized sectors (agriculture, transport, industry) in their programs for investment almost to the exclusion of regional planning. The latter is largely left to the states, even though the states have not been able to assemble adequate staffs. From the beginning the secretariats in New Delhi have appeared not to like cities, expressing the wish that people could be induced to remain in the villages. They did not support the larger urban areas until circumstances were becoming intolerable in the 1970s. India has, therefore, prepared no overall program for progressive urbanization, and so it can only compare projects with each other as they are submitted by the various metropolises.

Two policies are then open to the CENTRE. One of them will be to treat all claimants competitively, separating cost-benefit analysis from politics, and judge which cities get what on the basis of the social and economic growth per unit of investment that seems likely to be generated. With such criteria Bombay will do very well. The alternative is to minimize conflict by dividing up the available capital according to the number of voters lodged in the respective cities, to be used more or less as the cities see fit to employ the improvement funds. In the first instance the CENTRE might go further and take the best-looking projects to the international banks and other global sources of funding. If that occurs, Bombay's subway proposal or land-reclamation project would be competing with similar projects not only in India and elsewhere in Asia but also, to some extent, with all others in the world. To qualify for capital, a metropolis must demonstrate its vitality and competence, and it must have markets for some of its surplus in order to repay the loan. Therefore, it must deal with the multinational firms, which have built up their markets for manufactures and services but need urban labor to meet the demand. The human resources that are developed in its urban environment are drawn upon to back up a city's borrowing.

Actually the CENTRE almost always employs a mixed strategy. It funnels support to rural development groups, despite the lameness of their statistical justifications; it offers a steel mill, or a reasonable facsimile, to every state; it promises a factory from a national enterprise to every city; it subsidizes labor-intensive cottage industry production in the places with high levels of unemployment. The money is parceled out so as to keep the opposition from forming coalitions, since each faction can claim it obtained something for its constituency. The remainder of the capital at the CENTRE is matched with that obtained from overseas and assigned to the best prospects in the cities.

IMPROVING COMPETITIVE PERFORMANCE

We can judge overall excellence in a multifaceted metropolis by observing the choice-making behavior of the people and firms who actually have the option of locating in one place or another. What features are taken into account? We are particularly curious about the considerations that contribute to the choices made by persons with capital, entrepreneurial skill, technical knowledge, or other scarce characteristics, because they contribute to the improvement of future conditions within a city. Cities will die if they fail to produce conditions and opportunities that stimulate their own potential leaders and organizers, thus losing them to other urban centers, and also fail to attract equally competent replacements. They fossilize and become centers of depressed areas; few new organizations form in such cities. Through the sum of its actions each city creates a reputation for itself that may cause an individual to shun it, treat it with indifference, be intrigued by it, or be strongly attracted to it. How should a metropolis compete effectively? We can find out by looking at people's responses.

1. **Tourism.** Tourists are fleeing boredom with their home environment, so they look elsewhere for interest and adventure. The occasion for their coming to a city may be a holiday or convention, but they are also seeking excitement and variety. Most are willing to spend quite a bit more money per day than ordinary people and can therefore support an "export industry" of sizable dimensions, based largely on personal services. A study of the likes and dislikes of tourists, followed by local efforts to improve the quality of their experience, may not only increase tourism but should also have profound effects upon the internal organization of a city.[2] Of these feedback effects, three of the most significant will be introduced here.

Tourists strongly resent being accosted by beggars and touts. To prevent these unpleasant experiences, city authorities must spend scarce resources to provide alternative support for those who are dependent upon begging and hawking. An emergency relief program, good enough to get the casual beggars off the streets, has significant consequences for the social security of those who are so poor that they lack an address. They must also supply specially trained police to prevent re-entry and maintain orderly behavior in public places. Police control of touts and petty criminals should not become excessively visible, however, since recourse to the use of force is perceived by many tourists and some citizens as an assault upon civil liberties. Skilled management of overt threats, together with tolerance of some covert law breaking, is induced by subtle counterpressures brought to bear upon authorities controlling the police by small businessmen and committees of professionals concerned with ethical practices. These aspects of managing law and order are so shadowy that they are most clearly reported upon in novels, though some very insightful social analysis has been done in advanced cities where the poor are still numerous.[3]

Inside every tourist, it seems, is a bit of a pilgrim. He feels he must pay his respects to a place of worship, a historic site, a venerated institution, a celebrated occasion, or a local tradition. For each attraction an organization must be created which will assure that its unique features will be preserved. These are organizations that would operate much less effectively were it not for the interest, and often financial support, provided by tourists.

Often such high-grade urban services as fully equipped airports and large stadia could not be justified were it not for support provided by the tourist. The convenience, appearance, and luxury incorporated in those services to attract tourists will set a standard for affluent consumption that is markedly higher than the minimum adequate standard of living in a metropolis (unless the tourists are attracted mainly by the bargains made available by a well-organized free trading zone that excludes citizens) and will create a taste for conspicuous, frequently wasteful, consumption. Therefore tourism can be a corrosive force in the society—it adds to the key export industry sector, but at the same time it may enhance visible disparities in levels of consumption.

2. Capitalists. Without this second category of valuable persons who might be attracted to a city, many opportunities to create productive organizations will be lost. Even cities with a strong socialist ideology, such as Singapore, find it greatly to their advantage to create business conditions that attract capital. Normally this strategy involves the reduction to an absolute minimum of administrative control over flows of funds, which in turn requires a stable, convertible currency. Convertibility of currency demands major discipline within the urban sector of the country in balancing expenditures against revenue and imports against exports, although if the influx of capital is dependable it serves as a short-run substitute for exports. The great bane of the immigrant capitalist is inflation—when he discovers that money is printed without backing or credit is too rapidly expanded or wages rise much faster than productivity, he transfers his assets to another city.

Mobile capitalists build up trading services for both commodities and securities. They organize light manufacturing and must become knowledgeable about marketing. As a result they are also heavy users of the telecommunications channels, often providing their principal source of patronage while the channels are novel. Once there is confidence in the managerial competence of a city and the national administration that supervises it, much mobile capital can be induced to remain and back up longer-term investments, such as heavy industry, power plants, transportation, and housing. As a result the rate of a city's overall growth and physical development can be accelerated, though much of the increase in income is concentrated in the upper brackets. Switzerland is basically a very poor country that has become a collection of medium-to-small cities where even the poorest people live at the minimum adequate standard or somewhat above, largely by attracting capital and tourists. Hong Kong, Athens, Beirut, Singapore, San Juan, Sydney, Melbourne, Perth, Tel Aviv, and a number of smaller places have helped themselves significantly by their strong competition in the market for independent capitalists and the syndicates they form. It is to be hoped that some of these capitalists will create firms that grow up to become multinational organizations.[4]

3. **Managers and executives of multinational firms.** They are interested in much the same kinds of conditions as the syndicates of capitalists but have a more immediate potential for stimulating accelerated growth. If a metropolis is open enough and convenient enough, the managers of a multinational firm are able to employ and train workers in numbers up to the hundreds of thousands. By definition, these firms have developed a line of products, a technology of production utilizing ordinary labor, a system for quality control, and procedures for distribution; all that remains is that managers and executives must fit them to new legal systems and cultural environments.

Knowledge of specialized world markets is the most valuable asset multinational firms have acquired; consumer wants are anticipated, met, and the process is backed up with institutionalized research and development. With increasing frequency future managers and executives capable of moving this know-how to new metropolises will be persons with multiple citizenship. Most often they have technological or business training in the United States or Western Europe superimposed upon an earlier education acquired almost anywhere in the world. Although perhaps three-quarters of the multinational firms originate as American corporations, the management cadre begins to resemble a United Nations staff within ten years or so after the firm enters the world scene.

Each local enterprise started by a multinational corporation will import five to fifty staff members who must expect to live for years at a time with their families in an alien culture. The cities most successful in attracting these people will be those that have found a way of providing a nucleus of cosmopolitan services—shops with imported foods for holidays and parties, restaurants with gourmet cuisine, private schools using English, French, German, or Japanese to meet standards set in the respective societies for university entrance, churches and temples for ritual occasions, social clubs, sports facilities, circles for the review of contemporary culture, local vacation retreats, houses and apartments convenient for the entertainment of guests, familiar modes of health service and hospital organization, a complement of trained domestic servants, and so on.

Representatives of multinational managements and of the capitalist group can often be served by the same facilities that accommodate tourists. Their demand for cosmopolitan services is reinforced by the diplomatic corps, local top professionals, star performers in athletics, cinema, and other popular arts, and a rapidly growing body of technical consultants. Most such service facilities are readily financed with Euro-dollars or Euro-yen, thus imposing little if any net drain upon the capital resources of a poor but developing metropolis. A bewildering array of innovative organizations can be spawned by such a milieu, many of them unique. They are often self-serving, but a large share have the property of supplying an unfulfilled need in the modernizing sector of the metropolis.

4. Scholars and students. These comprise two related populations that can contribute to the competitive advantage of a metropolis over the long run even if they do not bring spectacular short-run gains. Scholars import ideas from elsewhere in the world, interpret them in terms of local cultures, and sponsor their transmission in the metropolis and the hinterland. Students need well-supported institutions in order to become scholars. The graduated students fill administrative slots in growing organizations. Some of them will become social entrepreneurs on the local scene. A metropolis that can attract high-grade students from a distance might very well attempt to sift out the best before they diffuse away and fit them into the really creative organizations in the locale and help them establish such organizations for themselves. Policies like these saved Boston from precipitate decline when its industries moved south; they are also one of the principal bases for the continued eminence of Paris, London, and Kyoto. Public investments must be made in libraries, laboratories, computer centers, data collection systems, museums, publishing facilities, and design studios. Often quick improvements in quality can be brought about by creating suitable posts for refugee scholars. London and many American cities made noteworthy gains by finding positions for scholars and artists fleeing from the Nazis and the Spanish Revolution. The scholars form independent circles and societies of creators and critics, drawing upon an already established cosmopolitan core for their enthusiasts, students, and patrons.

The metropolis that finds ways of attracting people with assets from elsewhere in the world is, therefore, really acquiring the germ cells and nutrients for new organizations. They reap the first fruits of a new capability before it spreads out into the hinterland or diffuses to less enterprising cities. Seminal organizations introduced in this manner from the outside may be branch facilities, franchises, consultant groups, clinics. laboratory groups, agencies, private schools, studios, or specialized communications networks. They provide a foundation for locally based corporations, government bureaus and offices, professional schools and departments in universities, technical training institutes, research and development groups, and securities markets for public and private offerings. The existence of a good supply of such backup organizations makes it possible to support executive headquarters for corporations of local origin that can go the multinational route (Bombay has four or five of Indian origin already, each with assets greater than a billion rupees, and is ahead of all others in the Asian continent except Hong Kong).

Henceforth, any new formula for doing business that is discovered and used successfully at a number of sites in a developing country has a promising future in the world at large. It could be a line of prepared foods, a new approach to insurance, a style of home furnishings, a technique of mariculture, or even a mode of meditation. The apparatus for making the leap into world operations exists everywhere that there is access to telecommunications, advertising, legal counsel, technical consulting groups, banking, and speedy private air travel. Then all that is necessary is the formation of a management team with a common concept and the ability to find an adequate replacement for any single key member, ensuring the survival of the group as long as the concept remains valid. This viability may last as little as a decade but could endure for many human generations.

To an increasing extent the multinational sector will be made up of public or nonprofit organizations (see figure 11.1). Some will be government corporations from socialist countries and mixed economies, a few alliances of cooperatives, quite a number of religious and communal organizations, and a repidly expanding component will be private foundations, supposedly eleemosynary in character, that arise from windfall capital gains.[5] Already there are hints of unusual hybridized forms, and chameleon types that are being discussed will appear soon. They would take on whatever formal kind of organization is most convenient in a given nation, whether it is a cooperative, joint enterprise with government, private firm, foundation, or professional association, and change as the government changes. An educational enterprise, like the Montessori, for example, could reshape itself into any of these. Asian inventions in this area have yet to be given names in the English language; they have often been regarded as social movements, sometimes even been seen as conspiracies.

Now it is possible to return to the protagonist for South Asian urbanization and to consider Bombay as it might transform itself in the course of successful competition with other metropolises, thus exploring its future in terms of the second of the approaches outlined above. Bombay is visualized here as becoming as much the habitat of complex organizations, many of them multinational, as Seoul or Singapore is today. (This future implies that competing metropolises will encounter political frustrations roughly equivalent to those identified in the gaming simulations for Bombay.) Once they are installed, the complex organizations would produce enough goods and services from local effort to support their participants (i.e., employees,

DYNAMICS OF THE URBAN TRANSITION

Figure 11.1 Niches for Multinational Organizations in Major Central Business Districts. Headquarters facilities tend to produce clusters of high-rise buildings that display organizational images. The new group using the electromagnetic spectrum resource tends to cluster separately, creating a precinct that with the aid of communications satellites operates around the clock. Nonprofit multinationals occupy positions of prominence but employ fewer people.

principal suppliers, distributors, and regular clients or members) at a minimum adequate standard and still generate a surplus when world prices are used as a basis for calculation.

In order for Bombay to register even this moderate success, the national government of India would be forced to modify its preoccupation with "Village India" and spend some time on "Metropolitan India." At first, if it is like other governments, it will believe it can control the urbanization process, largely by keeping people in the countryside and permitting orderly metropolitan development or urban infrastructure in a number of chosen centers. This policy is unstable, however; it builds up surplus populations in places where they cannot be supported in times of stress. A local drought or the outbreak of guerrilla warfare would generate tens of thousands of refugees who would normally end up encamped wherever roads and railroads converge—the cities. As in the crisis of 1971, out of which Bangladesh was born, authorities would be forced to relieve congestion by distributing them to other cities. By one means or another the surplus rural population arrives in huddled masses at the edge of existing cities, occasionally in virtually abandoned military installations. Those who have land or who have close surviving relatives will return to their homes when conditions become tolerable, but the landless are likely to remain. Their prospects, even as members of the powerless underclass, are better in the city than in the district where they were born. So a policy of control can be expected to crumble into one of coping with the apparently inevitable urbanization process. Events will always force the hand of planners for metropolises that are mostly poor.

The simulations of Bombay's future were conducted at a time when it was not known that drought conditions in Maharashtra and Gujerat would intensify to the point that many locales experienced two years of dry weather unprecedented in more than a century. By 1973 hundreds of thousands of refugee families crowded into a Bombay that was already extraordinarily, almost hopelessly, overcrowded. Bombay itself was on short rations of water and electric power, but planning that it had carried out earlier, meager though it had been, enabled the city to keep going when populous county-sized areas in the interior were being voluntarily evacuated. These harsh challenges to one or more must be anticipated at least once each Five-Year Plan, because India is a large country; they will occur even more frequently as surplus population in the hinterland becomes greater. Interestingly, they cannot be considered within a published plan, because if these reserves became widely known, regional politicians would be able to claim them by using publicity to build up the much more frequent moderate calamities into presumed national catastrophes—an example of the self-fulfilling forecast.

SPILLING OUT ONTO THE SEA

A third way of discovering incompatibility and conflict at the metropolitan level is to explore the difficulties encountered when urban settlement must invade new territory. Local power structures do not comprehend the magnitude of the forces rolling over them; so they litigate and delay until the family fortunes have been liquidated. Unsettled territory, on the other hand, requires hardy pioneers to find suitable adaptations to the previously hostile environment. Bombay's other choice must be considered.

People living in rural areas in the 1990s would be much more numerous (say 20-50% greater) than when counted in the 1971 census; most of them would be literate, and an important proportion would have picked up secondary education in addition to exposure to television. Family planning and postponement of marriage would have moved out of the middle classes in the city and be accepted by most of the rural cohorts born in the 1970s. Nevertheless, the village population would continue to grow, particularly in the more distant territories. Most households would have access to bicycles, and a network of bicycle paths would be superimposed upon the landscape. Small engines would be used to assist their movements in hilly areas. The railroad corridors would by then be quite heavily industrialized around the stations of smaller cities and on the buildable sites in between; the rail lines themselves would be mostly electrified so as to carry the added traffic. Increases in spatial mobility in Maharashtra and Gujerat would exert intense pressure upon the urban core, where the metropolis would be expanded into a polycentric megalopolis. Easily reclaimed land would have been used up, and the need for space well served with infrastructure would be intense. Land prices would hit astronomical levels. At that time, after perhaps a decade of discussion

and toe-wetting tests, Bombay could take to the surface
of the sea as a relief from crowding and congestion.

It was noted in Chapter 4 that sizable developments of
this sort would expedite the completion of the urban
transition in South Asia, but detailed discussion was
postponed so that the relationship with the new land-based
urbanism could be identified. Again, In Chapter 8, the
contributions of marine settlements to the strategy of
megalopolitan development were left to be taken
up later.

Marine surfaces act as huge buffers against pressures of
urbanization. When a metropolitan area begins to encounter
the escalating costs and risks associated with gigantism, and
word spreads that further development (it could be nuclear
power plants, jetports, bulk transport, recreational shoreline, or mass transit extensions) must be foregone because
of social and economic costs, designers will take on the
challenge of the sea. It can be a malleable environment,
one that is convertible to virtually any purpose that man
demands of land. As moving out to sea is risky and expensive, however, it may be viewed as a suitable solution only
when some kind of desperation motivates the search for
alternatives. An indication of the amount of added risk
is that insurance for a sea-going craft with living facilities
is about ten times as expensive as for a house at the shoreline that is equivalent in cost. In a place like Bombay the
arrival of the monsoon in June is a time to be feared;
extreme cyclonic storms and tsunamis may be even more
destructive though less frequent. Collisions become a
common source of damage as harbors fill up with craft.
Yet, in protected waters and with dependable mooring to
overcome these hazards, on-the-water living declines in
cost to the point where it is cheaper than nearby housing
with foundations fixed in soil.[6] The principal savings
would be in site development costs, but significant reductions in cost can come from factory assembly of the
structures.

In Bombay, the demand for greater variety in recreation
at reasonable cost is likely to lead the way to the sea.
Elephanta Island, standing in the middle of its bay, is
now reached by tens of thousands of people on a fair
Sunday; CIDCO recognized this when it assigned the fast
Hovermarine ferries to the Elephanta run. One of Bombay's
half dozen or so Chinese restaurants should soon perceive

that Hong Kong precedents may apply and so move to establish colorful dining on a barge. A Punjabi entrepreneur could counter with a replica of the Taj Mahal serving tandoori and curries. Economical hotel space could be introduced by leasing a retired ocean liner. Executives and technologists of the multinational corporations will bring with them marine avocations of many kinds, and they would be able to purchase the aquatic equivalent of villas, a form that has been evolving elsewhere in the world. The Arab oil exporters are in a position to capitalize a superport in deep water to the west, which would provide thousands of jobs at sea. They would probably draw upon Japanese marine technology, which should have a third-generation design available for use in the 1980s. Thus over the course of fifteen years a large component of Bombay's residents should become acquainted with the possibilities of aquatic settlement.

The billions of dollars of rents that could be derived from the use of the protected waters of the shallow estuaries around Bombay would attract proposals from sharp entrepreneurial groups inside and outside the government. Much of the capital that Bombay needs to build up its infrastructure could be obtained from auctioning options to use offshore space. The first real aquatic community in Bombay is likely to be made up of houseboats in abandoned obsolete naval installations, since they are already well served by breakwater jetties, fresh water lines, rail connections, docks, electirc power supply, and telecommunications. Later civil servants will be able to devise ways of reconstructing tidelands to create open water, channels, and reclaimed land so that the new activities could be readily integrated with earth-bound Bombay.

Ecological balance for a marine community will be achieved through procedures that appear quite different from those on land, though there may be some close equivalents. Because the life cycles of organisms living in the "deep scattering layer" and below are only now being unraveled, as are the relationships between the longer studied benthic species, the domestication of shellfish and fin fish has been late getting under way. With the publication of a comprehensive volume on aquaculture, this activity seems likely to be accelerated.[7] It is much easier now to define the niches that man, with his machines and automata, may occupy in the marine environment. The

chances of destructive perturbation are minimized, and
the basis for evolving a complex, ultrastable community
seems now to be present.

By the 1990s the United States and Japan should have
worked out improvements in method and equipment that
would transfer to any part of the world and could lay the
foundation for settlements with more services than those
dependent upon recreation and retirement.[8] Since neither
the United States nor Japan would be severely constrained
to conserve natural resources because their incomes seem
likely to move in the direction of still greater affluence,
and they will be able to pay top prices for the resources on
the world market, their designs are expected to be stylish
rather than economical. Less affluent countries must work
out economical modifications in the original designs. In
the neighborhood of Bombay, Djakarta, Dacca, and similar
locales attempts to design large communities around the
minimum adequate standard of living will be made. What
might such a cosmopolitan aquatic urban plan be like?
The following scenario introduces a designer with a community development agency as a client and a series of
cooperative banks and insurance companies as investors.
The community is supposed to grow to several hundred
thousand population.

**The principal resource that determines the form and
makeup of this community is the warm effluent from
a nuclear power plant. Earlier, the conservationists had
required that the plant distribute its "thermal pollution,"
as it was called, over a wide area so that no part of the
environment exceeded a natural temperature range. It
was eventually realized, however, that a warmer stream,
hovering around the optima for fish and thermophilic
strains of plants, could double or even treble the biomass
yield per unit area. Mariculture output for twelve valued
species was raised to several thousand kilograms per hectare
per year by bringing in pellets of alfalfa meal and granulat-
ed food-processing wastes. The husbandry of fish therefore
provides the common basis for small talk in this community—almost every third family has a member connected
in some way with the Fish Colony. The next community
down the coast is very different—it is made up mainly of
displaced Bengali who pride themselves on their aquatic
acrobatics.**

SCENARIO TEN

Creating a Marine
City for Living
at Minimum
Adequate Levels

This growing marine city is reached either through an underwater subway, an umbilical cord that connects it to Indian Railways and overland transport, or by ferry direct from Bombay Victoria. Thus the residents have access to a wide range of clerical, factory, and service jobs in Old Bombay and in the industrial estate that is coming into being adjacent to the nuclear power plant on the "power islands" designed in the 1970s. Dwelling units, service boats, and platform modules are produced four kilometers out to sea on a platform. Hulls are formed on site using concrete, ferroconcrete, steel plate, fiberglass, and internally foamed sheets of tough ABS (acrylonitrile-butadiene-styrene) resin—the kind used for nondenting autobodies. This busy construction center claims to be able to "launch" as many as a hundred units per day.

A cable grid was laid on the sea bottom, five to ten meters deep, before the tracts of individual houseboats were installed. Every forty meters it provides power, telephone, and television channel outlets on buoys. The pattern produced on the surface is a cluster of five or six circular or rectangular houseboats around the buoy. The blocks are hexagonal, the lanes undulate, and the directions, known as red, green, and blue (or blue-green, green-red, etc.), are appropriately color coded by night and day.

Boats move through residential areas daily, bringing fresh water and fresh vegetables and pumping out the holding tanks for the sewage. They contain the vendors who would normally be found in the tenement streets of the metropolis. Thus each home uses electricity for cooking and lighting, has a public telephone a few feet away, has its own store of fresh water and its own dory, paddleboat, or marine scooter with which to move about. People sleep on light net hammocks, which may also be used to keep small children from falling into the water during the day. Clothes are simple and kept in dry, watertight lockers. Often much of the floor space is used for cottage industries of various kinds, with materials in process arrayed around the television set. A small kitchen garden, planted in tin cans, is lashed to the top deck, farthest from the salt spray and splash.

Commuters take a passing launch, equivalent to a minibus, to a ferry terminal for their daily trip. Children get to school, and housewives to the weekly market, the same way. Community life centers around the temple, school, market, gymkhana and other clubs, the videotape production center, and the sweets shops specializing in ice cream and milk-based Indian sweetmeats. The community thus retains a peculiarly Hindu quality.

Closer to the Fish Colony are the apartment complexes assigned to full-time employees, mostly skilled. Thirty to fifty families live on a triple-decked barge. Many families that were tribal only a generation earlier have fitted into the fish-raising business very well. In very small things, such as the color of the women's saris, and the swagger of the men, unique village traits have carried over to these settlements. Each barge has its own coloring, although that is controlled by the need for orientation in a hexagonal layout, and its own flag. The two-to-three-hundred families around a utility service core tend to be brought together by a dominant employer and the sharpness of the water boundary; the people in the neighborhood develop an identity that results in a communal "landmark," such as a steeple or a dome, again differentiating the seascape and minimizing the likelihood of getting lost.

Designers note that the texture of a city form evolves quite naturally out of the diverse origins of the people, their capacity to help themselves once they have found employment, and the pride in community that shows up in athletic contests and some religious holidays. As the tracts fill up, they become quite densely populated—70 dwelling units to the acre (175 to the hectare) or well over a hundred thousand people per square mile. The ponds for sewage treatment and fish raising off to the side are not counted, nor are the marine gardens and aquatic sports pavilions. For reasons of convenience in getting about, and because people at sea have less attachment to accumulated personal property, human settlements on the sea are tightly clustered. The market system seems strange, because it is strongly decentralized to the tenders that ply up and down the water lanes. Therefore the central marketplace deals heavily in services such as festival decorations, marriage celebrations, graduation ceremonies, going-into-business floral decorations, burial rites, and other rites de passage.

The urban ecosystem that evolves is strikingly different from a land-based one. Not being moored to a dock, for example, allows man to escape from rats; he inherits the birds, however, which are likely to become as great a pest as pigeons in central cities, and measures for population control of wild birds may need to be instituted. The kitchen gardens need to have screen or plastic covers, for example. The "weeds" are marine organisms that collect on the hulls; "good" housekeepers keep brushing them off, but wherever the houseboats and barges grow old, along with the residents, the growth may be allowed to become luxuriant. A few dogs and caged birds emigrate along with their masters, but their population is aging and declines over time. A pet porpoise is a possible substitute, but it is a community project, because the cost in fish is very high.

The water surface is extremely subject to pollution by the high human density, since it can support flotsam and jetsam and blooms caused by nitrogen and phosphorus enrichment. The sea lanes must be cleared of floating litter by a service analogous to the street cleaner, and children taught a "water ethic" much stricter than any land ethic held by their parents before they arrived.

The mechanical components in the marine urban ecosystem have notable differences from land-based Bombay. Many fewer stationary machines are present, mostly because the footing is not truly stationary and requires more elaborate design to cope with forces transmitted by wave motion. A plethora of tiny personal vehicles is evident, ranging from the mass-produced two-man dories to the foam plastic "water shoes." Highly maneuverable launches with rakish long propeller shafts that are favored by the Thai boatmen (their techniques have now diffused to Bombay) chase up and down the boulevards. Most automata have been introduced from the navy. They are tucked into odd corners everywhere, the principal evidence of their presence being the geometrical wire sculpture that is found on many boats, obviously used for their antenna. Most automata are guardians of various sorts, and their installation is encouraged by insurance cooperatives.

Despite electric lighting, the marine metropolitan satelite city remains strongly diurnal. Only a few of the commuters to the central city are tied into round-the-clock operations, and they are joined by the maintenance men from the nuclear power plant. Save for central platforms containing celebrants, the city hushes three hours after dark and reawakens at the crack of dawn. An extra reactor

begins feeding energy into the grid, and water for tea is
put on galley stoves almost in synchrony.

Life in a marine city quickly reduces to a routine; people
must generate their own excitement. Each new cohort will
make up its own mind regarding the high points of life.
Their inventions will be much more surprising, even shocking, as they test the potentials of the new medium.

REDIFFUSION TO THE WEST

Asia's urgent needs will push it to evolve radically different approaches to the design of urban ecosystems, and
the Western metropolis cannot ignore these developments.
At present the momentum of overall social change in the
West causes the urban ecosystem to increase the consumption of energy resources toward levels that cannot
be supported, but splinter groups see most clearly the
debacle ahead and will buffer the inevitable shocks by
embracing some of the approaches worked out in the
Orient.

The incentives for paying attention to resource-conserving
life-styles are increased as prices rise, particularly in the
areas of meat and fossil fuels. The sharp upward swing
in those commodities experienced in 1972-1974 seems
likely to be maintained over the next two decades. Techniques for substituting communications for whatever
resource is scarce will be seized upon soon after a workable idea appears, regardless of its origins. Inventions born
of necessity in Asia and Africa will be picked up and
adapted to similar ends in the West before any economic
necessity arises.

Elements of sport or fun often contribute to diffusion,
since substitution may be undertaken in which no social
stress, price gap, or deeply conflictual problem is experienced. In America perhaps more than elsewhere, a novel
idea about consumption behavior may be put to use as a
hobby, tested, initiated elsewhere, and further improved
upon in several ways long before it is employed on a large
scale.[9] Thus a new sport will pick up cultural baggage,
such as a jargon of its own, artifacts, costumes, and rituals
from a number of traditions, before it is widely installed
as standard urban technology. This varied background
allows it to fit into many contexts.

Tracing the history of bicycles since the nineteenth
century, from gentleman's sport to the workingman's

substitute for a riding horse and the child's neighborhood plaything, illustrates repeatedly the rediffusion processes in world society; now Asia has become the predominant producer and is due to become the principal exporter.[10] A more recent illustration is that of the pocket radio. Japanese firms fitted together merchandisable designs with licenses and many components originally supplied by the West. Their versions quickly became a fad among American and European youth and were fitted into various recreational behaviors. In the poorer parts of the world the portable radio became an instant contact with the modern society and therefore a powerful status symbol among those with low incomes. Although a number of uses of the radios were purely recreational, the peasants outside the range of electrification began using them to become alerted to political shifts, weather changes, the availability of new products, and the timing of potentially significant events. The pocket radio prepared the way to the more complex agricultural practices required for increasing yields, while in the city its manufacture set the stage for a totally new industry. About a million jobs in electronics assembly were created in Asian cities in the decade from 1964 to 1974, the latest upsurge resulting from a line of pocket computers. These devices and their next-generation derivations will have a profound effect upon Asian organization because they will enable units with low capital-output ratios to carry out much more complex tasks than was possible before.

These discussions of the flow of innovating ideas provide too diverse and superficial a base for generalization. It is more useful to introduce a conceptualization of the diffusion between cities and greatly condense the argument. It presumes that increasingly reliable information will be collected on a variety of statistical series, similar to the statistical yearbooks of Tokyo and Seoul.

We begin with the total set of metropolitan places in the world, of which there are several thousand. Each must be economically, socially, and politically distinct, but they must also possess a single property in common, such as resident population or importation of fresh water. The list of metropolises can then be ranked, but with increasing uncertainty as one proceeds down the list. Kingsley Davis has been carrying out a population estimation exercise (where the number reported is quite sensitive to the definition of boundaries of the metropolis) using point estimates.[11] However, the *uncertainty* with which the population (or other property) is known is at least as important for understanding the future as the absolute value, because it is an indicator of the organization of a metropolis. Wherever uncertainties abound, we expect to encounter cities that are isolated from the others so that comparisons become difficult, or else cities in a great deal of political flux. Rangoon is an example of an isolated city, Saigon is in the throes of very rapid change, while Taiyuan (of the scenario in northwest China) fits into both groups.

Since point estimates of the population of metropolitan areas are presented by each major atlas, and uncertainties are suggested by comparing figures in different atlases, let us consider first a set of metropolitan populations. A number of crude generalizations based upon field observation combined with documentation can be offered regarding the diffusion of contemporary innovations.

1. Innovations in high technology (derived from recent advanced scientific research) tend to originate in large metropolitan areas of the West and diffuse unevenly toward the cities and towns in the West and to metropolises in the East at roughly the same rate.[12]

2. Consumer fads, styles, and novel traits of popular culture follow very much the same path as applications of high technology.

3. Innovations in the use of telecommunications channels and the mass media also start from the very large urban centers, but in both Eastern and Western hemispheres they then diffuse downward rapidly through the well-organized metropolises and finally outward to the least organized.

4. Notable improvements in urban services and administrative capability most often start in the less organized periphery (where they are needed to gain control of disorders) and move to the top of the hierarchy.

5. New religions start from smaller places in the East and grow by colonizing cities higher in their hierarchy; with increasing success they jump across the ocean to the largest Western cities and diffuse down the hierarchy to the less populous and less well organized.

This summarized experience regarding exchanges between world metropolises leads to the expectation that the West will be the recipient of new life-styles and modes of social

organization, accompanied by new faiths around which
a personalized system of values is constructed and transmitted to the next generation. Increasingly, they will
be associated with symbols and techniques previously
exported to the Orient. The most objective indicators of
successful transfer are found in the signs of the cityscape
(including scraps of music, characteristic noises, aromas,
stenches) and the neologisms incorporated into the local
language.

The exchange henceforth will be expedited by air travel,
which is not a very resource-conserving process, even when
allowing for the economies offered by very large planes.
At the current growth rate of 5-15% per year, international travel will quickly become a very significant
claimant for scarce natural resources. The true carriers of
innovation are people with ideas and a mission. They
often arrive from a distance, but they are supported by
symbols and imagery transmitted by a telecommunications
industry that is growing at even more rapid rates than
actual travel. As a result the structure of the global exchanges is strengthened and transformed.

Educational exchange transmits an understanding of
language and culture at a greater depth than tourism and
business. It has been increasing at a steady rate, but the
impact is even greater than the figures suggest because an
increasing proportion of the study in America and Europe
has moved from undergraduate general education, or
extremely specialized technical instruction, to graduate
and professional training. The recent rise in the cost of
tuition in Western universities makes popular the introduction of a year or more residence overseas, in which a
student can draw upon foreign educational facilities, together with joint faculties, without additional expense.
Although still very small, the export of educational services
from places like India, Israel, Singapore, and Egypt should
expand very rapidly because increasingly they are offering
bargains. The graduates from programs involving educational exchange are recruited by the large, rapidly growing
multinational firms or absorbed into a number of nonprofit
organizations that operate across international boundaries
with almost equal ease—the professional associations, labor
union staffs, cooperative alliances, eleemosynary foundations, and research institutes noted earlier. Within a quarter
century each metropolis in the West is expected to have

5-25% of its adult population contributing part of their time to these world-serving organizations. Through them the pressing needs of people in Eastern metropolises will become matters of personal concern.

The present world system, made up of nations jealously guarding their boundaries and building up loyalty to internally operated institutions, seems to be moving toward enhanced nationalism among the smaller, poorer countries. However, the increasing number of suppliers and distant customers, patrons and clients, teachers and learners who cut across national boundaries requires many more decisions and responses that also supersede purely national interests from an increasingly sophisticated leadership. One anticipates that the preoccupation with nation will start declining in a decade or so, as it has with the younger generations in Europe and America. Then a new system, based upon membership in one or more of the three thousand or so multinational organizations, will be superimposed upon the present United Nations assemblage of a hundred and forty nations and the mininations. The new layer will provide services that fit the interests of metropolitan citizens much better than archaic national institutions and will make possilbe new forms of cellulation among the minority of the population that dare to be different, because they are client-oriented, having the urge to persuade but not the power to demand.

The better-educated and widely traveled share of the population in the West will seek substitutes for the suburban community. People who wish to retreat to the close human contacts typical of a village but have income levels high enough to pay for books, travel, and other expensive uses of leisure are likely to form or join a specialized community. The concept of a voluntary therapeutic community, such as Synanon or Alcoholics Anonymous, is now widely accepted. Scores of religious communities already exist, and hundreds more are being founded of which scores will survive. The successful ones will maintain places for those with tentative commitments—apprentices, students, or novices—so that a fair amount of openness is maintained. Many will focus on gardening as a collective, nature-oriented activity and learn from, as well as teach, the urban villages that need to form in rapidly growing Oriental cities. One thinks of these cells as taking roles in future society not dissimilar to those of the monasteries and convents in past eras, and like those institutions there will be an international fraternal order or association that coordinates and promotes each particular way of life.[13] They will add strikingly to the range of life-styles found in a metropolis, complementing the respective cultural communities deriving from the different national or linguistic traditions that are expected to arise in the cosmopolitan cores of the cities.

The prospective division of labor in the global metropolis is worth some comment, because the patterns contain some sharp contrasts to conventional thinking. The best guess is that a disproportionately large share of the business of manufacturing artifacts for the world will take place in the cities of Asia and Africa. This assertion would have appeared incredible before 1965, but Japan's successes with cameras, watches, electronic appliances, automobiles, and ships in the interim makes the observation quite obvious in some circles. Items for householders—clothing, furnishings, appliances, interfaces with electronic equipment—will be produced most economically in the East, with newly urbanized labor that is still struggling to rise to the minimum adequate standard of living. The populations of machines will have most of their components made there, even if they are largely employed in the West. Mobile machines, primarily automotive, will be most efficiently produced in the coastal metropolises of Asia. Components for the automata will also be manufactured in Asia, although most of the designs will continue to come from the laboratories of the multinational corporations already set up in the West, and subassemblies would often be returned to the West for incorporation in complex apparatus. Obviously these transfers will not be complete, since even today the regions that nurtured the Industrial Revolution still have a few plants that produce textiles, pottery, iron castings, cutlery, soap, and dyes. The initiative in the marketplace, however, will belong to the newcomers.

What is there left for people in Western metropolises to do, if the expanding megalopolises of the Orient take on the tasks of producing most of their own food, constructing the equipment that conserves fuel for others besides themselves, building the machines, and doing most of the work on the automata? It is argued here that some Eastern metropolises will also engage in massive settlements of the nearby seas, thus creating quite new patterns of living, and a few will also be innovative in the design of new communities and philosophies. The contributions from the West appear to have great value wherever gigantic efforts are required—aerospace, telecommunications, nuclear energy, molecular biology in medicine, offshore drilling, and the like. Probably more important, though, is the application of fluid, hyperresponsive ad hoc organization. which the West has already developed to a degree hardly imagined in the Orient, to the tasks of image-making. The West will expend huge amounts of imagination on the projection of patterns, signs, and complex stimuli to catch people's attention and provide them with cues for guiding action. In marketing, where the image of a product, service, or organization is involved, the strategies will become even more elaborate. If competition is not strongly associated with the marketplace, the efforts are regarded as "cultural." The content of the urban communications channels, displayed in print, line, and color, will be invented by groups that come together for a while as a troupe or company to create a series of works and perhaps a style, but then dissolve, followed by a period of search, during which the participants find new connections or decide to retreat from the scene to recuperate.

Membership in the automotive and jet-set circles that continue to evolve in the West gives professionals an advantage in the intense competition that prevails at the cultural frontiers. Easterners that wish to participate may find it necessary to come West and earn their spurs in the studios, salons, and Madison Avenues of the present world capitals. Multinational organizations cannot catch up with the ad hoc groups in this field; large firms and foundations must invest too much in equipment, service staff, and structure-maintaining overheads to be able to compete on any front but that of the mass production of imagery at, say, the scale of Walt Disney. The growth of the huge enterprises, however, makes possible the founding and survival of many more small specialist groups who take on trouble-shooting, mediating, expediting, and pioneering roles.

The city holds people in its embrace by making possible more interactions and, with them, building various kinds of ties to the community. The possibilities of interaction are far from exhausted; the future experiments on almost every scale will draw upon themes and ideas from Asia but will be conducted primarily in the most open societies, now those of the Americas and of Europe. Pacemakers in these parts of the world are more concerned with the transmission of meanings from one individual to another across all kinds of cultural barriers than with the provision of some kind of personal security from the random fluctuations of nature.

1. It is standard practice now for firms to bargain simultaneously
with autonomous public agencies, such as port authorities, industrial
estates, and utilities in several cities in order to put together the
best possible deal. Investors in mortgages, bonds, and other long-
term commitments make equally close comparisons. In addition,
the unions of public employees are always alert to changes in
contracts made in comparable cities. Thus, through these channels
alone, urban administrators are reminded daily of the advantages
offered by their nearest competition; (see A.N. Christakis, "Regional Economic Development Futures," *Futures,* 4 (March 1972),
13-23.

2. A great deal of design effort is now being spent upon the fronts
of cities exposed to the tourist. Behind the exterior image that
must be apprehended and interpreted by almost everyone within
a few winks of the eye, most tourists like to find informality which,
within minutes, offers short cuts and other conveniences; often
within hours or days the educated young will then dig deeper to
find "reality." Beneath these levels one still finds a number who
probe for "intimacy" with the people and their environment,
still fewer who go "slumming" where only a minor amount of
fixing up is done for the visitor, and finally one might be accepted
in the back as a full participant. There folkways and kitchen gossip
direct the attention of the group. A successful, lasting program
for tourism must plan for contact at all six (or more) levels. Dean
MacCannell, "Staged Authenticity: Arrangements of Social Space
in Tourist Settings," *American Journal of Sociology,* 79 (November
1973), 589-603. The architect-planner reviews what is provided
for the affluent tourist elsewhere and then attempts to synthesize
a set of images that are different, but still more attractive. These
differentiations of product make forecasting of tourism a problematic operation. G.W.G. Armstrong, "International Tourism: Coming
or Going: The Methodological Problems of Forecasting," *Futures,*
4 (June 1972), 15-25.

3. The classic study of the ways in which police manage public
order in urban environments is that of James Q. Wilson, *Varieties
of Police Behavior* (Cambridge, Mass.: Harvard University Press,
1968). For instances where the predatory groups are juvenile gangs
that often arise among the first generation to be reared in the city,
he also contributed an article to the volume dealing with the larger
issues that was edited by Stanton Wheeler *et al., Controlling
Delinquents* (New York: John Wiley & Sons, 1968). One classic
contribution is that of Egon Bittner, "The Police on Skid Row,"
American Sociological Review, 32 (October 1967).

4. A listing of the multinational corporations with origins other
than that of the United States was prepared for a Special Report
by the McGraw-Hill economists and published in *Business Week,*
July 6, 1973, pp. 56-65. It shows quite clearly that firms in formerly imperial powers have found it relatively easy to put the international services to work for them when setting up branches across

national boundaries, and the firms of former colonies that became independent the earliest (Canada, Australia, Brazil) have recently been able to use the same one-way channels in order to expand overseas.

A review of the origins of multinational firms reveals that in almost every instance a socially useful production concept—very often an innovation that was not patentable—was launched by a top-rank organizer in a locale that was not unfavorable. He was a capitalist himself or he brought in partners who fulfilled that function. When the firm experienced phenomenal growth in national markets, it was forced to make decisions about expansion; normally it went to the banks for credit and perhaps also for help in "going public" in stock ownership. In the succeeding rounds of growth the organization was forced to seek new sites, both on the periphery of the city that fostered it and in other locales closer to the newly acquired markets.

One such success created a city; several together produced a metropolis. In the beginning the enterprises only considered decentralization to serve a nation; then they decided that greater returns were possible by delivering to markets in territories over which the home nation had economic hegemony (e.g., Sterling Bloc), and finally in foreign countries where exporting through agents became clumsy. In that case the headquarters activity became a substantial white-collar employer. Thus there has been an intimate connection between the growth of multinational firms and the growth of metropolises over the past half-century.

Most recently urban growth has been linked to the combined participation of dozens of such organizations locating in the same region. Presently many multinationals are seeking to overcome interruptions in the flow of manufactures which presently prevent service to customers as much as 5-20% of the time, and some remarkable stabilizing techniques have been invented. For example, automobiles may be manufactured for markets A, B, C, and D, with each having its own assembly plant, but subassemblies are made in only two countries, each with some surplus capacity. This arrangement not only achieves some economies of scale but also generates competition within the organization, improving its efficiency over time. Also, if a dock strike or political turmoil occurs in one country, deliveries can still be made in other countries, and enough time is allowed to find an alternative supplier in the world if it seems needed. One important result is that the multinational firm can survive conditions that would incapacitate a national firm. Thus, even though multinational firms seldom make exorbitant profits, they have a much greater likelihood of surviving.

5. A few examples are illuminating. Renault in France and Montedison in Italy are primarily government-owned, and the British government holds a large block of British Petroleum shares. The wholesale cooperative societies in Scandinavia, Great Britain, and Central Europe are member-owned, but they have a number of manufacturing arrangements whereby they serve each other and

the cooperatives in North America as well. The Church of the
Latter Day Saints engages in commerce (although primarily interested in the distribution of human services) all over the world
very effectively. New religions and professional associations are
experimenting with new modes of organization designed to penetrate international boundaries and provide such nonmarketed
services as counseling and advice.

6. The contribution of marine technology to urbanization throughout the world was taken up very early in the City of the Future
studies of C. A. Doxiadis and J. Papaioanou (ca. 1962). After
visits in Athens I wrote two assessments of the probable paths of
evolution after the early exploratory reviews: "Settlement of the
Seas I; Prospective Demands for Aquatic Surface," Ann Arbor,
January 1964, mimeographed, and "II: The Physical Development of Marine Communities," Ann Arbor, February 1965,
mimeographed. Some of this appears in Fraser Darling and John
P. Milton, eds., *Future Environments of North America* (Garden
City, N.Y.: Natural History Press, 1966).

7. John E. Bardach, John H. Ryther, and William O. McLarney,
*Aquaculture: The Farming and Husbandry of Freshwater and
Marine Organisms* (New York: Wiley-Interscience, 1972). The
interaction between rapid technological advance on economic
risk in this field is discussed by Lee G. Anderson, "An Economist
Looks at Mariculture," *Marine Technology Society Journal*, 7
(May-June 1973), 9-15.

8. Many will wonder why China, with its millions of water people
making up the predominant share of those living according to
aquatic life-styles, is not expected to set the pace in creating low-
cost modern communities. The reason I suspect that they will
follow rather than lead is that the present water people have
exceedingly low esteem, having been reduced to a very low castelike
relationship. They are now moving to the land and diffusing into
the city in search of factory and service jobs because improved
technology has led to overfishing. The cottage industry work
undertaken on the boats, such as plastic flower assembly, pays
very poorly. They are also strongly attached to a hull form and
overall vessel design that is efficient when hewn out of wood and
sailed on the Kwangtung coast, but will have to learn almost from
the beginning how to use such materials as ferro-concrete, fiberglass
plastic, and the tough foamed-resin sheets now being introduced. The
society of water people is close knit and adaptive but rarely engages
in innovation. Eugene N. Anderson, Jr., *Floating World of Castle
Peak Bay* (Washington, D.C.: American Anthropoligical Association,
1970). This monograph is unusual because it destroys conclusively
a number of well-established myths about the *tanka* (a term of
derision applied to people who had been living on boats) that
are circulated in Hong Kong and Taipei.

9. Rolf Meyersohn and Elihu Katz, "Notes on the Natural History of Fads," *American Journal of Sociology,* 62 (1957), 594-601; Neil J. Smelser, *Theory of Collective Behavior* (New York: Free Press, 1963), especially chap. vii.

10. Gary Tobin, "The Bicycle Boom of the 1890s," *Journal of Popular Culture,* in press, 1973.

11. Kingsley Davis, *World Urbanization 1950-1970* (Berkeley, Calif.: Institute for International Studies, 1969).

12. In general we look to Brian Berry for the refined arguments concerning central place hierarchies and the diffusion of innovations through them. Brian J. L. Berry and Frank E. Horton, *Geographical Perspectives on the Urban Systems* (Englewood Cliffs, N.J.: Prentice-Hall, 1969). The diffusion models are based upon the contributions of Torsten Hägerstrand, *Innovation Diffusion as a Spatial Process* (Chicago: University of Chicago Press, 1968).

13. More than 2,000 such cells formed in the United States in the period 1967, although only a minority survived. Those that have dissolved are quickly replaced by others. The communities for "alternate culture" are served by about 200 underground newspapers, 50 specialized journals, and at least 14 alternative telephone directories so that people can obtain goods and services to their liking. Communications are speeded up through the provisions of switch boards. They are served by 500 free schools and 50-75 free clinics. The concept of "alternate" is different from "deviant" in that the former attempts to design a total way of life different in orientation from the mainstream, and not insisting upon merely one or a few behavioral freedoms. Patrick W. Conover, "The Potential for an Alternate Society," *The Futurist,* 7 (June 1973), 111-116. An even larger number of people gain greatest pleasure from an organized avocation, so that participation in urban society serves as a source of income for engaging specialized sports or hobbies. With increased income, mobility, and communications it becomes possible for an individual to participate fully in several such cells, or communities apart from popular culture.

We live in an ecosystem in search of an utterly new climax
state. At climax a living system has stabilized with maximum diversity, minimized gyrations and swings in population size, developed an elaborate homeostasis to restore
relationships between species, and held biomass at a
constant level. Massive invasions and transformations
are no longer observed. The climax is not an equilibrium
but a balance of activity—a steady state.

   The previous climaxes—there were many separate biomes
reaching that state—were achieved after the ice ages, but
before cities. Man, the hunter, had already profoundly
disturbed many postglacial climax states, but with the
advent of cities human population became increasingly
dominant in the natural system. Societies that tilled the
land were ruled from cities that vastly expanded their
own membership as they brought forth a new class of
tool users; many families, genera, and species of machines
proliferated symbiotically with the specialization of urban
man. Giedion's masterwork, *Mechanization takes Command*
(1942), dramatized this transition.[1] One group of machines
remained sedentary, analogical with plants to such a degree
that the term for such an immobile mechanical facility is
"the plant." Another group of machines speedily evolved
to the point where they displaced animal-drawn transport
equipment and human-propelled equivalents (pushcarts,
rickshaws, galley ships). Then came an era of electrification
and telecommunications, providing almost instantaneous
transport of energy and information and providing a base
for the meteoric rise of another new population—automata.
The networks that distribute energy and signals are making
one ecosystem out of the world; they have annihilated the
effects of space because symbiosis can exist between
entities on opposite sides of the world and time lags
associated with the diffusion of a population are abolished.
The eventual One World concept applies not only to man
but to animals and plants, mobile and immobile machines,
and to automata—all are becoming tightly integrated and
interdependent. A steady state for these populations has
yet to be approached, but we can begin to describe it
through the use of the ecologist's experience with discovering order in such complex systems.

The basic data for defining the state of an ecosystem begin with censuses and population estimates together with an assessment of the carrying capacity of the environment. Starting from this information, noteworthy bio-geographical distributions and characteristic community structures can be deduced. From there ecologists go on to trace the energy chain and material transfers. It is then possible to summarize aggregate inputs and outputs for a specific community and to discuss the forces that work to restore equilibrium when, for any reason, it is disturbed. After this it is possible to discuss the potentials opened up for further evolution of the species. These steps constitute a logical order that will be followed in the closing arguments.

CENSUS TRENDS AND CARRYING CAPACITY

The numbers anticipated for the global metropolis when the world has completed both the demographic and urban transitions do not have great significance by themselves, but they seem to generate strong interest among those who have a horror of overcrowding and hubbub—demophobia. The etiology of the origin of this mental condition may be a simple lack of adaptive experience—these people have never lived in high-density surroundings themselves for even a short period of time, so they have no personal experience to draw upon to imagine what it might be like. The difference is simply that of living out one's life continuously surrounded by others of the same species rather than in a milieu in which other species are preponderant. Those who fear this often possess property, develop a strong territorial sense, and place a high value on privacy. Edward Hall would say that they have appropriated a big "space bubble" for themselves.[2]

Hardly any of the people who must decide whether to move into a city or remain away are interested in total population, either of the metropolis or the system of cities. Potential inmigrants are concerned about the availability of niches to fit into as individuals or as household units. The niches are defined by the number and quality of interfaces with others maintained by the city. Designers and managers can, with acceptable costs, manipulate the physical and organizational environment so as to maintain contacts with other humans in a thickly populated settlement at a low, high, or variable intensity. When allowing higher costs, it is possible for the individual himself to control consciously the intensity of contact. Intuitive reactions regarding future population size, therefore, should be treated as irrelevant to prospective welfare—unless the carrying capacity of the whole earth can be demonstrated to be at hand. People's feelings on the matter would definitely affect a voting outcome, but pluralities do not change ecological forces.

The most probable peak human population, based upon tracing a number of different developmental paths, lies in the range of ten to fifteen billion people. It should be reached four to five generations hence. John and Magda McHale have been engaging recently in exercises of global demographic extrapolation.[3] Basing my calculations on their work, if I were forced to gamble on a point estimate, I would wager at the present time on the figure of twelve billions. Almost all people, indeed almost all fauna (judged by biomass), would live in urbanized areas in order to gain secure access to food, shelter, and services.

The peak figure for human population is not very meaningful because nothing has been said yet about the population of automotive vehicles. On the average each of them requires an amount of urban space roughly equal to that needed by an urban resident. In studies of the most crowded ward of Tokyo, where legally required parking space for introducing a new car was equal to the average floor space per capita in dwelling units, it was found that one person left the community for each new vehicle registered—the total of people plus automotive vehicles remained constant.[4] Laws requiring off-street parking have been more lax in Europe and America, but comparable relationships can be observed. Therefore one should hasten to add an estimate of the motorized mobile machines. When estimated by means of the same multiple considerations by which population estimates were achieved, the number of automotive vehicles at climax ranges between two and three billions (the most probable figure is two and a half billions). However, the proportion of such vehicles in the territory outside the urban areas is due to be greater, so that only two-thirds of the total would be found within cities, even though they are expected to contain close to 90% of the human population. In addition, the supply of motorized vessels of all types used by a floating urban community seems likely to be higher than for a land-based community, because the swimming mode of movement is a poor alternative compared to the pedestrian mode, and pedal-operated vehicles are easily swamped.

The area required for this amount of urbanization is surprisingly small as compared to the total available. If one includes private and public areas with circulation space, parks, and sanitary districts (but not commercial food-producing gardens), then the point estimates become 1,500,000 square kilometers (600,000 square miles), or about 1% of the total land area of the earth. The remainder of the human population would be scattered all over the rest of the world in smaller cities, towns, villages, homesteads, and camps at thinner densities than at present.

The carrying capacity of the earth does not seem to depend upon a need for living space; it depends much more strongly upon the assumptions of the deciders—the human beings—regarding consumption levels over the long run. As such assumptions are required in order to propose immediate solutions to the task of urbanizing poor countries, the concept of the minimum adequate standard of living has already been introduced. It can be used as a criterion for discovering what scarcities are likely to be felt when urban population has reached these dimensions. Felt scarcities may be graver than represented here, but they are then traceable to unnecessary addictions to luxuries or inadequate control over destructive conflict.

The procedure for identifying a limiting supply of resources can be summarized as follows: (1) for each component of consumption in the minimum adequate standard of living identify what seems to be the most economic technology; (2) pick out the raw materials or commodities that appear to be insufficient to meet the needs of the peak population; (3) find substitutes or substitute technologies for the scarce material; (4) review the prospective supplies of the substitutes; (5) consider whether the external effects of using substitutes in such quantities would necessarily destabilize the environment, using current scientific evidence; (6) similarly, review what is known about the technologies for the substitutes concerning their impact upon each other (i.e., are they complementary and reinforcing activities, or are conflicts foreseeable?). Fortunately, the scientific and technological literature is quite well organized, so that such reviews can be carried out in a reasonable amount of investigative time. Yet misunderstandings remain common, so each serious investigator in this field must conduct his own search for the data that set actual "limits to growth" in order to be satisfied with these conclusions.[5] The opportunities for substituting for scarce inputs are almost always grossly understated in the quick, simple approaches to discovering limits upon growth.

When this procedure for the discovery of apparently adequate substitutes is followed, one finds quite consistently that increased energy is required per unit of the commodity consumed. Economies of scale are no longer obtained; the iron law of diminishing returns comes into effect. This is most evident when scrap is used to substitute for virgin inputs because collection, separation, and refinement require added transport and processing. Therefore in the final stage—estimating cross-impact—an accounting of overall energy requirements needs to be undertaken. At steady state, the allocation of energy to respective activities appears quite strange because of the reduced level of construction (table 6). The greatest uncertainty seems to remain in the demand for global travel that persists after the telecommunications devices have been perfected.[6] Nevertheless, sufficient energy exists to maintain a steady state dependent solely upon sunlight. It can be supplemented for a few centuries by expending moderate amounts for nuclear fuels, geothermal sources even longer.

It appears from this estimation of very long-range carrying capacity based upon energy and spatial considerations that the limits to growth are not likely to be approached so closely that strong stresses are induced in human society. Mammalian species other than man appear to be quite healthy when the population ranges between a quarter and a half of the estimated carrying capacity; man should be able to organize himself in such a way that the environmental stresses associated with overcrowding are minimal. There seems to be no verfiable reason why stresses should be any greater with a population of ten to fifteen billion looking forward to a steady state than they have been in recent history when a much more restricted area was occupied by two to four billion people anticipating growth.

This estimate of carrying capacity is most sensitive to the assumptions regarding net efficiency of solar cells.

Table 6
Energy Budget Estimates for Steady-State Resource-Conserving Urbanism

Demand

Food consumption (large-bodied individuals)	3,000 cal/day
Feed for animals	2,000
Fertilizer (virgin and recycled, process costs)	1,000
Transport of goods	4,000-6,000
Transport, local passenger	3,000-10,000
Transport, long distance (mainly airline)[a]	1,000+
Heating, ventilating, lighting (latitude dependent)	1,000-5,000
Materials of construction (climate dependent)	1,000-2,000
Manufacturing (other than for above purposes)	2,000-5,000
Communications (heavily aerospace)	1,000
Miscellaneous	1,000
	20,000-37,000 cal/day or about 7-14 X 10^7 cal/year plus air passenger movement
For 10-15 billion world population	7-20 X 10^{17} cal/year +

Supply

Sunlight intercepted by Earth	1.3 X 10^{21} cal/year
Available at surface after penetrating albedo[b]	2.0 X 10^{20} cal/year
Average net efficiency of solar cells, algae, and intensive agriculture	3-5%
Portion of surface of Earth utilizable for food production and energy collection	50%
Energy deliverable for human use	3-5 X 10^{18} cal/year
Energy-limited carrying capacity[c]	20-70 billions humans

(This allows for 5-10% of the surface for city life, 20-50% for intensive culture or energy collection, and 40-75% open space.)

[a]Many varieties of world organization are needed which are not yet proposed, and they require an indefinite number or airline trips which expend energy at a high rate, so the upper end could not be estimated.
[b]Penetration of the albedo is not an absolute limit, because it is already technically possible to convert the sunlight in outer space into narrow band microwaves which are not scattered or absorbed upon entering the earth's atmosphere and can be collected at the surface with antenna. (See note 15 for this chapter.)
[c]This limit assumes a freely interacting ecosystem with widely diverse communities, which is the major reason the range is so broad. Many more humans could be accommodated if, for example, the principal aim of world civilization was to maximize the number of egos, or souls, going to heaven.

Many engineering calculations in the journals report conversion efficiencies for solar cells in the range of 10-18%, but these figures do not allow for dust, variability of weather, or collection losses, all of which become very serious in completed designs. No mechanical system for the collection of solar energy has been outlined, to my knowledge, which would deliver large quanitites of energy from a solar source to a metropolis with a net efficiency of more than 3%. Higher efficiencies do not seem possible even if the economic value of power was several times greater than at present and therefore warranted much more investment per unit of output. Perhaps, however, in conjunction with geothermal sources or the use of tropical oceans as heat sinks, localized contributions from solar cells may be possible, but such designs have not been fully elaborated.[7]

The range proposed in table 6 could not have been safely argued for world-level conversion efficiencies if we did not have the performances of algae as photosynthetic converters to back it up. Shortly after World War II scientific work on photosynthesis, with conversion levels of up to 25% efficiency in the laboratory, led to speculation about a new capacity to meet prospective protein requirements. Optimism was short-lived because it was discovered that yields in stirred open cultures were disappointing. In the late 1960s, however, a new mass culture technology successfully emerged in Japan that could, if combined with methane or hydrogen fermentation, achieve a 3-5% net conversion efficiency in ponds constructed on flat wasteland in temperate to tropical climactic zones.[8] Yields seem likely to be enhanced if operations are conducted on a marine surface (but in a medium that is much less saline than sea water) where the waves contribute to the mixing and heat exchange helps prevent overheating at the surface. Technologically oriented investigators are now returning to the design of such schemes, so we must expect some interesting proposals in the near future.

Once the ten to fifteen billion population range has been reached and growth has apparently leveled off, some drifts in census counts may be anticipated. They are responses to longer-run adjustments that sometimes take centuries to work themselves out. Drawing upon Odum's analysis of the climax stage in an ecosystem for suggestions, we should expect that succeeding censuses and surveys would reveal:[9]

1. Constant or slightly declining human population.
2. Increasing average age.
3. Increasingly equal opportunities for newly born entrants.
4. Slowly rising biomass in domesticated animals, a noticeable increase in the population of wild animals.[10]
5. Raised standing crop of plant life.[11]
6. Roughly constant population of automotive vehicles, but increasing diversity.
7. Increasing diversity of immobile machines, along with rising population.[12]
8. Increasing utilization of energy, along with further electrification.[13]
9. Continuing rapid growth of automata, activating the responsibe environments.
10. Medium growth in communications flow rate, mostly because of added automata.
11. Steady increases in cataloged, organized knowledge.

Most of these expected trends derive directly from the observation that as an ecosystem reaches maturity the diversity of species supported thereafter also reaches a peak—diversity in this case being extended to man's differentiated social roles in the city of the future.

COMMUNITY STRUCTURES

At the human scale our image of the future city is aided by an analysis of trends in new towns. The urban transition was completed first in the United Kingdom, and it has expressed itself in the formation of complete new communities that fit the identifiable needs of urban man. The environment is specified in terms of concrete, glass, asphalt, greenery, layout, form of structure, and a complement of built-in services at costs that prospective residents can almost afford. By the time the model community is fully occupied, the designers hope that the enhanced productivity from sources of livelihood built into the community (and the effects of the ongoing inflation) will make bargains out of the facilities. These new towns are the peaks in civility as far as we can know it and bring it into being.

Scandinavia, like Britain, has had most of its rural population migrate overseas or voluntarily move into the city. In its new towns a few extra touches can be noted, expressing adaptations to a somewhat more rigorous climate and more extensive community activity. Ecologically, they too are "plantations" and share the property that all the components will grow old together. In the new towns of the part of the world starting this supposed steady-state urbanism, a thirty-year cycle is incorporated, because most people move in during the period when their families are young and expanding. It may take as much as a century to dampen the cycle and approximate a normal age distribution, the true steady state.[14]

In those painful years, over a century ago, when Adolf Hitler of the Nazi Reich was on the brink of conquering Europe, when cities were dark, windows blacked and covered, and food rations sparse and monotonous, planners dared to dream of bright, cheerful, open towns that would make a better life for their children. In the struggle to rebuild after World War II, their conceptions of what new towns should be were converted into blueprints, corporations were formed to implement them, and house-hungry populations were selected from the crowded precincts of the old metropolises to live in the new houses and apartments. As they walked into their homes, still so new that they smelled of wood, paint, and plaster, these people saw themselves as moving into the future of mankind.

Now a full hundred years later we can see what their future held. Satello-Vision takes us around the world from Europe—Harlow, Stevenage, and Hemel Hempstead in Greater London, then on to Stockholm, Helsinki, Munich, Moscow, and Warsaw—to America—Washington, Chicago, and then on to California. As we move to our first stop, we see a typical old-fashioned town. Our parents might have grown up among these weathered brick and concrete structures. Tall mature trees, greenery manicured at the front but seedy on the fringes, and patched-up asphalt surround them. Buses pick up draped figures from shelters at the roadside and drop them at the office towers (note the much newer facades) or at schools with wornout but partly modernized facilities. The town is, of course, fully electrified with wires underground, and the highest point is not the historical church steeple we might have expected only a few years earlier, but the familiar tower supporting microwave relays and laser beam directors that connect the activities of this community with all other communities in the world. Most noticeable of all is the

SCENARIO
ELEVEN

Post-World War II
New Towns Reach
a Century

quiet; in northwest Europe noise pollution was already one of the horrors of the professional classes and decision makers of the last century, so antinoise measures were strictly enforced from the beginning. Whistles, horns, bells, and amplifiers are required to operate at low-decibel levels, while the drilling, hammering, and pounding associated with construction is hardly ever necessary for a built-up community like this where dwelling units are expected to have a mean lifetime of a hundred and fifty years and commercial structures about half that.

People on the street are slow-moving and predominantly gray-haired, since children are not numerous in a steady-state community such as this and are segregated to places where the noise and disorder they generate can be contained. (When this town was built, the average age of the inhabitants in most cities was often as low as twenty-five years. Modern medical advances, especially the elimination of most cancer as a cause of death, have raised it to a more reasonable fifty years).

Active recreational behavior is devoted largely to environmental maintenance such as out-of-doors gardening, but most leisure here, as elsewhere, consists of interaction through an electric facility. The familiar fluorescent screen and keyboard provide drama and excitement in Hampden as in Hong Kong. So much of modern life is played out here that some observers have regarded city exteriors as no more than interfaces with the past and with natural surroundings.

Moving into the heartland of Europe, we see that people here also have spelled out ideals that should be put into new towns. Their versions from the 1950s and the 1960s are assembled with stacked apartments (slabs in the West and blocks in the East), central shopping areas partially protected from the winter, and many green parks. Transport was electrified from the start and often operated underground. These towns, too, have become good, gray, very much patched, sometimes quaint, well-trimmed, and almost as quiet as their British counterparts.

Swinging across the Atlantic Ocean, we see that America was forced by circumstances to be different. More than half of what it built used wood, and the mean life of a structure was seventy or eighty years. Each generation of owners transformed the landscaping, changed the exterior, and reconstructed the interior to suit their needs. Most

of the original designed community is gone; two-thirds of
the buildings have been replaced, and even the street
layout, which was intended initially for one-car families
but adapted for the generation of multiple-car families
and torn up again to make the dial-a-ride system work
better, has not persisted. Since the rise in the nostalgia
boom, it is still possible to find complete neighborhoods
like this. Whatever was not actually preserved from the
1980s stage of development has been restored: the three-
car garages have been converted to private apartments for
the youth and the elderly. Shrubs, lawns, and trees are
machine-trimmed, and the flower pots are delivered to
order each spring. The automatic irrigation systems installed by the second wave of occupants to keep the place
fresh and green until late in the autumn does develop
weak pressure areas; so in the evenings residents can be
seen watering by hand. each using a replica of old-fashioned
hoses. The lawns are shaded, and many of them appear
to be clearings in the forest, while the houses themselves
are now almost hidden in evergreen brush. The original
layout of the land was so spacious and is now so overgrown
that some say the old American suburbs (of which the new
towns of the 1950s were really a part) are ready to be given
back to the Indians. That illusion is dispelled, however, as
we rise and move West; many relics of the gigantism period
of the last century—skyscrapers, freeway interchanges,
massive bridges, telecommunications towers, and the
like—can be seen in the distance.

The people here in America are just as gray on the average,
but they are taller and more mobile than those in Europe.
The remarkable endowment of fossil fuels and the headstart in nuclear energy have made a difference. Americans
appear to have evolved a "no growth" stage that moves
more bulk, takes more trips, redevelops the urban environment more frequently—indeed, that recycles nearly everything more frequently than the Europeans. The statistics—
showing that Americans consume two to five times as
much energy per capita—bear out these observations. Also,
its population has a much higher Oriental component than
the European because the society remained open to people
who were attracted by the pace, the continuing fascination
with novelty, and the ideology of achievement. Each political disaster of the last century, and some of the natural
catastrophes, left a residue of immigrants in America. It

eventually absorbed, for example, a large fraction of the Palestinian Arabs, displaced a century ago by the acts of Israel, Jordan, Syria, and Egypt, who have now become leading entrepreneurs and managers. Much of Taiwan and Hong Kong found refuge here.

Japan's oldest new towns have not yet reached the century mark. Many of them are gone—they were razed and redeveloped in response to the extraordinary rise in land prices. The groupings that are left seem not to be prized, and maintenance is perfunctory. Life-styles for most Japanese changed drastically after they obtained their cars and redistributed the metropolitan populations over the mountainsides and bays. Upon looking closer, we see that the people living the old-fashioned lives of the "new towns" are those who have been stigmatized by society— the crippled, elderly, disfigured, cross-breeds, mentally subnormal, alien working-class immigrants. They are the people out of the mainstream in the social system, supported finally by a belated social security program from public sources. Japan itself is a fascinating cosmopolitan beehive that has incorporated the images of America, Europe, and China that represent its institutional commitments, but none of this was added to any new towns except the few assigned to academics.

If the scenario were resumed in order to examine cities in the underdeveloped nations, a far different picture would nave emerged. Latin America, at least the tropical parts of it, has a serious population control problem that will cause the urbanization process to drag out for decades to come. Cities in the temperate areas (Argentina, Chile, Uruguay) should take on a physical appearance similar to the cities of Europe; those in the tropics will almost certainly adapt to widespread use of the automobile North American style, even though the values of gringo urban culture are strongly disavowed in Latin America. Because the urban regions would contain five to eight times the population and ten or more times the amount of construction they have now (except for Buenos Aires, as urbanization has proceeded furthest there), the problems to be overcome are extraordinary, the capital costs monumental, and the achievement of equitable levels of living will not come for many decades.

Continental Asia is where the principal problems in achieving a steady state exist. That is why most of this study has concentrated upon coping with the shortages to be experienced in Asian countries. It will be at least two generations before most of Asia can come close to completing the urban transition; parts, along with Africa, will require a minimum of three. At that time a vast sea of slums will have been created, because the rural population can be absorbed into the city only at subsistence levels of living. After the urban transition it will take another generation or two to reconstruct the slums, imposing upon them the principles of order that make truly viable urbanism.

Physically, the dense central cities in Asia and Africa may find it more expensive to redevelop than New York, Tokyo, or Chicago at present, because an important fraction of the new metropolitan areas would need to run round the clock in order to compete effectively. Much of the reconstruction and redevelopment, particularly the delivery of materials to the construction site, has been carried out during the periods when the city was asleep; with round-the-clock operation much more careful planning is required for rebuilding. The solutions that occur to designers now require appropriation of some of the air space above the central area for a megastructure. With the aid of service columns to the utility corridors below the surface, it could support the added floor space needed for regrowth. Since these cities are in mild-to-tropical climates, they would also provide hanging gardens that restore plant life to a milieu that had crowded it off the surface except in malls with potted trees and ostentatious plazas with flower gardens. In those climates, the loss of blazing sunlight is not regretted, especially if it is not blocked out but is filtered by a shade of living green. Heroic measures may need to be taken to ventilate the fumes from the vehicles at surface levels, and more water will be required during the dry season, but even moderate prosperity should eliminate the sterility of contemporary downtown areas.

ENERGY CHAIN AND MATERIAL TRANSFERS

It has already been argued that energy need not be the limiting factor for a global metropolis containing up to fifteen billion human beings, because sunlight alone would allow the earth to carry many more. Nevertheless, the huge investment required to provide food and fuel will determine *where* urban communities are built first. The existing legacy of fossil fuel and uranium will be converted into urbanism wherever social systems can organize themselves well enough to attract funds or postpone consumption by their own members. The increases in biomass and the negentropy incorporated into the urban environment thus represent a more organized and structured form of the free energy that had accumulated on earth in isolated pockets over previous eons.

The sources of energy available for the maintenance of fauna were elaborated in Chapter 6, but a review of the total picture from an ecological point of view remains worthwhile. In the steady-state environment existing plant species grown in the irrigated plains of the world—cereals, sugarcane, oil seeds—make up the principal food supply, those sources would be supplemented by fats, fruits, and condiments from hilly areas and rain forests. Machine populations would assist in the harvest and process photosynthetic output, delivering the product to urban populations. fresh vegetables and fruits, as well as protein enrichment, would be obtained from recycling efforts within the urban area. Extra quantities of food could come from mariculture units and algae ponds floated on marine surfaces.

The energy required to make a difference between bare subsistence and convenient comfort is expected to be distributed in the form of electric power, gas (methane or hydrogen), and hydrocarbon liquid fuels. The locations of the deposits remaining during the reconstruction of the Ecumenopolis suggest greater concentrations of energy-intensive human activity in North America—metallurgy, machine building, automotive travel, aviation—while the equally large deposits in Siberia are mechanically exploited to provide the energy-rich materials of construction, such as chemicals going into plastics, rubber, and fibers. For the next three or four decades the Near East could provide these, along with automotive fuels and fertilizer, but its stocks are due to be exhausted well before Asian urbanization is completed. The Siberian resources will be required for the urbanization of China and the maintenance of Japanese activity. The trade engendered by this transfer should raise levels of living in the USSR.

During this period of dependence upon coal, tar sands, and shale, equipment for exploiting long-term supplies of energy will be built up. Breeder reactor stations, solar energy collectors, geothermal power generators, fusion energy reactors, aerospace satellite reflectors and converters are not yet in existence technologically but, with a likelihood in the order listed, may be expected to be operating on the fringes of urbanism all over the world.[15]

High-intensity fuels are converted into low-grade energy, which is diffused away from the urban areas. In general, the air and water around large-size conurbations will be raised 2-5°C above the surrounding regions, as it is now.

The funneling of materials from all parts of the world into the urban areas will be most noticeable. Pipelines, railroads, barges, and ships will converge upon the coastal metropolises because they are the natural locations for large-volume processing. Watersheds all over the world must be reconstructed so as to regularize the flow of fresh water and keep the barges and lighters moving. Once the skeleton of a metropolis has been laid down, the need for gravel, sand, stone, clay, lime, and steel greatly diminishes, but the demand for coke, salt, cellulose, sulfur, alumina, and more exotic materials will continue. The tonnage of food and fuel (whether liquid, solid, or gaseous) will remain roughly the same as it is now per million of urban population, and equal in volume of flow to the other inputs, despite the vast improvement in quality of life for the majority.

Most of the metabolic wastes from steady-state urbanism would flow out to sea, dissolved or dispersed in water, except for radioactive by-products, which would remain carefully segregated, probably incorporated in insoluble glass. Even the carbon dioxide added to the air through chimneys, exhaust pipes, and ordinary breathing would be absorbed mainly by the sea. A variety of bacterial decomposers would be given a last chance at the effluents of the city in the form of secondary and tertiary treatment. Pollution would occur, but primarily as a result of accident, human error, or temporary subsystem breakdown. The scale of the outputs presents no serious problems; known technologies are available for handling that volume and somewhat better ones are under investigation.

RESTORATIVE FORCES

The capacity of urban society to maintain a steady state must take into account all historic precedents of vulnerability, as well as other challenges that have never happened before but nevertheless have a finite and calculable likelihood. It is then, in principle, similar to a biological system in that restorative forces are directed toward the healing

of the wounds received as well as the repression of a burst
of growth. All significant deviations in populations, frequency of interaction, stockpiles, and consumption rates
must be identified quickly and returned to a point within
the normal range of variation. Once human society has
accepted the steady state as a norm and has come close
to achieving it, the social system may use moral pressures,
prestige attribution, the price system, tax schedules, special
prises, and a number of other devices to remove discrepancies.[16] As many philosophers, both amateur and professional, have repeatedly observed, the greatest contest will
occur between the growth psychology implicit in Western
outlooks, which is now spreading as an epidemic throughout the world, and a firm immobilism espoused by many
dogmatic environmentalists, which does not allow for
drift and substitution. The steady state will require continuous long-range planning—identification of potential
disruptions, designing of policies and projects that forestall
them, and then programs for implementation. Fortunately,
our models of systems seeking general equilibrium are
better than those intended to guide growth or contraction.

Disaster planning—the use of foresight to restore normal
conditions after an abrupt destructive episode—has already
been discussed in connection with a Malthusian catastrophe.
If the disaster is traceable to a failure of rainfall, the principal policy for alleviation of suffering is a building up of
buffer stocks of food and other commodities dependent
upon regular rainfall. Such stocks are more difficult to
manage in a rural area than in a city, where larger stores
can be afforded greater protection. Temporary dependence
upon stocks of foodstuffs that keep well is easier for city
folk than for country people, because the latter have less
opportunity to experiment with alternative dietary staples.
Contrary to common perceptions, therefore, urban populations may be expected to recuperate faster from a disaster
affecting nutrition and suffer less loss than townspeople,
villagers, or nomadic bands. Stockpiling can be equally
effective for meeting discontinuities in the supply of energy
and raw materials. New epidemics are different, although
antibiotic drugs can be stockpiled also, because the response
depends upon medical institutions being maintained in a
state of readiness and empowered to use measures like
quarantine and mass inoculation. Destruction by fire and

flood is foreseeable and, in cities at least, largely preventable. By requiring insurance and by insuring the insurer, cities can get healthy regrowth of households, firms, and other microdecision units—if the stockpiles are available to be drawn upon.

The future response to catastrophe of a world society made up of organized urban units is already recognizable from present institutional reactions when based upon good information. Any stricken portion of an urban settlement will have been maintaining active telecommunications contact with leading centers prior to the time it was hit by catastrophe. If these links should be severed, queries would be immediately raised with neighbors, and alternate paths through the web of communications would be tried, so that within minutes an affected area could be identified, an alarm of appropriate magnitude raised, and aircraft would be dispatched to get an overview. That report could be matched with the scattered reports emanating from the impacted area. The causes could include a stray hydrogen bomb in the hands of fanatic terrorists, a severe earthquake, a burst dam from a major reservoir, or a political coup triggering a massive communal riot.

Previously designated agencies at the national and international levels would call in radiation-monitoring teams or other specialists knowledgeable about the conditions to be expected, and some of them would be flown in with mobile telecommunications equipment. Most often the immediate problem in such grave instances is to cope with a fire storm or the possibility that one may get started, so precautions are taken to isolate combustibles. Simultaneously, emergency stocks are drawn from storage and routed to the damaged area, and ad hoc organizations are formed on the spot to direct the activity of teams of survivors engaged first in rescue and then in the provision of emergency services. Later the stocks arrive to prevent further losses from shock, depression, and exhaustion of rescuers, and newly mobilized relief groups appear to initiate its distribution.

In theory, the response to urban disaster would be carefully graduated to the dimensions of the destruction and loss of life. In all but the very largest catastrophes, however, we must anticipate overreaction and a scandalous (based upon hindsight) waste of supplies. People get excited in emergencies; alarm signals get amplified without conscious intent. The government makes grants to take care of relief, and it guarantees loans to organizations that appear viable. Insurance efficiently hastens the recovery, especially after it has become fully computerized.

The dimensions of this relief capability are, of course, limited. My own estimate is that the response required for ten standard hydrogen bombs going off simultaneously would be the limit to their capacity; even those dimensions would reveal some serious shortages, though in part that would be because this kind of catastrophe is unprecedented, even though long feared.[17] (Disaster may arise not from war, of course, but from a number of other events ranging from the impact of a large meteorite of the kind that has left big craters on the moon and Mars upon a populated area or to the waves caused by the ice cap of Antarctica slipping off into the sea.) In the long run, the level of destruction that can be responded to adequately enough to restore production and population within a few years (not necessarily on the same site) should certainly be equal to several hundred nuclear weapons. This implies a casualty rate of something under 5% of the world's urban population. Although recovery might well be made from much larger losses, it would require decades of effort. One of the features of the integrated Ecumenopolis that improves its abilities for recovery is its ability to operate with lower per capita levels of inventory than cities do at present because of its abilities to redirect flows of goods upon shifts in demand. It still must be able to stimulate new sources of production within a few months after a disaster, however, whether food, medicine, or materials of construction. The best way might be to make the reconstruction effort a source of demand functioning so as to replace normal consumption. When reductions in consumption caused by disaster are roughly equivalent to the outlays required to repair damage, the stimulus to overshoot equilibrium is repressed.

Exceeding steady-state levels—deviation in the opposite direction—calls into play response factors of an utterly different kind. It is difficult to know what kinds of localized growth constitute a threat since a steady state must drift so as to generate new opportunities to replace those that are dying out. Therefore the social indicators chosen to describe the steady state, and to raise an alarm if they move upward beyond the rate of normal fluctuation in any part of the world, will slowly become obsolescent. For example, the full-employment indicators, adopted after Keynesian theory was accepted as a basis for policy making, were based upon an estimation of the fraction of household units without a source of earned income. Later, juvenile unemployment arising from an invasion of the job market by cohorts of the postwar baby boom became a much larger component than adult heads of households. Then housewives and the semiretired began entering the job market whenever demand for labor was rising; they did this by declaring themselves unemployed. Still more recently an increasing segment of the population has opted for part-time employment for wages while working on a voluntary basis elsewhere on tasks that are deemed to be "more relevant," and presumably more productive. In developing metropolises, unemployment indexes rarely improve when conditions improve because the underemployed and self-employed start registering as unemployed. Shifts in employment indicators are increasingly difficult to interpret.

Indirect indicators such as shifts in prices and price indexes will, or course, be closely analyzed. These analyses are likely to stimulate rule changes intended to speed up equilibration. Lags of months or years are normally discovered from an analysis of market processes. Therefore great emphasis must be placed upon leading indicators of demand shift, often drawing upon social and psychological phenomena, such as requests for information, identifiable in the flow of communications. Greater interest in the overseas environments and meetings of specialists, for example, is responsible for the indeterminately strong demand for the highest-grade fuels in air travel.

It should be remembered that growth in moderate amounts can be immediately rewarding to influential people because the costs can be externalized so as to be felt by others and also can be deferred for a long time, often to a succeeding generation. Therefore, once steady state has been achieved, growth in one sector can be allowed only if there are evidences of decline in another. Displacement of one set of activities by another is what constitutes the "drift" that is required of a steady state, but the partially hidden secondary and tertiary effects will generate a great deal of concern.

Those arguments are not nearly as fundamental, however, as others that stem from the increasing knowledge accumulated under steady-state conditions. Knowledge is the serpent in the garden city of Eden prepared for the family of man four or more generations hence—if present experience provides any basis for forecasting. Continuing growth of knowledge seems likely to produce new insights, which must then contend with older ones. They will conflict as to the timing and methods for repressing growth. We get a taste of the differences that personal background, specialty, and institutional responsibility make among the seers when we see the pulse takers of modern economies today arguing about the proper growth policies for nations and common market blocs. The issues controlling "no growth" are much broader and cannot be reduced to economic magnitudes alone. Specific hints of the disagreements to come can be inferred from the paths by which political units attempt to reach the steady state.

APPROACHES TO THE NEW EQUILIBRIUM

What happens if a country or a metropolitan region loses its way along the developmental path of resource-conserving growth? Let us imagine that straying to the right involves the obsession of a ruling class with bourgeois values—particularly, conspicuous consumption of modern artifacts. Then losing the way to the left would mean commitment to ideologies of equity to the exclusion of openness, exchange, and diversity. In either case, resources would be wasted by choosing opportunities for investment much too narrowly.

Reading of recent history suggests that it is not unreasonable to expect that a third of the urban centers will lose the way, and that a few will not move onto the developmental track at all. At this time it is impossible to guess in what proportion they will veer to the right, to the left, get stuck and make no progress, or otherwise miss altogether. There is, of course, a possibility that other paths of development, distinctly different from that described in previous chapters, may be discovered. This alternative is highly unlikely, however, because a set of powerful innovations would need to exist that were very different from those already harnessed to this projection; existing technology indicates that much variation from this path would be difficult, if not impossible. Even if alternatives were to be discovered and taken up immediately by competent institutions, they could not have a significant impact upon even a few metropolises in less than twenty years.[18] This leaves the two kinds of deflections described above to be explored, together with the third alternative of "getting stuck."

An allegory, a future-oriented *Pilgrim's Progress* for a metropolis seeking salvation in the form of an ultrastable polyarchic state of being, could be constructed from recent political experience. The result would better illuminate the temptations and errors, but the tone of the argument becomes too moralizing. It seems best to translate the ecopolitical theory of succession into contemporary concepts that are illustrated as much as possible by recent events. Although their headlines emphasized nations as the actors (and scholars continue to discuss events in this way), the datelines and the arenas of action almost uniformly referred to large cities.

What are the penalties for straying to the right? The only historic models we can refer to are also the antecedents to pathological fascism (Berlin, Rome, and Tokyo in the 1930s). In those instances the original institutional patterns (relying heavily upon security markets, credit, and monetized exchange) had been subjected to financial crisis, then to bankruptcies, shutdowns, layoffs, and other failures to meet social claims and human obligations. Under these conditions a large share of the population is deprived of its social status; its members are bewildered by the necessity of filling less rewarding niches in the social system. Charismatic figures hoping to mobilize the disaffected can then arise, and some of them are able to achieve political power; characteristically, they pick out minorities as scapegoats, magnify threats from the outside, and often embark upon militaristic adventures. In the course of such a reaction to deprivation many intellectuals become refugees, and students enrolled overseas find excuses for not returning.

In Africa, where cities like Salisbury (Rhodesia) and Kampala (Uganda) seem to have been taken off in this direction by national decision makers, the general level of stress was already so great that much more trivial events than an economic crisis were sufficient to set off a sharp turn to the right. In those places civil war always seems imminent, and guerrilla warfare on the borders becomes endemic; services decline, funds are hoarded, development activities are abandoned, and neutrals are forced to choose sides. The communications networks are filled with reports of atrocities and demands for responses to them, widening the gulf between polarized groups (one of which may be alien and live across a disputed boundary). Many instances of damage to kinfolk, property, character, and person are experienced which call for private vengeance in years to come. Nevertheless, during a deviation to the right, the truly violent conflict is rarely brought to the cities and causes little lasting destruction when it does break out. If overseas alliances are made, the capital city, which is usually also the chief metropolis, often accumulates major, highly visible structures to commemorate the relationship. Totalitarian politics stimulate a domineering architecture; the structures, like the experiences, may still cast shadows a hundred years later.

Losing the way to the left of the developmental path imposes many of the same strains upon public order, but the rhetoric changes. Private capital is seized (often its owners become the scapegoats) and operated "for the people," although physical equipment tends then to be poorly maintained and gives less service over time. Top professionals and capitalists become the refugees. Intellectuals often embrace originators of the radical changes at first but later regret many of the consequences of revolutionary fervor. Although unemployment and bankruptcies are avoided, shortages of consumer goods become rampant, and rationing becomes necessary. Queues form wherever goods are made available to consumers. Metropolitan capitals like Rangoon and Havana took this turn in the 1960s, while Santiago (Chile) and Colombo (Ceylon) were ready to follow in the 1970s, but may rejoin the mainstream.

A gray, ossifying, quasi-stable condition may be reached on the left which can last for decades, but it resolves few, if any, of the pressures for urbanization arising from an overpopulated countryside—poverty has only been shared more equally. The metropolises that have been turned to the left by a national leadership are exceedingly vulnerable to crop failure. Experience shows that their predecessors, allies, and principal trading partners have never been very successful in agricultural programs and have not been able to accumulate significant buffer stocks from their own efforts.

Mistakes and accidents can occur on the high road to development as well. Whenever societies commit themselves to conspicuous production—fancy offices and presumptuous factories that glorify the organization but add nothing to the product—they may stall because of insufficient return on investments. They officially persecute no scapegoats and expropriate no significant amount of privately held assets, but they still do not attract enough mobile capital from elsewhere in the world. Factionalism can be raised to a violent pitch. Montevideo and Belfast come to mind as examples, while Santo Domingo and several smaller African capitals show some of these tendencies at an earlier stage of development. It is expected that quite a few more will be caught in these frustrations, where officials obey the rules in the book. They are late in doing so, however, and the road is rutted; so progress halts.

Almost certainly the worst is yet to come. When failures occur because of mistakes of right, left, or center, they have cumulative consequences. The internal reserves are drawn down to the point where they exist as fictions. Supplies of food, water, power, transport, and communications will be stretched to their limits, and most or all will break down simultaneoulsy. Queues then turn into mobs of angry rioters. Troops are normally called in to halt the looting, but discipline may be shaky, and some troops are likely to join the looters. Meanwhile, families quietly act upon previous arrangements, involving the return to the village of their origin or some other rural place where they have a stake, with women and children leaving first. When husbands see their jobs disappear, they also flee. In the course of this melting away of the population and dissolution of organization, much of the physical capital of the metropolis will be stripped for salvage. Nearby towns and villages recieve the portable loot, even if it must be moved by bicycle or cart. Cities may thus be almost vacated, with great loss of life among the elderly and the defenseless poor, but the actual casualties would not be reported because only fragments of the government would be functioning. The nearest historical parallel that comes to mind is the kind of life that was lived in and around the occupied and besieged cities of Europe during World War II, but the causes then were very different.

Bad policies lead to much suffering, but the original

causes may be so distant, in the popular mind, that they are not linked to the effect; because of this, succeeding regimes may make the same mistakes, though often mixed with different ones, so that repeated disasters affect the reconstituted metropolis. However, there is also a strong chance that the policies of successful states and their metropolises will be noted, most often because of refugees who come back to become leaders. The policies that seem to be associated with success are then imitated as closely as possible. A lost city may get back on the feasible development path once again, even after having experienced a bath of bankruptcies and dissolutions of organizations. The rebound can be extremely rapid. If the metropolis meets no serious obstructions, the lost ground can be made up over a period of one to two decades, because tested models for organization that require only minor adaptations to work effectively exist within it or are accessible to it.

A curious restorative force for cities that have retrogressed derives from the nature of the military as it is presently constituted in most developing countries. In emergencies, it is impelled to take over civil administration. Note that the officers in these armies are being taught management of some of the most complex technology in the world in staff training programs provided as military aid by the Great Powers and, to some extent, as an export industry of the Israelis. Thus the upper echelons have become sophisticated in organizational procedures and experienced in trouble shooting. Moreover, a military hierarchy faced with such technology must make most promotions on the basis of competence and performance. Thus the officer corps tends to become a meritocracy (often the only one in a struggling society) made up primarily of sons of lower-level provincial civil servants, ordinary professionals, and lesser landowners. It is pragmatic in outlook and more ready to borrow apparently successful formulas than an ideologically oriented elite. Military administrators of civil affairs are able to get public utilities back into operation and even to put finances in some order, but they are rarely able to bring themselves to stimulate the plethora of social, cultural, and political organizations, such as are needed for balanced development. Growth of that sort would need to be spontaneous, and spontaneity is often repressed by police surveillance and harassment.

Thus even for wayward metropolises the transition to urban climax is eventually expected to proceed, although the growth charts may show lapses of one or two decades. Such dips represent sequences of disastrous incidents that are very likely to be as costly in life and careers as all the wars experienced thus far in this century.[19] They also represent the introduction of scars and slow-to-heal injuries that affect the structure of steady-state urbanism over long periods of time.

We know from history that painful collective suffering can result in massive neurotic behavior. One illustration is the unreasonable reactions to signals that can be observed in cities years after any real stimulation has disappeared. In Europe the abnormal price of gold and the irrational warping of private investment practice can be explained by the strong reflex actions to headlines that can be popularly associated with the inflation of the 1920s, an era when the savings of many long-established families were wiped out. Similarly, experiences with unemployment in the 1930s created a labor union organization slow to accept changes in rules involving laborsaving practices. Wartime shortages made people ready to indulge in the hoarding of storable food items at the drop of a rumor. In China the memory of the hysteria of the Red Guard movement, which came near to causing a collapse of local government, and the fervent industrialization of the earlier "leap forward," will continue to influence decisions for decades to come. The great fear in South Asia is a recurrence of the insensate communal violence that occurred during the Partition and has broken out sporadically since that time. When indicators and omens associated with communal violence are evident, many civil authorities in South Asia go into shock, refusing to take action or even respond to questions.

Historians have speculated repeatedly on the bearing of disasters upon subsequent efflorescences of urban culture. Often, though receiving refugees and making relative gains by remaining outside a stricken area, a new set of centers has emerged to give leadership in innovation and organization.[20] Thus London, Paris, Amsterdam, and their satellites rose to eminence when the Hanseatic League and the Mediterranean cities were beset with warfare over religious doctrine. Hong Kong and Singapore have prospered with the aid of refugees from the Communist takeover of China. It is possible that the economic and institutional structure of the global metropolis will be shaped and differentiated much more by unspecifiable political disasters than by the more predictable natural catastrophes, the potential consequences of which were analyzed at length in Chapter 2.

THE PRODUCTION OF EQUITY

After the enthusiasms of patriotic display and discovery of ethnic identity have worked themselves out in developing countries, signs of inequality still remain. The really important function of urbanization is to produce conditions that offer equal opportunity for participation—a better use of human potential than can be achieved even through land reform, because possession of a specific plot imposes locational constraint. This implies an unprecedented outcome of ecological succession—a climax state cultivated and ordered according to the principle that each individual should be given a fair start in his, her, or its existence, and a fair share of resources during a full life cycle rather than one in which "individual welfare" is irrelevant unless it contributes to the maintenance of the species. Thus plant seed is selected, treated to prevent fungal infestation, fertilized, and irrigated. Animals are pure bred to specifications set by consumers or crossbred for vigor. Machines are subject to quality control both in design and in production and called back for reconstruction if defective, while components and assemblies for automata are selected for minimum error. Humans are to be guaranteed literacy and an opportunity to vote as an immediate minimum provision, and a generation or two later the guarantee should reach secondary education with a shot at the university. It will be recalled that the concept of a minimum adequate standard of living as a goal of urbanization was introduced primarily to cope with these rapidly building pressures for equity.

A full quarter of the world's population has seen the equalization produced by the philosophy of Mao Tse-tung. In China anyone living luxuriously is forced to do so in private and recognize that his good fortune will not last. Egalitarianism in the distribution of hard labor and its rewards has become part of the fabric of contemporary China. Whenever there is not enough to go around, scarcities are distributed with an even-handedness that appears to be unsurpassed. Expressed discontent within Chinese

society has been reduced to a new low, although the
borders must still be guarded to keep people from leaving.
All future programs in and around China will be consciously compared with Mao's to discover whether they produce
a comparable equity. China has achieved these levels of
equalization by re-educating the elite with manual labor,
requiring people to confess publicly all feelings of superiority and accept the censure of the group. It has been
accomplished at a cost, however, since the Chinese have
borrowed heavily from the future. Mao-style equalization
has meant cutting off contacts with modern nonmilitary
technology and urban culture elsewhere in the world.
Potentially elitist institutions of higher professional education have been virtually dissolved. Such policies have increased China's vulnerability to natural disasters, but to
an extent that can be tested only by time because a trade-
off seems to have been made that enhances team effectiveness. It has also increased the difficulties of transfer of
power at the national level, which will ultimately reflect
upon the cities in incidents leading to disturbances of
public order.

As steady-state urbanism is approached, each plan or
major program seems likely to be judged as much in terms
of the number of persons raised from subsistence levels
to the minimum adequate standard as in terms of equity.
(Living at subsistence, it should be explained, actually
means living noticeably above the minimum for some
periods but being unpredictably reduced to insufficient
levels during periods of "hard times"; fatalism dominates
personal decisions, and there seems to be little incentive to
save and invest for future improvement.) Before this point,
however, at the time of the most rapid inmigration a major
test applied to a proposed program will be the number of
niches within the city that can be produced in order to
provide places for surplus people from villages and towns;
that is, how can a social system minimize the cumulative
small-scale tragedies of the countryside without creating
conditions for massive tragedies in the metropolis?
Rising to a minimum adequate standard of living is now
a gradual process, but it appears that the transition may
become quite a sharp step and a readily measurable one.
The key factor will be the urban villages' apartment blocks
built to emphasize this standard, make it uniform, and
mass-produce it with major economies of scale. The score

of a government or an administration may very well be measured by the progress it makes in producing physical evidence of equity in consumption, or by a social indicator revealing that it achieves a growth rate in pulling people over this level higher than the growth rate in the GNP. Societies must retain graduated incentives for cooperation, effort, and performance, but these would take the form of prestige and rank, rather than levels of consumption that appear to be enhanced at the expense of the comfort and convenience of others.

These national and regional plans leave a global problem of inequity—the peak disparities are found in the high consumption levels in America and Western Europe. Standards associated with these cultural norms are already embedded in airport centers around the world, and they spread out from there into luxury suburbs, supermarkets, sport cars, motels, and the like in each metropolitan area of Asia, Africa, and Latin America. Their adoption by local people who are powerful and influential reduces the inequity of *elite* relationships with the Americans, but it virtually destroys local programs that are designed to reduce inequities. Such leaders lose the trust of their constituencies, even though respect for their ability to deal with the affluent societies may be retained.

Yet everyone admits that the Americans are likely to create, perfect, and export a larger share of the resource-conserving technology than any other society. They have the know-how for satisfying wants at the same time that they spread the infection of multiplying wants. Further, all the alternative sources of this kind of knowledge, such as might be provided by the representatives of their nearest competitors in Western Europe and Japan, are not noted for their restraint or abstemiousness. Walling them all out and closing a society to high consumption norms, therefore, is not only likely to exclude relevant knowledge and reduce economic growth over the long run but, because of this, would actually hold down the rate at which equity is approached.

A claim will be made repeatedly that the profligacy of Americans deprives others of scarce resources, thus preventing them from ever achieving adequate levels of living. Our estimation of the carrying capacity of the earth suggests, however, that it will probably be quite feasible for a billion people to consume energy at a rate ten times the minimum adequate standard and another five billion to consume at intermediate levels, if world population at steady state did not exceed fifteen billion. Thus the maintenance of some parts of world society at American levels really means that the maximum tolerable population would be reduced to a level much nearer the actual expected size. Inequity in energy use might well be traded off against rewards in some other medium that uses little energy—most probably related to communications.

The corollary argument, that American levels of living will retard the *rate* of progress toward equity elsewhere in the world, is more difficult to gainsay. In the 1975-1990 period the built-in requirements for hydrocarbon fuels for electric power production and transportation may raise prices for oil and gas to premium levels, thus slowing the spread of the Green Revolution (which requires oil and gas for economical fertilizer production). So far the effect seems to be small, however, and seems more than counterbalanced by the amount of foreign aid extended in the form of emergency food supplies and in energy-intensive equipment.

Most likely, also, a number of idealistic Americans (perhaps 10% of them when in their twenties) would voluntarily adopt a minimum adequate standard of living and perfect a variety of life-styles that fit low levels of consumption. Then if the tendency for emulation is a problem in a particular locale (as in China or Cuba today), American, Japanese, or European organizations may recruit these "Peace Corps types," or even members of the various technically competent countercultures, as their representatives. Multinational corporations are not organized to work this way at present, but many non-profit international non-government organizations, such as church service committees are already doing so.[21] In the long run it seems likely that adequate organizational interfaces can be prepared between societies struggling to achieve equity at minimal levels and those that operate far above them, even though the integrated character of the Ecumenopolis may enhance the exchange of persons a hundredfold and the exchange of images a thousandfold over present levels.

It appears quite certain that steady-state urbanism will

contain certain energy-intensive regions. The chemicals, plastics, and metal working of the world will be concentrated in those areas. Two such regions are found in North America (the Appalachian coal fields that extend to Illinois and Iowa form one, and the lower-grade bituminous beds that stretch from Canada to Texas under the Western plains the other), and they seem likely to be producing sizable quantities of coproduct liquid fuels for automotives at a time when the urban transition is completed. Deposits of equal size in different parts of Siberia offer less access to the world; those locations are expected to specialize in extremely energy-intensive areas of manufacturing, such as aerospace fuel. These areas would continue to be converted into man-made badlands until hydrocarbons from coal, shale, and tar sands cost as much as the direct conversion of sunlight. There is an environmental price that must be paid by those societies fortunate enough to possess more than their share of the world's energy reserves.

It is the American propensity to create extraordinarily disperse urbanism and to preserve vast areas in a close approximation of their original natural state that generates the long-run inequity in energy use. Spacious dwellings on large lots require personal, motorized transport in order to achieve the same number of face-to-face meetings and man-nature contacts as elsewhere. We can see from the foregoing analysis that the carrying capacity of the world is sufficient to support these tastes—there could be room enough at a steady state for a thinly settled North America, an almost empty Australia, North Africa, and Siberia, and a considerable quantity of energy potential would remain for transporting people to empty places for recreation. But overall equity demands that others must have some nonmaterial cultural or political commodity that they hold to be valuable to replace the freedom to move about in airplanes and autos. The commodity may be a privilege, such as the right to live in a residential college or a revered community, or a chance to have first choice when unique services become available. The true equity problem on the world scale resolves itself into a psychological issue; it involves a confrontation between the demand for participation on equal footing and the demand for continuing an already existing pattern of urban behavior.

A world with population and activity at a steady state implies that the sum of the earth's physical conditions will be constant. The analysis up to this point assumed that no significant changes (other than those induced by humans in their efforts to survive) would occur in the natural environment during the urban transition. This is the simplest assumption, and most likely it is valid. Nevertheless, the implications of some concrete alternatives bear investigation.

Recent geological and meteorological reports can be fitted together so as to suggest that a transition of the global environment may be imminent.[22] Studies from several different directions propose that a new ice age may be beginning and that the speed of onset is so rapid that the glaciers could be approaching their previous farthest extent in less than a hundred years—the time the urban transition is expected to be completed. The likelihood of such a spectacular climatic shift seems now to be somewhere between five and ten chances in a hundred and therefore real enough to take into account as an alternative future. Research leading to the formulation of an adequate theoretical explanation for glacial cycles is now very active, so that this estimate of the odds could move quite sharply upward within a matter of months from the time of writing.

With less energy reaching the surface of the earth, the overall carrying capacity for urban ecosystem would be diminished. At least as serious as the reduction in biological productivity on land and most seas would be the stranding of the maritime metropolises. Since the onset of a full ice age would cause the sea level to drop 100-200 meters, about 10-15% more dry land would be created. The Mediterranean Sea might start drying up altogether, as it has before. Until now advanced societies have located well over 80% of their capital investments in the narrow strips within the hundred-meter contour from navigable seas and streams. Thus new construction would have to be initiated to replace existing facilities, and continued at a pitch that is equaled only during wars for survival. Energy conservation would, of course, move up to top priority, and the manner of construction and its appearance would greatly change.

Every time a series of severe winters is followed by cool, wet summers, fears regarding the onset of another ice age have been expressed publicly in the areas that had once been glaciated. The images evoked are those of the return of the polar bear and the reindeer (though regrettably the woolly mammoth is extinct), with man occupying caves and forests at the fringes of the glacier. This picture, however, was that of a prehistoric era with an ecosystem that cannot be reinstituted; man has changed the world greatly in the interim. More solid grounds for suspicion that a new ice age could come quickly began appearing about 1970 among independent circles of physical scientists. Emiliani studied oxygen isotope distributions in deep-sea sediments in order to determine the temperature of the seas in which shell-making organisms lived, and discovered that there had been several more ice ages than had been deduced by land-based glaciologists. One implication of his work is that ice ages could come on very swiftly—perhaps within a century. Shortly thereafter astronomers became concerned about the upper-altitude dust that was being produced around cities. It not only limited the capacity of their telescopes to see out but also significantly reduced the amount of light that could penetrate to the surface. The Los Angeles Basin had already doubled the albedo—reflection of light back to outer space—and it was noted that another fourfold increase could cause the onset of a surface temperature reduction great enough to be associated with ice age conditions.

These kinds of reports alert one immediately to a possible rethinking of the future. During the course of this analysis we have been forced to visualize city building at a rate at least tenfold greater than at present. Could this construction process itself trigger climatic changes leading to its obsolescence? Accumulated astronomical records were compared, with the result that large cities could be absolved of blame. Their enhancement of albedo was shown to have a highly localized, rather than global, effect. The shift in blame might not affect the process, however, since a review of these same records indicated that volcanic explosions, such as that of Krakatoa, were large enough producers of fine particles delivered to the upper atmosphere to change the surface temperature. They are accompanied by richly red sunsets with strong aesthetic appeal.

Then a body of evidence arrived from another set of investigators. Geologists tracing the implications of the newly accepted continental drift theory reported that the tectonic plate—an island of crustal material—of Australia was colliding with the partially submerged plate that made up Southeast Asia. Thus the Indonesian archipelago will build up increasingly intense seismic activity over the next several hundreds of thousands of years. Large-scale explosions, bunched in time, could not be prevented. In this context we understand Agung (Bali) in 1963, Taal in 1965, and Mayon and Fernandina in 1968. Their effects would become worldwide as the upper atmosphere dust circulated farther away from the Equator.

The first shock would be transmitted by the effects of *tsunamis* and earthquakes. Tidal waves would cause much destruction of shipping and shoreline property, taking tens or hundreds of thousands of lives, particularly in densely populated Java. World response would be quick, and relief flown in to sustain the survivors, helping them to rebuild. The dust would affect local crops most strongly, but the extra-cold growing season would mean that grain crops all over the world would have a bad year. The cause—the clouds of not-so-fine particles—would thin out in the course of a year, washed out of the atmosphere by the rain clouds.

The next year would still be bad, but because it is possible to predict altered weather patterns, many measures would be taken in food surplus countries to maximize production. The cities that do not have rationing would take pre-cautionary measures, and potential catastrophe would be barely averted.

Even after coarse volcanic particles settle, the fine dust would remain in the upper reaches of the atmosphere. New eruptions make significant contributions. The jet stream in the Northern Hemisphere would drop a thousand kilometers south, and a new air circulation pattern would be instituted, with the Pacific storms battering coasts and transporting rainfall to regions that expect to stay relatively dry. Deviations from the previous norm swing to the kind of weather experienced in the winter of 1972-73 for reasons no one yet knows; the new mean around which the weather varies is a bit more extreme than that when measured in terms of temperature and precipitation.

Ice and snow accumulate in Scandinavia, Russia, Canada, Alaska, and Iceland. The ice packs on Greenland and Antarctica would also noticeably thicken, although much more of the Arctic would tend to become open water.

When it does, the energy it receives from the sun is much less reflected away but produces evaporation, which is later condensed on the periphery of the Arctic and accelerates the growth of glaciers. Sea water temperatures drop by 3°C in the Atlantic and Pacific, later by another step almost as large. The surface of the earth covered by ice and snow in November 1968 was 33 million square kilometers, while at the peak of a glacial period it is believed to be around 50 million. (Since 1968 the figure has advanced beyond 38 million.) Unprecedented cold fogs would develop in many locales, but wherever airports operate and cities depend upon automotive traffic, measures would be taken to disperse the fog locally, because that is the one kind of weather modification that can be undertaken with almost complete confidence of success. As snow accumulates more rapidly on land, the sea level would drop. This rate might exceed 10 centimeters per year. The combined effects would change the ocean currents, the areas of upwelling, the locations of the fisheries, and thus disturb the lives of people making their livelihood from marine activities. Note, for example, that almost all harbors would become too shallow to accommodate the ships designed to use them. At the same time many of the deserts would turn green. All these changes could be set into motion by an albedo change that reduced the energy absorbed by the surface by only 2-5% (see table 6).[23]

Much remains unknown about the fine particulate matter that is occasionally blown into the upper reaches of the atmosphere from volcanic activity. For example, there is increasing evidence that it is not the dust that is important but the ammonia and the sulfides. They oxidize to nitrates and sulfates and absorb moisture, thus becoming heavier. Can the process by speeded up? That remains to be seen. Meanwhile, it is worth speculating what might happen if man remains incapable of coping with natural forces of global scale.

SCENARIO
TWELVE

If a New Ice
Age Begins

Within a decade or so of the serious buildup of glaciation, most of the older ports become unusable, because the dredges can no longer keep up with the retreat of the tidewater. The tidal regimes themselves become erratic. Equally unusual effects are observed on the land, mostly in the form of storms, floods, landslides, and droughts.

Disaster relief activities become a special duty of expanded military forces, which find themselves taking on many different kinds of responsibilities. Crops fail three years in a row in some densely populated places, so that the discouraged, impoverished farmers are forced to abandon their land. Others, formerly in marginal territories, grow prosperous because the prices for exportable surpluses have risen so high.

A very sharp change occurs as ice collecting around Greenland, Iceland, and the Faroes Islands cuts off the flow of Arctic water into the Atlantic and shifts the direction of a weakened Gulf Stream. Over the next few years the Arctic itself becomes more open and increases the flow into the Pacific. Eventually the glaciers on land bridge the Bering Strait as well, thus transmitting a major shock to the Pacific circulation system. North Pacific climates paradoxically improve in many coastal regions.

A desperate counterattack is launched, led by the Russians. Hydrogen bombs temporarily break the ice bridges. Carbon black is dusted over spring snow around the cities to speed its melting and extend the growing season. A good share of the European livestock population is sacrificed because its maintenance, long dependent upon imported feed for wintering, has now become too expensive compared to synthetic milk and cheese substitutes. French cheesemakers move to the Atlas Mountains in Morocco, where the cattle population has been expanding as a result of increased grazing. After a few years the counterattack loses its momentum; by now the diagnosis has been conclusively reached that a huge, irreversible transition is under way. The only remaining strategy is to adapt to a new kind of world. Two hundred million Russians, three hundred million Chinese, a few Scandinavians and British, and some Swiss need to be resettled. The Southern Hemisphere has very few people affected, but also no increase in resources to succor the populations being evicted by oncoming glaciers.

Engineers again become folk heroes. They dig underground cities that conserve energy so that people can live in the places where they intend to remain. They build gigantic agricultural camps in the unused portions of the tropics for the production of food. Huge losses of population are experienced in North China, but finally, more in self-defense than anything else, the Arabs arrange for the

establishment of Chinese territories on the expanded
coastline of the Arabian peninsula. Despite increases in
rain, desalinated water is still needed for the support of
the Chinese settlers, who must learn from the Israelis
how to economize in the multiple uses of this precious
fluid. A corner of tropical Australia is similarly opened to
an enclave of Chinese. Huge public works, aimed at building cities directly out of the lateritic soil and sand, are
organized. With marvelous discipline, year by year, a new
Shanghai materializes, even though on some occasions it
does not know whether the food and fertilizer ships needed
to keep it alive will arrive in time. The changes in Italy,
Greece, Turkey, Egypt, and Israel come more slowly, but
it is evident that each of these societies must seek a new
home, because the Sahara is moving into their extended
borders.

More important than any physical change during this
period of ethnic transfer is the psychological effect of a
palpable crisis. Many will remain altruistic for years as
long as a crisis is at hand, though thereafter they are in-
clined to consider alternative choices. Thus people defer
consumption and double or treble the rate of saving. Their
attachments to site or recreational areas are greatly diminished because their attention has been deflected, and the
character of the places themselves greatly changed. Because
the administrations of the old high-density cities anticipate
that they may have to break the bonds that tie people to
their neighborhoods, a process of mutual disaffiliation
begins. The newer multinational organizations manage to
grow rapidly by serving as an alternative face-to-face
community and attract a remarkable amount of loyalty.
As a consequence of the environmental stress the multinationals are freed to place their operations almost anywhere on earth.

One would think that the loss of a hundred million lives
in Asia over the course of one terrible winter would make
the remainder of the population reluctant to produce
children. Logic suggests that couples need to remain mobile,
unencumbered with babies. In Latin America and a few
other miscellaneous regions the striking rise in abortions
indicates that the literate population is belatedly shocked
into a recognition of the importance of population control.
Elsewhere, however, a significant rise in the birth rate
occurs. Survey research interviews reveal that the increased

uncertainty of survival, combined with the enforced lack of mobility due to energy shortages, has the same effect as the onset of a war. In societies where one's identity depends upon family tradition, households try to assure maintenance of the lineage, and elsewhere the craving for human bonds is so heightened that children seem to be highly desirable, regardless of risks.

As a result of all these independent microdecisions the planners anticipate that the overall world population trend will remain about the same. However, much more effort and capital are to be expended henceforth to overcome the variability of food production. What had been spent in the military budget is now directed largely toward fighting back the oncoming glaciers until existing capital equipment—for example, the big dams in Quebec, Norway, and the USSR, the oil fields of the Alaskan North Slope, and the Sault Ste. Marie locks in the Great Lakes system— can be amortized. Thus a collective war, with close bargaining among allies, is being waged against cold and hunger.

Looking forward to the end of the twenty-first century: The global planners now expect that the glaciers will have reached their fullest extension about then and a steady state for human society will also have to be achieved. Birth rates have already been reduced to replacement levels, but the population will drift up to about twelve billion as the average age increases. More tropical land will be available to support them, because the oceans are due to recede a total of 140 meters, creating much new delta land. The Gulf current will resume its old path to the coast of Africa, the same that it maintained 17,000 years ago. Northern metropolises will have transformed themselves into largely underground settlements organized to operate round the clock; their surface is allocated to gardens, and the long summer days are becoming a continuous vegetarian festival.

A very high degree of interdependence is evolving. This is reflected in the agencies devoted to world and regional government. A polyarchic, polycentric basis for arriving at many big decisions seems to be operating informally; it is put into traditional legal form afterward by constitutional draftsmen. The bases for the decisions have become highly technical, and conflicts between firms, metropolises, or nations are resolved by experiment or simulation as the technique of arbitration. All this is attributed to the scale of resettlements and the effect of other responses to the advance of the ice.

REALITIES BEHIND THE SUBSTANCE

Whenever an unprecedented density, gradient, proportion, or rate is built into a plan, responsible professionals must view it with suspicion and ask for extra evidence of its feasibility. Thus far, reasonably adequate backing has been provided on the feasibility of the technological and economic aspects of our projections for resource-conserving cities, but there has been insufficient evidence for social, political, and cultural feasibility. For example, although great emphasis was placed upon the use of communications channels as partial substitutes for scarce natural resource, nothing has been said about the coding of communications—the language problems.

Long ago, Karl Deutsch, in his *Nationalism and Social Communications,* pointed out that language often becomes the sticking point in orderly institutional development.[24] It is an all-important system lying behind concrete reality; with it we manipulate a social system that, in turn, modifies the physical environment. Although the global metropolis will contain many more residents whose mother tongue is Chinese (the next in size is Hindi), those masses will arrive on the urban scene after the model for advanced cultural communications has been set. The most likely outcome, therefore, is that ordinary English, spoken with many accents, will become the dominant medium of discourse. Thus the language of the first country to start the Industrial Revolution and of the first to complete the urban transition, and that of the first to go through the mobility transition, will continue to be associated with the process of urbanization, although not without conflict.

In every urbanizing country minority groups place great store in the preservation of their language and culture. After agitation, and often also bloodshed, they receive the right to teach their language in public schools, while the literature and other communicable aspects of the culture become part of the core curriculum for teachers. As the literate population in this language expands, students discover that they are at a disadvantage in competition for seats in the centers of higher education. If there are as many as a million persons in such a group, they are likely to agitate for their own university. Although resistance from authorities may be strong, the ethnic dissidents almost always win. However, the new generation then discovers that the language which they have mastered is unable to grapple with the knowledge underlying modern professions such as medicine, engineering, and management; it also puts them at a disadvantage in the political games bureaucrats must play. They are likely to reject the language of the dominant group (Mandarin, Hindi, Urdu, Russian, Malay, Arabic, etc.) and choose an international language (English, French) in which to invest their effort.

When the native language is backed by institutions of higher education and by public associations for the preservation of drama, poetry, history, and ritual, a surprising community cohesion results. It is often backed by people with financial resources and status. Inevitably a demand for a separate self-governing state arises wherein the "mother tongue" is used to manage the whole political system. Sometimes peaceful solutions are found within confederation, as in Switzerland; but more often the demand for secession is resisted, and an endemic civil war results. Win, lose, or draw, the urge for self-government on the part of a special language group must be balanced by the need to conduct international relations; one of the international languages must therefore be taught in secondary schools and colleges up to a level of equal proficiency with the native tongue. English is almost always chosen (French was a strong contender until the mid-twentieth century), and it quickly displaces all other languages in the high culture. Ambitious students must know English well in order to have an opportunity to study abroad and achieve the highest levels of specialization; for the upwardly mobile component in the population, the principal lever for achievement is mastery of this alien tongue.

English has also become the language by which a major multinational organization is run. Even the Japanese, who restrict participation of outsiders in their organizations to rather minor roles, have found that knowledge of English is prerequisite to operations overseas. They achieved their astonishing successes only after discovering that mass marketing is a trade that is taught in the American version of English. The technology, the files, and the internal communications of such organizations are recorded almost entirely in English, even in regions where other languages dominate. Roughly 70% of the new scientific publications are printed in English; an even higher proportion of the material that commands respect appears first in English. Moreover, the proportion is growing over time. The names of the largest multinational organizations—IBM, General Motors, Bank of America, Exxon, General Electric, ITT, World Bank—are indicative of the momentum of English.

This is particularly significant because the programming languages by which automata function and communicate with each other will be restricted versions of the dominant language. As the codes for automata become more elaborate, they are expected to resemble what is now characterized as an "autonomous" style of spoken English. It is precise, unambiguous, and contains none of the paralinguistic features of communication involving intonation, gestures, and postures that carry through in human use of the language from the context of respective subcultures. The idea of autonomy is important for the new subspecialty of the linguists called generative semantics, which describes how the increased load of meanings presentable through language affects grammar.[25] Huge economies in secretarial labor are achievable if the man-automaton interface acquires finer distinctions. Increasingly the specialist in urban society will be taught technical material in a form that is compatible with a digital computer—from medical diagnoses to statistics to the search for legal precedents—even though no computer program may be involved.

If English only represented a medium associated with tradition and was a language preferred by alien imperialist corporations, it might be expected to be displaced by the dominant mother tongue of an urbanizing people in a growing metropolis. But English is becoming also the medium of exchange of information best suited to the expanded use of the electromagnitic spectrum, mainly because it is the source of the specialized languages employed for the representation of sociotechnical knowledge. Languages used in intimate relations—courtship, raising a family, organizing a gang, creating a team, expressing a sentiment, or building a friendship—will naturally draw upon a more traditional local dialect or else a version of spoken English that has borrowed much from local culture. Not to become literate in English in the city of the future, however, would entail a decision to retreat from the world

at large into one of the many enclaves set up for intro-
spective or retrospective meditation, where alternative
life-styles are propagated, and reclusive forms of urban
life are maintained away from the channels for exerting
economic and political power. In many of these enclaves
patterned novelties and preverbal images will be invented
or resuscitated and then peddled to society at large through
the telecommunications media. Music provides an excellent
example. When the images gain substantial acceptance,
they will be assigned a convenient label and join the
common lexicon drawn upon by English speakers without
a moment of hesitation. At the moment the world lacks
a good indexing system for preverbal images—one that will
encompass multiple millions of ideas with a lookup time
equivalent to that of a large dictionary or encyclopedia—
and does not seem likely to acquire such a system for some
time to come. Interfacing them with automata remains
very clumsy in the world of graphics and patterns.

It is easy to believe that preverbal images, as transmitted
by tape, film, music, graphics, and designed forms, will
become an exceedingly significant means of communication because of their cross-cultural potentials, and that a
large share of the cultural inventiveness of human society
will be expended upon the visual medium (the channel
capacity of the aural medium is a small fraction, say
about a quarter, of the visual). Language itself will be
expanding its lexicon, primarily to catch up. The lack of
adequate recall systems, however—the kind that use
specialized humans, such as archivists, or man-machine
combinations—for inventories of patterns or images is
likely to lead to early saturation. As much will be lost
as is acquired, and creative minds in film and videotape
will spend most of their creative time going over explored
territory, believing it is utterly virgin. So long as this
condition persists, the real growth of cosmopolitan culture
will continue to be recorded in the literary form and indicated best through indexes reporting upon items added
to the English vocabulary.

The normal city dweller in the future will be working **MOTIVATIONS**
much more with communications technology. He is expected to spend twelve to twenty hours per week, perhaps
even more, interacting with a screen, as compared to eight

to twelve hours in the public spaces of the city.[26] Altogether, there will be much more public life in the metropolis of the future than is obtained in any metropolis
today. The reward structure in the games that are played
between the citizen and the molders of the content of the
mass media will determine or reinforce mood, motivation,
belief system, and attitudes held by the citizen. Censorship
and strict control over content results very soon in distrust
of the media that have been so constrained, and a consequent reduction in the attention paid to it. Once a resident knows the languages, spoken and visual, he will choose
the channels that present information within a range of
complexity he finds comfortable, and he will select the
items that seem to be trustworthy. The interactive features
assure that the content of the media could be kept more
relevant and rewarding for all levels of sophistication.
What are the consequences for a largely postindustrial
society?

The social transactions involved in learning about the
complex environment of the global metropolis, and the
shared content of the mass media that keeps individuals
in contact with current developments, should together
produce some recognizable characteristics of a "mass
mind." At a given time in a given region certain generalized
motives are expressed and felt by a large share of the population. McClelland has identified three such factors by
analyzing the content of textbooks and publicly dissemin-
ated imagery—achievement, affiliation, and power.[27]
Extrapolating from his observations and measurements
of the motivational content of literature, drama, and visual
imagery of the mainstream culture, we expect that the
drive to build, to acquire skill, and to organize should
result in a strong emphasis upon achievement and performance during the construction of the global metropolis.
If history is to repeat itself as steady-state urbanism becomes integrated into an Ecumenopolis, there will be a
strong shift to an emphasis upon affiliation, accompanied
by the onset of a golden age in the arts. Among Charles
Morris's preferred "ways of life," which introduce somewhat more patterned value orientations, we must expect
that the rates of social change involved in accelerated
urbanization will cause new generations to adopt an outlook not too different from the American; they will prefer

tentative commitments and ad hoc situations, learning a little about a variety of ways of life.[28]

Some cautions and alarms must be raised along with these projected shifts of mass-mind motivation. Frequently, in the course of completing the urban transition, a need for power is superimposed upon a need to achieve—a combination that makes it possible for even a not-so-charismatic leader to gain control of the society through a virulent, aggressive political program involving the domination of others. Germany and Japan went through such a phase in the 1930s, and tens of millions of lives were lost in the process of resisting their pathological political systems. The violent elements among the few thousands of Arab and Irish extremists have caused enough world incidents to suggest that the global metropolis could become a very troubled place to live in if millions of powerless but power-seeking persons were to vent their frustrations upon the symbols of authority.

In the imagery of the mass media much fantasy is mixed with fact, myth with verified relationships. Very early in life a person develops a system of beliefs that includes myth, relationships to outside uncontrolled forces (such as a deity), and a set of proprieties, among other components. These systems undergo great stress during times of social change and the creation of larger specialized groupings as in urbanization. Incompatibility between traditional rural beliefs and experiences in the city leads to major reorientations sparked by social movements. In Latin America a turn to Pentecostal and fundamentalist Protestantism is commonly encountered in the *barriadas* and *favelas* sheltering the newly urbanized populations. The new belief system tends to fit the requirements for survival in a social system demanding postponement of gratification, autonomy, and reduced frequency of error in dealing with machinery and organizations much better than the abandoned anticlerical Catholicism.[29]

BELIEF SYSTEMS

The Red Guard movement in China also fits into the category of an enthusiastic adaptive cult. Stimulated by a living, canonized saint, it undertook a Maoist social action crusade that aimed to remove the barriers created by ascribed social status. Those with above-average rank were forced to confess their alienation from the masses.

Like a plague of human locusts, the enthusiasts boarded trains and scoured China in search of targets in the schools and the administration. Universities disbanded, schools recessed, production fell off, transport snarled, violent resistance for officeholders flared, foreign relations were cut off, and ambassadors were recalled to face a mob engaged in a holy war of purification.

The frenzy was halted by calling in the army, and the participants were largely distributed to villages for disciplined work and indoctrination. Five years after, production had rebounded and was scoring new records for output; but technological schools and universities operated only at the lowest levels, and scientific journals (except for medicine) were not yet published. Urban life was still suspect, and rustication was regularly imposed upon officials despite great cost to operations.[30]

Next time the crusade that shakes Chinese society might exhibit quite different fixations, but still with roots in Chinese tradition. The sequel for the society might well be civil war, with military cliques struggling to maintain power over their respective home regions.

India is subject to similar pressures, particularly since it is creating an increasingly large stratum of unemployed college and university graduates. As in the Maoist Naxalite movement, local violence is readily resorted to and can become substantial. Indians seem to be more schismatic than the Chinese, however, so that enthusiastic cults wishing to impose social change splinter early and begin to battle each other. (The police stood by and almost cheered in public while hundreds of assassinations took place among the factions of the Maoists in West Bengal in the early 1970s.) Institutions in India seem to be less seriously affected by such movements that in China.

When belief systems must change because outside forces affecting human lives seem to have modified the patterns of reward and punishment, some prophets will find ways of organizing people around less disruptive sets of beliefs that introduce new meaning into city life. The Pentecostal and fundamentalist evangelists in Latin America have already been mentioned; they will be found all through the partly Christianized areas of Asia and Africa as well. Such conversion often lapses and is replaced by missionaries from Seventh Day Adventists, Mormons, Lutherans, and other belief systems that provide more comprehensive doctrinal and institutional supports for achievement in urban society. In Africa and around the edges of Asia many syncretist forms of religion continue to be fashioned in order to cope with the stresses of urbanization A leader or guru may assemble tens or hundreds of thousands of followers before the sect begins to fade away; effective disciple-managers may even transform the religion so as to attract millions, build monumental places of worship, and perpetuate it institutions. The second-generation organizers of the Soka Gakkai in postwar urban Japan, seemed to have this appeal.[31] However, the opening to China in 1972 may have deflated the popularity of its Clean Government political program; very likely, enthusiasm will be deflected to a more generalized approach to cleanliness. The youngest generation of contemporary Japanese, knowing nothing but city life, television, and tours to resorts now appears to be attracted to a nature-worshipping emphasis upon environmental purification.

Some religions can have an enormous effect upon the livability of cities as long as the supply of goods and services is short of meeting requirements for the minimum standard of living. This is Karl Marx's "opiate of the masses" argument in modern dress. Even as minorities, the organized religions can negotiate coalitions that stimulate official campaigns for cleanup, reform, and the prevention of needless destructive exploitation of collectively held resources. A whole chain of consequences follows: for example, since the disappearance of garbage and litter in Chinese cities inside and outside Communist China, flies and rats do not breed; without flies, dysentery drops off significantly; without dysentery, babies are more vigorous and more likely to survive. The psychological effects of the slogans, the public approval of acts of cleaning up litter, or disciplined behavior in public places will have even longer-range consequences. Patterns for urban behavior arise from just such experiences.

The doctrines of such religions and the belief systems they encompass will have a larger and more immediate effect upon forging the life-styles of the Ecumenopolis than the kinds of resource-conserving technology depicted in earlier chapters, yet much less can be said about them. Technology must be based upon scientific fact if it is to work, and science offers a basis for forecasting. Environmental beliefs and publicly held myths have often disregarded both scientific and economic facts, but enthusiasms have still survived. They have greatly contributed to diversity in the metropolis as a result. In many instances prices paid by believers and unbelievers alike are registered in prohibitions or lost freedoms, such as not eating meat, for which there are no strong regrets if they have been replaced with other satisfactions.[32]

Once steady-state urbanism is achieved, its great crises could very well be epidemics of myth carried by word of mouth and reinforced through the channels of the mass media. These ideas start as curiosities but mutate into doctrines of movements. Enthusiasm carries them beyond the bounds of reason. Then resources are wasted, and property may be destroyed. Once the infrastructure for the spread of such epidemics of mind-set is established, the foreseeable future of urban life becomes a series of cycles, each great myth building upon the wreckage of previous ones, as in the history of China and the period of the great empires in the West. At climax many living populations are locked into such cycles as a basis for ritualized behavior.

An alternative view, and a more probable one, is that the huge capacity for developing competitive sets of images, now provided by our association with automata and links through communications networks, will bring about an equilibration at this metalevel as well. An exchange relationship between a myriad of social movements would come into being. Extremes in enthusiasm would be damped out by experience with prior formulas; populations stuffed with the drama provided by records of past human experience would become sophisticated in their reactions. The waves and cycles would still be noted, but would remain at the level of style in expression, and would not lead to the destruction of the life and images of nonconformers.

THE TRANS-FORMATION OF THE SPECIES

The modern social movements based upon alternative belief systems actually have a great deal of philosophical work to do. The accumulation of knowledge has had an erosive effect upon the dogmas and rationales still being held today, and a new formultion of doctrines regarding the self-image of man is required. The theory of living systems applied to the transition into a climax situation

can be fitted into a theory of human evolution. An ecosystem with plentiful food supply and a low level of variation in its overall biomass will generate many small niches
into which species can fit with enough security to survive.[33] Biologists have almost come into agreement that
man's physiological evolution has been halted, because of
crossbreeding and the preservation by modern medicine
of those who otherwise would not have reproduced; they
propose that evolution has been transferred to cultural
forms. However, they have neglected the effects of the
backward flow of that knowledge, along with other
features of human culture, upon man himself. The new
social movements will have to find a way of coping with
the feasibility of long-run differentiation in the human—of
preset, built-in, inequalities that last throughout life.

These major challenges to humanistic preconceptions
and beliefs, particularly those of the long struggle to
eliminate inequality in the endowment of individuals upon
their entry into the social system, arise from the progress
in biology that deals with "inside-the-skin" phenomena.
The recent wave of interest in organ transplantation
represents a small beginning. The parallel with the transformation of plant and animal species, where the rate of
evolutionary change was speeded up ten thousand times,
exists all round us.[34] New techniques would, of course, be
tested out thoroughly on plants and laboratory animals, by
determining their capacities to exist in a standardized model
environment, before they are applied to humans as therapy.

It can always be said that more education and imagination are required before the implications of similar
somatic engineering with enzymes and enzyme inducers
(such as hormones) can be understood. Until then a program for expanding the size of infants' brains, either by
adding natural growth hormone at a critical period or by
some similar violation of the integrity of self as defined
by the prevailing value system, cannot be proposed for
adoption. Nevertheless, these products will be used to
overcome damage to the organism, and doctors must
plan so as to obtain supernormal performance rather than
subnormal.

The production of multiple identical twins through the
technique of cloning was a shocking concept in the early
1960s, when it was first visualized as feasible in the fore-

seeable future. Now, however, as a wider variety of primary groups and households are experimented with in the West, it becomes increasingly acceptable to think of children being genetic replicas of each other, and perhaps also of a parent. The primary objection—that it could produce only personal tragedies because it clashes with a context of lives based upon standard households and human relationships—not longer seems persuasive. The argument for cloning, of course, is that "superior" genes would be selected, so that the best individual fits to a new wholly urban environment could be reproduced many times. This implies that the instances of bad fit would not be allowed to reproduce—at least to the same degree that cloning is introduced.[35] To keep population under control, a reproductive compact of some kind would seem to be required. Included in the pact must be some kind of review of the quality of replication because, thus far at least, the error rate in the cloning of frogs has been high, and theory suggests that it may always be somewhat greater than in sexual reproduction.

It is probably not going to be too difficult to get sufficient consensus within a community unified by a common belief system to aim at some idealized biologically perfect human being, since all the members have already agreed upon a formula of some kind that designates correct behavior. Every device available to biology and psychology would then be used to make each new human being into the intelligent, lovable, responsive, active, dependable person he could be according to theory. Molding man into that ideal would probably require a huge amount of organized human effort and use up more resources per capita than was provided for in the minimum adequate standard. If so, then portions of the Ecumenopolitan population would be voluntarily reducing their numbers so as to approach more closely an ideal human race—the logical extension of the quality versus quantity argument. People would identify with the whole human race as an extension of their own family, rather than limit the concept to a continuation of a blood line. Should the world prevent a multinational organization from carrying out these experiments in human racial evolution? Or an unusual metropolis or two from opting for such a vision of the future?

In the past few years an acceleration has occurred in the mapping of mammalian chromosomes. Given the number of scientific leads that exist, more advances are to be expected. We must anticipate that well before global metropolis has come into being, the complete genetic structure of a normal human being—from DNA and RNA to protein—will be as well known as the Mendeleev chart of chemical elements. Strong beginnings will have been made on determining the gene frequencies found regionally in the human population as a whole. The processes of interaction of genes with each other to give somatic expression will be cataloged. The natural result of such information will be to produce thousands of instances where recommendations for early abortion to avoid major birth defects will be clear cut; yet the evidence for "optimal" or eugenic selection seems likely to remain dubious and arguable. Since no more than a few percent of human conceptions would be aborted, this responsible approach to reproduction would not reduce birth rates significantly. Very likely, cutting off the least competent end of genetic distribution so as to promote equality of opportunity would only moderately affect the stability of the society. It would help counteract the depressing effects on the gene pool brought about by saving the lives of less fit individuals through application of modern medicine and allowing them to reproduce at will.

The quality of any gene complex can be judged only by it interaction with the environment—cultural, social, and political, as well as physical and biological. Therefore it seems likely that the extremes in urbanization may set quite different requirements for the ideal man from the cities of the temperate climate whose standards have dominated medical judgments in recent centuries. Should cities near the Arctic Circle set out to breed a polar man, psychologically stable against the long dark period? The floating cities, settled from the beginning with a strongly divergent cultural and social system, might see the value of an aquatic man. The Ecumenopolis as a whole might contemplate a caste of dwarf space-traveling men.

Very much more controversial would be the production of a deviant sentient type. The symbiosis of man and automaton (the manner in which a musician now fits himself and his life to his instrument has equivalents in

the way people become involved as designers and main-
tainers of complex computer programs) could lead to
serious proposals for "hybrids." An organism might be
designed with novel built-in transducers allowing it to
master sensations derived from distinctly different channels
of communication.[36] For example, what competitive
advantages would an organization or a community have
if each persona carried inside him a 10,000 line automatic
"telephone exchange"—a capacity well within the human
ability to recall specific names and associated patterns—and
had educated himself to be "on line" with others?

To repeat, these are a few of the issues that are raised
as soon as the task of completing the urban transition
appears readily soluble and within the scope of action of
already existing institutions. They are indicators of still
bigger problems that lie beyond the creation of a highly
integrated Ecumenopolis buzzing with transactions intended to equalize scarcities throughout the world. An ultrastable human habitat can be regarded here only as a stage
to higher levels of evolution where man makes man, internally and externally, individually and collectively, while
manipulating his animate and inanimate environment to
fit his varied ways of life.

WHAT IS CONSERVED?

What has been sketched out here is a series of the implications of ecological thinking applied to human organization.
It shows the path to a more highly organized, and therefore
interdependent, state of being that, from out vantage
point looks like urbanism. Economical modes of thinking
are only now becoming available for the consideration of
many alternative paths and steady states. We know from
experience with the development of science that as a body
of thinking becomes unified and intellectually powerful,
it is usually possible to express some central concepts as
laws of conservation. Such laws identify a property or a
condition that has been found to be invariant over the
time to which investigators have given attention. Thus
after a huge amount of careful observation, biologists
discovered that the gene pool of a species is conserved,
just as the chemists before them settled upon the chemical
elements as having a continuing existence, although they
might be transformed into a variety of compounds of
vastly different appearance. Similarly, physicists were

able to define energy in such a way that the first and second laws of thermodynamics could be stated for closed systems.

Laws of conservation make it possible to set up an accounting system to measure stocks and flows. Eventually, small but consistently observed discrepancies can be detected, and the unusual conditions where invariance seems to be violated can be defined. These findings are extraordinarily significant for a further understanding of nature. They are also fruitful in applications—which means that ways of changing nature locally can be designed and implemented. Very often it is accomplished through the design of control systems. In this way biologists accepted the Darwinian concept of evolution by which new species come into being, and physical scientists discovered that radioactive or fissile chemical elements are self-destructing exceptions to the rule—their mass is diminished and identity transmuted, but total energy held within a closed system is increased in a predictable way.

In *A Communications Theory of Urban Growth* I proposed that cities must operate so as to conserve information, or negentropy, if they are to survive.[37] More or less simultaneously, Margalef made similar arguments regarding the ecosystem. In this argument resources become highly significant. Biological systems studied by the ecologists receive their negentropy in the form of a steady stream of solar radiation, but cities depend largely upon exploiting the nonliving environment for nonrenewable resources, which become increasingly scarce over time. Thus the communications substitutes for such resources will become increasingly important; the channels convey information to members of the society, and their roles and functions in turn make a contribution to preserving the system. A potential limit to substitution was identified, since humans have a built-in channel capacity, which should soon be reached for a large share of the society living at a standard higher than the minimum adequate level. Automata that can handle simple situations have evolved, however, and there are no limits in sight for their transmission and storage of negentropy. If cities are to be maintained at the anticipated scale, it is apparent that automata must carry an increasing load of transactions. The urban system must also move toward dependence upon steady-state sources of energy (mainly sunlight, but geothermal sources may contribute a minor portion) if it is to become a long-lived open system.

At climax the longer-lived species tend to predominate. Again it is noted that the human species has some built-in constraints, and its members normally become senile in fourscore years or less. An assembly of silicon chips and servomichanisms can be constructed that is less fragile. Another feature of climax is that the populations of the various species are maintained at levels significantly below a theoretical carrying capacity based upon the availability of food and energy. By investing part of the available stock of fossil and fissile fuels in equipment for the efficient capture of energy, the carrying capacity of the earth appears likely to be stretchable to levels that would maintain somewhere between twenty and seventy billion human beings, a figure that is well above a relatively painless leveling off of the human population. It is possible to build a strong margin of safety from disaster while progressing toward the community of man. Thus almost all the present qualitative concepts of climax fit the city of the future very well and lead into the questions of evolution that have already been introduced.

One aspect of the evolution of the higher species appears to be exceedingly important when the future of cities is considered. It is believed to be a necessary, but not sufficient, condition for long-term survival. *Information can be invested in the environment so as to make it more ordered, structured, and secure.* All that has been proposed here as a path to resource-conserving urbanism represents just such an investment. Most of the information stored in the environment takes the form of precisely machined and assembled artifacts. We look at the surfaces of the artifacts and see synthetic nonorganic forms that are products created by machines, or are machines themselves. Printed matter constitutes a vast multileaved surface for the storage of information that guides behavior in cities. *Information incorporated in the surroundings regulates the range and direction for variation in the living species of the urban ecosystem.*[38] It accomplishes most of this redirection without plan, purely by reducing the frequency of encounters with critical levels of stress (attributable to accidents, errors, conflicts, crises). This regulating effect involves not only individuals but also their various communities. The protection afforded by the ordering of the environment allows the living system to build up more linkages, associations, and autonomous organizations. It enhances the overall volume of transactions. But those additions to the living system provide novel opportunities for further investment in the environment.

Thus a ratchet effect is obtained; an increasingly ordered and cultivated environment (with the frequency of disasters and destructive interruptions reduced) leads to a more diverse urban ecosystem, which from its accumulating transactional experience can invest added information, yielding more pattern and order in the environment. In present-day human society that investment shows up in geometrical, topological forms and as additions to networks first, and later as stocks of knowledge accumulated at points of easy access (nodes). The guidance provided by the paths and the files of experience that can be economically serached will enrich the transactions and shorten the time to completion. Going beyond, they expedite learning and mutually rewarding interaction. Society improves environment, and the new environment improves society, ad infinitum, or at least until some other major phenomenon intervenes. The concept has been speeded up by an order of magnitude or more in the modern metropolis.

As individuals we see and feel this process in a different way. Note that the richer transactions, their increased frequency via telecommunications, the added opportunity due to expanded networks, and the reduced frequency of error and conflict create new human bonds. We take responsibility for the welfare of others not always in our immediate vicinity, and they do the same for us. Initially the attachment is person-to-person, or loyalty to organization. Human organizations commonly invest 1-5% of their effort in codifying their knowledge and experience, usually under the rubric of "research and development," but they spend 10-30% of their effort in actively changing what they define as their environment. Most of this investment now goes to support the continuing increases in human population; important amounts are also spent in relatively uncoordinated attempts to produce equality of opportunity for individuals. If after the Ecumenopolis is built and population has stabilized the surpluses were to continue to be channeled in standard ways (with the recognition that institutions and their budgets are locked into present allocation ratios with little room for adjustment), they would generate more complex organization, and that would result in a still more highly networked, redeveloped urban environment.

Additions to the stock of knowledge itself seem to be the ultimate product of city building. For knowledge, there seems to be no practical limit. The idea of carrying capacity cannot be applied to stocks of information as knowledge can even be exported outside the planet. Previously, outsiders somewhere in the universe might have been able to tune in to the rising use of the electromagnetic spectrum for communications and perhaps decode some messages, but in recent years calculated efforts have been undertaken to export readily decodable messages—Rosetta stones for contemporary communications.[39] One can even envisage repositories on Mars and other planets, containing the product of urban culture on Earth and preserving it against the possibility of global catastrophe.

We would then have only to discover what part of the knowledge so laboriously accumulated in our cities and conserved over the generations is worth transmitting to extraterrestrial species. That knowledge would constitute the ultimate output of urban civilization.

1. The important phenomena were the standardization of parts followed by the assembly line. Much lower levels of skill were then required on the average to produce the machines and to keep them in repair. S. Giedion, *Mechanization takes Command* (New York: Oxford University Press, 1948).

2. Middle-class people—those who read and write books—create unusually large spaces for themselves, and their highly prized autonomy is visibly disturbed when it is invaded. Therefore, we must be conscious of a bias with regard to spatial density that is apparently not shared by the population as a whole. I observe that people who have a horror of large human numbers tend to place themselves on the distant side of Edward T. Hall's distribution in his study, *The Hidden Dimension* (Garden City, N.Y.: Doubleday, 1966).

3. John and Magda McHale prepared a report to the National Science Foundation on what they have called *The Timetable Project,* which brings forward the history of nearly completed demographic transitions and analyzes the alternative projections of the United Nations and others up to the year 2020 A.D. At that time the growth rate is still anticipated to be 1.1-1.4% per year. Tomas Frejka reported the implications for the distribution of this population in his article "The Prospects for a Stationary World Population," *Scientific American,* 228 (March 1973), 15-23.

4. R. L. Meier and Ikumi Hoshino, "Adjustments to Metropolitan Growth in an Inner Tokyo Ward," *Journal of The American Institute of Planners,* 34 (July 1968), 210-222.

5. Although the basic implications of the Club of Rome study carried out by D. H. Meadows, J. L. Meadows, J. Randers, W. W. Behrens III, *Limits to Growth* (New York: Universe, 1972), were known for decades, the sponsorship and the timing seemed to touch a nerve that led to an outpouring of reaction. A critique of that particular study was prepared by Sussex University in *Futures,* 5, nos. 1 and 2 (1973), and a reply to the critique in *The Dynamics of Growth in a Finite World* (New York: Wright Allen, 1973).

6. In the 1950s, when I was writing *Science and Economic Development,* the need for travel did not appear to be so strong, and an inadequate allowance was made in those projections. Since then I have come to agree with Zelinsky that postindustrial society brings with it a "mobility transition" fully as significant as the demographic transition. It will be possible to justify long-distance, energy-expensive trips as long as the capacity is available, because the threat of loss appears to be large as compared to the cost of flying. More often than not the need is put in nonmonetary terms, such as professional obligations, human affection, or the need for a vacation, which are difficult to gainsay. See Wilbur Zelinsky, "The Hypothesis of the Mobility Transition," *Geographical Review,* 61 (April 1971), 219-249.

7. Solar energy could be used to meet daytime peaks and produce hydrogen or pumped storage in a reservoir that would meet the evening peaks, while geothermal energy could provide the base power. Round-the-clock operation of the central city cannot be expected to remove all of the peaking in power consumption.

8. Several firms in Japan and Taiwan have been producing *chlorella* since the late 1960s in open ponds with yields of 7-8 tons dry weight of algae per hectare. The amount of sunlight energy converted to the algae was 8-12%; however, quite large and unstated amounts of energy are used for stirring, harvesting, and drying. (Personal communication, Michael G. McGarry, Department of Environmental Engineering, Asian Institute of Technology, Bangkok, December 1972.) The algae were used as an additive to fermented foods, contributing vitamins, minerals, protein, and some flavor; they remained too expensive to compete with soybean as a popular source of protein. Fortunately, the microbiological technology that converts to methane and hydrogen starts with slurries of algae, which can be harvested from ponds at reasonable cost after dark. The agitation required for stirring action in the culture—the bottom should move or be scraped—requires a substantial amount of energy.

9. Eugene P. Odum, "The Strategy of Ecosystem Development," *Science,* 164 (April 18, 1969), 262-270.

10. Striking improvements in the conversion of feed to flesh occur as the growing of livestock is rationalized. As the breeds are improved and the modern techniques for feeding are used, the same amount of original calories derived from the earth's surface will produce several times more flesh and a noticeable increase in biomass. The yield can be enhanced significantly by feeding urea instead of rough proteins to ruminants.
   The population of wild animals will increase, because the disturbance caused by cities invading new territory will gradually heal over. The periphery of cities can maintain particularly large populations of birds, deer, rabbits, and fish as conditions stabilize.

11. Once construction in the urban regions slows down to a steady state, the forests will be allowed to mature. The limit to the standing crop might then be set by the fire hazard caused by holding so much fuel in restricted areas.

12. The logic behind this conclusion, as distinguished from the previous one, derives from the possiblities of miniaturization. Vehicles are held to a common size because they carry humans, but many of the immobile machines can be devised to be smaller, thus opening new niches.

13. Each redevelopment or rationalization of a city at constant population seems likely to agree upon an excellent use of energy for cultural purposes that is believed to be worth the extra investment needed to extract it from the continuous sources or the

very low-grade mineral resources. Perhaps more important is the observation that higher mineral concentrations are being steadily depleted, while energy roughly proportional to the total bulk being processed must be expended. Moreover, transitions to more plentiful substitutes (e.g., copper to aluminum, silver to dyes, rainfall to desalinated sea water) almost always require more energy. The proposed move to the "hydrogen economy" is an example of the shift to electrification, since much of the hydrogen would be converted into power when arriving at the point of consumption.

14. The "new towns" literature is exceedingly rich, and most of the recent writers have absorbed the classics. The leading argument for new towns in America is that they provide a tabula rasa upon which institutional, and sometimes physical, innovations can be tested for their immediate implications: See Brown Miller, Neil J. Pinney, and William S. Saslow, *New Towns* (Cambridge, Mass.: MIT Press, 1972); James A. Clapp, *New Towns and Urban Policy* (New York: Dunellen, 1971); Gurney Breckenfeld, *Columbia and the New Cities* (New York: Washburn, 1971); American Institute of Planners' Task Force on New Communities, "New Communities: Challenge for Today," Washington, D.C., 1968. A group of experts was called together by the United Nations because of the worldwide interest in new town potentials, and these reports were collected in the volume *Planning of Metropolitan Areas and New Towns* (New York: United Nations, 1967), ST/SOA/65. The British approach is eloquently introduced by Frederic J. Osborn and Arnold Whittich, *The New Towns: The Answer to Megalopolis* (revised ed.; London: Leonard Hill, 1969). For a modern French analysis see Pierre Merlin (trans. Margaret Sparks) *New Towns: Regional Planning and Development* (London, Methuen, 1971); while for a national-istic, ideological approach see Alexander Berler, *New Towns in Israel* (Jerusalem: Universities Press, 1970). The periodical literature is a still richer source, but is heavily directed at the promotion of specific formulas for settlement or specific communities, with very few of the critical reactions reaching print until recently. No new towns worked out as intended, so the communities that survived combine the utopian visions of professional groups with the practical adjustments made by residents and local administrators.

15. Peter E. Glaser is reponsible for a proposal to use space satellites for collecting energy around the clock and beaming it to a receiver that supplies a city. The satellites are kept in synchronous orbit (i.e., they remain directly overhead the same point on the earth's surface). Each resembles a huge fan, about five kilometers on a side, amde up of solar cell arrays that convert solar energy directly into electricity. This low-voltage power would then be fed into microwave generators located between two satellites and trans-mitted to the earth's surface in any kind of weather. The efficiency of conversion can be raised theoretically to six- to fifteenfold over physical methods at the surface. The amount of power produced

would range between 3,000 and 15,000 megawatts, the latter presumably with the aid of mirrors. The receiving antenna would have to be about seven kilometers in diameter and would waste only about a tenth of the incoming radiation as waste heat. The satellites do not produce any appreciable shade at any point on the earth's surface; therefore, there is no reduction implied in the vegetation. A recent feasibility study suggests that much technological advance is required in solar cell design, their mass manufacture, the methods of fabricating such satellites in outer space, and in their reductions in cost. The lifetime of the cell should be increased from the present ten-year expectation to thirty years, and overall solar cell costs must be reduced by a factor of several hundredfold. *Chemical and Engineering News,* January 1, 1973, p. 17. It appears to be more economic, in my opinion, than electric power from solar energy in deserts, but not likely to be used before the twenty-first century.

16. The struggle to repress the instinct for physical growth that is so prevalent in Western society will be most severe. It has been eloquently introduced by John R. Platt, *The Step to Man* (New York: John Wiley & Sons, 1966), pp. 185-203. The momentum in Asia must be greater, assuming the prevention of major catastrophes, and so the psychological and institutional adjustments leading toward equilibrium may actually be more troublesome.

17. This account of disaster response represents a straightforward extrapolation from present policies and recommendations for improvement. Russel R. Dynes, *Organized Behavior in Disaster* (Lexington: D. C. Heath, 1970).

18. We are concerned here with an interdependent set of innovations that deal with such diverse phenomena as food, water, energy, communications, social controls, and learning. Even if several of them are potent enough to become significant in a decade or so, it seems most unlikely that the complement could take effect in less than two decades; the normal period being three decades or more. In order to diffuse rapidly, the ideas must not only be published but must also make a difference in the competition between already existing organizations so that the development process is accelerated. The potential shifts in competition cause comment; therefore, it is relatively easy to detect the introduction of practical ideas that might lead to radically different paths in the near term.

19. It always comes as a shock when estimates come in like those of the war of independence of Bangladesh combined with the Pakistan-India War of 1971, which had very likely even more casualties than the Viet Nam war during American involvement. Almost three million deaths and more than a half-million prisoners is not far removed from total Japanese losses in World War II, but recent loss of life was experienced over a much shorter period.

20. Pitirim A. Sorokin completed a classic review of the social effects of disaster in his *Man and Society in Calamity* (New York: E.P. Dutton, 1942). He ascribes the Crusades, the revival of flagellation, and ascetic Protestantism to famine, plague, and the consequent inability to resist invasion. Calamities are required to force mankind to make major steps in the synthesis of "a spiritual religion and a noble code of ethics," whereas "comparative stability, order and material well-being have scarcely ever given birth to a truly great religion or a lofty moral ideal." He wrote, as will be noted, at the darkest period of the war. William L. Langer in his Presidential Address to the American Historical Association said, "As historians we must be particularly concerned with the problem whether major changes in the psychology of a society or culture can be traced, even in part, to some severe trauma suffered in common" and went on to describe effects of the Black Death. *American Historical Review,* 63 (January 1959). For a more modern and more cautious review of the effects of disaster, see G. N. Baker and D. W. Chapman, eds., *Man and Society in Disaster* (New York: Basic Books, 1962), especially the contribution of Gideon Sjoberg.

21. The official approach in America toward saving energy requires a search for alternative technologies in shelter, transport, manufacturing, and transmission that may be used if proper incentives are offered. The government cannot coerce people to undertake changes in life-style. In a review of thinking in various laboratories in 1972, Allen L. Hammond came to the conclusion that the ultimate saving potential is "enormous"—as much as 25%, for shifts that often require as much as a generation. "Conservation of Energy: The Potential for More Efficient Use," *Science,* 178 (December 8, 1972), 1079-1081.

22. Carefully worded alarms were published in 1971, purporting to connect urbanization itself with the process of aerosol generation, claimed to be increasing by a factor of two in sixty years. P. W. Hodge, *Nature,* 229 (1971), 549. Theoretical calculations showed that global climate was much more sensitive to aerosol particles than to the accumulation of carbon dioxide, and only a fourfold additional increase would reduce surface temperature by 3.5°C., enough to bring about an ice age. Much of the original material dispersed in the upper atmosphere originated from volcanic activity. S. I. Rosool and S. H. Schneider, "Atmospheric Carbon Dioxide and Aerosols: Effects of Large Increases on Global Climate," *Science,* 173 (July 9, 1971), 138-141. More recent information collected from the astronomical observatories of the world suggests that previous trends were purely local (i.e., Los Angeles but not Arizona). P. W. Hodge, Nels Laulainen, and R. J. Charlson, "Astronomy and Air Pollution," *Science,* 178 (December 8, 1971), 1123-1124. Thus vulcanism remains the most serious known cause of surface cooling, and in this instance it is noted that one of the consequences of the verification of the continental drift theory is that the techtonic plate in the earth's crust known

as Australia appears to be colliding with another represented by Southeast Asia, with resulting very active mountain building and vulcanic explosions, such as the well-known Krakatoa event, increasing in frequency. Allen L. Hammond, "Plate Tectonics (II): Mountain Building and Continental Geology," *Science,* 173 (July 9, 1971), 133-134.

23. It is very risky to project responses to the onset of a new ice age because the existing theory is so fragile. The greatest uncertainties are encountered in the climatic shifts at the regional level—just where they have most significance for the growth of cities. I was struck by the implications for cities in the papers of Maurice Ewing and William L. Donn, "A Theory of the Ice Ages," *Science,* 123 (1956), 1061-1066; 127, (1958), 1159-1162, the critical comment by D. A. Livingstone and the authors' reply in *Science,* 128, (1959), 463-465. They invoked a wandering of the North Pole, whereas other proposals showed correlation with precessions of the equinox, although they should lead to a warming effect over the next 10,000 years. Emiliani has empirically shown a strong periodicity in paleotemperatures in the Caribbean using oxygen isotope rations, and that pervious generalizations regarding four ice ages are faulty. He finds eight occasions when water temperature there fell to 22°C in the last 400,000 years. The recent peak was 28°, but it has started dropping and was last reported at 27°. In the past, periods of high temperature lasted for only 3,000-10,000 years; ours already equals the longest. Cesare Emiliani, "Quaternary Paleotemperatures and the Duration of High Temperature Intervals," *Science,* 178 (October 27, 1972), 398-401. The Ewing-Dunn theory has not been updated, but recent continental drift theory adds plausibility to a variant of it. As the land masses drifted away from the original mass mainly in the Southern Hemisphere, they enclosed an Arctic Ocean producing moisture that froze and accumulated on land. This reflective surface finally reduced the temperature to such a low level that the ocean itself froze, thus cutting off the supply of moisture to the air. Then slowly and irregularly the ice cap shrank, the glaciers at the periphery retreated, and the cycle was repeated. See the conference report by C. K. Shedd, W. H. Berger, R. M. Born, and J. C. K. Huang, "Climatic Changes on Time Scales Ranging from a Month to a Millennium," *Bulletin of the American Meteorological Society,* 54 (May 1973), 425-432. The water-bearing cyclonic storms would move from the Atlantic into the Sahara. The monsoon would become still more intense than today, causing much flooding. The deserts of South Africa, Australia, and Chile-Peru should become well watered

Historians have described societal response to less than half this amount of cooling during the small scale climatic variations since 1000 A. D. by using reports on the quality of wine and bread, correlated with tree ring data and with the advance and retreat of glaciers, thus suggesting some of the more subtle effects. The stress seems to be greatest close to the leading edge of the glaciers, where mean annual temperatures have moved in a range of 5°C. LeRoy Ladurie, *Times of Feast, Times of Famine* (Garden City, N.Y.: Doubleday, 1971), trans. Barbara Bray.

24. Karl Deutsch, *Nationalism and Social Communications* (Cambridge, Mass.: MIT Press, 1953). An extension to this thinking is provided by Joseph B. Tamney, "The Scarcity of Identity," in Hans Dieter Evers, ed., *Modernization in Southeast Asia* (London: Oxford University Press, 1973). Tamney judges the capacity for survival of ethnic communities held together by a language or some other institutional complex by the willingness of members to risk life, or otherwise make sacrifices, in its support, Thus the greatest losses occur where commitments are strongest.

25. Very interesting analyses of the evolution of language are now under discussion. I have seen a draft of a paper by Paul Kay, "Language Evolution and Speech Style," November 1971 (American Anthropological Association, New York, Symposium on the Relation of Anthropology and Linguistics), and another by Brent Berlin, "Speculations on the Growth of Ethnobotanical Nomenclature," Working Paper No. 39, Language-Behavior Research Laboratory, University of California, Berkeley, March 1971. They suggest that we should henceforth be studying the expansion of lexicons in modern language as an indicator of the growth of conceptual richness and the power to communicate. The process of expansion is discussed by Martin Nystrand, "A Future-Shocked Language?" *English Journal,* February 1973, pp. 250-254, but I believe he is wrong in concluding that coded images are growing more rapidly than uncoded ones. He has forgotten to consider the effects of recording tape.

26. An insightful commentary has been provided by John P. Robinson in an analysis of cross-national time budget comparisons, "Televisions and Leisure Time: Yesterday, Today, and (Maybe) Tomorrow," *Public Opinion Quarterly,* 33 (Summer 1969), 210-222. He shows that, as the variety of television programming increases, people tend to spend more time with the set on and paying at least peripheral attention to it. The big difference, however, is between no television and the existence of any kind of popular program. The visual image generates an allocation four to six times as great as radio, in addition to possessing the capacity to transmit more information.

27. David C. McClelland, *The Achieving Society* (Princeton, N.J.: Van Nostrand, 1961); also with David G. Winter, *Motivating Economic Achievement* (New York: Free Press, 1969). For a personal reconsideration of what he has learned regarding both the achievement and the power motives by conducting large-scale experiments, see his interview with W. F. Dowling, *Organizational Dynamics,* 1 (Summer 1972), 56-72.

28. Charles Morris, in his *Varieties of Human Value* (Chicago: University of Chicago Press, 1956), notes that American college youth prefer a life that emphasizes "integrating action, enjoyment, and contemplation," and this predilection changed only to a small extent in a twenty-year period for a vastly expanded college stream. Significant decline was noted only in interest in the style emphasizing "preserve the best that man has attained." Charles Morris and Linwood Small, "Changes in the Conception of the Good Life by American College Students from 1950 to 1970," *Journal of Personality and Social Psychology,* 20 (1971), 254-260.

29. Emilio Willems, *Followers of the New Faith: Culture Change and the Rise of Protestantism in Brazil and Chile* (Nashville: Vanderbilt University Press, 1967), Bryan R. Roberts, "Protestant Groups and Coping with Urban Life in Guatemala," *American Journal of Sociology,* 73 (May 1968), 73-76.

30. Neale Hunter, *Shanghai Journal: An Eyewitness Account of the Cultural Revolution* (New York: Praeger Books, 1969); Ronald N. Montaperto, *Red Guard: The Political Biography of Dai Hsiao-ai* (New York: Doubleday, 1971).

31. The Soka Gakkai best filled the needs of persons who were uprooted and had to make their way in an urban environment that was replete with opportunity as well as threat. It appealed to persons in small enterprise and lower civil service primarily but did find some support in the work forces of the large industrial zones. The management of the growth of the religion demonstrated skills that are employed equally well in the top ranks of the *Zaibatsu.* James W. White, *The Sokagakkai and Mass Society* (Stanford: Stanford University Press, 1970).

32. For anyone who has reached these points in the argument about the uses and misuses of religion, it has become apparent that I do not possess an Olympian detachment. Brought up as a fundamentalist Lutheran, I embraced scientific humanism as a personal philosophy but remained intellectually eclectic; thus "science" could be recognized as operating like an established church. K. E. Boulding sees it that way also, and in his short article, "The Scientific Revelation," *Bulletin of the Atomic Scientist,* 26 (September 1970), 13-18, he noted that the gravest, most unpardonable sin in this organized faith is the formal publication of deliberately falsified results. Diplomats and political leaders do not blink, but scientists are cast into outer darkness. Great internal stresses are built up in the adherents to this revelation by the fact that curiosity, leading to novelty in reports, is highly valued, yet the communication of preventable error is highly sinful and discrediting in this "search for Truth."
In America at least it does not appear that a science-based religion will dominate the urban communities. In a way this is surprising, because already the priesthood of professional scientists—

the members of the respective scientific societies—is as numerous as the cleargy of the Christian churches, and they are still growing. Moreover, scientists have discipline, precision in communication, and commitment; their liturgy and dogma are cumulative rather than reiterative, and so it remains much more relevant than competing religions. Yet a system of belief based upon skepticism and doubt is hardly acceptable to the general urban population. Nor do they appreciate the suspicion of affect and the continual criticism of oversimplified systems of thought. The quickness of the scientist to castigate error forces such a person to lead a very self-conscious, almost inhibited life. It is claimed that this kind of social behavior is liberating, but the payoffs are reaped by succeeding generations.

Finally it is evident that commitment to science does not breed true—children brought up in scientific households more often reject that faith than accept it, so that the scientific church is populated primarily with converts. Most of the second generation go on to explore the plethora of sects and cults, most with roots in the classical religious myths, never really fixing upon any unless there is great personal need for anchorage—such as getting off drugs. It appears that the religions of the future will accept huge amounts of shared fantasy. Jacob Needleman, *The New Religions* (New York: Doubleday, 1970).

33. A fascinating and most unexpected extension of evolutionary thinking into the area of human culture has been introduced by Allen Lomax, "The Evolutionary Taxonomy of Culture," *Science.* 177, (July 21, 1972), 228-239. He carried out a comprehensive survey of human song styles and superimposed that information upon Murdock's *Ethnographic Atlas.* Song, as well as the organization of the chorus, was analyzed for differentiation and plotted according to degrees of similarity, showing complex pathways starting with African gatherers and proceeding to Old High Culture and European in a tree of culture which is flowering now. This is a particularly apt choice because it is one of the few elements of culture where the "tools" and the "environment" have remained virtually constant over all this period and all populations.

34. The *Bulletin of Atomic Scientists,* December 1972, put together a symposium reviewing the range of possiblities and the ethical problems posed for the healing professions.

35. John Maddox presents a sober view on cloning and other related possibilities that could very well predominate for the middle run in his *The Doomsday Syndrome* (New York: McGraw-Hill, 1972). I have relied more upon it than its speculative predecessors.

36. The highly instrumented experiments reported upon at a conference on "Transducing Membranes" (held in Tokyo, May 1972) stimulate one to think along these lines. Science fiction writers have, of course, been fantasizing such humanoids for a long time, but they have avoided coping with the limitations.

37. Richard L. Meier, *A Communications Theory of Urban Growth* (Cambridge, Mass.: MIT Press, 1962), chap. ix.

38. Among ecologists, R. Margalef, a marine biologist from Barcelona, is given credit for first seeing the connection between information theory and the diversity of species in a community. Certainly his empirical work supports the leap to that inference: see *Annual Review of Oceanography and Marine Biology*, 5 (1967), 257-289, "Some Concepts Relative to the Organization of Plankton." However, not even in his *Perspectives in Ecological Theory* (Chicago: University of Chicago Press, 1968), do I find a clear explanation of the reasons *why* there should be an equivalence between order in a community and order in a code for communication. What new hypothesis should follow upon this apparent connection? Is it that environmental changes in temperature and composition of the homogeneous media in flux provide a kind of "noise" that determines diversity at climax, and that spectral analysis of the environmental variations would suggest where increased stabilization could allow still more diverse communities?

39. The first of these attempts was formulated by NASA on short notice in 1972. It served primarily to identify our coordinates in the Galaxy and introduce others to our external appearance. If a higher civilization exists in outer space, our attempts to communicate more fully represent an application for admission, since the odds are almost a billion to one that a contacted civilization will have accumulated more knowledge than we with the cities we have built. If any contact is made the subsequent period would be one of "catching up" with an irregularly increasing amount of time and attention given to reconstructing cities so as to take advantage of information about higher levels of organization. Elaborate plans for the necessary hardware for exploring more deeply in space, as well as announcing our arrival as a civilization with extraterrestrial capabilities, have already been prepared. The building up of a constituency of backers remains. Although the equipment will be placed as far from cities as possible, because of their pollution of the electromagnetic spectrum, the ideas that lie behind its use and potential consequences have revolutionary implications for the further evolution of cities.